The NAACP Crusade
Against Lynching, 1909-1950

ROBERT L. ZANGRANDO

The NAACP Crusade Against Lynching, 1909–1950

Temple University Press
Philadelphia

Temple University Press, Philadelphia 19122
© 1980 by Temple University. All rights reserved
Published 1980
Printed in the United States of America

Library of Congress Cataloging in Publication Data

Zangrando, Robert L
   The NAACP crusade against lynching, 1909–1950.

  Bibliography: p.
  Includes index.
  1. Lynching. 2. National Association for the
Advancement of Colored People. I. Title.
HV6457.Z36   364.6'6   80-13926
ISBN 0-87722-174-X

Contents

	Preface	vii
ONE	At the Hands of Parties Unknown	3
TWO	The NAACP Confronts Mob Violence, 1909–1919	22
THREE	The Struggle for the Dyer Bill, 1919–1923	51
FOUR	In the Wake of the Dyer Bill: Transition, 1923–1933	72
FIVE	Need, Apprehension, and Hope: Renewing the Drive in Congress, 1933–1934	98
SIX	From Both Ends of Pennsylvania Avenue, 1935–1936	122
SEVEN	At the Peak and Beyond, 1937–1940	139
EIGHT	Expanded Programs of War and Postwar Years, 1941–1947	166
NINE	The Last Great Drive, 1948–1950	187
TEN	In the Hands of Parties Yet Unknown	210
	Notes	217
	Bibliography	281
	Index	305

This book is dedicated to:
Joanna Schneider Zangrando,
Margaret Troestler Zangrando,
and
Mary Troestler Hoerdt.

Preface

The lynching of young Emmett Till in 1955 and a wave of civil rights activism over the next ten years quickened my interest in the problem of twentieth-century interracial violence and the social dynamics surrounding it. As I studied these issues, it soon became apparent that this was equally a story of the NAACP—the National Association for the Advancement of Colored People.

With the collapse of Reconstruction, Afro-Americans became increasingly vulnerable to the caprice of white racism. Raw physical power and the authority of law rested preponderantly in white hands. A Jim Crow mentality prevailed, whereby southern whites practiced or excused violence as a necessary instrument of interracial control and northern whites greeted the news of lynchings with indifference or callous acquiescence. Finally, in 1909, a reform conscience took root with the establishment of the NAACP, an interracial group determined to safeguard black rights and challenge mob violence. The Association worked to bring black men and women wholly within the mainstream of modern American life; in doing so, the organization also wove itself into the fabric of an emerging liberal coalition of national proportions. By mid-century, the preconditions had been set for most of the civil rights advances that have marked the past thirty years, and the fight for a federal antilynching law, waged with determination during the period from 1909 to 1950, proved an essential part of those preconditions.

Curiously, lynching and its implications have received rather little scholarly attention. For decades, most white academicians ignored topics in black history or erroneously assumed that the failure to enact a federal antilynching law signalled a defeat of the entire drive to insure black rights. In fact, the inability to secure national civil rights guarantees represented a serious flaw in American democratic processes. Meanwhile, black scholars, who seldom enjoyed access to major publishing outlets until recent years, seemed reticent to explore the antilynching campaigns for a general audience. Perhaps they felt too much anger, resentment, and bitterness in the realization that any black man or woman could have been so brutally treated. The late field secretary of the NAACP,

Daisy Lampkin, once recalled that "We were so ashamed that whites could do that to *us*, that we hardly wanted to talk about it publicly."[1]

At one time, I had planned to make this a much more ambitious study, one that approximated a history of the NAACP from the perspective of its drive against mobbism. However, friends who read early drafts of the manuscript urged that I focus more sharply on the antilynching crusade itself. That is the book I have now chosen to write. Incidentally, some of the manuscript collections that I examined have since been moved; readers will want to bear this in mind, should they wish to use the same sources. For example, the W. E. B. Du Bois Papers are now being published through the University of Massachusetts. When I worked in these materials, they were held in New York City by Herbert Aptheker, who generously allowed me access. Similarly, I began my explorations into the NAACP Papers through the national office in New York City. That was before the Association shifted the collection to the Library of Congress in the mid-1960s. Accordingly, my notes make the distinction between the two locations, NAACP-NY and NAACP-LC, respectively. Throughout the Notes, I use the term "copy" to indicate that the collection in question has only a carbon or in some cases a transcribed version of the document being cited.

Grants from the American Council of Learned Societies and from the faculty research funds at Rutgers University and the University of Akron made it possible to complete this study. In addition, I owe a debt of appreciation to numerous individuals. Certainly I wish to acknowledge my mentors at Union College: Frederick Bronner, Robert Mendenhall, the late Sherwood Fox, Howard Rosenberg, Joseph Doty, and Clare Graves. At the University of Pennsylvania, I benefited enormously from work with Richard Dunn, Morton Keller, Wallace Davies, Jeannette Paddock and Roy F. Nichols, Martin Wolfe, Thomas Cochran, and Lynn Case. At the American Historical Association, Paul L. Ward and Henry Winkler were thoroughly supportive. Archivists at the many repositories I visited were unfailingly helpful; none more so than Roy Gee at the Schomburg Library in New York City. The persons listed in the interviews section deserve, and have, my complete gratitude. Of those affiliated with the NAACP national office, I want especially to mention William Hastie and John Morsell, both deceased, Judy Baxter, Henry Lee Moon, Virginia Brazington, Bobbie Branche, Jesse De Vore, Gloster Current, Maybelle Ward, and Lucille Black.

August Meier and Elliott Rudwick offered numerous suggestions and Warren Kuehl read a draft of the manuscript. Even when I disagreed with their recommendations, I appreciated the care and attention they exhibited. Special commendation must go to my faculty colleagues in the University of Akron History Department, who displayed high degrees of patience and good taste in never once harassing me for not completing the project sooner. I might not have finished at all, if, during long and crucial stretches away from my home base, professors Wilma Hall and Judith McDaniel of Skidmore College had not given me the unlimited use of their campus offices in which to write portions of this book.

At Temple University Press, editor Michael Ames was supportive and responsive at every turn; Dianne Sigler, Shirley Alves, Ann Marie Anderson, Michele Martin, and Doris Braendel transformed a raw manuscript into a book. I am delighted that Ronald L. Lewis urged me to take the project to them. Elsewhere, there was the steadily reliable typing of Janice and Michele Mursko, Diana Dickerhoff Battles, Diane Markley, Dorothy Richards, and Garnette Dorsey. The last two handled the closing stages of manuscript preparation with a proficiency and determination that were quite stunning. Frank Rivera, Davis Cole, Daniel Katete Orwa, Judy Hart, and Helen Horvath helped with specific tasks. Joanna Schneider Zangrando provided an indispensable mixture of historical insights, professional judgments, and personal good sense that made it possible to complete the book in a level-headed manner.

They have each my thanks, although what follows is strictly my own responsibility.

Saratoga Springs, N.Y.
January 2, 1980   R.L.Z.

    1. Personal interview with Daisy Lampkin, Morris Beach, N.J., Aug. 30, 1962.

The NAACP Crusade Against Lynching, 1909-1950

1

At the Hands of Parties Unknown

Lynching is a vicious practice in which members of a mob take the law into their own hands. On the pretext of seeking retribution for some wrongdoing, they injure or execute a victim in summary fashion, at times with great fanfare and public acclaim. Presumptions of innocence and proof of guilt are treated as afterthoughts, if at all. The accused may have broken a law, violated a local custom, or merely offended prevailing sensibilities. Outnumbered and overwhelmed, the victim has no means of redress, since the mob functions as self-appointed prosecutor, jury, judge, and executioner.

Dating at least to the Revolution and used initially to punish suspected criminals and Tories, lynching proved a popular mechanism for enforcing local mores; it took hold in settled communities and spread along the nation's expanding southern and western frontiers, as well. Gamblers and alleged murderers, desperadoes and horse thieves, antislavery advocates, blacks suspected of insurrectionary plots, Native Americans, and Spanish-speaking minorities comprised the bulk of its nineteenth-century targets. After 1890, immigrants, political radicals, labor organizers, opponents of the First World War, and kidnappers on occasion suffered the mob's fury.[1]

Primarily, however, lynching was a means to intimidate, degrade, and control black people throughout the southern and border states, from Reconstruction to the mid-twentieth century. The mob proved a ready instrument for enforcing racism, that disposition to proclaim all blacks inferior on grounds no more substantial than their physical characteristics. Choosing national harmony in place of older sectional animosities, turn-of-the-century whites, North and South, embraced a view of Afro-Americans that relied upon pseudo-scientific pronouncements of Nordic supremacy, racial hierarchies, and "natural selection." Just as western Europeans found these myths eminently suited to their pursuit of imperialist goals throughout Africa and Asia, Americans combined such beliefs with the use of naked force and the police power of the states to subordinate southern blacks. Stripped of their civil and political rights, men and women were flogged, dismembered, tortured with hot irons, and put to death by rope, flame, and gunshot.

Secure in the assumption that they served as agents for their white peers, lynchers acted with impunity. The magnitude and persistence of mob fury almost defy description, and lynching in its classic form involved hundreds of men, women, and children in ritualized murder, sometimes advertised in advance through the public media.[2] As Tables 1 and 2 supplied by the Archives at Tuskegee Institute reveal, 4,743 persons died at the hands of lynchers from 1882, the earliest date for reliable statistics, to 1968. Of these victims, 3,446, or 72.7 percent, were black.

However valuable, these statistics are not comprehensive. The tables include only *recorded* lynchings, and one can merely guess how widespread the phenomenon actually was. As opposition mounted in the 1920s and 1930s, the number of reported lynchings declined, but more subtle forms of brutality evolved. Worried that outside pressure might produce a federal antilynching law, some southern whites found it wise to suppress the news of mob violence. Although with less frequency, lynchers continued to terrorize and murder black people; but now select committees might be assigned to abduct, torture, and kill victims without public fanfare.[3] Further masking the realities behind the data was the phenomenon of "legal lynchings," whereby officials consented in advance to a sham court trial followed promptly by the prisoner's execution.[4]

Because it fit their racist beliefs and provided a convenient explanation, whites created the myth that lynching was a necessary protection for white womanhood. As Table 3 shows, this ranked among the most popular justifications for mob murder. In fact, less than 26 percent of those lynched were charged, let alone tried and convicted, of rape or attempted rape. And accusations of rape hardly explained the lynching deaths of several dozen black women. Nonetheless, the myth persisted at all levels, so that even a reformer like Theodore Roosevelt pandered to it while denouncing mob action.[5] Antilynching campaigners expended enormous amounts of time and energy in disproving rape as the cause of lynching. Certainly this was true for journalist Ida B. Wells at the turn of the century, Jessie Daniel Ames of the Association of Southern Women for the Prevention of Lynching during the 1930s, and Walter White throughout his public career with the National Association for the Advancement of Colored People (NAACP), from 1918 to 1955. Theirs, however, was an uphill battle.[6]

Some black males did assault white women, but neither that nor the greater frequency of rape and sexual harassment inflicted on black women by white and black men accounted for mob violence. Nearly 23 percent of the recorded incidents were clustered under "all other causes" (Table 3), and blacks were lynched for such transgressions of racial mores as sheltering a fugitive, disputing a white man's word, dating a white woman, testifying or defending themselves against whites, or just acting "troublesome." No, the reasons for lynching were hardly tied to sexual

Table 1. Lynchings, by State and Race, 1882–1968*

State	Whites	Blacks	Total
Alabama	48	299	347
Arizona	31	0	31
Arkansas	58	226	284
California	41	2	43
Colorado	65	3	68
Delaware	0	1	1
Florida	25	257	282
Georgia	39	492	531
Idaho	20	0	20
Illinois	15	19	34
Indiana	33	14	47
Iowa	17	2	19
Kansas	35	19	54
Kentucky	63	142	205
Louisiana	56	335	391
Maine	1	0	1
Maryland	2	27	29
Michigan	7	1	8
Minnesota	5	4	9
Mississippi	42	539	581
Missouri	53	69	122
Montana	82	2	84
Nebraska	52	5	57
Nevada	6	0	6
New Jersey	1	1	2
New Mexico	33	3	36
New York	1	1	2
North Carolina	15	86	101
North Dakota	13	3	16
Ohio	10	16	26
Oklahoma	82	40	122
Oregon	20	1	21
Pennsylvania	2	6	8
South Carolina	4	156	160
South Dakota	27	0	27
Tennessee	47	204	251
Texas	141	352	493
Utah	6	2	8
Vermont	1	0	1
Virginia	17	83	100
Washington	25	1	26
West Virginia	20	28	48
Wisconsin	6	0	6
Wyoming	30	5	35
Total	1,297	3,446	4,743

* Statistics provided the author by the Archives at Tuskegee Institute, February 1979. The data do not specify victims by ethnicity or by race other than black and white. Some earlier compilers tried to do so; see, for example, James Elbert Cutler, *Lynch-Law: An Investigation into the History of Lynching in the United States* (1905; rpt., Montclair, N.J., 1969), pp. 170–72.

Table 2. Lynchings, by Year and Race, 1882–1968*

Year	Whites	Blacks	Total
1882	64	49	113
1883	77	53	130
1884	160	51	211
1885	110	74	184
1886	64	74	138
1887	50	70	120
1888	68	69	137
1889	76	94	170
1890	11	85	96
1891	71	113	184
1892	69	161	230
1893	34	118	152
1894	58	134	192
1895	66	113	179
1896	45	78	123
1897	35	123	158
1898	19	101	120
1899	21	85	106
1900	9	106	115
1901	25	105	130
1902	7	85	92
1903	15	84	99
1904	7	76	83
1905	5	57	62
1906	3	62	65
1907	3	58	61
1908	8	89	97
1909	13	69	82
1910	9	67	76
1911	7	60	67
1912	2	62	64
1913	1	51	52
1914	4	51	55
1915	13	56	69
1916	4	50	54
1917	2	36	38
1918	4	60	64
1919	7	76	83
1920	8	53	61
1921	5	59	64
1922	6	51	57
1923	4	29	33
1924	0	16	16
1925	0	17	17
1926	7	23	30
1927	0	16	16
1928	1	10	11
1929	3	7	10

Year	Whites	Blacks	Total
1930	1	20	21
1931	1	12	13
1932	2	6	8
1933	4	24	28
1934	0	15	15
1935	2	18	20
1936	0	8	8
1937	0	8	8
1938	0	6	6
1939	1	2	3
1940	1	4	5
1941	0	4	4
1942	0	6	6
1943	0	3	3
1944	0	2	2
1945	0	1	1
1946	0	6	6
1947	0	1	1
1948	1	1	2
1949	0	3	3
1950	1	1	2
1951	0	1	1
1952	0	0	0
1953	0	0	0
1954	0	0	0
1955	0	3	3
1956	0	0	0
1957	1	0	1
1958	0	0	0
1959	0	1	1
1960	0	0	0
1961	0	1	1
1962	0	0	0
1963	0	1	1
1964	2	1	3
1965	0	0	0
1966	0	0	0
1967	0	0	0
1968	0	0	0
Total	1,297	3,445	4,742

* Statistics provided the author by the Archives at Tuskegee Institute, February 1979. The data do not specify victims by ethnicity or by race other than black and white. The slight discrepancy in totals between Tables 1 and 2 is not a typographical error; it derives from the complexities of recording mob action (Lillian B. Jiminez, assistant to the archivist, Tuskegee Institute, to the author, March 29, 1979).

Table 3. Causes of Lynchings Classified, 1882-1968*

	Number	Percent
Homicides	1,937	40.84
Felonious assault	205	4.32
Rape	912	19.22
Attempted rape	288	6.07
Robbery and theft	232	4.89
Insult to white person	85	1.79
All other causes	1,084	22.85
Total	4,743	100.00

* Computed from statistics provided the author by the Archives at Tuskegee Institute, February 1979. Percentages rounded to the nearest 1/100 of a percent. On the apparent discrepancy in the number of lynching victims, Table 2 and Table 3, see the explanatory footnote to Table 2.

conduct, real or fancied. Rather, mob violence transcended the victim's behavior and reminded all black people of white America's determination to impose its will and authority in a biracial society. Unable to vote, hold public office, or serve on juries in the Jim Crow South, blacks possessed no readily available means to alter the fact that more than 99 percent of mob members escaped arrest, prosecution, conviction, and punishment. Local white sentiment condoned their actions; public officials, answerable to a white electorate, either cooperated with the mob or sought refuge in silence and inaction. As a result, coroner's juries repeatedly found that death had come "at the hands of parties unknown," a sham verdict, indeed, since lynchers' identities were seldom a secret.[7]

At times, terror reached beyond individual victims of lynching. In race riots, for example, whites attacked and killed black men and women at random. While lynching increasingly took on a regional, that is, southern, character, riots from the 1890s to the early 1920s exhibited no such parochial pattern. Outbreaks occurred in North Carolina, New York, Ohio, Louisiana, Texas, Georgia, Illinois, Tennessee, Nebraska, Arkansas, Oklahoma, and the District of Columbia.[8] Riots and lynchings, however, had certain striking similarities. In riot situations, local or state law enforcement agencies occasionally abetted white mobs by a tardy response to the crisis, by a tendency to harass and punish blacks whether or not they actually fought their attackers, or by outright participation against black residents. Like lynching, riots often originated in rumors and false accusations against members of the black community. Riots showed a bitter determination among whites to employ force as an instrument of social control. And while some few prosecutions did occur, those were exceptions. Overwhelmingly, white rioters, like their lynching counterparts, expected and enjoyed immunity from the law.

Twentieth-century commentators have suggested a number of reasons for lynching's popularity in the South. Influenced perhaps by the harsh realities of the Great Depression, scholars of the 1930s and early 1940s tended to see economic factors as an underlying cause of mob violence. Planters and poor whites used violence to intimidate black workers or, upset by a decline in cotton prices, vented their frustrations on the black community. Analysts tried to establish that lynchings were more likely to occur in poor counties than those with a healthy economic base, although the idea of any direct relationship between mobbism and cotton prices subsequently came under challenge. In demographic terms there did seem to be an inverse correlation between the frequency of lynching and the total number of residents in a county, and blacks appeared more vulnerable the smaller their proportion in a county's population.[9] Such observations, however, offered a description rather than a causal analysis of the lynching phenomenon. More comprehensive explanations of lynching have emerged among Marxists, who have seen mob violence as an instrument to divide and oppress workers along racial lines in order to perpetuate the economic and political dominance of the capitalist class.[10]

Other interpretations have set lynching within a context of psychological, social, and cultural tensions derived from a biracial but racist atmosphere. W. J. Cash, for example, saw the South as "far too much concerned with bald, immediate, unsupported assertion of the ego," with "too great stress on the inviolability of personal whim," and "full of the chip-on-shoulder swagger." Such a posture was bound to have explosive consequences in communities that imposed few or no restraints upon white behavior. For poor whites, the mob reinforced group sentiments and provided a "safe" outlet for the diffuse frustrations they could not readily express without risking reprisal from those more highly placed in the socioeconomic hierarchy. For the latter, lynching not only fit the racist assumptions of the region but offered a means of deflecting lower-class anger.[11] In death as surely as in life, blacks served as a convenience.

A number of those who have studied the practice found that lynching or the simple likelihood of mob action afforded southern whites an exquisite instrument of social control. John Dollard explored the theme in *Caste and Class in a Southern Town*, and Gunnar Myrdal portrayed the connections between violence and the preservation of caste distinctions.[12] Sociologist Allen D. Grimshaw explained how lynching was employed to maintain dominance whenever it suited whites to reaffirm their mastery or blacks challenged or seemed about to test the established contours of their subordination.[13] More recently, an exchange in the *American Sociological Review* indicates that scholars may disagree about certain methodological and conceptual approaches but still perceive lynching as a collective enterprise meeting white needs.[14] And no attempt should be made to analyze racial violence apart from its collective functions within southern society, as historians Jacquelyn Dowd Hall and Pete Daniel have warned.[15]

Lynching has displayed a frenetic and brutal quality unmatched in

America's long saga of violent behavior. Mob members have engaged themselves for hours with a defenseless black victim and even fought among themselves for souvenirs of the event. In 1941, psychologist Hadley Cantril found that such action expressed an array of fears and stereotypes, provided a harsh but ready release for diffuse tensions, and encouraged an unusual degree of participatory involvement, however bizarre, in the resolution of real or imagined crises. For the individual ego and the group psyche, lynching was simultaneously exhilarating, cathartic, and strangely comforting. Furthermore, it reaffirmed prevailing sexual mores and embraced the behavioral code of the southern patriarchy. Cloaked in the myth of rape, lynchers symbolized the prerogatives to interracial sex that white males meant to enjoy. That left black women open to sexual attack, deprived white women of any options or voice in the matter, and made all black males stock targets for retribution.[16] The rape myth and the extreme sadism of sexual dismemberment that mobs exhibited reassured whites that their conduct had a certain rationale, a discernible beginning and end.

Of course, that could not be. Such violence defied neatly drawn boundaries. It had no sure limits, was inseparable from the larger public context that gave it roots, and could never be terminated by any logic of its own. Lynching was an extreme illustration of the group dynamics that Neil J. Smelser examined in his *Theory of Collective Behavior*. Acting from a general belief system, mob members seized any random occasion to express their mutual fears and release their shared hostilities. And social psychologist Roger Brown has affirmed the mechanism for social control that lynching involved. He found it an outlet for displaced aggression as well as an inducement to sadism in defense of the South's sexual mythologies.[17]

Of all the students of lynching, none has written with more knowledge of the practice than Walter White of the NAACP. He joined the organization's national staff in 1918 and became almost immediately involved with firsthand investigations of mob violence against the black community. His 1929 book, *Rope and Faggot: A Biography of Judge Lynch*, remains a primer on the topic. White's assessment of lynching was not at variance with most twentieth-century explanations; his was, however, considerably more detailed and outspoken. White explored and denounced the economic and political exploitation linked to white supremacist theories. He argued that lynching offered southerners a diversion from an otherwise dull existence, that lynchers were spawned by a culture that rejected new ideas, and that fundamentalist religions aggravated the sexual fears underlying the cruelty of the mob.[18]

Lynching declined after 1921 and seemed almost extinct by mid-century (see Table 2). Undoubtedly its spirit lingered in the bombings of black churches and homes, the assassinations of Medgar Evers and Martin Luther King, Jr., and the murder of civil rights workers in the deep South during the 1960s, but the mob no longer roamed at will nor did racist killers go unpunished.[19] Gunnar Myrdal speculated that lynchings dropped as the semi-isolation of southern life faded. Rural electrification and the radio, paved highways and the automobile, motion pictures and educational improvements, and, one might add, intercollegiate athletics offered alternatives to traditional beliefs and ritualized behavior.[20] Of course, the South was not transformed overnight. But for two consecutive generations, from World War I to 1960, the effects were cumulative. Various modernizing trends, including the mechanization of agriculture, industrial expansion, and the migration of blacks and whites from rural to urban areas within and beyond the region produced considerable change and mandated techniques of social control other than lynching. Northern investors and southern merchants preferred steady economic performance to the unsettling emotions of open race conflict. And, as sociologist John Shelton Reed has noted, advocates of industrialism—journalists, business managers, and public officials—rallied to suppress violence or the evidence of violence that might damage the region's image and retard its growth.[21]

In such a setting Social Gospelers could denounce the brutalities of mobbism, and expect at last to be heard. Against considerable odds, the Atlanta-based Commission on Interracial Cooperation (CIC) emerged in 1919 to rally influential white moderates and carefully picked black leaders. The CIC campaigned against mob violence, sponsored the Southern Commission on the Study of Lynching, abetted the Association of Southern Women for the Prevention of Lynching, and helped generally to hasten lynching's decline before transforming itself into the Southern Regional Council of the mid-1940s.[22] Throughout the interwar years and beyond, southern officials and juries would persist in their reluctance to punish mob members or delinquent peace officers. As early as 1933, however, scholar Arthur Raper was able to report some 704 prevented lynchings during the preceding nineteen years.[23]

Unquestionably, organized pressures from outside the South facilitated lynching's decline. That was the NAACP's great service. As early as 1916, the black academician William Pickens predicted that disclosures of southern brutalities would be an essential precondition to ending mob violence. Walter White consistently argued that the NAACP's investigations, exposés, and campaigns for a federal antilynching law awakened public concern, created a political dialogue on the topic of violence, and induced the South to reconsider its most blatant forms of racist aggression. Writing in 1939 and 1944, respectively, just after the peak of the Association's congressional drive, both Hortense Powdermaker and Gunnar Myrdal agreed with White's assessment.[24]

Altered cultural patterns, economic diversification, regional self-interest, moral suasion, disclosures of routine brutalities, public condemnation, lobbying, and threats of federal intervention were all powerful inducements to reduce mob action. More subtle developments played a hand, as well. Lynching had served as a powerful weapon in the white

South's campaign to reverse the implications of Reconstruction. From the 1870s to the 1920s, three overlapping generations had worked to oust blacks from public life, to forestall any renewed federal intervention in the region's internal governance, to "redeem" the South permanently. With a combination of Jim Crow laws, rigidly enforced segregationist customs, mob action, and a mythology of race that lent belief to behavior, whites thrust the black community into a subordinate status well beyond the reach of the Thirteenth Amendment. By the second decade of the twentieth century, the matter was largely settled as an item of "conventional wisdom," and the North, for the most part, concurred. Even the potential disruptions of black migration could be accommodated, because the employment and wage systems of the urban South lay firmly in white hands. That, too, made lynching less essential as an instrument of control.[25]

As the region became more securely fastened to the rest of America's socio-economic patterns, it found ways to adapt without sacrificing white supremacy. The movement of northern industries to the South after World War I, for example, opened job opportunities to whites for which blacks were seldom eligible. And with the Great Depression, New Deal relief and employment programs had multiple effects upon racial tensions. Crop reduction and acreage allotment programs drove black and white sharecroppers and tenants from the land, but whites found ready alternatives in the CCC, WPA, TVA, and other federally sponsored activities. Since the New Deal left on-site administration of such projects to local officials, it was easy to apply their Jim Crow preferences to work assignments. Blacks got only the most menial tasks, if any.[26] While not intended to have this effect, federally funded operations launched a pattern of dependency that lower-class, unemployed or underemployed black men and women would find a part of their existence into the present. While these newer patterns of dominance were transformed into social conventions, southern liberals more often acceded to than challenged the general racism of their region.[27] With blacks largely disfranchised, segregated, and economically victimized, supremacists could dispense with lynching as an everyday means of manipulation and control. Blacks, however, could never be certain that violence might not recur.

From the post-Reconstruction years to the mid-twentieth century, Afro-Americans were keenly aware of their vulnerability. Though exploited throughout the South and abandoned by the federal government, they exhibited neither passivity nor indifference. In the mid-1880s, for example, New York journalist T. Thomas Fortune advocated retaliatory self-defense. By 1890 he urged, instead, an orderly antilynching campaign through his newly established Afro-American League. Bishop Henry M. Turner of the African Methodist Episcopal Church hoped also to launch a drive against lynching with his short-lived Equal Rights Council of 1893. His motivation was quite explicit: "Until we are free from menace by lynchers . . . we are destined to be a dwarfed people."[28]

Meanwhile Frederick Douglass denounced the rape myth and its casual acceptance among influential and otherwise thoughtful whites. In the *North American Review*, he decried mob action and warned against goading black men to acts of desperation by treating them and their families outside the law.[29]

During the 1890s, Ida B. Wells was an active campaigner against lynching. She used her Memphis newspaper, *Free Speech*, until it was sacked by angry whites. She worked briefly with Fortune at the New York *Age* and then mobilized the Anti-lynching Committee in Britain to arouse foreign opinion against mob violence in America.[30] Prompted in 1898 by such atrocities as the lynching of Frazier B. Baker, a black postmaster in South Carolina, and by the riot at Wilmington, North Carolina, Wells and Bishop Alexander Walters of the AME Zion church, among others, launched the Afro-American Council for an attack upon lynching and other forms of racial injustice. When a mass meeting in Chicago adopted resolutions demanding apprehension of Baker's killers, indemnities for his survivors, and a federal antilynching law, Wells delivered the appeals to Washington. Joined by a delegation of Illinois congressmen, she made a presentation to President William McKinley. Subsequently, the black community was distressed, if not greatly surprised, when a federal court failed to convict any of those arrested in the postmaster's death.[31]

For blacks of the late nineteenth and early twentieth century, opposition to mob violence provided a common ground on which to stand, whatever their ideological and tactical difference on other matters. Nonetheless, disagreements did exist on how to handle the issue publicly. Some chose to leave the South rather than tolerate further brutality. Others proposed a workers' strike to disrupt white business activity after the next lynching. A few individuals echoed Fortune's earlier sentiments about retaliatory self-defense. Militant clergy like Reverdy C. Ransom and Francis Grimké openly condemned mobbism, while black newspapers like George Knox's Indianapolis *Freeman*, John Mitchell's Richmond, Virginia, *Planet*, J. Max Barber's Atlanta *Voice of the Negro*, William Monroe Trotter's Boston *Guardian*, and Harry C. Smith's Cleveland *Gazette* were generally outspoken on the topic. When blacks had a role in public affairs, an opportunity increasingly denied them throughout the South, they worked for legislative protections, as well. As a member of the Ohio General Assembly, for example, Harry C. Smith sponsored and won passage of an 1896 antilynching law that served for the next two decades as a model for other states willing to combat mobbism.[32]

It may be an index to the widely felt concern over lynching that those leaders who did hesitate found themselves on the defensive with each new evidence of mob terror. Booker T. Washington, for example, faced growing dissatisfaction with his accommodationist philosophy generally and was forced to accept a stronger line on lynching when he met with W. E. B. Du Bois and other dissidents at the Carnegie Hall conference in

January 1904. He never could appease them, for only ten months later he lamented to Oswald Garrison Villard, white liberal of the influential New York *Evening Post*, that northern militants had charged him "with cowardice" on the subject. He admitted not having protested each lynching, but argued that outspokenness would undermine his overall effectiveness.[33] Opposition to Washington took concrete form in the Niagara Movement of 1905; a year later, critics were denouncing his temperate reactions to the Atlanta riot that took at least a dozen black lives. Moreover, they publicly condemned President Theodore Roosevelt, with whom Washington was identified, for the summary discharge of 167 black troops following the Brownsville, Texas, riot of August 1906.[34]

Despite a general acceptance of or indifference to lynching among whites, a few of them decried the practice. Some believed blacks inferior but argued, nonetheless, that constitutional guarantees must be enforced for all. Others charged that illiteracy among blacks fostered not only crime but also suspicions of crime and thereby fed the lynching mania.[35] A counter argument, and one that attracted considerable support in the early years of the twentieth century, asserted that delays in jury trials and appeal processes made whites impatient and forced them outside the law to deal with black defendants.[36] For two reasons, none of these views could provide a sound basis for ending mob violence. They implied that black victims somehow shared in creating the conditions responsible for their own oppression, and they disregarded lynching's use as an instrument of interracial control.

Concurrently, the fear emerged that lynching damaged respect for law and order and harmed the nation's reputation. Because this view expressed a concern for the integrity of public institutions, it fit the perspectives of contemporary reformers and conservatives alike. It lent momentum to the passage or revision of laws dealing with mob action in several southern, border, and midwestern states during the 1890s and the early years of the twentieth century. Enforcement, of course, was another matter, and these laws were frequently ignored.[37] Indiana Governor Winfield T. Durbin, John Cardinal Gibbons of the Roman Catholic church, and various southern Protestant groups worried about lynching's erosion of public stability. So, too, did the Southern Sociological Congress, established in 1912, and one of its leading figures, Willis D. Weatherford of the southern Y.M.C.A.[38]

A few white and interracial bodies advanced more militant attacks, in which the plight of black Americans themselves took high priority. The National Citizens Rights Association, launched by Albion Tourgée in 1891, and the Constitutional League of the United States (commonly known as the Constitution League), founded in 1904 by John E. Milholland, another white reformer, fell into this category.[39] In November 1899, over 2,400 Union League members petitioned Congress to make lynching a federal crime, while among national magazines, *The Nation*, and especially *The Independent*, consistently denounced mob violence and other blatant forms of prejudice.[40] But these were like voices in a wilderness.

Public officials and major political parties remained wholly unresponsive to black needs. The federal government had abandoned its defense of constitutional and human rights in deference to states' rights, and a number of Supreme Court decisions, including the *Civil Rights Cases* (1883), *Plessey* v. *Ferguson* (1896), and *Hodges* v. *United States* (1906), lent sanction to this withdrawal.[41] Candidates for office either looked the other way or joined their noisiest constituents in race baiting. The atmosphere of the day honored white solidarity and old-fashioned virtues. Blacks, new immigrants, anarchists, radical labor unionists, Native Americans, the "little brown people" of America's expanding colonial domain in the Caribbean and Middle Pacific, and later, the socialist-pacifists of the First World War were all viewed as pariahs. The more pluralism loomed, the more avidly mainstream Americans embraced conformity.

The White House proved an unreliable source of redress for black grievances. Apparently Benjamin Harrison was its first occupant to advocate a federal law against lynching. He was prompted to do so because of the recurring violence against Afro-Americans and because of official embarrassment over the lynching of eleven Italians at New Orleans in 1891. Like other turn-of-the-century presidents, however, Harrison more often stressed the limitations of federal power in interracial matters and emphasized, instead, the importance of sectional harmonies. As governor of Ohio, William McKinley had opposed mob rule and supported the state's 1896 antilynching law. He was equally forthright in his first presidential inaugural address: "Lynchings must not be tolerated in a great and civilized country like the United States. . . . Equality of rights must prevail." Still, mobs faced no interference from the government during his presidency. Roosevelt encouraged others to denounce lynching but failed to dissociate it from rape in his remarks; and William Howard Taft preferred to leave the problem to the states.[42]

The mere handful of congressmen concerned with social justice could hardly put an end to lynching and other racist activities. The two best known pieces of federal legislation designed to assist black people failed to pass. The aid-to-education measure, sponsored by Senator Henry W. Blair (R–New Hampshire) was lost four times between 1884 and 1890; the bill to protect voting rights in the South, introduced by Congressman Henry Cabot Lodge (R–Massachusetts), suffered the same fate in the early 1890s.[43] In 1884 Senator John A. Logan (R–Illinois) had proposed a federal commission on the status of black Americans, but his bill made no headway; neither did Blair's 1894 resolution for a $25,000 appropriation to investigate lynchings.[44] During the early and mid-1890s, Senators John H. Mitchell (R–Oregon), William A. Peffer (Populist–Kansas), and Henry L. Dawes (R–Massachusetts), like Lodge and Blair, offered petitions from their constituents and from others around the country urging federal action against mob violence.[45] In January of 1900, Shelby M. Cullom (R–Rhode Island) laid before the Senate an antilynching petition with over 3,200 signatures. That same month, Congressman George H. White (R–North Carolina) sponsored an actual antilynching bill.[46]

Two Massachusetts Republicans, Representative William H. Moody and Senator George Frisbie Hoar, lent their prestige to the cause in December 1901 by introducing an antilynching bill designed by Albert E. Pillsbury, prominent Bostonian and former attorney general of the Commonwealth. Pillsbury defended the measure in the *Harvard Law Review*, but Congress was unmoved. The bill, however, would later serve as a model for NAACP-sponsored legislation.[47] In the spring of 1902, Jacob H. Gallinger (R–New Hampshire) tried unsuccessfully to secure a Senate inquiry into lynching and possible federal remedies. Taking a somewhat different tack, Congressman Edgar D. Crumpacker (R–Indiana) offered bills in 1902, 1905, and 1907 against the lynching of aliens.[48] Nothing came of these proposals for federal initiatives against mob violence. Instead, a Jim Crow mentality thrived, and the fact that Congress stubbornly refused to enact any civil rights measure from 1875 to 1957 suggests something of the frustrations felt by those who sought legislative remedies for black grievances.[49]

Meanwhile, there were too few black lawmakers, and their service was too brief, to have a substantial impact. From 1870 to 1901, only twenty-two black men sat in Congress. No more than eight ever held office simultaneously, and after 1877 their number slipped steadily. From 1892 to 1901, no congressional session had more than one black member, and so lasting were the effects of Jim Crow that not another Afro-American would win election to Congress until Oscar De Priest (R–Illinois) in 1928. Black legislators did what little they could, however. Senator Blanche K. Bruce (R–Mississippi) pleaded in 1876 for a federal inquiry into the violence that was stripping southern blacks of their civil and political rights; Thomas E. Miller (R–South Carolina) condemned lynching during a House speech in 1891; and George White introduced his antilynching bill during his final term.[50] Petitions from Philadelphia, New York, Virginia, Texas, and the District of Columbia showed support for White's measure, but it never came to a floor vote.[51] Hundreds of antilynching bills met a similar fate throughout the next five decades.[52]

By the early twentieth century, the civil status of blacks had deteriorated to an alarming degree, and there was a desperate need to combat the capriciousness and brutalities of lynching. Unexamined but widely held racist assumptions, public indifference, the inability or reluctance of officials to protect black lives, an ineffectual federal response, and a hesitant southern conscience in search of "good reasons" to deal with mob violence all conspired against racial justice. Matched against them, however, were two emerging forces: an interracial, reformist spirit impatient with Booker T. Washington's accommodationism, and a beleaguered but increasingly angry black community. The two intersected in the aftermath of the 1908 race riot in Springfield, Illinois, to form the National Association for the Advancement of Colored People.[53] Thereafter, black and white activists had an organization of national proportions with which to challenge racist beliefs and behavior.

NAACP leaders felt themselves recapitulating the work of William Lloyd Garrison, Frederick Douglass, the Grimké sisters, and other nineteenth-century abolitionists. At the same time, the Association's personnel fully reflected the early twentieth-century Progressive movement, with its tendency to attract well educated, professionally oriented, middle- and upper-middle-class advocates of urban liberalism. The NAACP's founding group was heavily comprised of authors, publicists, social workers, academicians, clergy, and lawyers, black and white, women and men, whose aggregate philosophies embraced such diverse causes as the Social Gospel, feminism, pacifism, socialism, and an old-fashioned enthusiasm for good government and public service.[54] An abiding commitment to the concept of equal rights induced NAACP organizers, whatever their differences on specific issues, to confront the needs of the Afro-American community in general and the horrors of mob violence in particular. Reviewing half a century of race relations in 1959, reformist clergyman John Haynes Holmes, who helped to launch the NAACP, remembered that, "it was to end this reign of lawlessness and terror and implement constitutional and statute decrees in the Negro's full interest as man and citizen, that the National Association for the Advancement of Colored People came into being."[55]

Progressives in general abhorred arbitrary force capriciously applied and sought through law to impose restraints. Ready to utilize the power of the people through democratic channels, they worked to obtain food and drug laws, antitrust legislation, child labor provisions, regulated railroad rates, a graduated income tax, the direct election of senators, votes for women, referendum and recall procedures, and other reforms. In their revulsion against all forms of mob violence, NAACP officials turned to the ultimate arbiter, the federal government, for antilynching legislation, once it became clear that local and state authorities would not or could not stop the slaughter. Like their contemporaries, NAACP personnel resorted to investigations, disclosures, conferences, publicity, negotiations with influential persons in government and business, lobbying, and litigation to achieve their objectives. Time after time, the Association would draw upon the values, attitudes, and techniques of the Progressive era from which it had sprung. For nearly half a century it would dominate and set the tone for and the style of interracial protest in America. Understanding this makes it possible to appreciate more fully the importance, vitality, and shortcomings of the NAACP campaigns for a federal antilynching law.

What follows is not a history of the NAACP; nor is it a social or psychological study of lynching and its practitioners. Rather, this book was designed to analyze the role that the Association played in the struggle against lynching and to explore the consequences of that role for the organization itself and for the emergence of the twentieth-century civil rights movement. No such movement for human rights could have occurred, in the form it took, without the NAACP's campaign against the mob.

This was a priority objective for the Association well into its fourth decade as an organization and long after the initial dimensions of lynching had receded into the historical background. Such persistence puzzled contemporary critics and has not been fully addressed by later historians. We need only look at the record. The fact that there were over 3,400 black victims from the early 1880s to the mid-twentieth century seems reason enough to pursue the fight against violence. Moreover, key Association leaders, like James Weldon Johnson and Walter White, confronted firsthand the evidence of mob action and were determined to end it, and every black person knew of family members, friends, acquaintances, and friends of friends who had felt the terror of summary justice. From a black perspective, there was ample justification for wanting to invoke federal protections, whether in 1918, 1922, 1937, or 1949.

While the campaign against lynching was essential and sincere on its own terms, the NAACP also realized that it could be used to draw attention to other racial inequities. Thus, lynching had dual implications, manifest and latent consequences: each killing justified a continued struggle against the mob, and the Association utilized each incident to educate Americans to the need for broader reforms. At a time when the public refused to honor voting rights, integrated education, equal employment opportunities, open housing, access to public accommodations, or social equality, the NAACP could gain a hearing by showing how violence threatened generally held Judeo-Christian and democratic values.

The drive against mobbism had multiple results. It was the Association's earliest and most sustained attempt to bring the federal government back into the field of civil rights enforcement. Lynching became the wedge by which the NAACP insinuated itself into the public conscience, developed contacts within governmental circles, established credibility among philanthropists, and opened lines of communication with other liberal-reformist groups that eventually joined it in a mid-century, civil rights coalition of unprecedented proportions. Lynching provided a readily acceptable issue around which to mobilize the black community, North and South. Once brought together against mob action, black people were better able thereafter to pursue other common objectives.

In organizational terms, the antilynching struggle provided the NAACP staff with opportunities to generate new membership and raise badly needed funds. But there was more. Since black men and women were routinely denied participation in major corporate, governmental, educational, and philanthropic networks, or were consigned to mere token roles in decision-making processes, the antilynching campaigns offered indispensable alternatives: training in public affairs, exposure to political practices at the highest and most sophisticated levels, insights into the mechanisms for effecting social change, and a direct, if sometimes harsh, appreciation for how the power brokers of this society function. For years Association officials would apply these lessons in other civil rights areas. Furthermore, the fight against mob violence brought the Association into direct working contact with southern white liberals, especially those in the Commission on Interracial Cooperation and, later, the Southern Regional Council. Finally, the antilynching drive stood as ready evidence of the NAACP's initiative on behalf of black people and helped, thereby, to deflect criticism levelled at the organization by certain black nationalist groups, like Marcus Garvey's Universal Negro Improvement Association in the 1920s, and various leftist organizations, like the Communist Party–USA in the 1930s.

Congress has never enacted an antilynching law as such. The closest it had come, before the NAACP began, was in segments of the civil rights statutes of the Reconstruction period, especially in the so-called Enforcement Act of 1870 and Ku Klux Klan Act of 1871. After the Supreme Court nullified portions of these laws, residual parts were incorporated into sections 51 and 52, later 241 and 242, of Title 18 of the United States Code. As interpreted and implemented, however, they proved insufficient for combating lynching.[56] The NAACP secured House passage of an antilynching measure on three occasions, 1922, 1937, and 1940, but each time it was killed in the Senate by a filibuster or the threat of a filibuster. Finally moved by a decade of intense public concern, Congress passed five civil rights measures from 1957 to 1968. The last of these established fines and jail terms for anyone who injured or killed a person seeking to exercise a wide range of federally protected civil rights—the nearest enactment yet to a national antilynching law.[57]

Throughout its quest for federal protections against mob violence, the NAACP faced a dilemma that has long confronted American reformers: the realities of a federal system that honors authority at the local, state, and national levels simultaneously. Abolitionists, suffragists, civil rights campaigners, labor union organizers, opponents of child labor, social welfare advocates, and proponents of the Equal Rights Amendment, to mention but a few, have all had to wrestle with the concept and practice of multiple jurisdictions. Realizing that local and state officials, and the white constituents to whom they answered, were not about to end mob rule, the Association sought a federal antilynching law. Time after time, opponents responded that lynching was murder, and murder was a matter for the states to resolve. Southern politicians and publicists, reformers among them, and constitutional conservatives elsewhere, evoked the image of states' rights to deflect NAACP efforts and to keep lynching beyond the reach of federal intervention. In the early decades of this century, such a tactic coincided with political expediency, sectional reconciliation, conventional wisdom, and the tenor of prevailing Supreme Court decisions.[58] But it made little practical sense to black victims and wholly defied the logic of a highly mobile and interdependent society that increasingly conducted its affairs across local, state, and regional lines.

The NAACP faced the enormous task of changing public attitudes as well as public law, if it hoped to involve federal authorities in a predictable and effective attack upon mobbism. Since the prosecution of individual mob members posed sticky constitutional issues, the Association was prepared to take a more oblique approach. This it did through the application of the Fourteenth Amendment, with its guarantees for all citizens of due process and equal protection of the law. NAACP strategists argued that the states had refused to protect black citizens' rights, that lynching recurred because officials and the general public condoned the mob's handiwork. Consequently, they maintained, delinquent officials must be removed, fined, or imprisoned, and the county, as the legal agent of the state, fined for each lynching within its jurisdiction.[59] The Association also hoped that the county liability provisions of any federal antilynching law would induce middle- and upper-income taxpayers to resist lynching after a review of their own economic self-interests.

Not surprisingly, critics of federal intervention were not quieted by this approach. They disliked any external review of locally elected officials and even more stubbornly opposed county liability. They proclaimed it an unwarranted interference in local affairs, argued that it unjustly penalized citizens who had nothing to do with the violence, and fought its inclusion in NAACP bills from 1920 to 1950. But there were state precedents to which the Association could turn. As early as 1893, Georgia had penalized sheriffs who failed to guard their prisoners against a mob, but the enforcement provisions were inadequate. By 1940, at least thirteen states, six outside the South, had legislated against delinquent officials. In 1896, Ohio enacted a strong antilynching law with a model county-liability provision; nine others utilized the Ohio statute in drafting their own regulations about county liability, and a dozen states, nine of them outside the South, had such measures by 1940.[60] Ironically, these laws were used by both sides as an issue in the debate over federal intervention. Since enforcement was uneven, skeptics doubted the wisdom of any further enactments; in any event, they conceded nothing beyond the propriety of state jurisdiction. The NAACP countered that the states, especially those in which blacks were most vulnerable, had not resolved the problems of violence. Consequently, federal solutions were imperative.

Throughout its existence, the Association has sought to transform American race relations. In ways that would prove vastly important for the nation, for the black community, and for the NAACP itself, the drive against lynching was an essential part of that objective for over four decades. This is not to discount the importance of the organization's victories in state and federal courts, its efforts for other legislative objectives, or its high-level negotiations with well-placed leaders in political, business, labor, academic, and civic circles. But the antilynching drive had an urgency, a public visibility, and a dramatic quality that no other civil rights activity quite matched. It was through the antilynching struggles that the NAACP gained much of its stability and recognition, learned how to deal with the complex problems of race in America, and placed itself simultaneously in the vanguard of black activism and at the center of national affairs.

2

The NAACP Confronts Mob Violence, 1909-1919

Afro-Americans had often enough been the victims of mob violence, but the race riot that ravaged Springfield, Illinois, in mid-August, 1908, evoked a special response among white and black activists. Of the city's 60,000 occupants, 4,500 were black. During the riot, whites lynched two and forced 2,000 others to flee. Property damage reached $120,000, business activity lay paralyzed for ten days, and the 4,000 militiamen used to restore order reportedly cost the State treasury $200,000.[1] Socialists William English Walling and Anna Strunsky personally investigated the incident and were shocked by what they learned. In the September 3 issue of the widely respected *Independent* magazine, Walling appealed for corrective action:

> Either the spirit of the abolitionists, of Lincoln and of Lovejoy must be revived and we must come to treat the Negro on a plane of absolute political and social equality, or Vardaman and Tillman will soon have transferred the race war to the North. . . . Yet who realized the seriousness of the situation, and what large and powerful body of citizens is ready to come to their aid?[2]

The Springfield riot led directly to the founding of the NAACP. The fact that such brutality had occurred in a northern city, indeed, in the capital of Illinois and the town so closely associated with the memory of Abraham Lincoln, helped to mobilize reformers in ways that previous racial disorders had not.

Walling and New York social workers Mary White Ovington and Henry Moskowitz turned for help to Oswald Garrison Villard. Grandson of abolitionist William Lloyd Garrison, Villard responded with his famous "Lincoln's Birthday Call" of February 12, 1909, which reviewed the extent of racial injustices and declared that,

> the spread of lawless attacks upon the Negro, North, South and West—even in the Springfield made famous by Lincoln—often accompanied by revolting brutalities, sparing neither sex nor age nor

youth, could but shock the author of the sentiment that "government of the people, by the people, for the people, should not perish from the earth."[3]

The Call carried the signatures of fifty-three prominent persons, writers, educators, social workers, publicists, and it roused considerable interest. But harder tasks remained. For this purpose a small group in New York City, calling itself the National Negro Committee, laid plans for a meeting in the late spring of 1909.[4]

The conference took place at the Henry Street Settlement on May 31 and June 1; among a number of topics, lynching was an omnipresent reality. Ida B. Wells-Barnett denounced "color line murder," excused but not caused by crimes against white women, as a "national crime" that "requires a national remedy." Arguing the need for federal action, she noted senator Gallinger's resolution to determine what steps Congress might take against mobbism, and a pending bill for federal prosecution of lynchers (again drafted with the aid of Albert Pillsbury).[5] Naming a Committee of Forty to handle organizational activities, the group made its position perfectly clear by denouncing "the ever-growing oppression of our 10,000,000 colored fellow citizens. . . . [who are often deprived] of their just share of the public funds, robbed of nearly all part in the government, segregated by common carriers, some murdered with impunity, and all treated with open contempt by officials . . . [and]held in some States in practical slavery to the white community." The conferees demanded that the president and Congress enforce the constitutional rights guaranteed in the Fourteenth Amendment, provide equal educational opportunities and a fair expenditure of public funds for black and white students, and protect voting rights under the Fifteenth Amendment.[6]

A year later, the National Negro Committee had completed its assignment and yielded its functions to the newly established National Association for the Advancement of Colored People, "its object to be equal rights and opportunities for all." The NAACP would use investigations and open meetings throughout the nation to discuss "peonage, public education, lynching, injustices in courts, etc.," with the proceedings to enjoy "the widest possible publicity."[7] Americans today may find it difficult to comprehend what it meant to have racism consigned to virtual obscurity, afforded little or no constructive attention in the public media, and, not infrequently, suppressed or misrepresented. As late as World War II, Swedish economist Gunnar Mydral, in his famous study of race in America undertaken for the Carnegie Corporation of New York, declared that, "to get publicity is of the highest strategic importance to the Negro people."[8] NAACP organizers understood this from the beginning, and their determination to expose injustices rested on their belief that a democratic society would respond constructively if only it had the facts at its disposal. This commitment to disclosure marked the organization's campaigns against lynching for the next forty years.

The National Negro Committee and the NAACP itself consisted of seasoned, vigorous reformers, interracial but white for the most part, very largely middle and upper-middle class, and drawn primarily from northern and midwestern circles.[9] While diverse in terms of particular views, experiences, and affiliations, they felt a common revulsion toward all forms of mob action. Such violence offended their sense of justice, because it violated individual rights, caused untold human suffering, jeopardized orderly, democratic procedures, and extended the victimization of an already oppressed race. As experienced activists, they had participated in other causes to protect all that the mob now threatened. Thus, lynching had to end, and through the NAACP they had a means to pursue that goal.

These reformers had the credentials to proceed. John E. Milholland of the Constitution League, economist Edwin R. A. Seligman, socialist and muckraking author Charles Edward Russell, and Ovington, Villard, and Walling were at the heart of the drive to establish the NAACP. So, too, was W. E. B. Du Bois, the noted black scholar-activist, whose 1903 publication, *The Souls of Black Folk*, had startled the public with its attack on Booker T. Washington's accommodationism.[10] By his emphasis on absolute equality in political, educational, and civil matters, Du Bois represented the philosophical thrust of the new Association. Recognizing America's contrived ignorance of racial injustice, he spoke of the veil separating the races. He argued, as well, that "the problem of the twentieth century is the problem of the color-line."[11] When Du Bois consented to leave Atlanta University in 1910 to become the Association's first Director of Publications and Research, and editor of its magazine, *The Crisis*, Mary White Ovington rejoiced that, "we nailed our banner to the mast. . . . From that time onward, no one doubted where we stood."[12]

Nor need anyone have misread their determination to work for social change. The NAACP's first president, Moorfield Storey, had a long familiarity with public issues. From late 1867 to the spring of 1869 he served in Washington, D.C., as secretary to Senator Charles Sumner of Massachusetts. As his career unfolded, Storey was a spirited patrician advocate of political and civic reform, president of the American Bar Association in 1896, and a turn-of-the-century opponent of American imperialism.[13] No less experienced were such NAACP mobilizers as Jane Addams of Hull House, Lillian Wald of the National Women's Trade Union League, Florence Kelley of the National Consumers League, Rabbi Stephen S. Wise, and black clergymen Alexander Walters and Francis Grimké.

Historians still debate the meaning of "Progressivism," and certainly not all NAACP leaders fit any single definition.[14] But lynching shocked northern reformers, who reacted with a demand not for force to counter force but for exposure, public education, judicial remedy, and legislation. Typical of this approach was a letter from Moorfield Storey to Congressman Frederick W. Dallinger (R–Massachusetts), whose antilynching measure was later merged with that of St. Louis Republican Leonidas Dyer (sponsor throughout the 1920s of the NAACP's antilynching bills). As a lawyer, Storey sought to resolve the problem of what the federal government could properly do about lynching.[15] "It has seemed to me," he wrote Dallinger in 1920, "a very doubtful question whether legislation by Congress against lynching in the States is constitutional, but I am very clearly of the opinion that it ought to be tried." The South expected the attempt and many southern citizens, opposed to lynching, would actually welcome it. He conceded that mob murder was customarily an offense left to the jurisdiction of the separate states, provided they actually did their best to prevent such crimes and punish perpetrators. If, however, the authorities should prove negligent, as they so often had, then the federal government should intervene. Storey concluded: "I hope your act . . . may become a law, for I feel very sure that unless lynching of colored people is stopped we are drifting into what may well become civil war."[16] No better illustration of a Progressive mentality, with its aversion to lawlessness, its fear of violence, its devotion to legal redress, and its reluctant acceptance of more sweeping procedures in the face of necessity, can be imagined. The Association would draw heavily and repeatedly upon the beliefs, aspirations, and the techniques of the Progressive era from which it emerged, as it proceeded over the next half century to combat lynching and to thrust itself into the center of the drive for national, interracial reform.

Progressivism laid the foundations of twentieth-century liberalism, with all its promises and shortcomings. Boasting a rich humanistic heritage, liberalism pledged more than it could deliver for the protection of black, other minority, workers', and women's rights. Dealing with the complexities of American life, liberals too often relied on legalisms, middle-class cautions, and deference to competing opinions in negotiations with entrenched economic interests and politically powerful, conservative forces. Despite the Fourteenth, Fifteenth, Sixteenth, and Nineteenth amendments to the Constitution, blacks, other minorities, workers, and women were left to rely on the very type of "virtual representation" that England had once offered the American colonists. As life in the twentieth century became increasingly bureaucratized, privileged white males, liberal and conservative, at the heart of the decision-making processes grew ever more distant from everyone else. Flawed by such exclusivity, neither liberalism nor the American Dream it professed to revere could fully meet the needs of America's "outsiders." While the favored few made and enforced the rules, these outsiders had to spend their emotional capital in protest and appeals, invest their energies and meager resources in carefully documented presentations legitimating their grievances, and, basically, wait their turn.[17] In very significant ways, the NAACP was faced with conditions beyond its means to remedy.

The Association had hardly begun to function when the issue of lynching was forced upon its agenda. In the year of Villard's "Call," 1909, 69 blacks had been lynched; 67 Afro-Americans suffered the same fate in 1910, 60 in 1911, and 62 in 1912. The comparable figures for white lynching victims were 13, 9, 7, and 2, respectively.[18] Individual cases in 1911 showed the brutalities involved. In mid-January, for example, a mob of twenty white men broke into the Shelbyville County jail, near Louisville, Kentucky, and seized three black prisoners. One, Eugene Marshall, had been convicted of killing an elderly black woman; the mob hanged him on a bridge outside town. The other two, Wade Paterson and James West, had been arrested on the vague charge of "attempting to detain" two white girls. When the mob ineptly tried to hang them both with the same rope, it broke, and they were shot to death while fleeing.[19] Three months later a more bizarre incident occurred in Livermore, Kentucky. Will Porter, who just minutes before had allegedly killed a white man, was tied up on stage at the local opera house and his body riddled with over one hundred bullets by mob members who purchased tickets to participate. Although thirteen people were later arrested for this lynching, neither this nor the Shelbyville affair seems to have produced any convictions.[20]

The NAACP reacted to the Livermore case with an appeal to President William Howard Taft and various congressional leaders. A group of ten Washington, D.C., citizens, headed by the black attorney Archibald Grimké of the Association's District branch, presented a resolution to Taft, who denied that the federal government possessed any authority to interfere in a state's internal affairs.[21] Meanwhile, the Association responded to two other lynchings, in Florida and Oklahoma. It wrote the governors involved, urged members to protest, gathered information from contacts within the states, and circulated press reports as the data became available.[22]

All this, however, was merely a prelude to the terrible events at Coatesville, Pennsylvania, not far from Philadelphia. On the night of August 13, a wounded black man, Zachariah Walker, suspected of having murdered an industrial guard, was seized at the local hospital and dragged, still chained to his bed, about half a mile from town. There a mob of some 4,000 lynched him by three times thrusting him into, and then withdrawing him from, a roaring bonfire.[23] Among reformers, Walker's death evoked a reaction similar to the Springfield riot three years earlier. Despite the Association's limited resources, Ovington, Villard, and others at the New York office stressed the need to secure evidence against the lynchers, not only because of the vicious nature of the murder but especially because it "had occurred almost at our door." If it could not bring mob members to justice in a major northeastern industrial state, the NAACP would stand little chance of achieving redress in southern areas where lynching had become such a commonplace. The Association's approach forecast the steps it would repeatedly undertake against lynching in the years ahead: on-site investigations, efforts at prosecution, fund-raising, protest meetings, news releases, and a campaign to win passage of appropriate civil rights legislation.

Martha Gruening, a volunteer social worker appointed to the staff the following winter, coordinated the NAACP's efforts, while Board members Mary Maclean and William Sinclair went into Coatesville to investigate local pressures against prosecution.[24] Thinking to expedite matters, the Association also employed the William Burns Detective Agency, but results proved costly and few. In mid-November more than four hundred men and women attended an NAACP antilynching rally at the Ethical Culture Society in New York City, and by the end of the year the Association had in hand an Anti-Lynching Fund of $400, which it used thereafter to fight mob violence.[25] But Coatesville produced no convictions. Local juries released those implicated in the crime, and by May of 1912 the district attorney had given up hope of obtaining any guilty verdicts whatsoever.[26] Apparently the North was not so very different from the South after all.

Meanwhile, the NAACP tried for nearly two years to get a Pennsylvania antilynching statute. In May of 1913, executive secretary May Childs Nerney wrote Board member Joel E. Spingarn that a friend of Villard's, Samuel B. Scott of Germantown, was introducing such a bill at Harrisburg and wanted an NAACP witness at the committee hearings. Nerney hoped that Spingarn would go, because "if after all our trouble over the Coatesville matter we could get this antilynching legislation passed, it would be a splendid victory for the National Association."[27] The implications in all this were clear: NAACP leaders found some of their best opportunities by working through a network of well-placed friends; others were prepared to see the Association as a source of expert testimony; and enactment would meet a pressing need and enhance the organization's reputation.

Throughout 1912, the NAACP had devoted considerable attention to mob violence, and the publication of a sixteen-page pamphlet, *Notes on Lynchings in the United States*, foreshadowed Association literature in the years ahead. *Notes* revealed that lynching created an atmosphere encouraging further crimes, rather than the other way about, as many southern white officials had argued. The pamphlet contained statistical data and bibliographical references. Essays by Villard and John Haynes Holmes stressed the humanitarian aspects of the antilynching crusade, and Pillsbury's article from the *Harvard Law Review* buttressed the Association's position. Because he viewed lynching as a national disgrace, Pillsbury cited laws, precedents, court cases, and legal arguments to show why the government in Washington could and should respond to mob violence. Whether or not antilynching legislation would violate the Constitution and state authority, as some opponents charged, could be resolved in the federal courts once Congress had acted.[28]

Always logical and carefully argued, the Association's position failed to move most public officials. In response to questions about the lynching of a black woman, Annie Bashdale, at Pinehurst, Georgia, in June of 1912, President Taft would go no further than to deplore mobbism, hope that her killers would be punished, and recite the need for better law enforcement in general. As the *New York Times* observed, however, the people of Pinehurst were strongly set against any prosecutions and convictions in the case.[29] And, at a governors' conference in Richmond, Virginia, the following December, Cole Blease of South Carolina rehearsed an old theme by announcing that lynchers in his state would go free, if their victims were black men who had assaulted white women. The Constitution, he shouted, simply did not apply to such matters.[30]

By this time the Association was increasingly dissatisfied with merely responding to mob murders as they occurred. Yet, it felt compelled to react to each new horror, since it still lacked the means to launch any major campaign that might reasonably forestall further lynching.[31] Searching for a broader approach in the fall of 1914, the national office distributed thousands of letters and fliers to elicit public support and to determine, in a congressional election year, where politicans stood on various race issues. Sent to all candidates in the Republican, Democratic, and Progressive parties, questionnaires asked for their positions on lynching, segregation, the possible reduction of congressional representation in states that violated the Fourteenth Amendment, proposed legislation against interracial marriage, and so forth.[32] Aside from putting them on notice, circularizing aspirants for public office had little immediate effect, but it was a tactic that the organization would regularly use in the future.

Not until 1916 did Association leaders attempt a more comprehensive approach. The mob had claimed fifty-six black lives the previous year, and the August 1915 lynching of Leo Frank, a Georgia white man convicted of rape-murder, had attracted national attention.[33] In such an atmosphere, Boston philanthropist Philip G. Peabody offered the NAACP a $10,000 grant on the condition that it devise a feasible campaign to end lynching. Responding to the challenge, the officers established the Committee on Anti-Lynching Programme in the late winter of 1916.[34] Members included Du Bois, Walling, Florence Kelley, and Joel Spingarn. Du Bois proposed that the money be used to gather evidence, rally support, prosecute sheriffs who allowed lynchings, and bring suits on behalf of the victims' survivors. Walling thought it might help to work more closely with such regional agencies as the Southern Sociological Congress, which had already indicated its concern, but Board member Owen Waller and Florence Kelley remained skeptical. The former doubted that legal action "stands any chance of success anywhere in the South," and the latter agreed that "neither persuasion nor an appeal to sentiment" would influence white southerners, although she favored federal intervention. Paul Kennaday, another Board member, urged the NAACP to remind chambers of commerce that mob violence hurt business by disrupting the smooth operations of the labor market.[35]

Peabody's offer represented an enormous incentive to an organization constantly strapped for funds. Accordingly, the national staff, under the direction of the recently appointed executive secretary, Royal Freeman Nash, prepared a "Memorandum for Mr. Philip G. Peabody on Lynch-Law and the Practicability of a Successful Attack Thereon." The Nash memorandum traced the history of lynching in America and examined what the NAACP might do, if it possessed the means. Various southern and border states had laws against mob violence, but public opinion precluded their enforcement. Nash assumed that, in spite of the prevailing trend, a growing dissatisfaction with lynching among southern liberals and moderates could lead to a responsive regional base matching the Association's efforts in the North and on the federal level. Accordingly, the new committee would gather and publish its data, attract southern whites to the campaign, prepare model antilynching bills for enactment by Congress and each of the states, solicit additional funds, and establish local committees to identify and prosecute lynchers.[36]

Headed by Moorfield Storey, a delegation met with Peabody on May 22; but he retracted his offer. He later informed Storey that "the small sum of ten thousand dollars" was simply not sufficient for the task. Moreover, the NAACP plan did not provide ample publicity in the northern press, and that would lessen the campaign's effectiveness. However, he enclosed a check for $1,000 with the promise that, if the Association found others more enthusiastic and could get $9,000 more, he would contribute an additional $1,000.[37]

Reactions to Peabody's decision indicated a great deal about the Association's stubborn determination to end lynching. "You will be sorry as I was to see that he is not satisfied with the plan," Storey wrote Nash, "but I do not think it should on that account be abandoned." He urged Nash to search for the additional money and promised $1,000 if the rest could be obtained.[38] The Board decided to appoint a three-member committee, chaired by Villard, to consider further actions and raise the $8,000 that would meet Peabody's and Storey's offers. But when Villard requested $325 to mail copies of an anti-lynching speech delivered by Willis D. Weatherford at the Southern Sociological Congress, other Board members hesitated.[39] They already faced bills of over $600, incurred in the Waco lynching investigation.[40] As so often happened, the NAACP found itself in a financial dilemma. Publicizing injustices and generating the resources necessary to combat them cost money the Association did not have.

Of the fifty-four reported lynchings in 1916, two—one in Texas and another in South Carolina—vividly demonstrated the deplorable conditions confronting the Association. In mid-May, Jesse Washington was burned to death at Waco. Suffragist Elizabeth Freeman, already on a speaking tour of the state, spent ten days investigating. Her findings, "The Waco Horror," appeared as an eight-page supplement to the July *Crisis*. Nash and his staff circulated the piece to 700 newspapers, with special illustrations of the lynching to fifty black papers; the supplement went to all members of Congress and was widely distributed with an appeal for funds. Finally, the Board voted to send Freeman on a two weeks' promotional trip "in the interest of the $10,000 fund."[41]

The Association had intended to bring suit in the Waco affair, and Nash looked for a Texas lawyer with whom the organization could work. But such matters, especially in the South, always involved great cost, lengthy delays, and uncertain results. In September, Storey explained that a Dallas attorney had offered to represent the Association for a $500 fee, with the expectation of an additional $1,000 if he could successfully institute grand jury proceedings. The Board felt it best to decline, with thanks.[42] Nonetheless, Nash believed the story had received more attention than any previous lynching.[43] Exposé thus served as a ready weapon, even if convictions in a southern courtroom remained elusive.

Soon after, Nash took personal responsibility for investigating and reporting the Anthony Crawford lynching in Abbeville, South Carolina, in the autumn of 1916. He found whites resentful of Crawford's prosperous and independent standing—the very sort of citizen that the late Booker T. Washington had extolled as the race's great hope for advancement. Publication of the secretary's findings in the December 11 issue of *The Independent* revealed once more the effective liaison between the NAACP staff and the prominent reform journals of the day. Perhaps *Independent* readers were heartened to learn that during the "calmer moments" following Crawford's murder, Abbeville citizens had publicly condemned the mob's action and discussed the necessity for state and federal intervention whenever local law and order collapsed, and that Governor Richard Manning had used the Abbeville incident to issue a strong statement against mob action. Nash hoped that "perhaps Anthony Crawford had not died wholly in vain."[44] Nevertheless, the NAACP and the black community at large still faced the enormous task of generating a sustained reaction against mob murders as a step toward interracial justice in America.

In pursuit of those goals, NAACP officials had undertaken a drive in 1916 that fell somewhat short of Peabody's target. Nevertheless, by August 31, there was a balance of $7,877; by October 7, it had risen to $9,297 in cash, with another $1,300 in pledges. The costs of gathering the money—staff salaries, travel, postage, printing, and the like—had run to $1,204, which meant that the organization enjoyed a highly respectable fund-raising ratio of about eight dollars gained for every one expended in the drive. Under Walling's chairmanship, the antilynching committee had done an amazingly effective job in a brief period. Of five special funds maintained by the Association at this point, no other exceeded $300; the antilynching fund had a balance on December 31 of $9,131; and all this occurred in a period (1912 to 1917) when the Association's annual income ranged between a very modest $11,000 and $15,000.[45] Indeed, in mid-

November, 1916, the Board had actually voted that the committee could spend up to $500 at its own discretion, without prior approval, so long as it reported such outlays at the next monthly Board meeting. Clearly, the campaign against mob violence, with its own major committee and special fund, had sufficient standing that it could and did take on a certain life of its own within the Association's total organizational program.[46]

In late November, the antilynching committee met at Moorfield Storey's Boston residence to reassess its activities and plan for the future. Members agreed that investigations and disclosures were primary weapons against mobbism. Beyond that, their conversations disclosed a certain restless search for newer techniques; some suggestions were creative, others seem quite fanciful in retrospect. They had not yet settled on the wisdom of trying for a federal antilynching law as a priority objective.

The group decided to send an agent through the South to explore the sources and extent of backing for an NAACP campaign. A Georgia white woman, Lily H. Hammond, whose husband formerly headed Paine College in Augusta, was proposed for this assignment, and the committee asked Walling to arrange reporter's credentials for her through the *Saturday Evening Post*, as a journalistic cover. This was a tactic the organization occasionally employed in later years, especially during Walter White's investigations of southern lynchings. The committee also planned to use Hammond's information as the basis for a major antilynching conference involving sympathetic southern leaders. Less vital was the idea of offering prizes in the South for the best high-school commencement addresses and college essays on the evils of lynching. Before adjourning, the committee decided to allot $5,000 for investigations and publicity, $2,500 for southern propaganda, and $2,000 for the prosecution of lynchers and for the legal defense of those accused of crimes and likely to become targets of the mob.[47] Exposé, it seemed, would remain the chief weapon.

Perhaps in thinking about a meeting of southerners, the committee hoped to replicate the success of the Amenia conference the previous August. At that time, Joel Spingarn had thrown open his country home eighty miles up the Hudson River from New York City to over four dozen leaders, men and women, mostly though not exclusively black, to discuss Afro-American issues.[48] But no southern-oriented meeting took place, despite Hammond's successful tour. Not until the spring of 1919 did the Association attempt such an ambitious antilynching conference, and that attracted largely northern participants.[49]

Two intervening developments helped considerably to transform the NAACP's approach to mob violence. First there was the addition to the national staff of James Weldon Johnson in late 1916 and of Walter Francis White in early 1918. Then, cutting across these appointments was America's involvement in World War I, which disrupted traditional civilian patterns of life and greatly increased racial tensions and violence. NAACP membership had risen steadily from 329 in 1912 to over 8,700 in

1916, and it would rocket to almost 44,000 during the war; monthly *Crisis* circulation exceeded 37,000 by the middle of 1916.[50] In its first half-dozen years, the NAACP was guided by a mixture of staff (always small in number, sometimes part-time in assignment) and Board members (forced to divide their energies among personal, business or professional matters, and the Association's work). And, there were occasional tensions among members of the two groups, especially when Du Bois protested the absence of any other blacks from major staff positions.[51] With greater demands on its services, the national office needed a larger and more harmonious work force.

The appointment of Roy Nash, a white man, proved merely an interim solution. He joined the organization as acting executive secretary in February 1916, became permanent secretary three months later, took leave in May 1917, to go to war, and formally resigned his NAACP office the following autumn.[52] Far more important, in view of the choice, was the selection of "a competent organizer or field agent whose chief duties shall be to supervise the branches."[53] For that purpose, the Board hired James Weldon Johnson in the fall of 1916.[54] Working as field secretary under two white executives, first Nash and then John R. Shillady, Johnson would eventually serve as the NAACP's first black executive secretary, from late 1920 to his resignation at the end of 1930. Once regarded as part of the Booker T. Washington network, Johnson began his involvement with the Association in unpretentious fashion.[55] He became a member in 1915, but there was nothing special in that. Then, Nash asked him in April 1916, to participate in an NAACP organizational meeting: "We wish particularly to enlist the college men and women of New York in a nation-wide fight against discrimination, segregation, lynching, and hostile legislation; and we want you to help us make the monthly meetings of the New York Branch an open forum on race questions that will attract liberal thinkers of all parties."[56] Shortly thereafter Joel Spingarn encouraged Johnson to attend the Amenia conference, and Du Bois scribbled "Do come" at the bottom of the invitation.[57] Johnson, then forty-five years old, fit smoothly into the Association's hierarchy. A former teacher, lawyer, and member of the United States consular service, and a successful Broadway lyricist, journalist, and author (his *Autobiography of an Ex-Coloured Man* appeared anonymously in 1912), he possessed the reformist attitudes and professional credentials of a Progressive, and he proved to be the one staff executive who won and held Du Bois's enduring respect.[58]

As a black man and a native of Florida, Johnson knew full well the horrors of mob action. All southern black people did. In fact, he had himself almost been lynched for no more serious a "crime" than having sat and talked on a park bench in Jacksonville with a woman journalist thought to be white by an angry mob of civilians and militiamen who put him under arrest. The near tragedy stayed with him for years thereafter, and certainly helped to inform and motivate the battle against lynching during his NAACP days.[59] In many ways, Johnson's work with the national staff had profound consequences.[60] He felt an urgent need to build a network of strong branches throughout the South. Perhaps wary of southern racism or disappointed in their own efforts to attract sufficient help from southern white moderates, some Board members objected that Johnson's proposal would cause the Association to compromise its overall stand on interracial issues. He countered that it was less important what was done for black America than what was done *by* black America, and with consent from the Board's majority set off in January 1917, to develop southern affiliates. During just such a field trip to Atlanta, he came upon Walter White, whom he induced to join the NAACP national staff as assistant executive secretary.[61]

Twenty-four years old when he arrived in New York City the following winter, White possessed none of his mentor's sophistication and wordly experiences. But there were bonds enough between them. Reared in Georgia, White, like Johnson, knew racism and the South firsthand. Both came from stable, middle-class family backgrounds, and graduated from Atlanta University, Johnson in 1894 and White in 1916. With blond hair, blue eyes, and a complexion light enough "to pass" when investigating lynchings and race riots for the NAACP, White, like Johnson, remained openly proud of his black heritage throughout life. And, like his older colleague, White had faced violence as a potential victim. He and his father crouched, weapons in hand, waiting to see if the mob would attack their home during the Atlanta riot of 1906. That incident had a lasting impact on White, and intensified his determination to combat racial violence.[62] Together, Johnson and White led the NAACP through a 1920s campaign to pass a federal law against lynching; thereafter, White as executive secretary pursued the goal indefatigably until 1949. In their hands, the antilynching effort became a number-one priority of the Association's public programs and the issue best conceived to redirect white America's perceptions of interracial realities. The appointments of Johnson and White and the initiative they demonstrated in office also provided the basis for a transition from white- to black-dominated leadership within the NAACP, a transition largely completed by the mid-1930s.[63]

Meanwhile, America's involvement in World War I raised new problems, as well as new opportunities for the NAACP and other advocates of interracial justice. A heightened spirit of intolerance directed at blacks, Jews, Catholics, and "foreign" elements had already taken visible shape in 1915 with the revival of the Ku Klux Klan. The release that same year of *The Birth of a Nation*, David W. Griffith's widely heralded motion picture about the Civil War and Reconstruction, was particularly offensive to Afro-Americans.[64] Based on Thomas Dixon's racist novel of 1905, *The Clansman*, the film prompted a spirited campaign by the NAACP to get it withdrawn or cut and re-edited.[65] Looking back a quarter century later, W. E. B. Du Bois still shared the opinion of his former colleagues that the production had unquestionably contributed to mob action and to the public's indifference to it.[66] Complementing the work of the national office, several NAACP locals entered the struggle, and the energetic Boston branch published a forty-seven-page pamphlet, *Fighting a Vicious Film*, as its contribution to the attack.[67] The Association also sought the creation of a movie that would portray black people in an honest, forthright fashion to counter the destructive effects of *The Birth of a Nation*, but the attempt fell through for lack of funds.[68]

As late as the fall of 1918, the Association still battled the Griffith film. It consulted the National Urban League to see what the two groups might do, tried to improve the image of black people in wartime Liberty Loan drives, and won support of the West Virginia Council of National Defense in suppressing *The Birth of a Nation* as detrimental to a united war effort.[69] Nevertheless, the picture enjoyed rather widespread success and would for many years thereafter. If the NAACP campaign accomplished anything, it helped to sharpen an awareness of the vicious consequences of otherwise complacently accepted racist stereotypes and, to a degree, brought the NAACP a step nearer to national standing as the black community's champion against race-baiting and the violence it encouraged.

NAACP programs took on new and larger meaning with America's participation in World War I. Intense patriotic fervor, repudiation of pacifists, enactment of sedition and espionage statutes, lynchings, and a frightful round of race riots all marked the war and postwar years as inhospitable to interracial justice. The year 1919 alone produced twenty-five riots, and seven of them—those in Charleston, South Carolina; Longview, Texas; Washington, D.C.; Chicago; Knoxville; Omaha; and Phillips County, Arkansas—attracted widespread attention and revealed the national scope of black vulnerability. Wartime dislocations, priorities for military production, conscription, labor shortages, migration of workers and their families, black and white, from rural to industrial areas all threatened the interracial status quo and created instabilities to which America responded in brutal fashion.[70]

Yet, the war offered a number of unanticipated dividends to the Association. The mobilization of human and physical resources greatly expanded the federal government's impact on American life, more so than did the Progressive reforms of peacetime. In response, the NAACP tried to involve the executive and legislative branches in the fight against lynching. With its augmented role in public affairs, the government had even less justification than before for rejecting the Association's appeals out of hand. Since the war highlighted black people's contributions to national needs, the NAACP sought to enlarge black citizenship rights generally. The struggle abroad for democratic goals generated fresh awareness of inequities at home. A nation concerned with the plight of Belgian children or self-determination in Central Europe ought certainly to guarantee protection of the law to its own citizens. The Association had logic on its side, even if American segregationists remained stubbornly resistant to change and their liberal counterparts were captivated by international crusades.

Whether an excuse for repression or an opportunity for reform, the war left the burden of proof squarely on the shoulders of those seeking justice. As historian Idus Newby has noted, racist politicians tried, by playing upon ingrained mistrust of black people, to preserve the status quo and prevent constructive changes of any kind. They turned to prohibition as an alleged means of keeping the black man sober, but simultaneously denounced the suffrage movement as an ill-disguised method for doubling the number of black voters. "Eventually everything to which they objected," he observed, "was labeled as an instrument for subverting racial purity."[71] Du Bois understood this. He knew that the war was an extension rather than a contradiction of white, western culture. The month the United States entered hostilities, Du Bois wrote bitterly that "a nation's religion is its life and as such white Christianity is a miserable failure." Referring to the war he declared that, "this is not Europe gone mad . . . this *is* Europe."[72]

Certainly racist hysteria was widespread. America rediscovered its fear of blacks, akin in some ways to the fear of slave uprisings and of subversion by free blacks that had marked pre-Civil War attitudes. On April 5, 1917, for example, the *New York Tribune* warned that German agents were trying to foment black rebellion throughout the United States, and cited racial incidents in Birmingham, San Diego, Harlem, Louisiana, and Mississippi. Roy Nash denied any implication of potential disloyalty among Afro-Americans. He conceded that black Americans resented the Wilson administration's racist policies and that black men were slow to enlist in a segregated military establishment, but he declared that black citizens loved the United States just as their white counterparts did. Association officials moved at once to refute talk of sedition by confronting the editor of the *Tribune* and alerting the entire black newspaper community to repudiate these rumors as well.[73]

Despite NAACP efforts, lynch mobs went virtually unchecked; they killed 36 blacks in 1917, 60 the following year, and 76 in 1919. Following the brutal death of Ell Persons, burned alive at Memphis in the spring of 1917, James Weldon Johnson investigated charges that Persons had been an "ax murderer." After ten days in Tennessee, talking with journalists, the sheriff, some white and many black citizens, he found no conclusive evidence of Persons' guilt. The tragedy spurred black residents to establish an NAACP local with Johnson's help.[74]

This reflected the continuing role of the antilynching campaign in the Association's overall program. While never misrepresenting the nature and extent of mob violence, the NAACP used the phenomenon to mobilize the black community, achieve recognition, add new members, both black and white, and solicit funds in the fight against lynching and racial injustice.

Back in New York, Johnson attended a Harlem rally called to denounce Persons' murder. Some 500 to 600 people assembled at St. Philip's church and formed an ad hoc organization to conduct a Carnegie Hall or Cooper Union protest meeting downtown. The NAACP's role became quickly evident with the selection of Dr. Hutchens C. Bishop (an NAACP Board member) as president, John E. Nail (Johnson' brother-in-law and treasurer of the New York City branch) as treasurer, and James Weldon Johnson as second vice president. The Board hoped to merge the group with its New York City branch.[75] Very shortly there were fresh and more compelling reasons to respond to mob violence, for on July 2, the East St. Louis, Illinois, riot erupted with terrifying consequences. The event had serious ramifications for the NAACP.

East St. Louis became a center of racial conflict for a number of reasons. An industrial site on the Mississippi, its rail stations bore the visible, daily traffic of black people leaving the Deep South on their way to the Midwest and North. Accelerated by the war, this migration was part of a national trend throughout the last decade of the nineteenth and first three decades of the twentieth century. Hoping to escape lynching and other forms of oppression and seeking new economic opportunities, black people left the countryside for cities in and outside the South. The eleven states of the old Confederacy showed a net, black migration loss of 242,400 in the years from 1890 to 1900; 216,300 from 1900 to 1910; 478,800 from 1910 to 1920; and 768,600 from 1920 to 1930.[76]

The black population of East St. Louis had tripled between 1900 and 1910, so that about one in ten of its nearly 59,000 residents was Afro-American; migration rates both through and into the city intensified in the period 1915–1917. Seeking a cheap, accessible work force, employers used railway and labor agents to gather blacks from southern states. White workers and union organizers grew anxious about job security, while Democratic politicians feared the role that black voters might play, legally or otherwise, under guidance from the local Republican party.[77] A prelude to the July riot occurred in late May, when a mob assaulted black people on the city streets, and the failure of authorities to deal satisfactorily with this lawlessness made it more difficult to contain the major riot five weeks later. Limited incidents of mob intimidation recurred in the second half of June, as well. Finally, events on the evening of Sunday, July 1, got totally out of control. As white assailants in a Ford automobile drove through a black neighborhood indiscriminately shooting into homes, they found that residents return their fire. Sent to investigate, a police car of similar make with two detectives in civilian clothes was fired upon. One officer died almost instantly, the other the following day. Some newspaper reports placed the blame on black "rioters" and even suggested the killings were premeditated. Rumors quickly spread of black "armies" mobilizing for a massacre. With their worst racist fears confirmed, white residents of East St. Louis promptly "retaliated."[78]

Thirty-nine blacks and eight whites died in the July 2 riot. Property damage through fire loss ran to at least $373,600, with some 244 buildings totally or partially destroyed.[79] The House of Representatives took some notice of East St. Louis. On August 3, a full month after the event, Representative Edward W. Pou (D–North Carolina) proposed an investigation of the riot's effects upon interstate commerce in those parts of Illinois and Missouri adjacent to the city.[80] The appointed committee submitted its report to Congress in early July 1918. It indicated that local police and members of the Illinois National Guard responded to the crisis with a mixture of inadequate riot training, general ineptness, callous indifference, and, in certain instances, actual support of and participation with white mob members: "It was a common expression among the soldiers: 'Have you got your nigger yet?' "[81]

The NAACP long understood the basic factors behind the riot. During the first half of 1917, the national office had authorized an investigation of black migration patterns, and Du Bois visited six southern states and secured additional data through agents in nearly all parts of the region.[82] In early July, he and Martha Gruening went to East St. Louis to study events firsthand, and her report later appeared in *Pearson's Magazine*.[83] Despite its limited resources, the Association did what it could for riot victims and their survivors. The St. Louis branch offered material aid to black refugees, tried to initiate legal action against the city and county in which the violence had occurred, and sought to defend innocent black people charged with inciting to riot. By mid-September, the branch had raised almost $1,000 for these purposes. Ovington informed the Board that many individuals and organizations had sent funds to the national office; among these, she noted, were several of the major black fraternal organizations which "heretofore had held themselves somewhat distant from the Association." The amounts involved were not unusually large, but assistance from such groups indicated a ready response to the riots and a fresh realization on the part of black people that they could turn to the NAACP as a vehicle for action.[84]

Because the riot drew national attention, the NAACP thought it timely to dramatize its own campaign against racist brutality.[85] Under the aegis of the ad hoc group recently formed at St. Philip's in Harlem, James Weldon Johnson organized one of the first mass demonstrations of black people in the twentieth century, the now-famous "Negro Silent Protest Parade." On July 28, 1917, some 9,000 to 10,000 Afro-Americans trooped down Fifth Avenue to the sound of muffled drums. Boy scouts distributed circulars explaining the Association's drive against segregation, discrimination, lynching, and other forms of racist oppression, as men, women, and children in the line of march carried placards that read: "MOTHER, DO LYNCHERS GO TO HEAVEN?"; "GIVE ME A CHANCE TO LIVE"; "TREAT US SO THAT WE MAY LOVE OUR COUNTRY"; "MR. PRESIDENT, WHY NOT MAKE AMERICA SAFE FOR DEMOCRACY?"; and "YOUR HANDS ARE FULL OF

BLOOD." The march literature clearly indicated the Association's philosophy, perspectives, and goals:

> We march because by the Grace of God and the force of truth, the dangerous, hampering walls of prejudice and inhuman injustices must fall.
>
> We march because we want to make impossible a repetition of Waco, Memphis, and East St. Louis, by arousing the conscience of the country and bringing the murders of our brothers, sisters, and innocent children to justice.
>
> We march because we deem it a crime to be silent in the face of such barbaric acts.
>
> We march because we are thoroughly opposed to Jim-Crow Cars, Segregation, Discrimination, Disfranchisement, Lynching, and the host of evils that are forced on us. It is time that the Spirit of Christ should be manifested in the making and execution of laws.
>
> We march because we want our children to live in a better land and enjoy fairer conditions than have fallen to our lot.

Johnson sent letters to all NAACP branches urging that they, in turn, organize parallel demonstrations throughout the nation.[86]

However valuable the use of magazine articles, appeals to members, and silent parades, the Association knew it must go beyond these diffuse tactics. For an organization of Progressive reformers witnessing the extraordinary expansion of federal powers in wartime, that meant turning to the national government. What happened, therefore, in the aftermath of East St. Louis was pivotal in the evolution of a sophisticated drive by the NAACP against mob violence. Within a month of the riot, James Weldon Johnson led a delegation to Washington. Unable to see Woodrow Wilson, they conferred instead with his long-time secretary, Joseph Tumulty, who promised vaguely that "the matter would not be neglected." The petitioners cited recent attacks upon black people and noted the more than 2,800 Afro-Americans lynched in the preceding thirty-one years, for which less than half a dozen persons had been indicted, convicted, and punished by the states. Accordingly, Johnson and his delegation left no doubt about their intentions: "We ask, therefore, that lynching and mob violence be made a national crime . . . and that this be done by Federal enactment, or if necessary, by constitutional amendment."[87]

Fully aware that appeals to the White House still had limited effect, the Association deemed them no less essential. They put politicians and the public at large on notice that the black community had organized itself and was determined to achieve redress; they indicated, too, the NAACP's commitment and that of its supporters to the orderly processes of reform grounded on data gathering, exposé, public protest, high-level negotiations, and lobbying. Such efforts also added to the Association's growing status as a nationally recognized group in the vanguard of interracial reform. Those three elements—alerting politicians and the public, mobilizing the black community, and strengthening the Association for more widespread assaults on racism—would continue to inform the NAACP's campaigns against mob violence in the years ahead. Thus, the fight against lynching had both direct and derivative results. To combat lynching was itself necessary; to have that effort stimulate broader struggles for interracial justice proved a crucial dividend.

The Ell Persons lynching in Memphis and the East St. Louis riot illustrated the violence that menaced black civilians. The case of the Twenty-fourth Infantry represented that same dilemma for blacks in military service. Stationed at Camp Logan near Houston, these soldiers suffered a fate similar to the Brownsville troopers during Theodore Roosevelt's administration, but with far more alarming consequences. Because southern whites had never taken kindly to the idea of black men under arms, the members of the Twenty-fourth were, by their very presence, an irritation to the local civilian population. The tensions of America's first summer at war contributed further to the riot that occurred on the night of August 23, 1917. Angered by the arrest of a black corporal who had sought to assist a black woman and a black soldier abused by a city policeman, Afro-American troops from Camp Logan stormed the town. In the ensuing riot seventeen white and two black persons were killed. Military authorities court-martialed sixty-three soldiers and summarily hanged thirteen of them "almost surreptitiously" before daylight on the morning of December 11, without benefit of the customary appeal to the president. The NAACP's retention of a local white attorney, A. J. Houston (son of legendary Sam), proved insufficient. In a second court-martial, fifty-one men were sentenced to life imprisonment, four to long prison terms, and five others condemned to death. Before the court finally adjourned, eleven more received the death sentence bringing to sixteen the number scheduled to die in the second round of executions.[88] Civil rights activists looked upon the entire episode as little more than a military lynching.

Although unable to get past Tumulty the previous summer to give President Wilson the facts of the East St. Louis riot, James Weldon Johnson headed a delegation to the White House on February 19, 1918, to ask clemency for the men of the Twenty-fourth. The group secured a half-hour interview with Wilson, during which it gave him a petition of nearly 12,000 names and a large number of telegrams from branches and individuals throughout the country. Johnson, moreover, raised the general question of violence against black people, such as the Illinois riot and three especially savage lynchings in Tennessee at Memphis, Dyersburg, and, earlier that month, Estill Springs. In addition to amnesty for the soldiers, therefore, the visitors asked that the president use the power of his office to make a public appeal against lynching and mob rule. The Association was determined to impress upon Wilson the fact that black people in all walks of life faced the hazards of summary justice and that the soldiers' plight, though dreadfully serious, was not an exceptional one.

The results of this White House conference varied. Wilson promised that he would have the records at the Twenty-fourth Infantry reviewed, and he said that he would "seek an opportunity" to say something openly against lynching. Shortly after the interview, the federal government announced the commutation of ten death sentences to life imprisonment; however, the remaining six men were executed.[89] Refusing to let the matter rest, the NAACP fought for two decades to free the imprisoned survivors of the Twenty-fourth Infantry. In late 1923, for example, it assembled petitions with over 43,000 signatures asking release of the ex-soldiers from Leavenworth Prison; the following spring the War Department informed the NAACP that fifty-four of the men were eligible for parole in staggered fashion over the next four years. Not until late 1937, however, could executive secretary Walter White inform his Board about the release of the last one.[90]

The Association also achieved some success in the matter of presidential willingness to speak out against lynching and mob violence. The statement, however, came neither quickly nor easily. One scholar has argued that Wilson remained "inexcusably slow" in using his authority to check lawlessness against black Americans, because he did not wish to precipitate a hot debate about race that might antagonize southern leaders or endanger white America's wartime unity. Two factors, however, forced his hand. One involved political considerations, the other the national war effort; neither sprang from a basic concern for black people. At Tumulty's suggestion, black leaders submitted a report to the White House on May 25, 1918, which alluded to the increased migration of black people from the South and summarized the added importance of black votes in forthcoming congressional elections. About the same time, Secretary of War Newton Baker informed the president of army intelligence reports about growing unrest among black Americans. Although the government had already sought to "appease" black citizens by appointing Emmett J. Scott (Booker T. Washington's former secretary) as special assistant to the secretary of war, opening a training camp for black officers at Fort Des Moines, Iowa, commissioning over 600 of the men, and relaxing some forms of segregation, Wilson now recognized the need for something more. Accordingly, on July 26, 1918, he issued his much-quoted denunciation of those who participated in mob action.[91] Even so, the much-respected *Survey* magazine, in an editorial entitled "Democracy Versus Demo-n-Cracy," found the message defective, because the president failed to deal specifically with the lynching of black people.[92]

Increasingly anxious to involve federal authority in a solution to lynching, the Association felt keenly the need of effective working relationships at both the White House and the Congress. Its earlier experiences with the Wilson administration, however, offered little encouragement. Relying on Villard, the NAACP had tried without success in 1913 to induce the new president to appoint a National Race

Commission, sustained by private subscription, to study the conditions that black Americans faced. Wilson's refusal greatly embittered NAACP leaders, several of whom had openly endorsed him in the 1912 presidential campaign.[93] Worse still was the pattern of segregation and discrimination in federal appointments and employment, which so angered the Association that Villard allegedly threatened Tumulty that Afro-Americans would institute protest marches in the District of Columbia with lynch ropes and antidiscrimination signs to dramatize their grievances.[94] But NAACP admonitions had little direct effect. After all, the organization spoke for a minority group long held in contempt by white America. Like the vast majority of their white constituents, administration officials exhibited the attitudes and behavior of an intensely racist, Jim Crow era. Even with an expanding membership, no group like the NAACP with limited resources could induce the public and the White House to embrace meaningful interracial reform, certainly not to embrace it promptly or openly. At the other end of Pennsylvania Avenue, the broad issues of Afro-American participation in the war, whether as officers, enlistees, draftees, or workers, forced on the NAACP a lobbyist role far broader than it had previously experienced. Association leaders found themselves increasingly in contact with congressional personnel, and this proved an invaluable experience on which the Association later drew when pressing for various domestic and nonmilitary reforms, including a federal bill against lynching.[95]

Midway through the war, in January 1918, the Association appointed a trained social worker, John R. Shillady, as executive secretary. With an eye to routine and organizational detail, he reorganized the work load among staff members and coordinated a national drive that raised membership from 9,869 to 35,898 by July 1. During his brief stay in office, about two-and-one-half years, Shillady relied heavily on his associates, Johnson and White, especially in the campaigns against mob violence.[96] He fully shared their concern with mobbism and sent two researchers to the Library of Congress to tabulate information on all known lynchings. They uncovered names, dates, locations, sex, age, manner of death, and charges against the victims, and in April 1919, the NAACP published the data as *Thirty Years of Lynching in the United States, 1889-1918*. One particular value of the report lay in its documentation of the fact that less than 20 percent of the more than 2,500 black people lynched in that thirty-year period had been accused, let alone tried and convicted, of rape. Although *Thirty Years of Lynching* could not forestall future mobs, it was used, along with the annual supplements that the NAACP thereafter published, to help refute the stereotyped belief that lynching was somehow essential to the protection of southern womanhood.[97]

When a black sharecropper, Jim McIlherron, was chained to a tree and tortured to death with heated irons and a bonfire at Estill Springs, Tennessee, in February 1918, Shillady sent Walter White, armed with a press card from the New York *Evening Post*, to investigate. To Shillady's and Villard's distress, White retained the card and subsequently used it to investigate the mass lynchings of late May in Brooks and Lowndes counties, Georgia. Ten black people died there, including one victim's pregnant wife, whose unborn child was ripped from her body and trampled by a member of the mob. Walter White not only assembled considerable evidence in this case but showed the courage and flair that would mark his entire NAACP career by posing as a reporter to reach Governor Hugh M. Dorsey, as well.[98] Although the Association provided Dorsey with full details, including the names of two ringleaders and fifteen mob members, his *pro forma* response was a genuine disappointment. Nonetheless, three years later, in the spring of 1921, Dorsey released a pamphlet of his own entitled *The Negro in Georgia*, which exposed 135 serious violations of black people's rights—a pamphlet that the NAACP promptly put to use in its own system of press releases and appeals to public officials.[99] Perhaps White's initiative paid dividends in ways that he and his colleagues had not initially perceived.

The unrelenting sadism of the mob and the growing strength and competencies of the NAACP national staff were on a collision course by 1918, when the Association entered a five-year period in which it gave priority to the fight against lynching. In preparation, the group wrestled with the controversial but fundamental question of how to define a lynching. At its meeting in late November 1917, the antilynching committee had declared it "not only the illegal killing of an accused person, but also the killing of an unaccused person by mob violence."[100] Mobs had not restricted their handiwork merely to those charged with a crime. Yet, southern white moderates, among others, liked to argue that more expeditious legal procedures (swift apprehension and prosecution, trials completed without undue delay, and so forth) would lessen the incidence of lynching. The NAACP, on the other hand, insisted that any black person, not simply a criminal defendant, was vulnerable to mob attack, whether in a lynching or race riot setting. It was, after all, the indiscriminate use of violence that gave the mob its real utility as an instrument of intimidation and control in a racist society. This, and not just the mechanical issue of procedures, the NAACP was prepared to challenge. Having assembled its special antilynching fund of about $10,000, expanded its appeals that branches challenge local and state officials to action against lynching, and increased its own news releases on the topic,[101] the Association now stepped more deliberately in the direction of Congress.

Of the handful of congressmen prepared to work with the Association toward interracial reform, Leonidas Dyer (R–Missouri) was the most persistent. He served the twelfth congressional district, an area that comprised much of the heavily populated and industrialized sections lying along the Mississippi River on the south side of St. Louis.[102] Since entering Congress in 1911, he had shown his interest in the black community by twice proposing bills to erect a monument to black soldiers and sailors and by extolling in floor debate the loyalty of Afro-Americans.[103] Greatly troubled about the East St. Louis riot, Dyer called for a joint House-Senate investigation and declared that the incident involved "the most dastardly and most criminal outrages ever perpetrated in this country."[104] Undoubtedly the relocation of many black survivors into St. Louis quickened Dyer's interest in black Americans.[105] In March 1918 he and the Association joined in urging a full disclosure of House findings. And, Dyer asked for NAACP support to sponsor a bill that would make lynching a federal crime.[106]

In April 1918, Dyer and Merrill Moores (Republican of Indianapolis) each introduced an antilynching bill. Dyer's (H.R. 11279) became the prototype for subsequent NAACP-sponsored antilynching measures. Bearing a strong resemblance to the bill drafted in 1901 by Albert Pillsbury, it defined a mob as three or more persons acting without authority at law and held them liable to prosecution in federal court for a capital crime. Designed to invoke the Fourteenth Amendment, the bill would guard "citizens of the United States against lynching in default of" state action, which had denied victims the equal protection of the laws. Delinquent officials who allowed a lynching to occur or failed to prosecute lynchers were subject to imprisonment for up to five years and fines of up to $5,000, while the county in which the crime occurred would have to pay from $5,000 to $10,000 to the victim's heirs. Members of lynch mobs and those sympathetic to lynching were barred from serving on federal juries trying any cases under the act.

Aside from federal prosecution of mob members, a provision dropped after 1922 in deference to constitutional conservatives who argued that only the states could punish murderers, the NAACP retained the basic features of this Dyer bill in almost every antilynching measure it sponsored over the next three decades.[107] In the late 1940s, however, the Association argued that altered patterns of mob violence required more comprehensive legislation, and it once more advocated direct federal penalties for lynchers themselves.[108] The Dyer and Moores bills were similar, but the Association tended to work more closely with the Missourian, in part because he more actively solicited NAACP cooperation. After an extended conference with Walter White, for example, Dyer asked the Association to organize the witness list for committee hearings and to prepare an argument on his bill's constitutionality.[109]

The Board of Directors explored its options in mid-May. Walling's committee urged the appointment of an antilynching publicist in Washington. It stressed the need to participate in House hearings and gather support nationally for the Dyer or Moores bill ("whichever . . . [may] have some chance of passage"). The Association recognized "the opportunities for favorable publicity which this bill would afford even if it could not be passed."[110] Despite Board approval, certain problems remained. Most perplexing was the question of constitutionality, an issue eagerly seized by critics of federal initiative over the next three decades, and one that troubled the NAACP itself in these early years. Could the federal government assume any jurisdiction whatsoever in lynching, if one insisted that mob murder was just that, murder, and therefore a crime properly prosecuted and punished by the states? Anticipating the dilemma, Walter White wired Moorfield Storey on May 1 to ask that he appear within two weeks before a congressional committee to argue the matter. Storey pleaded the impossibility of preparing that quickly, so White had to inform Moores that the Association could not send an attorney on such short notice to discuss constitutionality.[111]

In light of the Association's subsequent efforts, its conduct in 1918 seems curious and hesitant. The NAACP actually declined to make an open push for either the Dyer or Moores bill on grounds that the measures were not constitutional as written and could not, even if revised, be made so. This was the group's first formal confrontation with congressional antilynching legislation, and it was clearly feeling its way. The national staff relied heavily on advice from its eminent lawyer-president, Moorfield Storey, who at the time took a very conservative, traditional position. By the spring of 1922, in frank recognition of the failure of state governments to move against lynching and mob violence, and upon reconsideration of the Fifth and Fourteenth Amendments and the application of certain Supreme Court decisions since 1876, Storey had shifted to an open defense of the antilynching bill's constitutionality.[112] That altered view, though, did nothing to help Dyer and Moores or Walling and White in 1918.

While still cautious in mid-1918, Storey conceded an alternative, one that claimed the federal government could respond to lynchings under its wartime powers and national emergency needs. On July 11, he endorsed this course of action in a letter to Walter White. But it was Major Joel Spingarn, then serving with an Army intelligence unit, who made it possible. He found Congressman Warren Gard (Democrat from Hamilton, Ohio) willing to sponsor the measure, testified before the House Committee on the Judiciary on June 6, and secured a supportive brief for the committee from his associate, Captain George S. Hornblower, on July 12. During the hearings, Spingarn reported that the discouragement pervasive among black Americans might adversely affect the war effort, especially if mob violence continued unchecked. He declared that Congress possessed sufficient authority in wartime to legislate against this lawlessness, and it should do so swiftly to assure black citizens the justice at home they were allegedly defending overseas. "That is a common argument in these colored newspapers—that is, that while they are fighting abroad, their relatives and dependents are being injured and lynched here."[113]

Through the ingenious device of appealing to the federal government's wartime needs and responsibilities, and on the lucky opportunity of his commission in the Army's Military Intelligence Branch, Spingarn had found an answer, however temporary, to Storey's concern over deficiencies in the Dyer and Moores bills. To some degree Dyer had already anticipated this ploy by trying to link antilynching legislation to the national emergency. On May 7, he took the floor during a debate over questions of military service and punishment for disloyal and abusive language against the United States. He reminded his colleagues how foolhardy it seemed to seek an end to oppression abroad while simultaneously acquiescing in the brutalities of lynching at home.[114]

The Association and its collaborators understood that an appeal couched in terms of national defense was best suited to win a sympathetic hearing during the tense months of mid-1918. Surely the advocates' connection with Military Intelligence put a good face to the whole matter for public officials uneasy about a federal position against lynching. Whether or not materials and arguments supplied by Congressman Dyer, Major Spingarn, and the NAACP formed any sufficient part of the Army Intelligence report that induced President Wilson to denounce mob violence in late July is uncertain. It seems unlikely, however, that such evidence could have escaped consideration when Tumulty, Baker, and other confidants formulated policies with the president. In any event, the Spingarn-Hornblower approach convinced Storey, even though he sensed its limitations. Storey advised White that the measure would affect only persons of draft age and cover them only during wartime, and he questioned any extension of federal protection to relatives of military personnel. Moreover, he suggested that, to win passage, there should be no intimation that the bill was designed to protect black men and women especially; the measure would suffer "if our Association were to become prominent in pressing it."[115]

The Association followed Storey's advice and muted its role as lobbyist for an antilynching bill.[116] But in no sense did it relent in its determination to fight mob violence, and it took great care to record its activities for members and other interested parties. The *Ninth Annual Report*, covering 1918, for example, reviewed the special investigations of lynchings in Brooks and Lowndes counties, Georgia, and Estill Springs, Tennessee; and of race riots and disturbances at Camp Merritt, New Jersey; Brooklyn, New York; and Philadelphia, Pennsylvania. The Association intermittently sent President Wilson, Attorney General Thomas Watt Gregory, and the executive committee of the American Bar Association memoranda on lynching, while pertinent materials on mob violence went to editors of leading newspapers on a regular basis, and members of the national office repeatedly referred to lynching in their various public addresses. The *Report* noted that "The Negro Question," Storey's speech on race conditions and lynching before the Wisconsin Bar Association in June 1918, had gone to all Cabinet members, all state governors, the mayors of several cities, newspapers and periodicals, and selected prominent citizens; and it received even wider circulation early in

1919.[117] Table 4 indicates the Association's efforts to influence key political and business leaders in states plagued by lynchings. It also reveals the rather spotty, even meager nature of the acknowledgments from those areas most directly affected by mob violence.

The antilynching campaign was having some impact. Addressing the executive committee of the American Bar Association in May 1918, the attorney general recommended an educational campaign against lynching and mob violence; the Wisconsin Bar Association responded to Storey's speech with a resolution condemning lynching and calling upon the legal profession to invoke the law against mob rule; the Chattanooga Chamber of Commerce and the *Nashville Banner* denounced lynching; the Tennessee Law and Order League was established to suppress lynching and encourage similar actions in other southern states; North Carolina Governor Thomas Bickett employed troops to assist officials of Winston-Salem in preventing the lynching of a black prisoner; the governor and attorney general of Tennessee asked Shillady for help in preparing a state antilynching bill; and both Kentucky and Wyoming took legislative action to reduce mob violence.[118]

Financial data also reveal the accelerated pace of the Association's antilynching campaign during and immediately after the war. The antilynching fund had far exceeded the three or four other special reserves maintained apart from the general operating budget, and showed a balance of $7,977 at the end of December 1917. Two years later, the organization announced that, not including any share of administrative expenses, it had spent $15,793 during 1919 on the antilynching campaign alone, which made that the largest single-issue expenditure in the budget.[119] Reaffirming the importance of the campaign, Walling's committee had met on December 5, 1918, and unanimously agreed to allot at least $10,000 for the antilynching drive during 1919. Moreover, the committee pledged to raise whatever was needed to maintain that figure "each year so that at no time would there be danger of the Fund's being exhausted and no funds in sight for the work." The implications are apparent if one realizes that the Association's total proposed budget for 1919 was only $50,690. In other words, the organization, always strapped for available cash to meet the unending burdens involved in the quest for interracial justice, was planning to maintain a separate reserve, equal to almost one-fifth of its total operating budget, just for the fight against lynching and mob violence.[120]

At the end of 1918, Walling's committee proposed, and the Board agreed, to convene a national conference on lynching. The idea was hardly new; it had been discussed two years before. Now the Association had sufficient status, and it sensed a measure of public concern. These together held a reasonable promise of success. An enthusiasm for high-level negotiations prevailed. The conference, for example, would "be called by a group of the most substantial and influential leaders of public opinion in all fields"; the "governors of the states, particularly the Southern States,

Table 4. NAACP Communications and Replies on Summary Justice, 1918

State	Telegrams and Letters of Protest, Inquiry, and Commendation			Acknowledgments			
	Governor	Chamber of Commerce	Other Official Persons	Governor	Chamber of Commerce	Press Stories	Other
Alabama	2	10	-	-	2	1	-
Arkansas	1	-	-	-	-	1	-
Georgia	5	2	-	2	-	8	-
Kentucky	1	-	-	-	-	1	-
Louisiana	7	11	-	-	2	9	-
Mississippi	2	-	-	-	-	2	1
North Carolina	3	1	1	2	1	3	1
Oklahoma	1	-	-	1	-	2	-
South Carolina	-	-	-	-	-	1	-
Tennessee	5	9	7	2	3	9	2
Texas	3	-	1	1	-	3	-
Wyoming	1	-	-	1	-	1	-
Total	32	33	9	9	8	40*	4

* In listing by states there are duplications in cases where a single press story includes matter affecting more than one state. The total "40" is the actual number of press stories, eliminating the duplicate count by states.

Source: NAACP, *Ninth Annual Report* (New York, 1919), p. 33.

[should] be especially invited to attend"; and, finally, "the chief idea . . . [is] to secure the cooperation of men with national reputations whose signatures to the call . . . and whose participation in the conference" would attract new recruits to the fight against lynching.[121]

The Association overreached itself only slightly. Walling's committee had wanted the meeting for Lincoln's birthday (February 12, 1919), but it was delayed until May; and, the conference fell somewhat short of involving the nationally prominent figures initially projected. In any event, the NAACP found itself on the eve of its ten-year anniversary with a sizeable membership; a degree of recognition in Washington and throughout the country; a solid, competent staff; a general list of programmatic objectives that included the antilynching campaign as an item of pressing priority; and, the previous December, new headquarters at 70 Fifth Avenue.[122] Preparations for the conference occupied the opening months of 1919, with Shillady directing the publication of *Thirty Years of Lynching in the United States*. It appeared a month before the meeting. In May, Herbert J. Seligmann became the NAACP's first full-time publicity director, which further facilitated the use of press releases as a mechanism of exposé and propaganda.[123]

The conference posed certain procedural and political dilemmas. The Association wished to assemble a powerful group, but it had, in the fashion of moderate reformers, to weigh questions about the representative nature of those invited, and to guard against any possible embarrassment at the hands of those deemed too militant. The sessions, after all, would put the NAACP on full-dress parade. It was vital that the meeting have "a non-partisan and non-sectional atmosphere," Storey wrote Shillady in late March. "If I had my way I should be glad to have . . . Judge [Charles Evans] Hughes, Attorney General [A. Mitchell] Palmer, Governor O'Neal [Emmett O'Neal, former governor of Alabama], and Anna Howard Shaw [of the National American Woman Suffrage Association]" as speakers, he concluded. Thus, the Association would have the Republican party and the bench represented by Hughes, the Democratic party and the Administration by Palmer, the South by O'Neal, and women activists by Dr. Shaw.[124]

Carefully balanced "ticket splitting" proved harder to achieve in the matter of key black participants. In mid-March, Shillady informed Storey that Robert Russa Moton, the late Booker T. Washington's successor as head of Tuskegee Institute, and Emmett J. Scott, Washington's secretary, had both declined to sign the call initiating the conference. Shillady suspected that Moton's reluctance stemmed from the advice of philanthropist George Foster Peabody, on whose good will so many southern black educational ventures relied, and with a bit of rare bluntness added that it was "about time for the undertaker to come for Mr. Peabody," his good health notwithstanding. James Weldon Johnson had approached Scott, but he proved unwilling to step forward, if Moton would not. Having lost support from prominent blacks on its right flank, the Association sought to reduce the forces to its left by declining to invite William Monroe Trotter, the fiery editor of the *Boston Guardian* and head of the all-black National Equal Rights League. Johnson feared that Trotter was "so temperamental as perhaps to upset matters for us if he should come to the meeting." With his independent spirit and suspicions of the interracial NAACP, Trotter was hardly a universal favorite at 70 Fifth Avenue, and only the previous autumn the Association's Board had declined an opportunity to participate in his National Race Congress.[125] Trotter and Moton aside, preparations for the meeting nicely matched the Association's overall needs. For example, in March Shillady wired Storey to use his personal stationery for an appeal to Madame C. J. Walker, the wealthy black cosmetologist: "THERE IS PROSPECT FOR CONSIDERABLY SIZED CONTRIBUTION TO ANTI-LYNCHING FUND." Within three days, Walker informed Storey that she would gladly sign the conference call, would give the NAACP her check for $1,000, and hoped to demonstrate her support in an even more material way later.[126]

The antilynching conference took place at New York City's Carnegie Hall. Demonstrating his customary attention to details, Shillady compiled a list of state laws on lynching and distributed it for the conferees' use under the awkward but descriptive title, "Summary of Laws Relating to Lynching of the States (except Texas) Having More Than 25 Lynchings in Past Thirty Years."[127] The staff left little to chance. It had obtained 120 signatures on the formal call, including those of Attorney General Palmer, former Secretary of State Elihu Root, Minister to the Netherlands Henry Van Dyke, Charles Evans Hughes, four governors, three former governors (Emmett O'Neal of Alabama among them), and seventeen sponsors from southern states. The list of signatories was interracial and included both women and men. Moorfield Storey's opening address set the reformist tone for the gathering when he declared that:

> This conference has been called for the purpose of considering what measures should be adopted to end the barbarous practice of lynching. It is not sectional, it is not partisan, it is American. . . . We come together as Americans; not to apportion the blame but to find a remedy; not to deal with the past but with the future. We know what the causes are and we know what the facts are. They are matters of record. The question is, what can we do to unite all the forces of law and order and of Christianity in this country in a movement to make life and liberty secure for every citizen, securing for every man charged with crime a fair trial.

Among the principal speakers were Hughes, O'Neal, General John H. Sherburne of the Ninety-second (black) Division, and Anna Howard Shaw. With some 2,500 persons in attendance, the conference had to be considered an enormous success and, at least momentarily, it thrust the question of mob violence to the center of public attention. Conferees resolved that lynching be made a federal crime, that the NAACP establish committees to work for comparable state legislation, and that its antilynching drive include a sustained fund-raising and advertising campaign. After the conference, the NAACP drafted "An Address to the Nation on Lynching," signed by 141 persons including Palmer, the governors of seven states and three ex-governors, three former attorneys general of the United States, ex-President William Howard Taft, Root, Hughes, several college presidents, and twenty leading white southerners. The NAACP moved quickly to distribute some 24,000 copies.[128]

One especially revealing aspect of the "Address" was the fact that it avoided a direct appeal for federal legislation and stressed instead a congressional investigation of lynching. In his letter of June 9 to Moorfield Storey, Shillady explained that the constitutionality question still lingered.[129] The Association was reaching for southern support and still pulling its punches on the matter of a federal statute. Despite this momentary deference to Storey and to a traditionalistic legal position, however, the organization's overall activities and the larger force of events throughout American society were already combining to push the NAACP into the arms of those who openly proposed federal antilynching legislation. Even Storey finally acceded to that as the Association moved more boldly from advocate to adversary.

3

The Struggle for the Dyer Bill, 1919-1923

From an organizational standpoint, the NAACP benefited enormously from its experiences in the antilynching fight from 1919 to 1923. Although the staff would lose Shillady, James Weldon Johnson and Walter White more than ably filled the gap. After some hesitation, prominent white Board members swung around to support Johnson and White's drive for a federal law against mob violence, and that effort thrust the NAACP into the heart of national political affairs.

Much like their party predecessors, Republican leaders expressed concern for black needs but failed to deliver the statutory guarantees required to protect those needs. In terms specifically of the antilynching bill, GOP regulars professed support but declined to confront and overcome a threatened Democratic filibuster against the measure. Republican liberals, meanwhile, labored under a second-class status within the party and hungered for some renewal of the prewar, progressive coalitions that had lent shape to their reformist tendencies. They felt little inclination, however, to make black rights the basis for new political ventures. Liberals across the country could not then or later agree on how much priority to accord those rights. The issue posed more of a divisive than cohesive force, especially when addressed beyond the limits of certain congressional districts.

Thanks to the unsettling experiences and opportunities of World War I and its aftermath, black men and women had adopted a more militant perspective about themselves and their goals. Moreover, their mass migrations into heavily populated urban centers in the North and Midwest had established the foundations for black political action. This was not perfected overnight, its impact was still limited in the 1920s, but its expression was quickened by the antilynching campaign. The NAACP's intensive drive from 1919 to 1923, therefore, was a reflection of contemporary realities and a portent of more aggressive civil rights activism in the future.

The Association barely had time to savor the triumphs from its 1919 antilynching conference when a startling, wholly unanticipated event dramatized anew the violent side of American life: Shillady was physically assaulted in Austin, Texas. This marked the first time in the organization's ten-year existence that any officer or staff member had been attacked in the line of duty. Like the white abolitionists who ventured South in antebellum days or their civil rights heirs of the 1960s, Shillady learned firsthand that whites striving to defend black rights could become, momentarily, as vulnerable to racist retribution as any Afro-American.

It all began routinely enough. Fearful that the state of Texas might suppress the Association's work, Shillady had tried in August of 1919 to confer with the governor and attorney general about its purposes and programs. Unable to see either official, he met instead with the acting attorney general. What followed that interview was bizarre, to say the least. Shillady was detained by a constable, served with a subpoena, and forced to undergo heckling and hostile questioning before a secret court of inquiry. The following morning when he attempted to see the president of the Association's branch, a group of assailants intervened and beat him severely. His attackers included a county judge and a constable.

The NAACP discovered that no effective redress could be had through the state government. Governor William Hobby publicly condoned the treatment given Shillady, and admonished the NAACP that "your organization can contribute more to the advancement of both races by keeping your representatives and their propaganda out of this state than in any other way."[1]

The governor was not the only indifferent Texan, for the NAACP could not find an in-state lawyer of stature to handle the case. Even Moorfield Storey, former head of the American Bar Association, made no headway; all the attorneys he approached hesitated to risk their reputations in an unpopular cause. Undeterred, he announced: "we shall . . . be able to state to the county that the conditions are such that a citizen of New York travelling in Texas on lawful business is beaten, and all the authorities of the state and members of the bar decline to interfere."[2] As the Association had so often to do, it tried to turn oppression and official inaction into campaigns of public awareness, and the staff set to work on a report of the Austin incident for widespread circulation.[3] Making the best of unsatisfying alternatives had long been the lot of minority-group leaders, but in the aftermath of Shillady's beating at least some NAACP staff members must have viewed with heightened skepticism the high promises of the May conference and its projections of help from southern moderates. As black activists reared in the Jim Crow South, Johnson and White were never much deceived about the limitations of "good white people's" assistance, and the Shillady incident fired their own resolve to get a federal law enacted.

Other than protests and a quickened determination, however, the NAACP could do little about Austin. Certainly the event left its mark on

Shillady. His efforts for an open exchange of ideas with duly elected officials had earned him nothing but physical reprisals. But Shillady experienced more than the force of blows in Austin; he suffered the loss of an ideal. All his statistics, meetings, press releases, and assurances of cooperation from prominent people had not saved him from a mob. Shillady now felt that the public and its representatives were irrevocably beyond his reach. Like so many of his contemporaries—liberal reformers stunned by the carnage of war or the terms of the Versailles Treaty, appalled by the Palmer raids, or confused by the vagaries of prohibition— Shillady confronted the gap between ideals and practice and decided to withdraw. Remaining at work long enough to complete some pending tasks, he submitted his resignation in a mood of severe pessimism.[4]

His departure left the way open for James Weldon Johnson to become acting secretary in September and executive secretary in December 1920. Du Bois had recommended him for the office in June, and once officially installed as head of the staff, Johnson and his assistant, Walter White, proceeded to lead the Association in a two-year campaign of unprecedented vigor for a federal antilynching law.[5] Important in its own right, the effort also served as the model for NAACP antilynching lobbying during the next three decades.

Black America generally was in no mood for temporizing. The war had generated fresh visions of a better life, at home and abroad, and awakened strong currents of resistance to white oppression. While thousands rallied behind the NAACP's interracial commitment to American citizenship rights, perhaps millions endorsed Marcus Garvey's black-nationalist, back-to-Africa movement—the Universal Negro Improvement Association—founded in Jamaica in 1914. Based in Harlem after 1916, Garvey found lynching and race riots endemic to white control over black people and warned of race extermination in nations where African peoples did not control their own governments.[6] Meanwhile, the needs of a world-wide black community inspired Du Bois to organize the first of several postwar Pan-African Congresses, which attracted fifty-seven delegates from sixteen nations to its Paris meetings in February 1919.[7] And, boldly paralleling Du Bois and emulating Ida B. Wells's campaigns of the mid-1890s, William Monroe Trotter journeyed to Paris in May of 1919 to register international protests against the exclusions, proscriptions, disfranchisement, and lynchings inflicted upon Afro-Americans.[8] That very month a Du Bois editorial in *The Crisis* captured the new air of militancy. Black soldiers had fought for the United States but still faced lynching, job discrimination, unequal educational opportunities, disfranchisement, and general insult. Things, he warned, must be different, would be different:

> But by the God of Heaven, we are cowards and jackasses if now that that war is over, we do not marshal every ounce of our brain and

brawn to fight a sterner, longer, more unbending battle against the forces of hell in our own land.

We *return*.
We *return from fighting*.
We *return fighting*.

Make way for Democracy! We saved it in France, and by the Great Jehovah, we will save it in the United States of America, or know the reason why.[9]

The editorial aroused a great deal of agitation throughout the South and in Congress, for it raised the specter of black people who would not reaccommodate themselves to the Jim Crow patterns of prewar days.[10] In the aggravated Red Scare atmosphere of 1919, postal authorities withheld the May *Crisis* from the mails for seven days.[11] But there was worse repression than censorship. The number of reported lynchings of black people rose from sixty in 1918 to seventy-six in 1919, and that same year some twenty-five race riots erupted.[12] In one such tragedy of late September, a mob of several thousand, generously sprinkled with returning servicemen in uniform, burned a black man to death across the street from the federal courthouse in Omaha, and very nearly lynched mayor E. P. Smith because he refused to assist the mob. Desperate for help, municipal and state authorities requested, and got, Army troops to restore order. Storey termed this federal intervention a "very important object lesson" for Americans. If the riotous destruction of property and the near murder of the mayor did not make people realize that lynching had to stop, "they must be very peculiar." While sorry for the horrors "coming thick and fast," he supposed that "they pave the way for a better day."[13]

In the aftermath of such indiscriminate violence, the Association discovered two congressional alternatives. Leonidas Dyer had made good an earlier promise and reintroduced his antilynching bill (H.R. 259), and he also sponsored a resolution for a congressional inquiry into mob violence (H. Res. 319). Meanwhile, Senate Majority Whip Charles Curtis (R-Kansas) introduced his own resolution for an investigation (S. Res. 189).[14] Dyer's action surprised no one, but what of Curtis? Perhaps it was his personal identification with another beleaguered minority group, for he was part Kaw and part Osage. A more immediate motivation probably stemmed from his devotion to the best interests of the Republican party, his reputation as a GOP "regular," and his determination to strengthen the party's image in the forthcoming presidential race as the traditional friend of the black voter. Within a year and a half the NAACP would have second thoughts about the utility of congressional investigations into lynching, because it felt that there was ample public evidence of mobbism—much of which the Association itself had provided. Moreover, it feared that a legislative probe would merely offer Senate and House members a convenient way of postponing a floor fight and a vote on federal antilynching bills.[15] However, in 1919 and 1920 the organization welcomed any collaboration from members of Congress, and explored what it could do to boost the Dyer and Curtis measures.

Admittedly, the prospects were mixed. Dyer had asked the Association to draft a brief in support of his antilynching bill's constitutionality, prepare the necessary data on lynching's causes and effects, and coordinate the presentations of friendly witnesses at the hearings.[16] His request signified the recognition the Association had won as a competent lobbying group in the Capital. But certain problems arose. One of Johnson's expert witnesses was Albert E. Pillsbury, former attorney general of Massachusetts and author in 1901 of an antilynching bill that Congress had refused to consider. That bill now served as a model for Dyer's own version. Pillsbury consulted the congressman, but was not impressed. Cautious to a fault, he complicated matters further by claiming to speak for Storey, as well, in warning Dyer that open investigations should precede federal legislation and that, in any event, no bill should be offered that its own friends could not agree to endorse on constitutional grounds. In light of Storey's customary wariness, that narrowed the field of action considerably. Pillsbury subsequently predicted nothing but delays in congressional committees and reported to Johnson that an old friend, House Speaker Frederick H. Gillett (R–Massachusetts), doubted whether any action was possible.[17]

All of this had little direct effect at the Association, where the judgments of in-house leaders increasingly prevailed. Pillsbury had already earned himself something of a reputation for gloomy predictions, while Johnson, White, and the NAACP staff were prepared to test the mood in Congress.[18] As in many membership organizations, the Board had the ultimate authority for designing policy, but it relied upon the paid staff for information, guidance, and the implementation of programs. The fact that Ovington, who chaired the Board, and the Spingarn brothers, also resident in New York City and close to office matters, tended to support the secretariat vastly strengthened Johnson and White's determination. None of this was necessarily unusual. Elected officers and sympathetic advisors are often caught up in their own professional activities and operate at some remove from the day-to-day hopes and anxieties at headquarters. They tend to adopt a more cautious, less impassioned view of matters than do the staff executives. The latter function at the center of a communications and interest-group network that by its very nature quickens the sense of needs and possibilities. Pillsbury and Storey had no deliberate intention of impeding the fight against lynching, but their reasoned, constitutional concerns simply did not coincide with the secretariat's eagerness to get things done in Washington. This was especially true for a staff increasingly dominated by two black southerners all too familiar with the implications of mob violence against Afro-Americans.

In late January 1920, Johnson, attorney Arthur Spingarn, and Archibald Grimké of the Washington, D.C., branch represented the

NAACP at House Judiciary Committee hearings on the antilynching bill. William Monroe Trotter also appeared as did congressmen Dyer, Moores, and Dallinger.[19] Meanwhile, Storey had written a member of the Senate subcommittee reviewing the Curtis resolution, William P. Dillingham (R-Vermont), who reportedly doubted that Congress had the authority to undertake a general investigation. Working his own way through qualms about constitutionality, Storey cited the words of his famous mentor, Charles Sumner, that Congress "is the grand inquest of the nation," able to examine conditions whenever they threaten national peace and domestic tranquillity. If congressional jurisdiction to legislate against lynching was not absolutely clear cut,

> much may be said in favor of the proposition that where in a state the right to a trial by an impartial jury is denied and lynching mobs are tolerated by the authorities, and no attempt is made to punish the lynchers and that system has continued for years, so far as the colored people are concerned there is no republican government, and it should be possible for Congress to pass laws so as to ensure so large a section of our population their rights as citizens.

Storey argued that Congress could not meet its legislative responsibilities without a full investigation and that congressional disclosures would arouse public opinion against further mob abuses. If Congress, with a Republican majority, failed to act "it would seem to the colored people that they have nothing to hope for from the law, and I am afraid the consequences may be disastrous."[20]

Congress, however, did not respond, so Curtis and Dyer promised to press the matter in future sessions.[21] Meanwhile, the 1920 presidential campaign offered its own opportunities, and Du Bois prepared a questionnaire for all presidential candidates. First among his several inquiries was the question, "will you favor the enactment of laws making lynching a Federal offense?"[22]

With its powerful southern segregationist wing, the Democratic party seemed an unlikely instrument for racial reform. But the Association did send James Weldon Johnson to the Republican national convention, where he conferred with party chairman Will Hays, Senator James Watson of Indiana, who chaired the Resolutions Committee, and Harry Daugherty, Warren Harding's campaign manager and the future attorney general. Johnson and other black advocates got a scant twenty minutes before the Resolutions Committee; he used the occasion to stress the need for a plank against lynching. The results were mixed: the GOP platform did "urge Congress to consider the most effective means to end lynching," but Johnson came away feeling that "the Republican Party desires, more and more, to get rid of the Negro."[23]

Johnson, however, kept pressing. On August 9, he and Harry E. Davis, a Cleveland resident and member of the NAACP Board of Directors, visited candidate Harding in Marion, Ohio, to ask that he issue several pre-election statements on race issues. These involved voting rights, segregation in federal departments, passage of a federal antilynching law, an investigation into the American occupation of Haiti, federal aid to education, opportunities for blacks in the armed services, and Jim Crow restrictions in interstate travel. Harding expressed concern, in principle, with each but declined to make a campaign issue of any except conditions in Haiti, which might embarrass the Democratic administration in a national election.[24] Eager to capitalize on any legitimate possibility, Johnson investigated the Haitian occupation further. He wrote four articles in *The Nation* that GOP strategists did, in fact, use to good advantage in the party's drive to victory. The new president subsequently commended Johnson for the help, but using such acknowledgements as leverage in the drive for an antilynching law proved another matter.[25]

On January 15, 1921, Johnson returned to Marion to discuss a governmental inquiry into conditions facing black Americans, federal appointments for blacks, amnesty for the men of the Twenty-fourth Infantry, black voting rights, and the fight against lynching and the Ku Klux Klan. Though cordial, Harding seemed less anxious to promise action than he had the summer before. Johnson felt that the president-elect, though an "average, decent American citizen," was really "a man of very little imagination and seemingly of very little human sympathy."[26] On April 4, he met with Harding once more. Would the president, Johnson asked, include in his first message to Congress a clear-cut recommendation for the passage of a federal antilynching law? Harding responded a week later when he declared that Congress "ought to wipe the stain of barbaric lynching from the banners of a free and orderly representative democracy." The *New York Times* noted that the president's remarks on black people drew "applause and then silence" from House and Senate members.[27]

Aware of the hurdles that lay ahead, the Association welcomed Harding's endorsement, as it did some other hopeful signs. At the opening of the new Congress, Dyer introduced H.R. 13, his latest antilynching bill. The Association's St. Paul branch led a drive for passage of a Minnesota antilynching law, and Governor Jacob Preus sent a copy of the bill to the national office.[28] Meanwhile, a more exciting development, considering its source, took place when Governor Hugh Dorsey of Georgia released a pamphlet entitled *The Negro in Georgia*. It cited 135 instances of lynchings, peonage, and lawless oppression against black people within the state, and the Association quickly distributed extracts to the press and to the White House. The NAACP had long known and reported on the data contained in the pamphlet, but publication by a governor from the Deep South greatly enhanced their significance. "In some counties," Dorsey reported, "the Negro is being driven out as though he were a wild beast; in others, he is being held as a slave; in others no Negroes remain." Only two of the 135 cases involved the question of rape, that old southern rationale for racist crimes, and the governor concluded:

> To me it seems that we stand indicted as a people before the world. If the conditions indicated by these charges should continue, both God and man would justly condemn Georgia more severely than man and God have condemned Belgium and Leopold for the Congo atrocities. But worse than that condemnation would be the destruction of our civilization by the continued toleration of such cruelties in Georgia.[29]

The son of an eminent Georgia jurist, Hugh Dorsey had begun legal practice in his father's law firm and served as solicitor general of the Atlanta judicial circuit. In that capacity he had prosecuted Leo Frank, the Jewish factory owner who died at the hands of a lynch mob in 1915 after being convicted of rape-murder. Walter White, who lived in Atlanta at the time, believed that Dorsey derived considerable political profit from his courtroom success in the case. A two-term governor from 1917 to 1921, he had not always responded as forthrightly to mob violence as the NAACP had hoped. But now he condemned lynching and peonage and, despite public criticism, argued that racial conditions could be markedly improved through investigations, publication of the facts, compulsory education for both races, proper religious instruction, and interracial conferences.[30] Dorsey's report spoke especially to a group of southern liberals distressed with the more blatant forms of racial injustice. They had found an outlet for their concern in the work of Will W. Alexander and the Commission on Interracial Cooperation. Established in Atlanta in 1919, the CIC resembled the young, contemporary NAACP, particularly in opposing mob violence. It bore a likeness to the Association, too, in the composition of its leadership, which—drawn from both sexes and both races—reflected an intellectual, professional, and culturally sensitive group of clergy, journalists, educators, lawyers, and social workers.[31] It was, in many ways, a southern expression of urban Progressivism.

Amid these encouraging developments, the Association opened an overly ambitious drive for a quarter of a million members and moved to broaden its contacts among legislators.[32] An air of quiet confidence prevailed. In late February, White had told Storey that however little the Association really knew about the incoming Harding administration's intentions toward antilynching legislation, "we have reasons to believe that a Bill will be introduced and passed." He also hinted at the importance attached to recognition and perseverance: "Of course, our desire is to get a Bill through regardless of the credit for . . . passage. . . . Yet, since the NAACP has done more work than any other organization in a fight for the Bill, we want to continue the work up to and following such passage."[33] These declarations seem, in retrospect, a frank expression of the organization's goals, and a determined attempt by the black-led secretariat to assure prominent white Board members that the former had everything in hand.

Two months later White gave further indication of the staff's optimism and of the maturing of its attitudes and objectives as a result of favorable Washington conditions. He informed Storey of thirteen bills, nine promising, on the question of lynching. However, two would provide for an investigative commission, and,

> We shall not, of course, support any such measures and, if need be, we will actively oppose those two bills and any similar ones that may be introduced in the future. Such a commission will not serve any purpose other than to give a few jobs and defer action by the Congress against lynching for several years. Our position is that a commission on lynching is no more necessary than a commission on murder or treason.

The spring of 1921, then, witnessed the Association's first open rejection of a congressional investigation into lynching, on grounds that it represented a diversionary tactic. With but few exceptions born of strategic necessity, the NAACP maintained that attitude over the course of the next thirty years. That did not mean, however, that the group opposed a more broadly cast inquiry into racial matters. Quite the opposite. So long as a probe was divorced from the lynching issue, which the Dyer bill so ably addressed, the NAACP could and would support a serious federal examination of race,[34] as it had wanted in the early months of the Wilson administration and would welcome in 1946–1947, during Truman's first White House term.

In late May, Dyer expressed confidence that his bill would be reported from committee. Accordingly, Johnson alerted Curtis of the Association's decision to back an antilynching bill rather than congressional investigations, and the senator concurred. Next, Johnson spoke with Republican Congressman Martin Ansorge of New York, whose own antilynching bill, the Association felt, called for little beyond investigative powers. Ansorge, too, agreed to subordinate his measure to the interests of the Dyer bill.[35] Clearly the NAACP was getting the type of cooperation established lobbyists come to expect, and that gave further testimony to the organization's growing recognition on Capitol Hill.

Constitutionality continued to be a sticking point, however. Would, in fact, any federal law in this area infringe on the power of the states to deal with murder? Storey had by this time fully resolved his own doubts in favor of federal action, but unfortunately for the NAACP and the black community, a number of important congressional figures lacked his flexibility.[36] No doubt some had genuine reservations, while others found it politically expedient to question the wisdom of national remedies. In either case, their hesitation played into the hands of stubborn segregationists and ultimately helped to prevent passage. When the Association sought legal precedents that might sustain an antilynching law, they were difficult to find, largely because of the conservative tendencies of the Supreme Court since the 1870s. The NAACP had, for instance, thought of invoking certain Reconstruction laws, but Assistant Attorney General Herron explained that the Court in recent years had found against the Justice Department when it took that approach.[37]

The Association also tried to secure favorable opinions from legal authorities of such unimpeachable stature that their endorsement of an antilynching law would outweigh any objections in Congress and in the public mind. At various times the organization looked to Louis Marshall, Charles Studin, Albert E. Pillsbury, George W. Wickersham, and Storey for such service, but their counsel was not always what the staff wanted to hear. When, for example, both Wickersham and Marshall confessed doubts about constitutionality, Walter White merely exhibited the determination that marked the black secretariat's drive against lynching: "these statements while a bit discouraging, will not deter us" from working for passage.[38] And if the Supreme Court should declare against the statute, White asserted, "we will then have gained a point . . . [to be used] in securing an amendment to the Constitution." Bold words, but even as they acquired further support for the bill, Association leaders could never fully free themselves from the snare of constitutionality.[39]

Neither Wickersham nor Marshall was callous to the horrors of lynching and neither wished to hinder the Association's work. The former Attorney General of the Taft administration had already confided to the NAACP in 1919 that "common humanity" required "some action be taken" against mobbism, while Marshall, president of the American Jewish Committee and attorney for the Leo Frank appeal to the Supreme Court, had unassailable credentials in the fight against discrimination and mob violence.[40] The real problem was that American society and its constitutional experts had not yet devised a system of federal responsibilities in areas traditionally left to the states. Progressivism and the mobilization of resources during World War I had served merely to point the way. It would take a decade of economic disaster in the 1930s and the exigencies of World War II and the cold war to swing the tide in favor of an enlarged federal presence in community affairs. In civil rights, the impact would occur during the 1950s and 1960s under the pressures of non-violent, direct activism. Thus the crusade for a federal antilynching law was a harbinger of later, national remedies, a prospect that segregationists understood and feared. No wonder they fought the NAACP at every turn.

For their part, Johnson and White were wise to push forward despite the reservations of eminent counsel, especially when support emerged momentarily from other quarters. In July, Guy Goff, assistant to Attorney General Daugherty, endorsed the constitutionality of the Dyer bill at House committee hearings, and the attorney general himself publicly concurred in early August. Congressman Moores, who had played an important role in revising the Dyer bill to allow potential lynching victims to petition for federal protection, anticipated passage. Always sensitive to official and public opinions, the NAACP staff set out to publicize Goff's testimony and Daugherty's approval. The only admonition came from Dyer, who now worried about timing. Why not postpone further action on the measure until after the congressional recess expected in mid-August?

He feared that the combination of weather and heavy workload might put legislators in a bad mood, and saw no purpose in jeopardizing his bill at that point.[41]

When Congress returned in the fall, the House Judiciary Committee finished work on the Dyer bill and ordered it favorably reported.[42] The NAACP knew its efforts had begun to pay dividends but could not accurately gauge how far its influence reached. To hasten consideration and passage, the Association wired its twenty-seven largest and most active branches to apply pressure on their congressmen. Bidding for public support, it sent releases to the black press and distributed special slides and exhibits to a half-dozen movie theaters in New York City. But on October 24, Dyer again turned cautious. He told Johnson that little else could be done in that session and suggested the bill take its place on the calendar and await its turn on the floor. Fearing that such an uncertain course might take months, Johnson could not accept the prospect with equanimity. He admonished Dyer that the staff in New York had exerted all its energies and that it "would be very difficult, if not impossible" to do so again.[43]

The first session of the Sixty-seventh Congress met from April 11 to November 23, 1921, the second from December 5 to September 22 of the following year. What lay behind Dyer's complacency? Did he perceive correctly that few controversial measures could weather the drive to close the session, and that on those grounds his antilynching bill ought not be endangered needlessly? Or, had he received signals from GOP leaders who felt that the party had done enough to redeem its pledges to the Association and now preferred to let the issue die quietly without risking southern Democratic cooperation on matters of higher priority to Republicans? Caring less about motives and more about moving the bill, Johnson went directly to GOP Congressman Martin Madden of southside Chicago, who chaired the powerful Appropriations Committee and had a political reputation of befriending the burgeoning black community within his district.[44] Madden promised to speak with certain party leaders that same day. Johnson next visited Speaker Gillett, Majority Leader Frank Mondell (R–Wyoming), and other influential House Republicans on the Steering and Rules committees. Unless they were "willfully deceiving me," Johnson informed the Association in some excitement, the measure would probably come up, and they all felt that "the Bill will be passed in the House, if it is brought to a vote."[45]

In this atmosphere, Dyer took the floor on October 31 to move immediate consideration, but the Rules Committee still had to act. Meanwhile, a minority of five on the Judiciary Committee, headed by Hatton Sumners (D–Texas), dissented on constitutional grounds and charged that the measure threatened to destroy both local responsibility for law enforcement and the traditional balance between state and federal jurisdictions.[46] Such criticisms carried sectional and political as well as constitutional overtones. The majority, however, had offered imposing arguments on behalf of the antilynching bill, which clearly reflected the work of NAACP lobbyists and legal advisors.[47]

The Dyer bill's status remained promising but precarious. The NAACP had assisted in and fully welcomed the exposé of Ku Klux Klan violence published by the New York *World* in a nationally syndicated series that September and October. But discursive, week-long hearings on the Klan by the House Rules Committee in October had little effect on the status of the antilynching bill.[48] In deference to its powerful southern wing, the Democratic party avoided questions of interracial reform, and the Harding administration seemed unwilling to launch a lengthy struggle on Dyer's behalf. Despite its sizable numbers (299 representatives, 59 senators), the Republican majority on the Hill was no more aggressive.[49] In fact, what the GOP attempted next was a classic illustration of political expediency when, in early November, two prominent black Republicans, Henry Lincoln Johnson and Perry Howard, publicly suggested changes in the Dyer bill.[50]

The Johnson-Howard amendments would have gutted the bill by invoking federal intervention only when prisoners already in custody were taken from an officer or from a jail to be lynched. The majority of mob-inflicted deaths did not fall into those categories; besides, officials and mobs could easily fabricate conditions to circumvent such stipulations. The NAACP was furious. It appeared that important elements within the Republican party hoped for a political windfall from the passage of an antilynching measure, even though it failed to protect the black community. Or, the proposed changes might throw the bill back into committee, where revived but unresolved debates on constitutionality could delay floor action indefinitely. With a vigorous counterattack, the Association scuttled the Johnson-Howard recommendations. Then further problems emerged with Dyer's evident willingness to accept compromises in his bill. He had developed an "extreme anxiety" to have his antilynching law enacted, James Weldon Johnson reported in mid-November. Acknowledging this perfectly human and political desire, Johnson urged Dyer to accept defeat on a strong measure rather than have his name associated with a worthless statute.[51]

With black lives continuously at stake, the NAACP had no intention of compromising. Just three weeks before, White had urged Storey to handle the Supreme Court appeal of the Phillips County sharecroppers: "Having put our hand to the plow in the Arkansas cases, the Dyer bill, the Haitian investigation, and the relief of the Tulsa [riot] victims, it is impossible for us to turn back." And Mary White Ovington echoed these sentiments as well.[52] In that very spirit, Johnson, using the specter of political reprisal, set about shoring up his attack in Washington. In mid-November he sent urgent letters to Republican House leaders warning that congressional delays or alterations in the Dyer bill would be viewed "as a betrayal" by Afro-Americans, who "are no longer in a temper to be played with." In response to a personal visit from the NAACP secretary, Dyer agreed to get, and did get, a reaffirmation of support from the attorney general. Next, Johnson went directly to Madden, who accompanied him on urgent visits to Majority Leader Mondell and Chairman Philip Campbell of the Rules Committee (R-Kansas). All this turned the tide, for Campbell promised the bill would get a special rule that would set the terms of debate and clear the measure for consideration on the floor.[53]

Thanksgiving recess came and went and Christmas was in sight when the Republicans, under pressure from Johnson, finally went to the House for a special rule. But southern Democrats refused to cooperate, and it proved necessary on two successive days, December 19 and 20, to maintain a quorum by locking the chamber doors and issuing warrants for errant members. Forced to participate, opponents tried without success to filibuster against the antilynching bill, or they fell back on stereotyped accusations that rape was the essential reason for lynching. Johnson left the gallery, called Dyer from the floor, and armed him with the figures to refute those charges. Meanwhile, Walter White had been rounding up strong editorial support in the New York *Times*, *Tribune*, *Post*, and *Globe*, selected copies of which Johnson circulated among Republican leaders.

With a rule successfully adopted, southerners conceded the probability of House passage but hoped the measure could eventually be stopped in the Senate. For his part, Minority Leader Finis J. Garrett of Tennessee had kept enough Democrats out of the House at one point on the twentieth to force an agreement from Mondell that the antilynching bill would lay over until after the Christmas holidays. Once the GOP leader yielded, phone calls went out across Capitol Hill for "the boys [absentees] to come on over," as the *New York Times* so vividly put it.[54]

As the NAACP would discover year after year, many congressmen treated antilynching as an expendable issue. They, their friends, and family were not the mob's targets, so the entire issue remained a mere abstraction, constantly vulnerable to more expedient definitions of priorities. After the Christmas recess, for example, Johnson found a strongly organized opposition among southern Democrats, and more disappointing, a certain vacillation on the part of northern Republicans. Madden, of all people, told him that appropriations would take preference over the Dyer bill and that the latter might not come up until the following June. A frank discussion of political consequences induced Madden to cut his estimate to two weeks, and on Wednesday, January 25, the House agreed to debate the Dyer bill.

Once again, however, it proved necessary for the Speaker to close the chamber and send the Sergeant at Arms in search of absentees.[55] Mondell honored his party's commitment by speaking in favor of the bill. Across the aisle, however, William Driver of Arkansas chose to attack black activists:

> This is the stuff which your type of Negro offers his race, and which the National Association for the Advancement of Colored People and

other kindred organizations are circulating over the country, breeding discontent and inviting enough serious trouble without the aid of this body or encouragement by special legislation.[56]

Baltimore Democrat J. Charles Linthicum charged that Dyer simply wanted to woo the black voters of St. Louis, but Democrat Anthony J. Griffin of New York's twenty-second district, which included Harlem, countered with a citation of numerous southern newspapers that had taken an indulgent position toward the antilynching bill.[57] His compilation suggested the use of materials distributed by the NAACP.

Debate grew increasingly heated. When Mississippi's Thomas Sisson equated lynching with the need to protect southern women, Wisconsin Republican Henry Cooper objected to this open endorsement of mob violence. Sisson retorted by calling Cooper "idiotic."[58] While the chair tried in vain to restore order, the large black audience in the galleries rose and cheered Cooper, and the House was reduced to chaos. Southern Democrats leaped to their feet, shook their fists, and cried, "Sit down niggers," but voices shouted back "We are not niggers, you liar[s]!" The excitement continued for several moments.[59]

The *Afro-American* reported that over seven hundred blacks packed the galleries during the debate, because "there seemed a general understanding that colored people should crowd the Capitol for the effect it would make."[60] With the issue now in the open, Republican leaders had no opportunity for evasion and little enthusiasm for political embarrassment. They demonstrated their ability to advance a measure whose urgency and merits they could no longer discount. Utilizing all necessary parliamentary tactics, they defeated a motion by Hatton Sumners to recommit; instead, they called the measure to a vote earlier than originally expected. On the afternoon of January 26, the antilynching bill passed, 231 to 119.[61]

The NAACP launched its drive for Senate passage with a special memorial signed by various governors, mayors, college presidents and professors, editors, jurists, lawyers, and other prominent citizens. On March 1, a mass audience at New York City's Town Hall adopted the memorial, listened attentively to the principal speaker, Congressman Dyer, and contributed $670 to the antilynching fight.[62] Johnson had planned to present the document to Vice President Calvin Coolidge, the Senate's presiding officer, but Butler R. Wilson, a black attorney from Massachusetts, thought it wiser to use Majority Leader Henry Cabot Lodge. Accordingly, on May 4, Wilson, Johnson, and Archibald Grimké met with Lodge at his Capitol office; two days later he submitted the memorial to the Senate.[63] Turning to Lodge served two purposes. It utilized the most important senior Republican in Congress and also put Lodge, running for re-election in November, on notice that the Association and its backers intended to force him into a public commitment.[64]

On April 10, Johnson appeared before the law enforcement committee of the American Bar Association to testify on lynching as a crime. The committee agreed to endorse the Dyer bill, and in August the American Bar Association, meeting in San Francisco, officially announced that "further legislation should be enacted by the Congress to punish and prevent lynching and mob violence."[65]

The NAACP had still to win approval from the Senate Judiciary Committee, however. The subcommittee assigned the bill consisted of two southern Democrats and three Republicans from states that had no large black constituency.[66] The chairman, Republican William Borah of Idaho, took great pride in his reputation as a constitutional authority; had he been willing to champion the measure, its future would have been assured. As it turned out, he took the opposite approach and entered into an adversary relationship with the NAACP for the better part of two decades. The Association understood that Borah was central to the bill's progress. In the hearings, it tried to win him over with expert witnesses and carefully drawn briefs by attorneys Storey, Herbert K. Stockton of New York, James Cobb of Washington, D.C., and Butler Wilson and William H. Lewis of Boston.[67] But it never anticipated the unyielding personal opposition he would exhibit.

In early February Borah warned Storey that he would not support a measure he thought unconstitutional merely to bring the question to Supreme Court review. Three months later he informed Stockton that in light of past Court decisions "it may be a perfectly vain thing to pass this particular measure." On June 1 he told Storey that he could not possibly vote for the bill; it was unconstitutional. However, he would not obstruct its progress, if a majority in the Senate wished it passed—a prospect all the less likely because of his opposition. And Borah wrote an attorney friend on June 27 that "I've just had a visit of nearly an hour with a number of colored bishops upon the Dyer Anti-Lynching bill, . . . which I think as proposed is wholly unconstitutional."[68]

Aside from his convictions in the matter, Borah had much to gain from Lodge's political embarrassment if, legitimately or not, the majority leader could be charged with failure to pass an antilynching bill in fulfillment of party pledges. As Borah's attitude hardened throughout May and June, NAACP officials found themselves caught in the crossfire of latent antagonisms between the two men. Indeed, after Lodge ordered the measure reported from the Judiciary Committee, Borah seemed increasingly unwilling to give the Association the benefit of the doubt on the question of constitutionality. Lodge chaired the prestigious Senate Foreign Relations Committee, followed in seniority by Porter McCumber of North Dakota and Borah. Capitol Hill insiders calculated that if the other two failed of reelection that year, Borah would have the coveted chairmanship, and it very nearly happened. Lynn J. Frazer soundly defeated McCumber in North Dakota's June primary. In the fall, Lodge retained his seat, but by the slimmest plurality of his entire career, and there was some talk of reversal upon a recount. Moreover, in the summer of 1922 some liberal

Republicans tried to launch Borah as a candidate for the next presidential campaign, a prospect that threatened to reopen the party's conservative-progressive wounds of 1912 and renew more recent tensions over a GOP stance on Wilson's League of Nation's Covenant.[69] Any such divisions endangered party harmony on the antilynching bill, which already faced solid opposition from southern Democrats and had yet to enjoy priority standing among Republicans.

Anticipating that Lodge would face a stiff campaign for re-election, and that the Dyer bill could prove important to his chances, Johnson visited White House secretary George B. Christian, Jr., and Senator Lodge's secretary in mid-June.[70] The black vote in the Bay State was relatively small for a northern industrial area, but the Association did everything possible to maximize its effect. Lodge had to contend with public pressures generated by Butler Wilson, William H. Lewis, and their associates in the Boston branch, and he also had to confront the more radically outspoken black militants headed by William Monroe Trotter of the Boston *Guardian*, who was already on record in support of the Dyer bill. Unlike Borah, Lodge never openly opposed the bill. In fact, thirty-two years before he had sponsored a federal elections measure, the so-called "Force Bill," which was favored by black activists. No, the problem in 1922 was not his outright opposition but the limited and detached nature of his response.[71]

As early as mid-February 1922 Lodge had assured the Association that he probably would support the measure, but he admitted not having studied it carefully. His correspondence with the NAACP bore the same guarded tone three months later. Meanwhile, he told an opponent of the bill that no citizen of Massachusetts could refuse to oppose lynching.[72] In an extraordinary move against a senior member of his own party, Dyer spoke under NAACP auspices to a Boston audience in May and urged that his listeners work for Lodge's defeat that autumn unless he got the antilynching bill through.[73] The senator understood what was called for, and his pressure on the Judiciary Committee brought a reply from Borah in early June that there was "no intention . . . to abandon . . . or unnecessarily delay" the bill.[74] Soon thereafter, Lodge confided to Johnson that he was "following the matter very closely," that he felt "strongly the need" for such legislation, and that he had done everything possible to get committee action and would stay at it.[75] Finally, on June 30, the Judiciary Committee endorsed the Dyer bill, 8 to 6, with Borah joining five Democrats in opposition.[76]

Now, could the bill get to the floor? In early July, Johnson worried about press reports that Republican conferees, meeting at Lodge's home, had agreed to abandon the measure, but this brought a quick denial from the senator.[77] Still, talk of GOP indifference, at both ends of Pennsylvania Avenue, persisted. In mid-September, Lodge assured Johnson that "the President had no thought whatever of turning down the Dyer Bill."[78] And, there were false starts as well as rumors. At one point, Senate Republicans Lodge, Curtis, William Calder of New York, and James Watson of Indiana discussed a possible deal with southern Democrats whereby the latter might be dissuaded from filibustering against the Dyer bill, but no such trade-off occurred.[79]

Despite periodic reassurances, the bill's fate remained in doubt. It always took a backseat, as NAACP strategists realized, to such items as the tariff, veterans' bonus, and ship subsidy bills, the rail strike, and the disarmament conferences. Besides, whatever leverage existed in the upcoming fall elections was completely ephemeral, because threats of political reprisal would fade for another two years once the returns were in.[80] So Johnson, White, and their colleagues kept pressing, and when an opening developed in the Senate's business in late September, the Association found its opportunity.[81] GOP leaders decided to present the measure in the closing days of the second session, and made arrangements for the chair to recognize California's junior senator, Samuel Shortridge, for that purpose.

Nothing so much revealed the low priority that the Republican leadership accorded the antilynching bill as the selection of this untested legislator, whatever his personal enthusiasm. On September 21, Curtis helped clear the way for the Dyer bill, which, for a brief instant, caught the opposition by surprise. Shortridge addressed the chamber but quickly found himself the victim of clever parliamentary tactics. New to the Senate and anxious to serve in the grand tradition of Webster and Calhoun, Shortridge twice yielded on points of controversy only to discover that the president pro tem had given the floor to Democrat Byron (Pat) Harrison of Mississippi.[82] One can imagine the sense of relief among Republican leaders once Harrison had control of the debate. So long as southern intransigents made action on the bill impossible, Lodge and the GOP had a great weight lifted from their shoulders, and thereafter Republican apologists from the White House down consistently attributed the loss of the Dyer bill to Democratic refusal to let the measure come to a vote.

Determined to forestall action, opponents called for a quorum. When only twenty-seven senators answered the roll, no vote was taken, and the bill went over to the next session.[83] Republican leaders quickly assured the Association that the only unfinished items of business on the Steering Committee's agenda were the Liberian Loan and the Dyer bill, and they promised that these two measures would be taken up and disposed of before any other legislation.[84] With that, members of Congress went off to make what they could of the antilynching issue in the pending political campaigns.

Not only the NAACP felt ill-used because of the abortive attempt to bring the Dyer bill to a vote; Shortridge let his own disappointment be known. On October 6, he wrote to Lodge that "I, too, regretted your forced departure when I was making an earnest effort to bring up the Dyer

Bill. . . . when I noted your absence I felt like saying . . . 'Call you this a backing of your friends?' " Shortridge lamented the fact that the lack of a quorum had made his efforts futile, because,

> friends of the bill who were in the Senate and saw and knew the situation should have remained there,—I have in mind certain gentlemen who left to "keep dinner engagements." I hope my remarks served to placate many who are so deeply interested in this bill and who were disposed to think we were indifferent to its fate.[85]

Lodge replied defensively that he had to get back to Massachusetts to attend the state convention. Perhaps the pressures of his re-election campaign explained but they hardly excused the willingness of the Majority Leader, once present on the floor, to walk out on the antilynching bill and its novice GOP sponsor. The state meetings, after all, were not scheduled to open until two days later.[86]

As the November elections drew near, forces in and outside Massachusetts continued to urge that Lodge secure enactment of the Dyer bill. Trotter and his National Equal Rights League represented one persistent source of pressure, and in early October Lodge wrote Harding that the League wanted passage in a special congressional session.[87] On October 11, Trotter headed a delegation that met with Lodge in Boston. With petitions from several states, the group asked that the Dyer bill and the Liberian loan be put on the calendar of any special session. Lodge agreed to make the effort and consented to press for the Dyer bill first.[88] Meanwhile, the NAACP stepped up its drive. In search of funds White, in late October, wrote philanthropist Julius Rosenwald of Sears, Roebuck to explain the status of the bill and the Association's immediate plans. He reported confidently that the measure "is not yet dead and we have not yet stopped fighting." Prospects appeared "good," with the Dyer bill as the first order of business in any special session. Consequently, the Association wished to generate a groundswell of public support that would move the Senate to act. This would be implemented "through full-page advertisements in newspapers of the widest circulation, by bill boards, and other methods of publicity that reach the millions." The American Fund for Public Service (the Garland Fund) had voted on October 11 to appropriate $2,500 for this campaign, if the Association could raise a matching $2,500, and another grant might follow.[89]

The fall elections came and went with very little direct consequences for the Dyer bill, except that the NAACP was now denied whatever threat of swift political reprisal it had or claimed to have. Meanwhile, a number of Republicans had lost their seats in November, and with his own priorities to serve, Harding called a special session of Congress for late November to get what he could from a lame duck legislature. It was an odd situation. The Sixty-seventh remains the only Congress ever to meet in four sessions, the third from November 20 to December 4, 1922, the fourth from that day until March 3, 1923.[90] Johnson pressed for immediate debate on the Dyer bill. However, GOP leaders, especially Watson, Curtis, and the re-elected Lodge, wished to delay, since the White House was eager to pass its ship subsidy measure. Johnson's protests, a rally by the Association's District of Columbia branch on the day before the third session opened, and general NAACP lobbying efforts helped momentarily.[91] But as opponents of mob violence had seen in the past and would find in the future, the antilynching bill was about to be displaced by the indifference of its friends and the strategy of its enemies.

Johnson and White had done impressive work as lobbyists. However, once the bill went to the Senate in late November, matters were largely beyond their control. The struggle was brief. Pat Harrison and other Democrats launched a series of parliamentary maneuvers that stopped poor Shortridge and his listless Republican colleagues. Minority Leader Oscar Underwood of Alabama reminded Lodge and Curtis that the South would never consent to an antilynching statute and that, unless they withdrew it, the Senate could transact no further business. Faced with these obstructions and the threat of a lengthy filibuster, the Republicans prepared to surrender.

Alive to the situation, the Association could do nothing. Johnson noted that aside from Shortridge, Walter Edge (New Jersey), Frank Willis (Ohio), and Harry New (Indiana), majority senators had made no fight for the bill. Rather, Lodge, Curtis, and Watson contented themselves with allowing southern Democrats to go on record in their opposition and to bear immediate responsibility for the bill's defeat. Johnson urged the three to resist intimidation from across the aisle, but he soon saw how easily pledges of support were disregarded.

On Saturday night, December 2, the Republicans held a caucus to review their legislative problems. After two heated hours they decided to abandon the antilynching bill altogether. Although nine members refused to concur in the caucus decision, neither they nor Johnson with his urgent appeals to Harding and to the Senate majority leaders could salvage the measure. On Monday the fourth, Lodge assured Underwood from the floor that Republicans would not press the matter any further at the session ending or at the one about to begin. "That is," asked Underwood, "between now and the 4th of March?" "Between now and the 4th of March," replied Lodge.[92] In other words, the bill would not come up again during the Sixty-seventh Congress. This effectively canceled the Association's legislative drive to that point, since the bill could not become law in the Sixty-eighth without clearing *both* the House and the Senate.

Having succumbed with little pretense of a fight, Republicans now tried to mollify the Association. On December 4, with one session closing and another opening immediately, Lodge dispatched a personal letter, "receipt requested," to Johnson by special messenger. The urgency of the act and the letter's anxious tone suggested the senator's eagerness to be absolved from responsibility:

I received your telegram of last evening. I do not know what you mean by saying that I said to you in our conversation that "the bill would not be abandoned on terms laid down by filibusterers." I never said anything of the kind. I never mentioned terms to you in any way. There was no question of terms. The bill was either to be laid aside or kept before the Senate. There was no question of terms at all. I explained to you that the bill could not become law even if the effort to take up the bill was continued until March 4th, that it was equally impossible to change the rules, and that the only question that the conference would decide was whether they would give up all business of the session,—put aside the ship subsidy bill, the farmers' extension of credits bill and all the supply bills, and in addition a large number of confirmations—or whether they were to withdraw the Dyer bill and not press it during the coming session, which begins today. The conference agreed not to press the bill further and instructed me to say precisely what I said in the newspapers, so far as I have seen the newspaper report. I wish to repeat to you that I said nothing whatever about terms because nothing of that sort arose, and the words you attribute to me were never uttered by me. Nothing of that sort was said.[93]

Indiana's Watson invited Johnson to his Senate office to discuss the whole affair. When the NAACP secretary argued that public sentiment would have sustained the Republicans in confronting a southern filibuster, Watson confessed that he viewed matters in practical terms and did not believe the Dyer bill warranted such a risk. He declared, according to Johnson, that the GOP planned, in an extra session, to change the rules governing unlimited debate, and added that the measure "will be passed before the next elections."[94]

Neither Lodge's hasty disavowals nor Watson's bright promises tempered Johnson's keen disappointment. And for a time, some Republican leaders seemed unwilling in political terms to let the matter rest. The NAACP received several letters from senators, which indicated the party's concern about the bill's defeat. On December 8, Harding's secretary, George B. Christian, Jr., sent Johnson a tardy but revealing message. The whole problem, Christian declared, stemmed from the Democratic filibuster. Only a change of the rules would alleviate that, but such an effort would itself elicit a filibuster. "Frankly, it does not seem possible for a revision of the rules to be effected at the short session," he concluded.[95] Apparently, the White House and Senator Watson were dispensing conflicting bromides.

It remained for the NAACP to put the matter into perspective, and on December 13, the Association addressed an open letter to the Senate asking what its members intended to do about mob violence. The letter claimed bluntly that the blood of lynching victims rested on the heads of those southern senators who had obstructed even the discussion of remedial legislation and equally on the Republican majority "who surrendered with hardly a struggle to the lynching tactics of the Democrats." The Association bitterly proclaimed the bill's failure a license to kill with impunity, as the four lynchings between December 4 and 12 seemed to show.[96]

The November elections had provided no hope that the new Congress would treat lynching much differently. Republicans retained control of both houses. However, their majorities, as so often happened to parties that rode to power in a presidential election, dwindled in the off-year returns to fifty-one senators and 225 representatives. By existing Senate rules, a filibuster could be broken and debate terminated (i.e., cloture) only if two-thirds of those present and voting agreed.[97] That meant help from northern and western Democrats, and the Association resented the fact that GOP leaders never made a serious effort to mobilize such cooperation, never tried to challenge or break a filibuster on an antilynching bill.

If GOP conservatives, like Lodge, Watson, and Curtis, professed the customary Republican concerns about the Afro-American community even when failing to deliver, party liberals or progressives were usually less responsive. Looking for alternatives after the Senate defeat, NAACP leaders wondered if they could rouse La Follette and some of his political allies to reopen the antilynching question in the closing months of the Sixty-seventh Congress.[98] Nothing came of it. Insurgents possessed little power within national GOP circles, and the party had impressed upon them the absolute necessity of "staying in line" ever since the progressive diversions of 1912. Furthermore, Borah opposed the antilynching bill, and La Follette had other matters on his mind and would make his last run for the White House on a splinter ticket less than two years later. Indeed, none of the prominent Republican progressives championed the Dyer bill.[99]

The Republican party had underestimated both the black community and the Association and would pay dearly for this indifference in the future.[100] An emerging black political presence in northern and midwestern urban centers, the result of migration patterns and black initiative, was evident but not yet strong enough to achieve its goals alone or in coalition with interested whites. That would come later. For the moment, however, the Association had made an impressive three-year drive in Washington and begun the lengthy but essential process of re-educating politicians and public alike to the need for interracial reform. With the antilynching bill the NAACP had taken a civil rights measure farther through the legislative process than ever before in this century; not for fifteen years would it get another such bill through either house. And while making itself a key lobbyist for black rights, it had, especially through the work of Johnson and White, established an organizational competence that could be utilized for other tasks. Now the Association had to fold its campaign against violence and summary justice more neatly into its overall, evolving program for black America.

4

In the Wake of the Dyer Bill: Transition, 1923-1933

The Senate's defeat of the antilynching bill in December 1922 forced the NAACP to redirect its energies. As they unfolded, the 1920s proved less and less hospitable to civil rights legislation, and not for over ten years would it seem politically feasible to launch another sustained drive in Congress. The gradual decline in the number of reported lynchings (see Table 2) served both sides of the controversy: it offered some consolation to those opposed to mob violence but lent credence to conservative arguments that the states could handle the problem without federal intervention. The NAACP, of course, was not convinced; it never felt that basic issues had been resolved. Staff members were pleased, therefore, with Dyer's willingness to reintroduce his measure session after session, even though everyone realized the unlikelihood of enactment.

During the years 1923 to 1933, the Association found itself in transition, and the staff and Board wrestled with the question of "what next?" However, organizations committed to minority-group rights seldom have the luxury of picking their targets before the fact. Such groups have limited resources, under the best of circumstances, and much of their time and energy is spent reacting to conditions beyond their control. In retrospect the period smacks of adaptation, even uncertainty at times, if one looks for an orderly progression to issues other than the antilynching campaign. The NAACP measured alternatives, felt its way along, and responded to crises as they arose. By the late 1920s, however, it had settled on a major new venture: a drive for black rights through the courts on a broad and systematically chosen basis. That was a task intimately connected with the crusade against violence and destined to have an extraordinary impact on American race relations.

The failure of passage notwithstanding, the struggle for the Dyer bill had provided an essential rallying point for black activism: "unfortunately the Negro vote is not yet a sufficiently united body for us to rely upon," Walter White declared in late November 1922, *"except in this one instance of unity on the Dyer Bill."*[1] And staff member Robert Bagnall conveyed more than consolation when he wired Johnson from Chicago on December 3:

> ALTHOUGH WE DID NOT WIN WE WENT FURTHER THAN EVER BEFORE AND DROVE THE ENEMY TO DESPERATE MEASURE[S.] MUCH GOOD WILL RESULT FROM OUR WORK ON THE BILL IN THE AROUSING OF PUBLIC CONSCIOUSNESS CONCERNING THE BILL AND IN THE UNIFICATION OF OUR GROUP[.] WHAT IS NEXT FIGHT[?] HAD MANY TELEGRAMS SENT YESTERDAY[2]

At the national office, Du Bois pressed the questions of "what next" and "how" in writing some fifty-six prominent black leaders. Respondents understood the importance of the Association's antilynching campaign. They stressed the need for nonpartisan, coalition politics rather than any dependence upon the Republican party, and urged that the Dyer bill and the plight of black people generally be made key issues of reform.[3] This fit nicely with Johnson's feelings about possible action during the coming year. In early February 1923, the national staff submitted to the Board of Directors a "Tentative Draft of Proposed Activities of the N.A.A.C.P.," which reviewed the antilynching campaigns and made specific suggestions about the future. The draft called for expanded education, propaganda, and advertising for "reaching the uninformed." It also stressed the need to maintain pressure on Congress and to capitalize on Republican apprehensions about political reprisals from the black community.[4] NAACP officials and their black allies never lost sight of the antilynching campaign's political implications. Johnson had repeatedly warned Republicans of recriminations over the Dyer bill's defeat, and two leading black Chicagoans, Oscar De Priest and Jesse Binga, made the same point to Harding during a White house visit and to John T. Adams, head of the GOP National Committee, in early 1922.[5] These admonitions reflected an emerging black discontent.

Eager to build GOP strength in the South, president Harding had already antagonized the Afro-American community. In a speech at Birmingham, Alabama, in October 1921, for example, he pandered to white prejudices by referring to allegedly fundamental differences between the races. A few weeks later he declined to endorse the Dyer bill in his December message to Congress.[6] In April 1922, the *Afro-American* noted pointedly that thirty senators faced re-election campaigns, while an editorial in mid-June condemned the majority for its deference to Democratic feelings on the antilynching measure. One month later the paper declared bluntly that no Republican for national office should expect support until the party's pledge on the antilynching bill had been met. When several thousand people participated in a silent protest march in the District of Columbia on behalf of the Dyer bill, reporter Ernest Harvier wrote of significant black defections from the Republican party. He cited developments in Harlem, Brooklyn, Queens, Chicago, Philadelphia, and

Kansas City, and linked them to the GOP's inept handling of the antilynching measure. A year later, an article in the black *St. Louis Argus* still decried Harding's Birmingham address, denounced segregation in federal employment and at presidential ceremonies, and attacked Perry Howard, Senator Joseph Medill McCormick (R-Illinois), and Congressman Madden for doing so little for the Dyer bill.[7] Events in the political world did not revolve around the antilynching question alone; but the black community and its leaders were keenly aware of the topic and willing to make it a test issue in public discussions.

The fight for the Dyer bill had produced certain repercussions in the 1922 elections and given the NAACP the first opportunity to test its capabilities for selective political reprisals. The results, though mixed, were generally heartening for the national staff. Admittedly, it is always difficult to assign any candidate's fate to a single issue, but the NAACP and its allies had not hesitated to introduce lynching into the campaign at carefully chosen points. This was compatible with the Association's nonpartisan policy, since it addressed individual positions on key race questions. For example, the national office and the Michigan branches openly opposed Patrick H. Kelley in his primary bid against the incumbent GOP senator, Charles Townsend. Kelley had voted against the Dyer bill in the House, while Townsend favored the legislation. The senator won renomination, although he eventually lost his seat in November. Nevertheless, a branch president who had worked for Townsend's re-election reported that "Every hamlet, village, and city was organized as a result of the [NAACP's] fight" for the Dyer bill.[8]

In New Jersey, the Association publicized Republican Joseph Frelinghuysen's absence from the Senate chamber during crucial roll call votes on the Dyer bill. When Frelinghuysen sought to improve his image by recommending a presidential commission to study lynching for one year, the NAACP dismissed the proposal as threatening unnecessary and dangerous delays.[9] The Association also undertook active campaigns, in cooperation with local black communities, against Republican Congressmen E. Wayne Parker of New Jersey and Caleb R. Layton of Delaware; each had voted against the Dyer bill. Like Kelley and Frelinghuysen, each lost, and the Wilmington *Evening Journal*, a Republican paper, attributed Layton's defeat to the antilynching question.[10]

Adding to the climate of political retribution, the *Chicago Defender* criticized the Senate and suggested that White House "indifference if not clandestine hostility" had killed the Dyer bill. Both the *Defender* and the *Afro-American* used cartoons on their editorial pages to express graphically black America's distress over the measure's defeat, and the Norfolk *Journal and Guide* noted that Republican leaders had become increasingly suspicious of the NAACP because of the organization's recent election activities. The paper went on to denounce lily-white Republicans as well as those black leaders "bought" into the party's support.[11] The reference to Perry Howard was unmistakable.

Black activists especially resented Howard's efforts to weaken the Dyer bill and his criticisms of the NAACP. Following the November 1922 elections, Howard, special assistant to the attorney general, had written Senator T. Coleman Du Pont to denounce the Association and those who used it to defeat "some of the best friends that we have." He urged that Republican leaders "ignore and give the back of your hand" to men like Du Bois, James Weldon Johnson, Robert Nelson (of the Wilmington *Advocate*), Robert Vann (of the Pittsburgh *Courier*), and others—"these political bolshevists should be annihilated as the basest of ingrates."[12] Howard angrily denied any complicity whatever in the defeat of the Dyer bill and charged that Walter White and Nelson had aided Democrat Thomas F. Bayard's successful drive to unseat Du Pont.[13]

Convinced, however, that Howard had deflected support from the Dyer bill, the Association secured a copy of this letter, which it circulated to black newspapers in Chicago, Pittsburgh, Baltimore, Atlanta, New York, Wilmington, and elsewhere. As White explained to his colleague, Robert Bagnall, we must "make Perry Howard's name anathema in the minds and hearts of all colored people in the United States."[14] The controversy was widely aired throughout the Afro-American community, and black attorney James Cobb of the District of Columbia suggested that NAACP branches protest directly to the Justice Department about Howard's "pernicious activity."[15] Wounded and embittered, Howard found other occasions to retaliate. A year and a half later, for example, he urged the White House to ignore the NAACP and curry favor among black Americans by *increasing* the size of segregated units in selected federal agencies. Informed of this advice, Secretary of War John Weeks warned that black residents in the District of Columbia were likely to resent any such expansion of Jim Crow practices.[16]

The defeat of the Dyer bill magnified black dissatisfaction on a number of fronts. In early April 1923, the *Afro-American* condemned ten Republican senators for voting against the confirmation of Walter Cohen, a black man, as comptroller of customs in New Orleans. The Pittsburgh *Courier* noted that Harding might reappoint Cohen; such a step would prove significant at a time when the GOP was discovering that "neglect, indifference, and double dealing are prices that bring disaster."[17] In late spring, congressman Dyer, on one of his national tours to help the NAACP, told a large audience in Chicago that Republicans must bear the blame for the defeat of his bill; if black people really wanted federal protection, they must not vote for men like Senator McCormick, absent in Europe when the bill was called to the Senate floor. The *Courier* reported Dyer's remarks with enthusiasm but predicted that the GOP would merely repeat the rosy pledges made against lynching in the 1924 campaign. That summer, the *Afro-American* reviewed the policies of the late President

Harding toward the black community and found them wanting; progressive black voters had already switched to Harding's political opponents, the paper declared.[18]

Nor were Afro-Americans much happier with Harding's successor, Calvin Coolidge. Six weeks after becoming president, he received a letter from Tuskegee's R. R. Moton, who reported the black community's anger over the selection of C. Bascom Slemp, lily-white Republican and a former Virginia congressman who had voted against the Dyer bill, as Coolidge's executive secretary. The NAACP had already criticized that appointment because of Slemp's vote on the antilynching bill and his efforts to bar black delegates from the 1920 Republican convention in Chicago. Black disenchantment with the Republican party might have occurred anyway with the mass migration to metropolitan centers. There, Democratic strategists increasingly cultivated working-class, ethnic, and minority-group voters in the second quarter of the century. But the GOP's failure, to some observers its reluctance, to win passage of the Dyer bill induced black leaders and constituents to reassess their Republican loyalties that much sooner.[19]

By the late summer of 1923, the makings of a black revolt against the Republican party took added shape in a conference of some 200 delegates from 17 states, who met in Chicago to form the Non-Partisan National Association of Colored Voters. The delegates passed resolutions condemning the Slemp appointment and went on record against the Ku Klux Klan, the government's concessions to racism in the Tuskegee Hospital affair, and the defeat of the Dyer bill. Designed to break black voters from Republican ranks, the conference sent messages of commendation to Senators William Bruce of Maryland and Samuel Ralston of Indiana, William G. McAdoo, and Governor Alfred E. Smith of New York, and to "other leading Democrats" who had endorsed Bruce's call for a governors' conference to devise measures against lynching.[20] In an atmosphere of growing disaffection with the GOP, the Dyer bill and the question of lynching continued to serve as effective reference points. With an embittered comment on the party, James Weldon Johnson warned black voters to avoid all appearances of "being a mere tool and monkeypaw of alien Yankee domination." His experience with the Dyer bill left its scars. The man who endorsed Hughes over Wilson in 1916 and supplied data to the Harding campaign four years later had lost all zest for partisan endeavors. In his autobiography, Johnson admitted that for some time his Republican fervor had waned, until by 1928 it was quite dead.[21]

Republican leaders had ample warning from black advisors who sensed that disappointment at the loss of the Dyer bill was breeding a legacy of resentment toward the GOP. Accordingly, in the fall of 1923, William Lewis of Boston (who would later bolt the party) urged the White House to court the Association through judicious appointments. The president could award a federal judgeship to James A. Cobb in the District of Columbia, assign Johnson a high-level government position, and provide all expenses for Du Bois to represent the United States at the forthcoming inauguration of President C. B. D. King of Liberia. Lewis prophesied that such maneuvers would silence antiadministration sentiments in the black press and neutralize *The Crisis*. Otherwise, "we shall not be able to hold the colored vote. . . . I am not predicting a revolt; it is on; it is an actual existing thing." He added that Coolidge should also urge passage of the antilynching bill, especially since Congressman Dyer continued to make a public issue of Slemp's House vote against the measure.[22] Lewis was not alone in sounding the alarm. Recorder of Deeds for the District Arthur G. Froe sent the White House a set of newspaper clippings in late November on "the question of unrest, which I explained to you." And Melvin J. Chisum, field secretary of the National Negro Press Association, complained on several occasions about the damaging consequences of Republican policies toward the black community: "Of course if the administration does not care, then I am wasting your time and mine."[23]

Beyond the matter of public and political support for interracial reform, the NAACP believed that its program, especially the campaigns against lynching, would serve to mobilize the black community. With the Dyer bill, black America suddenly had a single, major legislative issue that it could champion throughout the nation, even to the White House and Capitol steps, in the very terms endorsed by white America. Who could deny the right of personal security and the principles of judicial redress in a nation that had so long professed individual rights in a society of laws? White America was not yet ready to condone equal opportunity in education, transportation, housing, employment, and voting, but a straightforward campaign against summary justice was something different, or it could be in forcing white Americans to implement fundamental Judeo-Christian and democratic beliefs. Furthermore, the Dyer bill appealed to Afro-Americans, who fully recognized the implications of mob violence. Through the network of friends and relatives, North or South, the sense of a shared heritage and destiny, and random experiences with police and mob brutality, black people, from whatever region, understood their vulnerability to force and intimidation. So the quest for a federal antilynching bill had special merit, because it addressed a real problem and could evoke a favorable response from most white Americans.[24]

The specter of lynching and mob violence cut deeply into the consciousness of black Americans. When Jake Brooks was lynched in Oklahoma in 1922, editor Roscoe G. Dungee of the Oklahoma City *Black Dispatch* sent reports to President Harding and to Dyer for distribution to members of Congress.[25] Late that spring, the black community in Washington demonstrated its concern. Headed by Shelby J. Davidson of the NAACP, some five thousand black people picketed the White House and the Capitol on June 14 to protest lynching and endorse the Dyer bill.[26] During the summer a group of concerned women proposed to raise one million dollars for the suppression of lynching and the establishment of an NAACP legal defense fund. An overly ambitious objective, it nonetheless represented the type of ad hoc committee that the organization would occasionally utilize for fund-raising and special promotional work. Eventually known as the Anti-Lynching Crusaders, the group originated with sixteen women at the Association's annual conference in Newark, New Jersey, and came under the direction of Mary B. Talbert of Buffalo, New York. By the end of summer she had addressed women's groups in Richmond, Washington, and Baltimore, distributed four hundred letters, and identified some nine hundred key women in New York, Rhode Island, Indiana, Colorado, Maryland, and South Carolina. Mrs. H. K. Harring, who had helped to prevent a lynching at Manassas, Virginia, promised to submit a list of one hundred southern white women who would join the effort. All nonoperating funds achieved from the drive, designed to run from July to late December, would go to the NAACP, which gave the group a $500 loan, advice and coordination in publicity matters, and some 10,000 pamphlets dealing with mob violence.[27]

Blacks recognized the importance of passing an antilynching law, and Senator Shortridge received letters of encouragement that summer from black citizens and organizations across the nation.[28] By the time the first extended campaign for antilynching legislation met defeat in the Senate, the Dyer bill had become directly identified with the general search for interracial justice. Early in 1923, the *Afro-American* ran a political cartoon showing a determined black man challenging a "White Supremacy" pirate for the possession of a treasure chest labeled "Negro Rights." A scroll entitled "Dyer Bill" lay beside the treasure chest, and the black man declared, "FOR FIFTY YEARS I HAVE BEEN PLEADING FOR THAT WHICH IS MINE—NOW I AM GOING TO FIGHT FOR IT."[29]

A more telling indication of the campaign's meaning for black Americans was Dyer's sharp criticism of certain local black clergy, whom he charged with giving insufficient support to the NAACP and to his bill. Speaking on May 18, 1923, to a gathering at Omaha, where a famous lynching had occurred less than four years before, the Missouri Republican declared that because of the seriousness of the antilynching fight those black pastors not present in the hall, and not ill, should be retired. According to the *Defender*, Dyer marked them as "not fit to fill the pulpit." It was an incredibly revealing incident. After all, Dyer was a white congressman with a large black constituency in St. Louis, and he was on a speaking tour for the NAACP.[30] That he dared to attack an established leadership element without fearing the consequences for himself or the Association affirmed black people's enthusiasm for the antilynching bill. And that included those in his immediate audience as well as the thousands who would read his remarks in the black press. Even a year later the bill carried such prestige that the well-known speaker and organizer, Mary Church Terrell, could use it, paradoxically, as a GOP campaign theme among black voters. She urged them to reject the Democrats as the party that "recently prevented the passage of the Dyer Anti-Lynching Bill."[31]

Black leaders other than those affiliated with the NAACP could not ignore the implications of the antilynching fight. For example, William Monroe Trotter continued to lobby for the Dyer bill, even after its defeat in the Sixty-seventh Congress. His National Equal Rights League had issued a call to organizations fighting lynching for a meeting of officers to discuss mob violence, discrimination, and segregation. In the fall of 1923, he led a NERL delegation to the White House in search of redress for a long list of problems, including lynching. Trotter specifically asked Coolidge to announce his endorsement of the Dyer bill.[32] While the National Urban League concentrated on employment opportunities and job training, it was always sympathetic to the antilynching fight, supportive of NAACP efforts, and hopeful about the end of mob violence.[33] Meanwhile, cautious whites perceived the impact of the antilynching fight on black Americans and their organizations. During the campaign for congressional passage, Eben W. Burnstead of the Massachusetts Civic Alliance warned Senator Lodge that the Dyer bill had evoked near-treasonable assertions and was "apparently arousing a sleeping giant."[34]

In rallying the black community against mob violence, the Association also pressed certain state governments to draft appropriate legislation. That worked best where there existed a sizeable urban black electorate. In the spring of 1923, for example, a measure almost identical to the Dyer bill passed the Pennsylvania House of Representatives, and not long after the *Courier* reported a new law in New Jersey against mob violence, Klan-like activity, and lynching.[35] Black politicians recognized the importance of the antilynching campaign. In mid-summer 1923, black delegates from fourteen states assembled at Atlantic City for a Republican conference. They approved a number of resolutions, including one for passage of the Dyer bill.[36] Certainly the black press backed the NAACP's drive. This represented not merely a commitment among the publishers but their awareness of the topic's importance to readers. The Chicago *Defender*, for example, was a relentless opponent of mob violence and an advocate of federal protections.[37] In the spring of 1923, the Pittsburgh *Courier* serialized Walter White's articles dealing with his investigations of lynching.[38] Throughout the black community, the fight for the Dyer bill evoked support and encouraged further group activity.

Even the black nationalists of Marcus Garvey and his Universal Negro Improvement Association flirted with the desirability of securing a federal enactment against lynching. In early summer 1919, Garvey's weekly *Negro World* had dismissed the NAACP's antilynching drive as wrongheaded; the best answer lay in self-defense not fund-raising, the paper declared. Still, the question was too important for Garvey to ignore. Early in 1922, he wired Congress in support of the Dyer bill, and afterward tried to claim some credit for its enactment in the House. In March, the *Negro World* complimented the NAACP for its campaign, and over the next few months UNIA and NAACP representatives occasionally shared the lecture platform and paraded jointly on behalf of Senate passage. But self-determination and not federal legislation was Garvey's chief concern. Garveyites still criticized and, by 1923, openly attacked the NAACP's approach, while Association personnel were well along with their efforts to discredit UNIA.[39]

That the NAACP and UNIA could have agreed, though tentatively and briefly on the Dyer bill, when so much separated them on ideological grounds, affirmed the basic enthusiasm among blacks for the fight against lynching. In the 1920s, black America was adapting itself to an urban-industrial atmosphere, testing its strength, and alerting whites that it would no longer accept an assigned secondary status. On its own merits and as a symbol, the Dyer bill performed signal service in that awakening. In 1933 James Weldon Johnson, a man not given to false boasting, declared that the measure had "brought out the greatest concerted action I have yet seen the colored people take."[40] Garveyites, then as now, might demur, but surely for those blacks to whom the antilynching campaign meant new opportunities within America, Johnson's assertion was valid.

The NAACP not only led the antilynching drive, it benefited from it. The more the organization did in this area, the more people recognized its leadership in the fight against race violence and its service as an agency for black rights generally. Board minutes throughout 1920 and 1921 show an intense concern with lynching and mobbism. The amount of material devoted to mob violence and to the Dyer bill in the secretary's reports and those of the publicity department for 1922 is literally overwhelming. Board chairwoman Mary White Ovington observed that "the one big job for the past few years has been work against lynching," and early in 1923 she proudly credited the Association with moving the Dyer bill further along "than any piece of legislation . . . in so short a time."[41] Of course, the intensity of the publicity work and lobbying took its toll. In early 1923 Board member Joseph Loud warned Ovington about Johnson's physical condition and the fear among his friends that the secretary might "break down unless he takes a much needed rest soon." Accordingly, the Board voted Johnson the vacation that his efforts for the Dyer bill had prevented during the previous two years.[42]

While the NAACP roused public opinion against lynching, it utilized the issue for endorsements, membership enrollments, and financial contributions to the Association itself. In other words, the antilynching campaign, with all its legitimate objectives, also generated organizational feedback to the benefit of the NAACP. Early in 1921, the Board scheduled an antilynching conference to coincide with the membership drive. Branches were encouraged to coordinate their meetings, and the staff selected three new antiviolence pamphlets as literature for the drive. In

March, Johnson reported a reprinting of the pamphlets *An American Lynching* and *A Ten-Year Fight Against Lynching* for use in membership work, and director of branches Robert Bagnall announced arrangements for a mass antilynching rally geared to the close of the membership drive.[43] The national economic recession interfered with the plans to enroll new members, but a year later "Lynch Law Must Go" served as the slogan for the spring membership drive designed to culminate with an antilynching conference at Newark in late June.[44] The annual meeting in January 1923 further revealed the importance that lynching had assumed in the Association's total activities. The featured speakers included Mary B. Talbert, Spingarn Medalist for 1922 and head of the Anti-Lynching Crusaders; Dan Kelly, a white Texan sent by the Association to investigate the triple lynching in Kirvin, Texas; Dyer bill lobbyist James Weldon Johnson; and Rabbi Stephen S. Wise, who condemned both the Ku Klux Klan and the failure of the Dyer bill. Herbert K. Stockton, whose legal brief had helped in getting the Dyer bill favorably reported by the Senate Judiciary Committee, was elected to the NAACP Board of Directors.[45]

Another measure of the antilynching campaign's impact on the Association can be found in the organization's financial statements. By early 1921, the NAACP had expended more than $35,000 in a ten-year fight against lynching, and monthly NAACP treasurer's reports showed a persistent drain on the antilynching fund from December 1921 to the end of the next year. At the height of the Senate struggle for the Dyer bill, deficits of $1,997 on November 30, 1922, and of $3,260 on December 31, 1922, stood as proud badges of involvement when year-end balances for the other two special funds, the Arkansas Defense and the MacLean Memorial, totalled $1,072 and $74, respectively.[46] Of course, the figures also represented a level of intensive activity, sustained in part by the special fund-raising of the Anti-Lynching Crusaders, that no black protest organization of limited resources could maintain indefinitely.[47]

The search for a federal antilynching law also gave the NAACP staff invaluable lobbying experience in Washington and broad contacts in reformist circles. Each carried residual benefits for the years ahead, and nothing indicated this so well as the help provided by the Garland Fund. In 1920, Charles Garland of Massachusetts received a sizeable legacy from his father; after first refusing, the young man formally accepted the money in 1922. He gave $200,000 to his estranged wife and used the remainder to found the American Fund for Public Service, an organization designed to dispense the money, as Johnson expressed it, "*as quickly as possible, and to 'unpopular' causes, without regard to race, creed, or color.*"[48] At a crucial moment for the Dyer bill, Arthur Spingarn, chairman of the NAACP legal committee, turned to the Garland Fund. Writing on September 19, 1922, he reported that expenditures of $40,000 had depleted the special funds and created a deficit of over $1,900. Spingarn explained the need for an immediate publicity campaign that would move the great mass of

Americans to write hesitant senators on the bill's behalf. Nothing less than $10,000 would do, and the subject was so sharply controversial that standard philanthropic sources proved too conservative to involve themselves. Spingarn closed with a mixture of hope and pessimism: "The political situation is less unfavorable to the passage of the Bill at this time than ever before. If the present opportunity of pressing the Bill to a final vote in the Senate should be lost, it is doubtful whether such an opportunity for action will occur for a long time to come." Following a further exchange of letters, Roger Baldwin, head of the fund, advised Spingarn in mid-October of a $2,500 grant, provided the Association secured pledges for an equal amount. It was this money that helped to finance extensive antilynching advertisements in the New York *Times*, Chicago *Daily News*, Atlanta *Constitution*, Washington *Post*, Kansas City *Journal*, Kansas City *Star*, San Antonio *Express*, and *The Nation* while the Dyer bill was pending in the Senate.[49]

This early cooperation between the NAACP and the American Fund laid a basis for more extensive collaboration in the years that followed. By 1928, the American Fund had contributed over $26,500 to the NAACP defense fund, and on November 8, 1929, it voted a single appropriation of $100,000 to the NAACP. Although the fund's executives later blamed the depression for their inability to transmit the total $100,000, the Association used the portion received to finance the so-called Margold plan of the early 1930s, a plan that led directly to the historic Court decision of May 17, 1954, in *Brown* v. *Board of Education of Topeka* (347 U.S. 483).[50]

Productive working relationships between the Garland Fund and the Association further showed that the NAACP and its staff had come of age and achieved a certain stature among reformers in the nation at large and about New York City in particular. James Weldon Johnson moved with facility in circles that included Mary E. McDowell, Carl Van Vechten, William Z. Foster, Sidney Hillman, Dr. Harry F. Ward, Lillian Wald, Norman Thomas, Roger Baldwin, Robert Morss Lovett, and the like, and he eventually became president of the Garland Fund. In the 1920s especially, the Algonquin Hotel on West Forty-fourth Street served as unofficial meeting house for major figures of the theatrical, reformist, and literary worlds, and the Johnsons (James Weldon and Grace Nail) enjoyed access on the most cordial terms. Nearby stood the recently formed Civic Club, to which Johnson belonged, while his wife joined the Heterodoxy Club, an organization composed mostly of younger women interested in social, literary, and feminist matters.[51] Enriched by experiences in the theater, politics, diplomacy, law, education, literature, journalism, reform, and public affairs, Johnson's career epitomized the intellectual-activist climate of the age, and the contacts that he and his associates forged proved of inestimable value to the Association in its work for interracial justice.

Meanwhile, a common concern for justice, a shared sense of standing as beleaguered minorities outside the mainstream of America's prevailing Anglo-Saxon culture, and a mutual abhorrence of violence (whether lynching or pogroms) induced NAACP officials and leaders of the Jewish-American community to embrace each other as allies. Henry Moskowitz, Stephen Wise, and the Spingarn brothers had played important roles in the NAACP's founding years; Martha Gruening worked on antilynching matters for the NAACP staff, and her brother Ernest, a journalist, assisted the Association in a number of ways. Louis Marshall of the American Jewish Committee provided legal assistance, and his son-in-law, Jacob Billikopf, helped to forge contacts between Walter White and various Jewish contributors to civil rights funds, such as Julius Rosenwald. The Council of Jewish Women aided the antilynching drive of the early 1920s, and associations with Louis Brandeis, Felix Frankfurter, Herbert Lehman, Jacob Schiff, and others meant untold dividends in good will, public support, or financial backing for NAACP causes.[52]

All told, the antilynching campaigns had been necessary in themselves and had also strengthened other aspects of the Association's work. But the inability to win passage of the Dyer bill compelled the NAACP to reorder its priorities. During the years from 1916 to 1923 it had concentrated heavily on mob violence and given secondary consideration to a range of other issues; from 1923 to 1933 it reversed that pattern. With the overall decline in the number of reported lynchings after 1922 (see Table 2), a reversal made sense. This was all the more true because the antilynching campaign had given the NAACP a platform from which it could attack more varied and subtle forms of racism.

The shift of emphasis, however, was always one of degree. Early in the summer of 1923, with little hope of pushing the measure through Congress, Dyer was back on the stump for the Association before large and enthusiastic audiences at Providence; Springfield, Massachusetts; Buffalo; New York City; and Philadelphia. He wrote Johnson that the Clerk of the House had promised to reserve House Bill no. 1 for his antilynching measure. The following winter, after the Judiciary Committee had once again reported the bill favorably, Dyer assured the NAACP that "I will be glad to have the continued splendid assistance of your organization until the legislation is written into law." But by December 1924, a friend of the measure, Congressman Theodore Burton (R–Ohio), warned Johnson that the Democrats would prevent passage at all costs.[53]

The 1924 national elections presented special problems, because the Association feared that the antilynching question would be exploited for partisan purposes. In the spring Johnson guessed that Senator Watson's need to pacify both strong Ku Klux Klan elements *and* black constituents in the Indiana primaries led him to just such behavior. Certainly Dyer, Madden, and Burton had no confidence in Watson's discreet professions of concern. Meanwhile, it seemed possible, by pressure on the Rules Committee, to jam the bill through the House with the help of some northern Democrats offsetting the uncertain Republican majority. Congress, however, would probably adjourn without Senate action, and then party strategists could artfully use the issue to their own benefit. Neither Johnson nor Dyer wanted black voters and their supporters to feel tricked or to hold the Association or the congressman guilty of complicity, stupidity, or both. So, the NAACP prepared an expository memorandum for Dyer's use on the floor, while a matching NAACP press release explained the sponsors' reluctance to see the measure become a mere political convenience. The Association promised to seek action in both houses after Congress reconvened.[54] Once more, the NAACP was left with the consolation that its efforts had alerted the country to the horrors of lynching and contributed to the decline of mob action. Congressional supporters averred that the simple fear of federal intervention served as a deterrent. And they felt that additional work in Congress followed again by House passage "will do still more to curb mob violence and lynching regardless of what action the Senate may take."[55]

There would be no House passage, however, until 1937, thirteen years later, and that occurred only because the NAACP had vigorously reopened its drive for enactment at the end of 1933. By then, of course, southern Democrats possessed not only the filibuster but control of major committee chairmanships throughout the New Deal years. Consequently, Senate approval for an antilynching bill would still elude the NAACP. But in the mid-1920s, the Association could do little more than keep the issue before the public, reaffirm the need for statutory protections, and seek to weave the problem of lynching into the many concerns facing black America.[56]

In February 1926, for example, Johnson appeared at Senate Judiciary subcommittee hearings on a companion measure to the Dyer bill, introduced by Republican William McKinley of Illinois. The NAACP secretary lamented the federal government's studied inability or refusal to move against mob violence. He declared that lynching was truly a form of anarchy that wrongfully superseded the processes of indictment, prosecution, and conviction, and asserted that the states had forfeited jurisdiction by their failure to act. He also cited the NAACP's successful Supreme Court appeal of 1923, *Moore v. Dempsey* (261 U.S. 86), which had saved the lives of a dozen black sharecroppers from what William English Walling used to call "legal lynching."[57]

This was the last committee hearing on the antilynching bill at which Johnson represented the NAACP as executive secretary. He would take an extended leave of absence in 1929, and resign a year later. His report for April 1926, moreover, showed the organization's continuing transition to other questions, while NAACP press releases further confirmed the decline of the antilynching bill. Of fifty-four releases, only one was devoted to the Dyer bill. Meanwhile, the Board voted to transfer $2,500 of the antilynching fund from a checking to a savings account, where it would earn 4 percent interest.[58] The very thought that this special fund, so often strained by heavy demands in the recent past, should now show a healthy balance and be partially immobilized in a time-deposit account fully indicated the cessation of an intensive campaign to secure federal legislation. For their part, Dyer and Johnson kept in close touch, and the congressman faithfully re-introduced his antilynching bill. In February 1928, he told Johnson the measure might pass the House, despite the impossibility of Senate action. He wondered about asking some influential senator to introduce and defend the bill "merely for the effect of making an impression of the facts upon the Senate and, through publicity, upon the country."[59] The proposal must have seemed anticlimactic to the NAACP staff at that point.

Having failed in the 1920s to secure a law that would invoke federal prosecution against mob violence, the Association fell back upon the burdensome task of handling individual cases of injustice. This brought the voluntary legal committee more to the fore than had been the case during the antilynching lobbying, but the issues involved were not at all incompatible with the campaigns for the Dyer bill. Three cases, for example, graphically illustrated the NAACP's determined fight against summary justice, regardless of the setting. One involved the Arkansas sharecroppers; a second concerned the prolonged imprisonment of the Twenty-fourth Infantrymen; and a third dealt with the trial of the Sweet family.

When black farmers in Elaine (Phillips County), Arkansas, attempted to organize and improve their economic conditions in the fall of 1919, whites in the area responded with savage mob rule. According to White, who investigated—and very nearly got himself lynched—these reprisals took the lives of over two hundred black men, women, and children. Charging seventy-nine black croppers for the initial violence in which a white man had died, local authorities conducted a sham court trial. Black witnesses were whipped until they consented to testify against the defendants, an all-white jury followed the proceedings in the midst of a mob that threatened lynchings if no convictions ensued, and the defendants' court-appointed counsel asked no change of venue, called no witnesses, and put no defendants on the stand. The entire trial lasted less than an hour and in five minutes the jury had voted a dozen black men guilty of murder in the first degree. The court sentenced the twelve to death and sixty-seven others to long prison terms.[60]

In a series of protracted, dramatic developments, the Association eventually won freedom for all seventy-nine defendants. Working through its Arkansas branch, and through two lawyers of the region, a white named U.S. Bratton and a black, Scipio Africanus Jones, the NAACP brought the case to the United States Supreme Court. There Storey successfully presented the appeal. Justice Oliver Wendell Holmes, Jr., spoke for the majority on February 19, 1923, in *Moore* v. *Dempsey:*

> In *Frank* v. *Mangum*, 237 U.S. 309, 335, it was recognized of course that if in fact a trial is dominated by a mob so that there is an actual interference with the course of justice, there is a departure from due

process of law; and that "if the State, supplying no corrective process, carries into execution a judgment of death or imprisonment based upon a verdict thus produced by mob domination, the State deprives the accused of his life or liberty without due process of law."

Holmes cautioned against the excessive use of habeas corpus, by which NAACP lawyers had tried to save the farmers, but he concluded:

> If the . . . proceeding is a mask . . . [and] counsel, jury and judge were swept to the fatal end by an irresistible wave of public passion, and . . . the State Courts failed to correct the wrong, neither perfection in the machinery for correction nor the possibility that the trial court and counsel saw no other way of avoiding an immediate outbreak of the mob can prevent this Court from securing to the petitioners their constitutional rights.[61]

In mid-January 1925, Scipio Jones telegraphed the national office that the last of the Elaine prisoners had been released.[62]

Beyond freedom for the defendants themselves, the case had a number of important long-range consequences. A few days after the Supreme Court decision, the Association received a substantial check from Louis Marshall, who had previously failed to secure just such a ruling in the mob-dominated Leo Frank case. It was *Moore* v. *Dempsey* that induced Marshall to join the NAACP legal committee.[63] The case and the NAACP gained a good bit of attention in both the white and the black press. Nine years later that master of public relations, Walter White, turned the affair to good account when the Supreme Court in *Powell* v. *Alabama*, 287 U.S. 45 (1932), reversed the death sentences in the Scottsboro case and granted the defendants a new trial. Embroiled in a lengthy dispute with the International Labor Defense and its sponsor, the Communist Party–USA, White gleefully asserted that *Powell* had reaffirmed the Association's earlier work in *Moore*.[64]

The fate of the Twenty-fourth Infantrymen further illustrated the Association's abiding commitment to judicial processes, and its genuine distaste for the retributions of summary justice. Having kept some of the soldiers from the gallows, the NAACP worked for two decades thereafter to secure federal paroles for all the men involved. The last prisoner was released in 1938.[65]

If the Elaine episode showed the oppressed state of southern black farmers, and the case of the Twenty-fourth Infantry revealed that military justice could match its civilian counterpart for severity, then the third major event of the period confirmed the fact that mob violence against black people knew no geographical or regional limits. In the late summer of 1925, the residents of a Detroit neighborhood tried through organized intimidation to prevent the family of Dr. Ossian Sweet from occupying a newly purchased home in an all-white section of the city. During the conflict that followed, one man died and the Sweets found themselves arrested and charged with murder.[66] Segregationist responses had assumed ominous, ugly proportions in cities faced with black mobility. Alive to the problem, the NAACP had won a unanimous Supreme Court decision in 1917 against a residential segregation ordinance in Louisville, Kentucky. It also involved itself in 1925 with a Washington, D.C., housing segregation case that later reached the Supreme Court.[67] In October of that year, Johnson termed the matter "acute" and listed fifteen cities other than the District plagued with some form of discrimination or intimidation in housing.[68] The violence was too prevalent to ignore. After sending White to investigate the Detroit situation, the Board and staff decided to make a stand there. For this purpose, they secured the services of Clarence Darrow.

The Association launched a publicity campaign to raise money, and Storey wrote the American Fund for Public Service for help in assembling a $50,000 defense fund. He predicted that a verdict against the Sweets would encourage further mob action against Detroit's black population and asked, "is the mob to dictate where colored people shall and shall not live?" The AFPS responded with a contribution of $5,000 and offered to contribute an additional $15,000 if the Association itself could raise the remaining $30,000.[69] The national staff accepted the challenge, and by early 1926 Johnson wrote the American Fund to announce that the NAACP had met its goal in only seven weeks; indeed, the total stood at $49,544, including the Garland Fund's initial $5,000. Because they dramatized every black person's vulnerability to violence and the hazards of legal proceedings, the Sweet trials produced a lively response among branch members. Though generously given to check lynching in years past, branch contributions to the national office in 1925 exceeded those of any other single year in the decade.[70]

After a mistrial, the second Sweet trial began in mid-April 1926, this time with Henry Sweet, Dr. Sweet's brother, as sole defendant. Detroit had grown into a large industrial city that proved attractive to both black and white labor from the South, and they brought their interracial tensions with them. Ku Klux Klan activities had aggravated the desire of many neighborhoods to preserve an all-white character, and not a few elected officials found it convenient to acquiesce to organized Klan pressures. Clarence Darrow demonstrated that the schoolhouse in the Sweets' neighborhood had been used the previous summer for a meeting to preserve all-white occupancy and that at least one speaker had advocated violence to that end. In a stunning seven-hour summation, Darrow said the case was one of race prejudice and not murder. He discredited prosecution witnesses and other whites from the neighborhood who seemed ready to perjure themselves to keep a black professional family from their block. And he asserted that had the situation been reversed, had a crowd of blacks attacked a white home whose occupants fired in defense of their lives and property, no indictments would have followed. Finally, the fatal bullet did not fit and could not have been fired from Henry Sweet's gun. Darrow's skill carried the day, and the jury returned a verdict of acquittal.[71]

The Sweet trials revealed a set of conditions larger than the question, crucial in itself, of the family's fate. They demonstrated that the Association could mobilize its branch structure in a crisis and make the contacts required to bring the most prominent lawyers and reform-minded organizations to the aid of black victims. The role of Darrow and of the American Fund for Public Service confirmed that. Moreover, Arthur Garfield Hays of the American Civil Liberties Union, who shortly before had collaborated with Darrow in the famous Scopes trial in Dayton, Tennessee, served as consultant. The episode also marked the Association's early involvement with Frank Murphy, the trial judge. He later served as mayor of Detroit, governor general of the Philippines, governor of Michigan, member of the NAACP Board of Directors, and justice of the United States Supreme Court. In the late 1930s, he was the United States attorney general who established a civil liberties unit in the Justice Department that served as forerunner to the more powerful Civil Rights Division.[72] Most especially, the Sweet affair symbolized a problem, still unresolved, of how black Americans could fully enjoy the added mobility and choice of lifestyles that might normally be expected to follow socio-economic advancement. The case served as a thunderous portent of tragedies to come and underscored again the absolute need to oppose the Ku Klux Klan and all Klan-like activities. And, the organization's defense of the Sweets, like its campaign for the Dyer bill, appeals for the Arkansas sharecroppers, and pleas for the Twenty-fourth Infantrymen, fit neatly into its over-all search for interracial justice through predictable processes of legal-judicial redress.

If the choice had been theirs in the years from 1923 to 1933, NAACP leaders would have preferred a range of statutory, civil rights guarantees. But the nation displayed no mood for legislative experimentation, and the Association lacked the means to overcome congressional hostility. Thus, the Association was left with the Sweet trials and dozens of less publicized instances, and the tasks of pleading, negotiating, and when possible, litigating on behalf of black citizens. On one or two occasions, this produced notable effects. Supreme Court victories against the all-white primary (*Nixon* v. *Herndon* in 1927 and *Nixon* v. *Condon* in 1932) come to mind.[73] Even these, however, were but early battles in a very long war for suffrage and not until the Votings Rights Act of 1965 would Congress react in a resounding and affirmative manner. Along the way, the NAACP did what it could, when it could. This willingness to respond to individual cases of injustice and harassment might have seemed defensive, when more imaginative, offensive maneuvers were needed. Those would evolve. Meanwhile, black people appreciated what the Association tried to achieve, especially in its constant resistance to mob violence. That the

NAACP program and the community's needs did complement each other is further suggested by the attention given to lynching and riots in the works of the Harlem Renaissance.[74]

James Weldon Johnson had presaged this in *The Autobiography of an Ex-Coloured Man*, published anonymously in 1912 and reissued at the height of the Renaissance in 1927. Witness to a savage lynching by fire, the book's central figure remembered that,

> I walked a short distance away and sat down in order to clear my dazed mind. A great wave of humiliation and shame swept over me. Shame that I belonged to a race that could be so dealt with; and shame for my country, . . . where a human being would be burned alive. My heart turned bitter within me.[75]

Less famous than the NAACP secretary, two younger contemporaries devoted considerable portions of their literary efforts to lynching. Born in Boston in 1880, Angelina Weld Grimké, daughter of Archibald, niece of Francis, grandniece of the Grimké sisters of pre–Civil War abolitionist and feminist fame, was no stranger to social protest. Her play, *Rachel*, was produced for the Washington, D.C., branch of the NAACP in early 1916 and published in book form in 1920. The story involved a cultured, hardworking black family stung by the awful tragedy of a double lynching. In the September and October 1919 issues of Margaret Higgins Sanger's *Birth Control Review*, Grimké returned to the same theme in short-story form. In this work, a young black couple in New York were joyous at the birth of their child. But on hearing of her brother's death and dismemberment by a Mississippi lynch mob, the mother gave way to grief and smothered her baby, because, "There is a time coming—and soon—when no colored man—no colored woman—no colored child, born or unborn, will be safe in this country."[76]

Georgia Douglas Johnson, born in Atlanta in 1886 and educated at Atlanta University and at the Oberlin Conservatory in Ohio, enjoyed more literary attention than Grimké. Her books included *The Heart of Woman* (1918), *Bronze* (1922), and *An Autumn Love Cycle* (1928), but she still found time to compose a number of short plays specifically devoted to lynching: "Blue-Eyed Black Boy," "Safe," "A Bill to Be Passed," "And Still They Paused," among them. The last two dealt with antilynching legislation pending in Congress, the very issue that had brought her husband, Henry Lincoln Johnson, and Perry Howard into open controversy with the NAACP.[77]

Jamaican-born Claude McKay used poetry to make some of the most unforgettable commentaries on mob violence. "And little lads, lynchers that were to be, Danced round the dreadful thing in fiendish glee," he observed in "The Lynching." "If We Must Die," his more famous piece, announced that:

> If we must die—let it not be like hogs
> Hunted and penned in an inglorious spot,
> While round us bark the mad and hungry dogs,
> Making their mock at our accursed lot. . . .
> What though before us lies the open grave?
> Like men we'll face the murderous, cowardly pack,
> Pressed to the wall, dying, but fighting back![78]

Not all Renaissance authors discussed mob violence, of course, but the theme recurred often enough to indicate its importance. No more than the NAACP lobbyists, black writers would not, perhaps could not, let the matter drop. In *Cane*, for example, Jean Toomer included a poignant episode entitled, "Blood-Burning Moon." Here Bob Stone was a young white man who had been intimate with Louisa, the cook at his parents' home. His antagonist, Tom Burwell, was black and fiercely possessive of Louisa's affections. When Bob went spoiling for a showdown, and pulled a knife on Tom, he paid for it with his life. But so did Tom, promptly roasted alive by an angry white mob unforgiving of any form of black aggression against a white. Sadly, it was a familiar scene to Toomer's contemporaries: "Now Tom could be seen within the flames. Only his head, erect, lean, like a blackened stone. Stench of burning flesh soaked the air. Tom's eyes popped. His head settled downward. The mob yelled."[79]

No one had to explain mob violence to Walter White. In his thirty-seven-year career with the NAACP, he would investigate forty-one lynchings and eight race riots. The Renaissance atmosphere encouraged him to write two books that dealt with lynching, and, as Johnson's colleague and protégé, he was understandably eager to have his own part in the fast-paced literary activities of the decade. First he tried a novel, *The Fire in the Flint*, which appeared in 1924. It involved a northern-trained black physician who returned to Georgia to help his people. Because he showed too much concern for their organizational efforts, the doctor was summarily lynched.

White's other book on the topic was a scholarly investigation. The project derived from his own NAACP experiences but was greatly facilitated by a Guggenheim Foundation fellowship awarded in 1926. *Rope and Faggot: The Biography of Judge Lynch* caused considerable interest when published three years later, and it has remained a standard work in the field ever since. In addition, White maintained close contact with a national audience through his articles in black newspapers; there, too, he seldom allowed readers to ignore the implications of mob violence.[80]

Although the organization won its share of applause, not everyone was enamored of the NAACP. It came under fire in the 1920s from three groups whose views of race relations differed strikingly from the Association's and rather sharply from each other's. Among black nationalists, Marcus Garvey and his Universal Negro Improvement

Association were most vocal; from the far Right, the racist ideologies of the Ku Klux Klan were particularly in evidence; and from the Left, the Communist Party–USA especially found NAACP solutions defective. Garvey believed that the NAACP eroded racial pride and jeopardized racial solidarity. The Klan saw the Association's interracial policies as a threat to white dominance. The CP-USA argued that the NAACP's legal-judicial emphases prevented any fundamental, structural changes in an exploitative, capitalist system. Indicative of the central role of violence in race matters, each had its own position on lynching and summary justice.

Garvey had come from Jamaica in 1916, and found an enthusiastic audience among the black masses of urban America. His extraordinary success jeopardized the membership rolls of other black activist groups. As for the NAACP, basic differences separated it from the UNIA, and these could not be resolved. Garvey, after all, felt that Afro-Americans could never achieve justice in the United States, while Du Bois, Johnson, White, and their interracial associates pressed unrelentingly for reforms within the American system. At several points in the spring and summer of 1922, Garveyites sought to draw NAACP officials into some forms of peaceful coexistence; this coincided with UNIA's momentary endorsement of the Dyer bill. But Du Bois and NAACP field secretary William Pickens declined the overtures.[81]

What particularly outraged the Association was Garvey's trip to Atlanta that year for a conference with Edward Young Clarke, Imperial Kleagle of the Ku Klux Klan. Convinced that all whites were racists and that lynchings and mob violence would persist in American society, Garvey apparently wished to forestall Klan harassment of UNIA and to determine if Clarke would endorse his program for relocation to Africa. Such dealings with the hated KKK, whose members so often joined in violence against blacks, helped to rally Garvey's critics and enemies. But Garveyites were neither dismayed nor silenced. Instead, Assistant Secretary General Robert L. Poston assured UNIA's annual convention in mid-1922 that the Dyer bill was a poor alternative to black people's best hope, the establishment of a strong, independent state in the African homeland. And Garvey subsequently prophesied that NAACP and Chicago *Defender* programs for racial justice would "only lead, ultimately, to further disturbances in riots, lynching and mob rule."[82]

It is tempting to imagine that competition between the NAACP and UNIA had persuaded the former to undertake its five-year struggle for a federal antilynching law, at precisely the time of Garvey's greatest public success. In that event, his trial and conviction on charges of mail fraud in 1923, incarceration in 1925, and deportation in 1927 would have offered the Association an opportunity to relax its Washington efforts. That Association personnel played a role in Garvey's downfall was true; that the NAACP had less to worry about in organizational terms thereafter was also true.[83] But the nature of its interracial visions and legal-judicial programs and the realities of racist violence, not Marcus Garvey, had launched the NAACP's federal campaigns. The inability to secure passage of the Dyer bill in 1922 and the unlikelihood of doing so throughout the rest of the decade, not Garvey's removal, caused the Association to temper its drive for a federal law—until renewed violence and a changed political climate in 1933 forced a reconsideration of priorities.

Meanwhile, there was no way that the interracial, reformist NAACP could reconcile itself to the activities of the anti-black, anti-Jewish, anti-Catholic, and anti-"alien" Klan that was reorganized in its "modern" form by William J. Simmons in Atlanta in 1915 and vastly expanded by Edward Young Clarke and Elizabeth Tyler in 1920.[84] During the war, the Association had urged federal officials to take "immediate and strong action" against the Klan, and throughout the early 1920s NAACP branches worked openly to undermine the group locally. Moreover, the national staff took heart from congressional inquiries into Klan activities and contributed information to the New York *World's* 1921 exposé of the Invisible Empire.[85]

Perhaps the most dramatic example of the Association's war on the Klan occurred in the fall of 1926. A mob seized three black people (Demon Lowman, age twenty-two; Clarence Lowman, fifteen; and Bertha Lowman, twenty-seven) from the Aiken, South Carolina jail and shot them to death a mile and a half from town. The victims had been falsely accused of murder and sentenced to death in a courtroom jammed by armed Klansmen. When the State Supreme Court reversed the convictions, and when developments at the retrial indicated the three might go free, the mob intervened and killed them. State action had once again proved totally insufficient.

Under cover of a press card from the New York *World*, White joined the paper's star reporter, Oliver H. B. Garrett, in a personal investigation. On October 28, White wrote an amazing six-page, single-spaced letter to South Carolina Governor Thomas McLeod, in which he extensively outlined the conduct of the Klan and the actions of the mob in the Aiken lynchings. Always quick to take command of a situation, White advised the governor that he was returning to New York, which "will allow some forty-eight hours for action before any of the material I have gathered will be published." White's report documented the premeditated conduct of the mob, the collusion of prison officials, and the identity (with addresses and occupations) of promiment mob members: a bonded constable from the courthouse, a magistrate's constable, two deputy sheriffs, a captain of the chain gang, the town's superintendent of streets, two of the governor's special state constables, two policemen (one of whom wore his uniform to the lynching), a local attorney, a three-time member of the state legislature, a constable from a neighboring community, the town jailer, the town traffic policeman, and the sheriff of the county. White also mentioned in passing that three cousins of governor McLeod were among the spectators.[86] Although the NAACP little expected and never secured effective redress in this case, that hardly dampened the staff's determination to expose the Klan.

Among its informational publications, the NAACP prepared and distributed a pamphlet entitled *The Recent Record of the Ku Klux Klan— As Set Forth by 2 Alabama Editors*, which utilized editorials of September 1927 to denounce the brutalizing, sadistic tactics of the Klan.[87] Meanwhile, White gave considerable attention to the organization in his book, *Rope and Faggot*. Affirming his support of Progressive remedies, he declared that "agitation for legal weapons" was essential for reform:

> Lynching—rule by rope and faggot and tar-bucket instead of by orderly and civilized processes—has for too long been a curse to America and an affront to decency and humanity. Against it is needed a larger, more effective, more valiant, and more articulate public opinion to restore sanity, truth, and the reign of law. If that organized opinion and action are not forthcoming, sad and terrible days, not only for the lynching states, but for all of America, seem inevitable.[88]

Although the Klan was in a state of decline by the late 1920s, and the number of reported lynchings had dropped,[89] the Association felt that the violent, racist spirit that drove Klansmen onward was nowhere near extinction. Accordingly, the NAACP asked President Herbert Hoover's Law Observance and Enforcement Commission to study lawlessness against black people in the form of lynching, disfranchisement, peonage, mob violence, and discrimination in schools, places of public accommodation, and residential occupancy. James Weldon Johnson submitted a brief to the Commission chair, George W. Wickersham, with whom the Association had discussed the Dyer bill after World War I. Johnson declared that "lynching constitutes the quintessential form of law-breaking and brutal disregard for human life and Constitutional guarantees in the United States." The secretary accompanied his brief with copies of the House and Senate committee hearings of 1920 and 1926, respectively; *Thirty Years of Lynching* and its supplements; the statement of Governor Hugh M. Dorsey on the oppression of black people in Georgia; several pamphlets and reprints on lynching; NAACP *Annual Reports*; and copies of White's *Rope and Faggot* and Herbert Seligmann's *The Negro Faces America*. The Association argued that lynching, in its social, political, and economic overtones, served as a mechanism of terror that maintained the subjugation of black men and women. Furthermore, since the plight of black people symbolized that of other minority groups, it posed a test of the democratic system itself. Finally, the Association advocated commission endorsement of a federal antilynching law that would empower federally impaneled juries to assume jurisdiction when local authorities failed to prosecute and convict in cases of mob violence.[90] Unfortunately for the NAACP and the black community, the Wichersham Commission focused on crimes that dealt with bootleg alcohol and gangland activities, and gave little attention to lynching and race.[91]

Disagreeing hotly with Garvey's black nationalist UNIA, and unalterably opposed to the white racist Ku Klux Klan, the NAACP also discovered an organized challenge, the Communist Party–USA, on its left flank. The party emerged from the leftist factionalism of the postwar years, achieved unity under pressure from the Comintern, and by mid-decade was prepared to denounce the Association for allegedly exploiting the antilynching campaign to its own benefit.[92] Hoping for grassroots membership, in 1925 the Communists established the American Negro Labor Congress, which published a thirty-one-page pamphlet entitled *Lynch Justice at Work*. The author, B. D. Amis, depicted the NAACP and the National Urban League as "the misleaders of the Negro masses" and "the agents of the white ruling class," but applauded the American Negro Labor Congress for its drive against lynching.[93] In 1928 the CP-USA, pursuing a strategy charted in Moscow, turned to the creation of dual organizations to intimidate, immobilize, or displace the NAACP, the Urban League, and other agencies that the party could neither capture nor control. Accordingly, by 1930 the nearly dormant ANLC was transformed into the League of Struggle for Negro Rights. It advocated mandatory death penalties for violence against black people. Meanwhile, the party had also developed a legal unit, the International Labor Defense, which would conduct "a persistent and militant struggle against lynchings and the entire lynch law system" in cooperation with other class-struggle groups. In the spring of 1930, the ILD held a meeting in New York to condemn lynching and announce plans for mass protest demonstrations, the distribution of one-half million antilynching pamphlets, and an ILD membership drive.[94]

Quite clearly the CP-USA recognized the importance of lynching and mob violence and was prepared to address the issues as a way of establishing its credentials among Afro-Americans. But, of course, the NAACP and the Communist party came to interracial matters from very different directions. The Association was reformist but not anticapitalistic, while the party viewed the erosion and destruction of the capitalist system as a necessary goal. The NAACP invoked the instruments of legal and judicial redress, while the CP-USA argued that legislatures and courts were simply the faulty mechanisms of a corrupt, capitalist system, and were to be used as forums to discredit that system. The Association took its reformist orientation from the liberal-pragmatic tactics of the Progressive era, while the Communist party (while hardly without its moments of compromise) presented a more ideologically oriented public image that not infrequently reflected the cues and positions adopted by Communist groups outside the United States. And, finally, the NAACP started from a position of primary concern with the rights of black people and spread its attentions out to other questions of justice and equal rights, while the CP-USA cast the problem of social, political, and economic change in an all-encompassing

Marxist framework and attended to black people's needs within that context. Accordingly, the two groups mistrusted each other. Only the facts that they were both interracial, that both needed the protective umbrella of civil liberties to function effectively, and that they sometimes found it expedient to cooperate on specific objectives tempered the tensions and competition that usually characterized their relationships.

Overall, the period from 1923 to 1933 proved a strangely important one for the Association and for its campaigns against summary justice. The era contrasted sharply with the bustling, uncertain years from 1909 to the start of the war; it differed from the intensive, anxious years, from 1918 to 1923, of trying to win public action, especially on the federal level, against lynching, race riots, and other forms of harassment; and it served as a mere prelude to the Association's more varied, comprehensive activities during the Franklin Roosevelt and Harry Truman eras. The decade from 1923 to 1933 was one of transition and adjustment. Federal antilynching legislation remained an objective, but it was not pursued with the vigor that marked either the earlier or the later periods. The campaigns against physical intimidation assumed a broader focus, with Association work through the courts regularly complementing its efforts at redress through legislative and executive means. Meanwhile, the organization expanded its contacts among liberal-reformist sympathizers and generally strengthened its capabilities to work with politicians and with the public on behalf of civil rights. Finally, the Association's public confrontations with black nationalist, white racist, and politically radical groups sharpened its own self-definition, impressed the NAACP's image more clearly on the public mind, and prefigured the conflicts that the NAACP would have with similar organizations (the Nation of Islam, US, and the Republic of New Africa; the Klan and the White Citizens' Councils; and the CP-USA, the Du Bois Clubs, the Progressive Labor Party, and the Black Panthers) later in the century.

During the period from 1923 to 1933, the NAACP staff and Board reexamined their plans and programs for the future. Having achieved stability, the NAACP began a subtle but sustained shift in emphasis from defensive to offensive measures. Investigations of lynchings and disclosures of mob violence, the handling of court cases for victims of mob action or distorted legal procedures, the broad fight against summary justice, and the pursuit of a federal antilynching law all carried certain defensive connotations. In these, the Association responded to lawless patterns initiated by white Americans and demanded, at least, minimal guarantees of justice. Though not unrelated, offensive action involved a quest for expanded rights and opportunities. Of course, the fight for a federal antilynching bill contained elements of both: defensively it symbolized the reaction against the mob; offensively it represented a search for predictable legal-judicial processes grounded on a federal statute that could itself be used thereafter as a point of departure for additional civil rights legislation. Moreover, in offensive terms, the antilynching bill implied open access to federal courts, potential jury service for black people, and even the indirect possibilities of effective state and local reform by officials and citizens eager to avoid the need for federal intervention.

The Association had tried on occasion to undertake offensive action, but was too often caught in the crossfire of pressing demands and limited resources.[95] When writing the American Fund for Public Service for financial help in June 1923, Mary White Ovington explained that the workload in fighting "almost every form of discrimination that could be practiced against an oppressed people" placed a heavy burden upon the organization and its branches. Moreover, "if we persistently neglect such cases we lose our branch support, and yet we must neglect them unless we can receive other help than that which comes to us through our regular channels."[96] In view of the Association's need to develop long-range offensive programs without jeopardizing its innumerable day-to-day tasks, the American Fund came to play a pivotal role—the same American Fund whose first contribution to the NAACP in 1922 had been for the Dyer bill.

In 1929, a three-member Committee on Negro Work, consisting of Morris Ernst (New York City attorney), Lewis Gannett (journalist and literary critic with the *Nation* and the New York *Herald-Tribune*), and James Weldon Johnson, submitted to its parent body, the American Fund for Public Service, a twenty-two-page memorandum that outlined a broad campaign for interracial justice. Citing the Association's past work, contacts, and achievements, the committee suggested that the American Fund release $100,000 to the NAACP for a series of lawsuits on behalf of equal educational opportunities, jury service for black people, and nonsegregated travel facilities. The memorandum also included a drive for civil liberties in general and the use of "intelligent and extensive propaganda" to expand public awareness of the Association's activities.[97] Ernst, Gannett, and Johnson understood that such a massive effort might well trigger reprisals against the black community and prompt "secret assaults on those Negroes active in the campaign." Accordingly, they advocated a special $10,000 allotment for "defensive action." Thanks in part to NAACP pressures for federal intervention, lynching patterns had shifted somewhat from the mass orgies of an earlier day to the less obtrusive torture and execution of victims by small, select groups seemingly immune from prosecution. The committee, therefore, wanted the financial means to investigate every such incident, lest recurring intimidation undermine its overall program.[98] The history of this ambitious master plan of 1929 had important repercussions for the fight against lynching, but not quite in ways that the NAACP had anticipated.

The American Fund did vote a $100,000 allocation, but the depression intervened. In October 1931, the fund announced that the collapse of the national economy had so badly eroded the returns on its investments that it had to curtail the authorizations.[99] White responded with a revised program and a reduced budget. An extended joust between the American Fund and the NAACP followed. Each protested its impoverished condition; both pleaded that the other temper its requests for help and remit monies already due (quite apart from the major grant, the NAACP had borrowed $5,000 from the fund in February 1929, and the AFPS wanted the remainder paid).[100] Refining the master plan still further, White sought $20,000 in May of 1933 specifically for campaigns against discrimination in education and interstate travel. The AFPS voted $10,000 on June 7, but the final payment was not made until seventeen months later, in November 1934. The master plan—sometimes called "the Margold plan" after attorney Nathan Margold, who was hired to help design and implement it—had stalled.[101]

The period from 1923 to 1933 proved a significant one for the Association's general objectives and for the enlargement of its capacities as the leading black protest organization of the day. However, throughout the early 1930s, the Association found its options limited by the depression and by a growing workload.[102] Hopes for extended legal-defense activities and for a frontal attack on racism through the courts faltered in the face of financial problems, endless pleadings, and a constriction of resources that affected the selection of issues and cases. Had this not been so, had the full $100,000 been available, and had the Association been able to move as planned, the staff and legal advisors might possibly not have had the time, energy, or inclination to reopen a full scale lobbying effort for a federal antilynching bill. Still, minority groups seldom have the luxury of choice. Given the nature of racism in America, the specter of mob violence persisted. When the number of reported lynchings rose to twenty-one in 1930 and jumped to twenty-eight in 1933 (see Table 2), the Association responded. Its renewal of an intensive campaign for a federal law against lynching seemed sudden, but the reasons behind this decision in 1933–1934 stemmed from a mixture of necessity, apprehension, and hope.

5

Need, Apprehension, and Hope: Renewing the Drive in Congress, 1933-1934

Until 1933, the NAACP had no fully conceived nor sustained plans to reopen the drive for a federal antilynching law. Overall, there seemed good reason for assuming that Association efforts might be expended on other matters. In May of 1928, Johnson had reported the smashing of a thirty-nine-year record: no reported lynchings for the first four months of the year. When they did recur, lynchings fell to eleven in 1928 and ten in 1929.[1] Beyond that, the 1928 political situation offered no promise of working to the NAACP's advantage. The GOP had done nothing since the great fight for the Dyer bill in 1922. Candidate Herbert Hoover seemed more interested in cracking the Solid South than in championing civil rights and was, in any event, thoroughly identified with the two previous Republican administrations in which he had served. "Rum and Romanism," not civil rights, were the major campaign issues. And Democratic presidential candidate Alfred E. Smith proved unwilling and unable to risk alienation among powerful southern elements in his party by any forthright stand on the conditions facing black men and women.[2]

With the Association pinched for funds in the winter of 1930, Johnson suggested drawing on the residue from the Anti-Lynching Crusaders of 1922. They had donated the money "for antilynching work, for legal defense, and for general use at the discretion of the Association." Johnson's proposed that $1,300 or $2,000 be taken out of the antilynching fund "*from which it is not expected that much money will need to be spent in the future.*" Joel Spingarn concurred.[3] The officers even discontinued the antilynching group as a standing committee of the Board.[4] Once a headline issue, lynching was relegated to the sixth chapter of the *Twenty-second Annual Report*, and the volume gave no hint of plans for a revised federal campaign.[5]

For all of its disinclination to reopen a drive, however, the NAACP faced a combination of circumstances in the early and mid-1930s that forced its hand. To begin with, the incidence of reported lynchings rose abruptly, dipped, and rose again. After an encouraging three-year decline, lynchings for the period, 1930–1935, were 21, 13, 8, 28, 15, and 20, respectively.[6] The Association could hardly ignore this and still claim to be a leading advocate of interracial justice. White had investigated the double lynching at Marion, Indiana, in August 1930,[7] and explored the feasibility of a new federal effort. But his role the previous spring in helping to prevent confirmation of Hoover's Supreme Court nominee, John J. Parker of North Carolina, had soured relations with the White House. When the administration ignored its overtures, the NAACP put aside throughts of a revived drive in Washington.[8] But the problem would not disappear, and with an escalation of competitive pressures from the far left, the NAACP eventually renewed its quest for a federal antilynching law in ways that thrust the organization into the center of national, reformist affairs.

The Association and the Communist Party–USA had feuded for years, but the leftward drift of the depression decade intensified their mutual hostility.[9] In testimony before the House Select Committee on Communist Propaganda, chaired by New York Republican Hamilton Fish, Jr., White disavowed any NAACP connection with the CP and charged, instead, that lynching, disfranchisement, segregation, and economic inequities all served Communist propaganda needs. The Association regularly asserted that its program, if implemented by federal action, promised the best defense against political radicalism.[10] Pursuing the same line, Joel Spingarn advised White in early 1932 that putting two or three southern liberals like Will Alexander on the program at the annual meeting would help "bring home the fact that we are a safer bet for the South than the communists."[11] To the CP-USA, White and other alleged friends of black America totally missed the implications of lynching by refusing to admit that mob violence stemmed from inherent evils in the capitalist system. In 1933, the Communist party's League of Struggle for Negro Rights announced that black people must abandon the so-called race leaders of the NAACP, who groveled before whites in the fashion of Booker T. Washington.[12]

The *cause célèbre* of the early 1930s that highlighted these strained relations was the Scottsboro affair. It had all the earmarks of a legal lynching. On March 25, 1931, nine young black males, thirteen to twenty years of age, were forcibly removed from a Chattanooga-to-Memphis freight train and taken to the nearby town of Scottsboro, Alabama. A local jury convicted them of raping two white women on the train and sentenced all but the youngest to death. The entire episode took sixteen days. The case had its full measure of drama and controversy: racial and sexual overtones; a southern, small-town setting; swift trial and conviction without adequate legal defense; threats of mob violence; and the customary all-white jury. But the fact that the Communist party's International Labor Defense and the NAACP soon engaged in a heated public struggle over which organization would represent the defendants and best serve their needs quickly raised the Scottsboro affair to national and even international proportions.[13]

From the very start, the ILD had the better of the tussle. Poor Walter White, elevated in 1930 to the post of executive secretary when Johnson retired to the faculty at Fisk University, suffered the agonies of a leader whose organization had won second place in a two-way contest.[14] Unlike the Elaine sharecroppers case, the Association had no one on the scene to match Scipio Africanus Jones. Unlike its work for the men of the Twenty-fourth Infantry, it could not appeal directly to a national leader for leniency. Unlike the Sweet trials, it was not dealing with a solid, middle-class professional family defending home and property rights in a northern, metropolitan community. In the Scottsboro affair, the Association's regional representatives proved ineffectual; it had to negotiate with local and state officials who, for the most part, openly shared the racist attitudes of the rural South; and it was confronted with the explosive issue of sexual assault that, however untrue, worked in an Alabama setting to prevent any presumptions of innocence. Moreover, the NAACP found few allies sympathetic with its dilemma. Most of the important black newspapers on whom the Association had previously relied for making its positions clear grew impatient with its hesitancy and ineffectualness. Plagued by the depression, most black Americans lacked the time or inclination to condemn the CP-USA for its assaults against the established order. The NAACP discovered that liberal white southerners, clustered around the Commission on Interracial Cooperation and its two auxiliary units (the Southern Commission on the Study of Lynching, and the Association of Southern Women for the Prevention of Lynching), were neither willing nor able to champion the NAACP in Alabama or throughout the region generally.[15]

The steady threat of Communist incursions alarmed the NAACP. Despite a high turnover rate (black involvement rarely exceeded 7 or 8 percent of the party's membership in this period), the CP-USA recruited blacks with great fanfare in the early 1930s. The Association watched uneasily the growing use of black delegates, often in positions of leadership, at CP-USA conventions, party training schools, and party-sponsored Unemployed Councils. The CP-USA ran James W. Ford, a black man, for vice president of the United States in 1932, and would do so again in 1936 and 1940.[16] Elsewhere, the party exhibited initiative in areas once presumed to be the province of the NAACP. Early in the summer of 1933, the ILD announced that it had sent its own antilynching bill to Washington: a "Bill of Civil Rights for the Negro People," sponsored by the League of Struggle for Negro Rights, endorsed by the National Scottsboro Action Committee, and transmitted to the president and Congress by the Free the Scottsboro Boys Marchers.[17] On the grounds of its drive against lynching and other forms of summary justice, the ILD was making inroads at the American Fund for Public Service.[18] For example, the 1934 annual resumé of AFPS gifts included $10,000 to the NAACP for its program of court cases, but $35,361 to the International Labor Defense.[19]

Faced with this quickened competition for allegiance and limited resources, the NAACP had to reassert itself. Walter White fully sensed the implications. No executive secretary of the country's most prominent black protest group could afford to ignore them. No leader, elevated from the relative obscurity of an Atlanta insurance company to national prominence as an author, investigator, and lobbyist, could allow the pressures from the far left to continue unanswered. The NAACP had become Walter White's whole life, it represented "enough religion" for him, and he could not risk his personal reputation nor the stature of his organization. No man so vain yet energetic could accept with equanimity the challenge from the Left designed, as he and his associates interpreted it, to destroy their organization.[20] A revived antilynching campaign seemed to offer the NAACP one ready answer.

Meanwhile, there emerged a new sense of urgency within the black community itself, as expressed by the influential Chicago *Defender*. From the time he brought the *Defender* to prominence in the early part of the century, Robert S. Abbott had championed a list of major objectives, one of which was federal action against mob violence. Late in 1933, Abbott announced that the *Defender* would undertake a nationwide drive against lynching and for a federal law. Accordingly, he arranged for an open editorial to Franklin Roosevelt to be hand-delivered to presidential advisor Louis Howe.[21]

Pressed to renew the antilynching campaign or see others do it, White and his colleagues perceived three hopeful signs: the liberal-reformist atmosphere generated by the Roosevelt administration, stirrings among southern white liberals to put lynching to rest, and White's recent successes as a Senate lobbyist.

The year 1933 was one of high political drama. The New Deal contrasted sharply with the demoralization of its predecessor and with the detachment and seeming complacency of the Coolidge and Hoover years. The "Hundred Days" excited public imagination, and the NAACP hoped that black Americans might share in the political and socio-economic advances underway.[22] For reasons more evident now than at the time, NAACP expectations went largely unfulfilled. The needs of the black community continued to have very low priority for national politicians. The Democratic party, whatever might be said of its northern and liberal wing, still housed an inordinately powerful southern element that would tolerate no federal action on racial matters. Roosevelt and most of his advisors, apart from general humanitarian sentiments, had little understanding of or basic concern for the black community; the administration's major goals centered on reversing the depression and re-establishing some semblance of economic stability. And New Dealers were, whatever else they might have been, thoroughly political animals, and in the hard-nose give-and-take of Washington, officials knew that black advocates had relatively few rewards to offer in return for whatever risks a politician or a party might take on their behalf.

White informed his Board early in November 1933 that the legal committee was preparing a new antilynching bill with the aid of Professors Karl Llewellyn and Joseph P. Chamberlain of the Columbia University Law School. Meanwhile, the Association sent a message to President Roosevelt asking for federal intervention to stamp out lynching.[23] Less than two weeks before, James Weldon Johnson had written White about the "terrible throwback" in a recent Maryland lynching. With no indication of whether White had broached the subject, Johnson noted the trend toward greater centralization and increased federal powers, and he volunteered "that it would be a good time to make another try for an antilynching Federal law. We came near doing it ten years ago; I believe the chances today are better."[24]

White and his associates also looked to the growing protest against mob violence within the South itself. This sentiment seemed fairly widespread, but its focus lay with Dr. Will Alexander and the Commission on Interracial Cooperation in Atlanta. In mid-1930, the CIC began a quiet, relentless campaign against lynching and the mythologies that condoned it. This involved research and publicity, community education, and the work of the Association of Southern Women for the Prevention of Lynching (ASWPL). Robert Eleazer and CIC secretaries in the several states implemented the overall program, while Jessie Daniel Ames set about organizing women on a local, federated basis. Alexander got the young editor of the Chattanooga *News*, George Fort Milton, to chair the newly formed Southern Commission on the Study of Lynching, which included such prominent white personalities as Howard W. Odum of the University of North Carolina; Julian Harris, news editor of the Atlanta *Constitution*; Dallas attorney Alex Spence; Nashville's W. P. King, book editor, Methodist Episcopal church, South; President W. J. McGlothlin of Furman University; and such major black figures as R. R. Moton and Monroe N. Work of Tuskegee Institute; John Hope, president of Atlanta University; sociologist Charles S. Johnson of Fisk University; and B. F. Hubert, president of Georgia State College in Savannah. In November 1931, this panel published part of its findings in an eighty-page pamphlet, *Lynchings and What They Mean*. Two years later, under the Commission's aegis, the University of North Carolina Press published *The Tragedy of Lynching*, by Arthur F. Raper, and James Harmon Chadbourn's *Lynching and the Law*.[25]

Over the years a healthy rapport developed between the CIC and the NAACP. Although White occasionally thought that Alexander worked too closely with the southern power structure, and though Alexander, in turn, sometimes found White a bit too egocentric, each recognized the ability and goodwill that the other brought to mutual tasks.[26] Both worried, too, about Communist party exploitation of such interracial incidents as the Scottsboro affair. In mid-1932, for example, they exchanged letters about the identity of one "Mary King" who had condemned Johnson, White, and Du Bois to Alexander. He remarked that "she did not get very far" with such an attack. White and Alexander discovered that "Mary King" was, in reality, a member of the American Fund Board who had tried to divert appropriations from the NAACP to the ILD.[27]

The CIC and the ASWPL sought to develop local and regional pressures against lynchings and against public officials who allowed them to occur. As Jessie Daniel Ames noted in a general letter on procedures distributed in the summer of 1932:

> One course suggests itself to me. Watch your daily papers closely for any news stories which might end in a man hunt or a lynching. When you see one, write instantly to anyone you know in that county to support and encourage the sheriff and other official [sic] in all efforts to handle the situation within the law.
>
> If a mob does form and does attempt to act, suggest to the county officials that they file charges against the leaders for inciting to riot.[28]

Pamphlet literature in the late 1920s and early 1930s indicated the CIC's thrust. *Mob Murder in America* asserted that public sentiment, stiff determination by law officers, the work of pulpit and classroom, a change of venue for prosecution, and the use of a state constabulary under the governor's control—and thus shielded from local pressures—were effective ways to end lynching. *The Cost of the Mob*, an eight-page sermon of 1933, argued that increased education for blacks and whites and a wider recognition of the sanctity of the individual were essential cures for lynching. A 1933 ASWPL pamphlet noted that since January 1931, the group had organized in each of the thirteen southern states and issued statements against lynching for *any* alleged crime.[29]

During the second half of 1933, mob violence and summary justice were very much in the news. The lynching death of three black prisoners at Tuscaloosa in August and September underscored the need for federal action, especially since local officials there had previously proclaimed their ability to maintain order. The ILD, CIC, and NAACP all reacted publicly to the incident, and CIC investigators charged that county officers had actually abetted the mob.[30] Not long afterward, the Upper South in general and Maryland and Washington, D.C., in particular, were caught up in the aftermath of the George Armwood lynching of October 18 at Princess Anne, Maryland. Two thousand people had participated in what the *New York Times* reported as "the wildest lynching orgy the state has ever witnessed." I. Amter, national secretary of the CP-USA's Unemployed

Councils, wrote President Roosevelt to ask that he remove Governor Albert C. Ritchie from office because of the state authorities' failure to bring the lynchers to justice.[31] Five weeks later, Amter's fears were realized when the governor announced that Maryland intended no further action in the Armwood case. Ritchie believed that the local courts could handle the matter satisfactorily, although a *Times* inquiry in Somerset County revealed a prevailing skepticism about the prospects for any prosecutions and convictions.[32]

Meanwhile, a lynching in California created a national sensation of another sort, when governor James Rolph foolishly attempted to justify the mob murder of two white men, kidnap-slayers, at San Jose in November. Even former President Hoover became publicly embroiled in the controversy, when he condemned the governor's endorsement of the mob.[33] With Tuscaloosa, Princess Anne, and San Jose fresh in their minds, a number of groups, in addition to the NAACP, demanded remedial action. The Socialist party called for an antilynching law; 2 Catholic archbishops, 24 bishops, and 350 priests adopted a resolution deploring mob action; and 400 members of the CP-USA's League of Struggle for Negro Rights met in Harlem to denounce Armwood's death and the treatment given the Scottsboro defendants.[34] The NAACP begged Roosevelt to take a public stand against mob violence, and on December 6, he responded in his nationally broadcast radio address commemorating the twenty-fifth anniversary of the Federal Council of Churches of Christ in America. Calling lynch law "collective murder," the president warned against those "in high places or the low who condone lynch law."[35]

This emerging outrage against mob violence reinforced southern liberals' inclinations to combat the phenomenon, but it also left them in a somewhat awkward position.[36] In their public opposition to mobbism, they were usually ahead of their neighbors though still lagging behind the evolving national sentiment for federal solutions. Will Alexander understood this dilemma and sought to deal with it constructively. He knew that the NAACP planned to open a new congressional drive but believed that southern congressmen would prevent passage of any antilynching measure. Although he would get behind a federal law, "if there is a chance that it will be effective," he chose instead to counsel Edwin Embree of the Julius Rosenwald Fund that "we should take advantage of the agitation for a federal law to work aggressively for more effective legislation on the part of our Southern states and for a more determined and aroused public opinion generally in this section."[37]

On December 9, however, Clark Howell of the Atlanta *Constitution* forced the issue with an editorial that endorsed the concept of a federal antilynching statute,[38] and Alexander was prompted to write CIC members and major newspapers throughout the South to tap their reactions. Most respondents argued that campaigns of better education in race relations at the local and state levels, and not a federal law, were best designed to rid the

South of lynching.[39] However, Harry M. Ayers of the Anniston, Alabama, *Star* openly favored a federal statute, while Douglas Freeman, though advocating state action first, admitted that a federal law "is a remedy to which we must resort if the states do not act to prevent lynchings."[40]

A month later, the Association of Southern Women for the Prevention of Lynching, which claimed a membership in excess of one million, came dramatically close to advocating federal initiative, if not the NAACP's formula. Acknowledging that it preferred a uniform antilynching statute in each of the forty-eight states, but admitting that state and local officials had failed to curb violence, the ASWPL resolved "that some plan should be devised by which state and federal authorities may cooperate in eradicating this evil." Throughout the decade, southern liberals occasionally flirted with the idea of federal intervention; its value was grudgingly conceded by the CIC in April 1935. But, despite NAACP encouragement and some breaking of ranks, they failed either to lobby as a group for such a solution or to resolve their ambivalence about a national law.[41]

For its part, did the NAACP have any reason to expect that it could influence Congress, especially the Senate, in a renewed antilynching campaign? It did, for as recently as May 1930, Walter White had played a significant role in the Senate's refusal to put John J. Parker on the Supreme Court.[42] Black people were pleased that one of their own could influence national policy, and that Hoover's next nominee for the seat denied to Judge Parker seemed a far better choice to them. Owen J. Roberts of Philadelphia was, unlike Parker, a liberal on the race issue, and for many years a trustee of Lincoln University in Pennsylvania. Meanwhile, the NAACP moved quickly to capitalize on its success. Over the next several years, it worked against the re-election of eleven senators (a former ally, Shortridge of California, among them) who had voted for Parker.[43] While the Association's opposition was but one factor in Parker's rejection, the incident greatly enhanced its reputation and that of its aggressive new staff leader.[44] Even Du Bois, who had reservations about White's leadership in other areas, admitted that the campaign was "conducted with snap, determination, and intelligence never surpassed in Colored America and very seldom in White."[45]

Between Parker's defeat in 1930 and the decision in 1933 to reopen the antilynching drive in Congress, the Association enjoyed a second, though less publicized, Senate success. The issue dated to the last years of the Coolidge administration, when extensive flooding of the lower Mississippi Valley led to the appointment of a cabinet committee, headed by Herbert Hoover, to assist the Red Cross and other relief agencies. Federal officials allowed the racist patterns of the area to dominate the rehabilitation work. Black families got less help than their white counterparts, and black workers were, in some instances, forced to labor against their will in conditions of semi-peonage.[46] The problem persisted during Hoover's presidency. Acting on federal grants, private contractors hired black and white workers, but under discriminatory employment and wage conditions. When NAACP investigators submitted their complaints to Hoover and Secretary of War Patrick J. Hurley, little was done. With the 1932 elections pending, however, Hoover appointed a special investigative commission; but it had no funds and seemed a poor joke. Accordingly, Walter White urged black newspapers and the Association's larger branches to press for a Senate inquiry, and the NAACP's main ally, Robert F. Wagner, introduced a resolution to that effect. After much maneuvering, the New York Democrat secured passage by unanimous consent in late February 1933.[47] When White, Charles Houston (recently appointed head of the NAACP legal staff), and John P. Davis (of the ad hoc Joint Committee on National Recovery) toured the Mississippi flood control camps in the summer of 1934, they found conditions noticeably improved.[48]

In his brief years as head of the national staff, therefore, White had enjoyed two important Senate victories. Even his mentor, Johnson, had never succeeded there. The reopening of the campaign for a federal antilynching law, then, came about in the face of increased mob violence, with the NAACP's program through the courts stalled by a reduction of Garland Fund grants, under visible competition and incessant criticism from the far Left, and in anticipation that New Deal liberalism, an expansion of southern interracial activities, and recent Senate victories all augured well for the attempt. Put more succinctly, the Association renewed its federal drive against lynching under conditions of necessity, apprehension, and hope.

Meanwhile, a number of complications within the NAACP during the early and mid-1930s further induced Walter White to push for a federal law against mob violence. The depression had cut traditional sources of income but intensified calls for help from an increasingly impoverished black population. In the fall of 1932, for example, White informed the Spelman Fund that 75 percent of the Association's working budget came from contributions and membership fees within the black community. This spelled disaster in hard times. The branches were $7,000 behind their 1931 remissions to the national office. A year later he confided to Johnson that "appeals . . . have trebled . . . income has been sharply cut . . . this work has been done with a greatly reduced staff; and . . . already low salaries have been cut three times in less than two years."[49] At one point the Board considered vacating the 69 Fifth Avenue offices, if it failed to get a rent reduction.[50]

Moreover, in this atmosphere of stringency, White had come under fire from his salaried associates. In a December 1931 memo to the Board, Du Bois, William Pickens, Herbert Seligmann, Robert Bagnall, and assistant executive secretary Roy Wilkins complained about his handling of finances, his reports to the Board's Budget Committee, and the economies they suspected he might undertake at their expense. Joel Spingarn had his doubts, too, about White's money-management capabilities. A review of matters produced tighter oversight of the newly installed executive secretary by officers like the Spingarn brothers and Ovington, on whom he especially depended for backing in any event.[51] White survived the embarrassment, but badly needed to reaffirm his leadership abilities. It seems fair to suggest that, for him, the antilynching campaign offered such an opportunity, once developments outside the Association made the undertaking necessary.

There were other difficulties at national headquarters. Troubled at least in part because his suggestion of a second Amenia conference produced no results in mid-1932, and restless over the NAACP's inability to change America's interracial temper, Joel Spingarn submitted his resignation as president and chairman of the Board on March 6, 1933.[52] Prospects of losing Spingarn alarmed White and his associates, and the secretary pleaded with James Weldon Johnson to intervene.[53] The crisis persisted for three months, during which the Board voted its approval of another Amenia conference and convinced Spingarn to withdraw his resignation.[54]

By 1934, a more ominous staff problem, involving Du Bois, arose. Tension had existed for some time between Du Bois, the aloof and senior scholar of black protest, and Walter White, the flamboyant, energetic, vain younger staff officer. The former had led the staff's protest against White in 1931.[55] Moreover, there was a long-standing controversy over how much autonomy Du Bois should enjoy as editor of *The Crisis*, especially since the journal had lost money regularly since 1929. White, among other NAACP officers, argued that the depression would no longer permit the organization to subsidize the journal indefinitely. Accordingly, at the end of 1932, the Board organized the Crisis Publishing Company as a legal maneuver to limit the Association's liability for the magazine's future debts. This, plus the influence that White increasingly exercised through the *Crisis* editorial board, brought Du Bois to the point of rebellion.[56]

Du Bois suggested a reorganization of the NAACP hierarchy with a general displacement of white by black decision makers. Using a series of *Crisis* editorials, begun in January 1934, he advocated a program of self-help and economic autonomy for the black community. Because other Association leaders interpreted this as an open endorsement of segregation, Du Bois and his colleagues were on a collision course.[57] After he announced in the April *Crisis* that NAACP programs were ineffectual and that Walter White's Caucasoid features shielded him from a full awareness of racist oppression, the Board disavowed all unauthorized public disclosures of internal matters and declared that no salaried officer could use the journal to criticize the "policy, the work, or officers of the

Association."[58] The final rupture came in June, when Du Bois submitted his resignation.[59] Twenty years before, in a similar but less disruptive controversy, Ovington had sided with Du Bois. Now she expressed relief and satisfaction, especially because of "all that White had gone through . . . since the depression and Du Bois has made it infinitely harder. . . . Now we are rid of our octopus, for of late he has been draining our strength, I hope we shall do better work."[60]

By any measure, then, White's first four years as executive secretary were far more unsettled in organizational terms than anything his predecessor had experienced. Not only had he come under criticism from colleagues at the national office, but Joel Spingarn's threatened resignation and the breach with Du Bois had put White, as the executive officer, in a very tenuous position. By the summer of 1934, he had weathered his storms, but there still remained the unanswered question of whether or not he was, in fact, the man to unite the NAACP internally and coordinate the activities of black protest on a nationwide basis. And there was really no way to establish an answer quickly and convincingly, unless he should prove capable of winning a clear-cut major victory on behalf of black Americans. Granted, he had helped to defeat Judge Parker and to secure an investigation of the Mississippi flood basin, but other problems had arisen. As a leader whose prestige had been challenged, White needed a major issue in which he could prove successful. Not a lawyer, he could hardly enter into pleadings before the Supreme Court. Untrained in economics, he could not formulate and implement a sophisticated program to alleviate the effects of the depression on black men and women. But he was dynamic, and persuasive, and energetic; few exceeded him as a lobbyist and publicist. In the first six months of 1934, despite the fact that his authority was simultaneously under attack in the Du Bois affair, he nearly brought an antilynching bill to debate and vote in the United States Senate. He thirsted for that legislative triumph. Given the nature of racist brutality in America, the black community needed such a law, and both White and the NAACP could have turned its enactment to good advantage.

In the early 1930s, the Association faced several hard decisions about objectives and programs. It had resolved at least part of that dilemma with plans for a concerted attack through the courts, but the scarcity of American Fund for Public Service monies impeded implementation.[61] Even NAACP officials who favored litigation feared the approach was too cautious to help segments of the black community needing immediate protection. For example, in early 1933, assistant executive secretary Roy Wilkins wrote Arthur Spingarn that the Association must broaden its legal defense program. "The courts and the police are very close to the Negro. He is more familiar with them than he is with ethics and philosophy and great principles of racial justice," Wilkins argued. Black people wanted help on a daily basis in getting out of jail, in escaping the endless, small injustices from indifferent judges, police, and court-appointed lawyers. If only the

Association would come down from the high plane of abstract victories and commit itself to black defendants in the lower courts, it would have a program that "would bring money, prestige, loyalty and support from the friends and relatives of rescued people and, most important of all, would effectively get rid of the charge that this is a highbrow organization." In a moment of unrestrained candor a year and a half later, Ovington confirmed the Association's tendency to restrict its commitments. She admitted to Villard that the NAACP had hesitated at first to enter the Scottsboro case because "we did not want to defend boys guilty of rape." While the NAACP investigated further, "the communists jumped in."[62]

When the Amenia conference finally met at Joel Spingarn's estate in the mid-Hudson Valley in August 1933, the nearly three dozen participants represented a variety of perspectives. Four main themes emerged: the fight against segregation and racial discrimination in any form, the applicability of Marxism to black people's needs, collaboration among disadvantaged black and white workers, and the legal-judicial approach of the NAACP.[63] Unable to agree upon and certainly incapable of implementing any one approach, the Amenia conferees accomplished very little; but they did help to prod the NAACP to a fresh examination of tactics, programs, and goals.[64]

Two young black men had already made efforts on their own to do something about the economic disabilities facing black people and about the failure of federal programs, like the National Recovery Administration, to benefit the black community sufficiently. Four days before Amenia, Roy Wilkins wrote White about John P. Davis and Robert C. Weaver, who wished to use their own work in the Negro Industrial League as the flywheel for a coordinated effort among black leaders and their organizations. Wilkins reported the success they had already experienced with Washington bureaucrats. Davis and Weaver were "considerably disappointed and disillusioned" at the apparent indifference of the National Urban League and the NAACP, and Wilkins declared that "I think we ought to join with them[;] . . . they are the only Negroes in Washington who have their hands on the situation." Wilkins suggested they had better talk about this at Amenia, and no doubt they did. By mid-November 1933, White was writing to James Weldon Johnson that the NAACP had joined with seventeen other organizations in the Joint Committee on National Recovery, the Davis and Weaver coordinating group, "to see that Negroes are dealt with fairly under the N.R.A."[65]

Confronted with pressures from a variety of sources—the depression itself, the efforts of Davis and Weaver, the Amenia proposals, Du Bois's call for black economic autonomy, and the ever-present competition from the CP-USA—the NAACP Board established a special Committee on the Future Plan and Program, in June 1934. Chaired by the black economist Abram L. Harris, it delivered a preliminary report on September 25. In essence, the Harris committee urged that the Association move deliberately into economic activities by designing projects that would unite black and white workers in a recognition of their common problems. Meanwhile, John P. Davis, short of funds but eager to continue what he and Weaver had started, sought to have the NAACP hire him and assume responsibility for the Joint Committee on National Recovery.[66] White and those who controlled the NAACP Board remained, for the most part, philosophically cool to the Harris and Davis proposals and reluctant to shoulder such added responsibilities. White feared that implementation of the Harris report would divert the Association's resources to economic projects only partly under his and the Board's control.[67] A majority of the Board backed the secretary, so that no merger with the Davis committee occurred, Davis did not become a regular NAACP staff member, and Harris resigned in frustration from his NAACP committee work. Disappointed, Charles Houston warned White that winter of the need for an Association lobbyist in Washington: "you need an expert on economics on your staff . . . there is too much popping everyday in the field of economics which slips by us for lack of detailed knowledge and familiarity with this field. Lip service won't do." He had already complained that "you are topheavy with white-collar interests and attitudes."[68]

Suggestions for changing the basic programmatic activities of the NAACP and for adding new staff members competent to work in areas that directly affected black labor and black economics won little endorsement from Association leaders. They recognized the plight of black working men and women during the depression and did try to respond when they felt they could.[69] But for the most part NAACP officials had too long involved themselves with legal-judicial redress, only recently reinforced by the Margold study and the AFPS appropriations, to undertake any basic reorientation. Key leadership figures still reflected the highly educated, upper-middle class, professionally inclined, and somewhat elitist element that had established and guided the organization since the Progressive days. A continued emphasis on working directly with their counterparts in government, foundations, and reformist groups seemed to them far better and more appropriate than suddenly plunging the organization into direct and sustained contacts among the black masses.[70]

Consequently, of the several alternatives facing the NAACP in 1934 and the winter of 1935, a renewed, intensified effort to secure a federal law against lynching seemed best designed to fulfill customary NAACP objectives. Such a campaign coincided with traditional NAACP philosophies and skills. Moreover, it would capitalize on existing contacts in high places and generate the level of national awareness that the Association persistently sought. And, as historian Raymond Wolters has observed, the Association knew that it could more safely rely on financial contributions from individuals and foundations, if it attacked so blatant an injustice as mob violence rather than venturing into the more complex issues surrounding workers' rights.[71]

When White reopened the antilynching campaign late in 1933, no one could have fully anticipated what followed: seven years of intense effort, passage on two occasions in the House (1937 and 1940), but a recurring failure to surmount southern obstructions in the Senate. Throughout, White's handling of the venture bore a marked resemblance to Johnson's work on the Dyer bill: investigations, press releases, meetings, petitions, congressional testimonies, appeals to the White House, high-level negotiations, use of *ad hoc* groups, fund-raising and membership drives, to note the most obvious. In pursuit of a statutory enactment, the NAACP sought further to educate the public and its elected officials about the need for, and wisdom of, interracial reform, to mobilize support within and beyond the black community, and to strengthen the Association. If White persisted much longer than Johnson had, this reflected the former's personality and the atmosphere of the 1930s rather than any alteration in Association strategy. White's dogged determination and the seductive prospects of New Deal support reinforced each other. Unfortunately for the executive secretary, liberal politicians repeatedly discovered priorities that outranked black needs; despite expressions of concern, the antilynching bill would once again be allowed to die.

The question of resuming the battle in Congress was discussed at Joel Spingarn's home in October 1933. On December 7, the Association convened a meeting in New York City of several organizations called jointly by the NAACP and the American Civil Liberties Union to coordinate all efforts behind a single antilynching measure.[72]

At one point the Association felt it could improve chances for passage if a southern congressman would sponsor the bill. That proved impossible, however, and the Association turned to Senate Democrats Robert Wagner of New York and Edward Costigan of Colorado.[73] Noting the recent "shocking reversion to primitive brutality," Wagner decried not only the inaction of elected officials but the even more regrettable circumstances under which some law officers condoned and connived with mass murder. Long an advocate of liberal social measures, and a major sponsor of New Deal legislation, Wagner declared that pragmatic necessity justified federal initiatives. Moreover, he felt that "the most painfully won and precious gain in mankind's long march from savagery to civilization has been the subordination of mob rule to constituted authority and the guarantee that constituted authority will dispense equal justice to every race, creed and individual."[74]

Less famous nationally but no less committed to liberal and humanitarian reforms, Costigan brought all the finest credentials to his sponsorship of the antilynching measure. He had successfully defended seventy-nine miners indicted for conspiracy in the Ludlow massacre of April 1914, and throughout his career supported federal and state work projects; the child-labor amendment; accident, sickness, old-age, and unemployment insurance programs; increased tax levies on the wealthy; a

National Labor Relations Board; the regulation of holding companies; an independently functioning tariff commission and reciprocal tariff agreements; and revised banking legislation to increase federal control over credit and currency.[75] Costigan's Senate comments against lynching in the spring of 1935 best conveyed the sympathies he shared with the NAACP:

> If one can mention, much less picture, such appalling facts as I have recited without being revolted, he is indeed hardened out of all semblance to humanity. They destroy our claim to civilized life. They must not be permitted to multiply. Every repetition of mob brutality denies its victims the right of speedy and impartial trial and the equal protection of the laws guaranteed by the Constitution. No man can be permitted to usurp the combined functions of judge, jury, and executioner of his fellow men; and whenever any State fails to protect such equal rights, I submit that the Federal Government must do its utmost to repair the damage which is then chargeable to all of us.[76]

Eager to promote the new campaign, White hit upon a tactic that allowed him and his colleagues to tap the extensive friendships they had made in literary and journalistic circles. On December 1, he wrote Johnson about adding the latter's name to the newly formed Writers' League Against Lynching. With the buoyant self-assurance that he always displayed and sometimes used to bring others into line, White said he was sure Johnson would not object and added that the group would serve chiefly as "a hell-raising committee to influence the country through writing, pronouncements, and the like."[77] Within a week, White submitted to the NAACP Board a rather imposing list of League participants, including Dorothy Parker, Sherwood Anderson, Heywood Broun, Edna Ferber, Fannie Hurst, and Drew Pearson. While such people were not likely to frighten southern sheriffs and magistrates, they proved valuable in drawing attention to the cause. Accordingly, the league sent a message to Franklin Roosevelt and urged California Governor Rolph to retract his defense of lynching.[78]

Wringing a sustained commitment from the White House proved an arduous matter. Prior to Roosevelt's election in 1932, his mid-Hudson Valley neighbor, Joel Spingarn, had sent him a "Statement on Negro Problem" that reviewed a half-dozen issues, including lynching.[79] In 1933 the Association twice tried, without success, to get a conference with the new president. Not until the end of the year did its appeals have any impact on the White House.[80] Even then, despite his address to the Federal Council of Churches in December and some guarded remarks against "organized banditry, cold-blooded shooting, lynching and kidnapping" in his January message to Congress, Franklin Roosevelt kept his distance from the antilynching campaign.[81] Absorbed with fighting the depression, forced to deal with the powerful southern wing of his party, and operating from limited knowledge of the black community, the president was not a man to reveal his position easily in such matters. Perhaps it was some consolation to the NAACP that even influential southern liberals had difficulty deciding where the president stood on the new Costigan-Wagner bill.

In early December 1933, for example, Will Alexander confided to Edwin Embree that, even after being in touch with Roosevelt, it was hard to gauge the president's opinion toward a federal antilynching bill. A month later, journalist Mark Ethridge of the Washington *Post* advised Alexander that Senator Byron (Pat) Harrison (D–Mississippi) had predicted in confidence that Roosevelt would not back the Costigan-Wagner proposal. Furthermore, Ethridge announced that the NAACP "does not expect— and really does not care for—the bill to get through, but is rather using it for the moral effect." Alexander responded placidly that he had imagined that all along.[82] Southern liberals, it would appear, were sure that they could penetrate the black psyche. They also relished the belief that they had an inside track with the president, particularly because he spent so much time at the polio-treatment center in Warm Springs, Georgia. Trying still to sharpen his impressions of White House intentions, Alexander implored philanthropist George Foster Peabody of Warm Springs to tell him "confidentially whether or not this Costigan-Wagner bill is in line with the President's wishes." Reading Roosevelt's mind was a favorite sport, even when poorly played—as it invariably was.[83]

Like many civil rights advocates diverted by presidential finesse, White and his colleagues sought relief through Eleanor Roosevelt, with whom they developed an easy and effective relationship.[84] White conferred with her at her New York apartment late in the winter of 1934 about a number of issues, including the role of black families in the federally sponsored Arthurdale housing project, and the Virgin Islands Advisory Council to which the president appointed him. They talked about the Costigan-Wagner bill, and Eleanor Roosevelt apologized for her inability to deliver a radio broadcast, as White had asked, against lynching. The president felt it would arouse unnecessary antagonism toward the measure and asked that she wait until later. She did indicate, however, that her husband was actively though quietly supporting the bill and wanted it to pass in the current session.[85]

With the antilynching bill stalled in the Senate several weeks later, White wrote a lengthy letter to Eleanor Roosevelt following another of their meetings. He enclosed statements from twenty senators and thirty-two representatives favoring the Costigan-Wagner bill, and reported that a recent Senate poll had indicated the support of fifty-two members—if the measure could be brought to the floor. Only White House insistence would guarantee a vote, he added, because politicians preferred an early adjournment in an election year. White cited examples of widespread endorsement for the bill: the Federal Council of Churches; the National Board, Public Affairs Committee, and Student Council of the YWCA: certain Catholic clergy; the Women's International League for Peace and

Freedom; the Congregational church; the ACLU; the Woman's Missionary Council of the Methodist Episcopal church, South; and of course, the Writers' League Against Lynching, and the NAACP.

White suggested, with more optimism than the realities warranted, that editorial support for the bill by various influential southern newspapers had lessened the prospects of a filibuster, that a few southern senators might even vote for the bill, and that some others reportedly planned a convenient absence from the debate. He predicted partisan advantages in having a Democratic Congress pass the measure, and argued that it could be applied to the Ku Klux Klan, Fascists, and other reactionary groups known to employ violence against minorities other than black people. His most pointed reference stemmed from an incident at Hernando, Mississippi, where a judge had saved three black defendants from a mob by asserting that "there is pending in Congress a bill to give the federal government authority to end lynching—if you lynch these Negroes you will insure passage of that bill."[86] In response, Eleanor Roosevelt arranged a face-to-face conference between her husband and White shortly thereafter. Their discussions proved cordial and informative, but the bill still languished in the Senate.[87]

The 1934 Costigan-Wagner bill (S.1978) initially followed the general outlines of the earlier Dyer measure, and represented fairly well the type of legislation that the Association tried to obtain from Congress from the first World War through the Truman administration. Designed to upset the normally complacent acceptance of mob murder and to make lynching too hazardous a pastime for local mobs to practice, the bill was to "assure to persons within [the] jurisdiction of every State the equal protection of the laws, and . . . punish the crime of lynching." Among its components were:

Section 1 defined the mob as a group of three or more persons, lacking a legal basis, who set about to harm another or to deprive him or her of life.

Section 2 provided that in the event the state or governmental subdivision should fail to protect its citizens, this legislation would come into effect.

Section 3 provided that any state or local official who failed to protect citizens or to arrest or prosecute violators of the law would become liable for a fine, not to exceed $5,000, or a jail term of up to five years, or both.

Section 3b stated that any law officer who aided or assisted the mob would face a prison term of five years to life.

Section 4 allowed the federal district court and its law enforcement agency to enter the case, if after thirty days both the state and local agents of the law had failed to react to the lynching.

Section 5 proposed a $10,000 fine on the county in which the lynching occurred.

Section 6 held both counties mutually liable for the fine in the event the victim was seized in one county and put to death in another.

Section 7 applied the coverage of the bill to all citizens of the United States and to all foreigners whose countries were associated by treaty with the United States.[88]

One important point about the Costigan-Wagner bill should be underscored: it involved no direct federal action against lynchers themselves. Rather, the bill was aimed at law officers who, by indifference or collusion, permitted lynching, and at the counties in which the mob action occurred. Not surprisingly, the measure elicited criticism from both ends of the political spectrum. Communists denounced the measure for its failure to impose a mandatory death sentence upon lynchers, while traditionists and strict constitutionalists rejected the plan to penalize all taxpayers when only some were violent and lawless.[89]

The NAACP, however, considered the bill wisely drafted. Its investigations revealed the way local officials and citizens unashamedly winked at lynchings, and the Southern Commission on the Study of Lynching concurred. The Commission's report of November 1931 had observed that fifteen of the twenty-one lynchings of 1930 produced no grand jury indictments whatever, and only four of forty-nine defendants were convicted in the other six incidents. The Commission found that coroners' inquests announced with callous regularity that death had come "at the hands of parties unknown."[90] Weary of southerners' cynical attitudes in pleading their inability to identify, prosecute, and convict mob members, the NAACP hoped that the antilynching bill would stimulate corrective action locally and utilize federal jurisdiction as a shield for judges and juries, attorneys, and witnesses against the most intense forms of community pressure.[91] True to its Progressive heritage, the Association continued to argue that federal intervention was necessary once state and local officials had proven unable or unwilling to cope with the problem. Similarly, penalizing the county to induce remedial action by the "better" taxpaying elements disclosed certain assumptions about economic motivations and the existence of a thrifty, stable, law-abiding, and property-holding middle class.[92]

The Association faced some hard decisions in Congress. Oscar De Priest (R–Illinois, the lone black member of Congress) and five other House members introduced separate bills, while freshman Congressman Thomas Ford (D–California) offered the NAACP his services for the same purpose. White conferred with Wagner's assistant, Leon Keyserling, and with Costigan's secretary, Lee Johnson. The trio found the De Priest measure too weak and felt that Ford lacked the prestige and influence to carry the burden alone. One Shortridge fiasco had been enough. Consequently, they decided to invite Charles West of Ohio to join Ford in sponsoring the Association's bill and then move the other six behind the West-Ford-NAACP measure at an appropriate time.[93] However, the big test would come in the Senate, where opponents had the use of the filibuster. Since they already had two major New Deal advocates there,

White and his colleagues decided to make their stand in the upper house. That would seem to belie southern liberal assumptions that the NAACP cared more for publicizing the evils of lynching than for winning passage. Choosing the easier House route, where black urban votes had a direct impact, with the option of Senate action thereafter, would have brought ample notoriety, had that been the major objective.

White threw himself into the task of assembling witnesses for Judiciary subcommittee hearings, although at times his enthusiasm led him to claim more than he could deliver. He hoped, for example, that the Commission on Interracial Cooperation would be an instrument for attracting prominent southern liberals, but Alexander wondered whether the hearings would actually materialize, and some CIC leaders thought that the NAACP had released a list of possible witnesses prematurely.[94] Although he courted them incessantly, White found that commission members, individually and collectively, remained uncertain and divided among themselves about the wisdom of a federal law.

Basically, CIC leaders wanted to build upon the work that their organization had already accomplished by means of the Southern Commission on the Study of Lynching and the Association of Southern Women for the Prevention of Lynching. They wished to publicize the recent Raper and Chadbourn books and to win the passage of new, or the updating of existing, laws that dealt with lynching in each of the southern states.[95] A federal antilynching law, sponsored by a black protest organization based in New York City, threatened to upend these carefully developed plans. In mid-January, Will Alexander told CIC member (and NAACP supporter) Albert E. Barnett of Nashville that neither the central council of the ASWPL nor the "majority of the Commission" approved a federal measure; but this picture was somewhat clouded when a predominantly black splinter group within the Association of Southern Women for the Prevention of Lynching independently informed White that they would publicly support his antilynching bill.[96]

Will Alexander worked with White in honest and straightforward fashion, but never could fully resolve the complex situational difficulties of trying to lead a campaign of southern white liberals against racial injustice. The strain showed at times. Ten months after the first Costigan-Wagner antilynching bill was introduced, for example, Mrs. R. P. Neblett, secretary of the Committee on Interracial Cooperation of the Women's Missionary Society of Northern Mississippi, wrote to Alexander to say that the group wanted him to take the lead and design a federal bill against lynching that could win general southern support. Alexander called the task impossible, since a successful federal law must depend upon local cooperation, which seemed beyond reach. He preferred to develop community sentiment that might eventually make a federal law effective in practice. And then, in what seemed an unnecessary and rare expression of sectional sensitivities, Alexander reminded her that the Costigan-Wagner bill was drafted wholly by New York lawyers without benefit of help from other regions of the country, and that, "no one had ever sent me a copy of the bill until this last week." In fact, White had sent him a draft of the bill on January 2, 1934. Moreover, one wonders about a major southern leader in the fight against mob violence who, ten months after the bill had become a national issue, would admit by implication that he had not taken the time to secure a copy.[97]

All the while trying to pull together a team of prominent southerners to testify, White kept in touch with the Baltimore *Sun*'s H. L. Mencken about the structure and functions of the hearings. The salty journalist thought White's list "not very promising," a group of mere "uplifters" who would "go to pieces" under cross examination from "any sharp Southerner." Mencken admonished White against confining the testimony to expressions of opinion, and advocated instead that the NAACP stage "a sort of lynching clinic." The committee could make arrangements to subpoena all the evidence and witnesses that Maryland Attorney-General W. Preston Lane had diligently assembled in a futile attempt to secure an indictment and conviction against the George Armwood lynchers. Mencken admitted that until that tragedy he had opposed a federal law; now he believed "that nothing else can really fetch lynchers."[98] But Mencken's plan for what we would now call a "guerilla theatre" presentation fell through when, in response to White's inquiries, Senator Wagner thought it unwise and Keyserling warned against dramatics.[99]

The hearings took place on February 20 and 21, and White's testimony was a masterful restatement of the NAACP's position for the previous two decades. He reminded the subcommittee that over 4,500 lynchings had occurred from 1882 to 1934, with about 70 percent of the victims being black people and 94 women—17 white and 77 black. Attempting to dispel old myths, White referred to the recent works by Chadbourn and Raper to show that no connection existed between lynching and the alleged need to protect southern white women. In only one-sixth of the incidents had the victim been accused, let alone proven guilty, of rape. Thirteen of the twenty-one victims in 1930 had committed no crime whatsoever. White briefly reviewed the history of the Dyer bill. Despite southern assurances that local initiative could remedy the problem, 277 lynchings (22 white and 249 black) had occurred since the last great drive for a federal law. The NAACP secretary reported the growing sentiment throughout the South against mob violence; he cited southern newspapers, churches, youth groups, and educators, and noted that even reluctant proponents of federal action agreed that any loss of states' rights stemmed from the region's own failure to end lynching. Furthermore, states' rights had a hollow ring when critics of the Costigan-Wagner bill so willingly accepted federal money for relief, public works, aid to education, and the like. In any event, questions of constitutionality could be left to the United States Supreme Court. White warned that failure to act might encourage the spread of lawlessness against any unpopular element in society—immigrants, radicals, and other minority groups; and he returned to the familiar argument that black people needed their share of justice in America if they were successfully to ignore Communist propaganda.[100]

Arthur B. Spingarn, chairman of the NAACP's national legal committee, also testified. He observed that the individual states had an unqualified record of failure in prosecuting and punishing perpetrators of mob violence. In the more than 3,500 lynchings from 1900 to 1930, there were only 12 convictions involving 67 offenders.[101] All of this had occured, Spingarn observed, despite the fact that, starting with Georgia in 1893, state after state had enacted its own antilynching legislation; indeed, since that time Georgia itself had had 402 lynchings. Obviously local authorities could not or would not provide adequate protection. Another NAACP witness, attorney Herbert K. Stockton, argued that a federal antilynching act would give support and encouragement to law-abiding elements at the community level, and he declared that Congress possessed ample precedents to enforce equal protection of the laws.[102]

In sharp contrast to its drive for the Dyer bill a dozen years before, the Association had relatively little trouble getting its proposal favorably reported in the Senate in 1934. Dated March 28, *Report No. 710*, which drew on many of the Association's arguments and statistics, recommended passage of the Costigan-Wagner bill with certain amendments. Fines against counties were set from $2,000 to $10,000, instead of the latter figure alone; the money, paid to the victim's survivors, would be legally immune from expropriation by any creditors. The bill, moreover, was to apply only to victims taken from peace officers. The first posed no threat to the bill's purposes, and so the NAACP offered no objections. It did, however, protest the reduced coverage, because less, if only slightly less, than half the lynching victims since 1918 had been taken from custody.[103] The Association knew how easily "cooperative" officials could subvert the new stipulation. On April 12, the Judiciary Committee reported the Costigan-Wagner bill favorably to the Senate, but White sensed "an under-the-surface movement . . . to keep it from coming up for a vote." Itching for enactment and certain that he had enough senators committed to the bill, White turned to the administration.[104]

He heard from Eleanor Roosevelt that she had discussed the bill at great length with the president. However, she reported, "as I do not think you will either like or agree with everything that he thinks, I would like an opportunity of telling you about it, and would also like you to talk to the President if you feel you want to."[105] Through her good offices, White spent an extraordinary hour and twenty minutes on the White House veranda on Sunday, May 6, taking tea with the president, Eleanor Roosevelt, and Sara Delano Roosevelt, and reviewing the bill at length. He discovered that a discreet campaign to discredit the measure was further along than he had realized; the president expressed concern about the county fines.[106] White assured him that this involved no new principle in American law, that a number of states (including South Carolina, Connecticut, Kansas, North Carolina, Pennsylvania, Nebraska, Illinois, Minnesota, and New Jersey) had such provisions in their own statutes, and that financial penalties of this sort had been imposed and upheld by the courts. By the time tea, pleasantries, and hard, substantive discussions had ended, Roosevelt, according to White, agreed to urge a vote before adjournment, but did not promise to hold out against a lengthy filibuster if one developed.[107] Obviously pleased, White wrote Eleanor Roosevelt that while the Association felt it had sufficient votes to win passage, "it would be preferable by far even to have the bill voted on and defeated than to have it die through inaction."[108]

As the session moved on, inaction prevailed. On May 24, Roosevelt conferred with Costigan and Wagner at the White House. At the senators' suggestion White did not participate. Because presidential appointments secretary Marvin McIntyre was reputed to favor the southern position on the bill, the sponsors considered White's absence a necessary discretion. Roosevelt confessed that he had made inquiries and felt certain the bill would easily pass if brought to a vote, but he also recognized that some senators would bitterly oppose such action. Anxious to salvage the measure if he could, White got Max Stern of the Scripps-Howard chain to ask Roosevelt about the antilynching bill at a press conference in late May, but the president merely responded with hopes for a vote before adjournment. "It is almost heart-breaking to have put as much work into this struggle as we have . . . to have a small, recalcitrant group of senators prevent a vote being taken," White complained to Eleanor Roosevelt. Recalling what Johnson and Villard had done in 1917 in New York City, White even thought of holding a silent protest parade in the District of Columbia, if the Senate showed no intention of voting on the measure. However, Elizabeth Eastman of the YWCA (who had cooperated with White in lobbying for the antilynching bill), Senators Costigan and Wagner, and Charles H. Houston—perhaps recalling the bonus march disaster two years before and certainly conscious of the augmented southern influence that accompanied the return of a Democratic administration to the city—warned against such a tactic.[109]

Though they tried, friends of antilynching legislation could do little in Congress to ease the Association's disappointments. On June 11, a week before adjournment, Costigan wrote Senate Majority Leader Joseph T. Robinson of Arkansas to say that he and Wagner had received a message from "a responsible New York citizen" (he carefully avoided White's name), who had recently conferred personally with the president and Eleanor Roosevelt about the Costigan-Wagner antilynching bill. Costigan explained that on the evening of June 8 she had told this anonymous source, "If the sponsors of the bill will go at once to Senator Robinson and say to him that, if, in a lull, the anti-lynching bill can be brought up for a vote, the President authorizes the sponsors to say that the President will be glad to see the bill pass and wishes it passed." Costigan asked that the bill come up and assured Robinson that neither he nor Wagner would engage in any time-consuming explanatory statements from the floor.[110]

There is no need to doubt either Eleanor Roosevelt's or Costigan's sincerity, any more than one would realistically expect a ranking Arkansas Democrat to take very seriously a report of presidential wishes obliquely conveyed at the eleventh hour through a network of intermediaries that included the cosponsor of the legislation, the president's activist wife, and an unidentified Yankee from New York City. Costigan informed White four days later that Robinson had not replied, that all signs pointed to adjournment without action, and that he, Costigan, had learned through the Clerk of the Senate that Kenneth McKellar of Tennessee planned, in any event, to block consideration of the measure. The prospects, Costigan admitted, were "not favorable."[111] White's appeals for a special presidential message to Congress had no effect, South Carolina's "Cotton Ed" Smith rallied opponents against one last, desperate floor attempt, and on June 18 the NAACP secretary conceded defeat.[112]

So ended White's first effort as executive secretary to wring a major piece of civil rights legislation from a New Deal Congress. In spite of the failure, prospects for the future seemed encouraging. White had secured a favorable report from the Senate Judiciary Committee, and had done so with relative ease; he also enjoyed the sponsorship of two leading New Deal senators. In addition, a majority of senators had expressed support, and a group of eager representatives stood ready to champion antilynching bills in the House. Moreover, White had, in Eleanor Roosevelt, the unique assistance of a White House "insider"; he had public expressions of sympathy from a powerful president, even if Roosevelt would not risk open battle for the bill; and sentiments for reform were generally widespread. All of this formed a far happier picture than the one confronting Johnson in the winter of 1923, and a man of White's enthusiasm and competitiveness could be excused if he believed it wise and necessary to try again and again over the next half-dozen years.

White's efforts also extended the NAACP's lines of communication to other reformist groups: southern white liberals, even if they did not yet concur on specific objectives; the influential corps of Washington journalists covering the national scene at both ends of Pennsylvania Avenue; and that crucial network of congressional aides, legislative assistants, secretaries, and liaison personnel responsible for so much of the vital, behind-the-scenes legwork in the daily life of official Washington. He re-established the NAACP's entrée into the capital's power structure, on a level, and to an extent, that exceeded anything Johnson had accomplished. Moreover, the connections that White was building would confirm him and the NAACP as the ranking advocates for black America.

White was a master publicist. He understood, for example, the advantages of radio broadcasting. Thanks in no small measure to his perceptiveness, the 1934 Costigan-Wagner proceedings set radio history. It was the first time that a Senate committee hearing had been carried on a nationwide network. And, when the NAACP and the ACLU protested the editing of Joel Spingarn's radio speech on February 11 (apparently all references to segregation, lynchings, and riots, and to the Dyer and the Costigan-Wagner bills were deleted), NBC production manager John F. Royal averred that the network had intended no censorship and that the NAACP might have fifteen minutes of prime air time during which any speaker could say anything he or she chose about lynching and the Association.[113] In all this, White stole the limelight from his competitors, especially those in the CP-USA, and provided himself and his colleagues with vital lobbying and public relations experiences that would later benefit the NAACP in its support of a wide range of socio-economic, New Deal and Fair Deal legislation valuable to black Americans.

However, a number of crucial sticking points remained. Former Congressman Leonidas Dyer warned the NAACP in January 1935 that a Democratic Congress would never enact a meaningful antilynching law.[114] That may have been a partisan admonition, but the political structure within Congress, dominated by entrenched, senior Democrats from the South, did plague the Association and the civil rights movement for another thirty years. And Senate rules about unlimited debate were to leave reformist measures captive to filibusters for just as long.[115] A divided, indifferent public still needed to rethink its acquiescence to racist patterns; some argue that we have not yet resolved that dilemma. Finally, there was a liberal administration whose leader refused to jeopardize economic and social programs by championing a national law against mob violence. As late as March 1936, a president known world-wide for his governmental initiatives still sought refuge in pieties about local remedies for lynching.[116] Apparently, a double standard of priorities and prescriptions prevailed in matters that touched black lives: the more ardently Walter White struggled to secure White House aid, the more hostile some presidential staff members, like Stephen Early, seemed to become.[117] Determined, nonetheless, to invoke federal protections, White, with the experience of 1933 and 1934 behind him, explored fresh approaches to these persistent realities.

6

From Both Ends of Pennsylvania Avenue, 1935-1936

Throughout the summer and autumn of 1934, Walter White carefully laid his plans for a new drive in Congress. He maintained contact with Wagner and Costigan and urged all branches of the Association to stage benefits, entertainments, picnics, and the like for an antilynching war chest.[1] He seized every opportunity to push the campaign against violence. In September, for example, while conferring with Assistant Attorney General Joseph D. Keenan about the Texas primaries,[2] White decried the indifference that Attorney General Homer Cummings had displayed toward antilynching legislation. Keenan believed that the drafting of a constitutionally sound bill was possible, and promised to look into it, if the Association would send him pertinent materials. White complied. Meanwhile, his national staff drafted a memorial to the White House and secured the American Civil Liberties Union's files to compile a list of well-known liberals who might sign the document.[3] In some ways, it seemed very much like 1922 all over again.

Before the Association had its opportunity to present the memorial, however, a blatant example of mob violence confirmed the inability of southern states to prevent lynchings, and underscored the persistent difficulties of securing any help from the executive branch in Washington. On October 19, 1934, a young black man named Claude Neal was arrested in Marianna, Florida, and charged with the murder of Lola Cannidy, a local white woman. Responding to an ugly public mood, officials moved Neal from one jail to another, but on Friday, October 26, the mob seized him in Brewton, Alabama, and transported him back to Marianna, where a crowd of more than 4,000 awaited his lynching. In a sadistic orgy that lasted through the night, the crowd stabbed, kicked, mutilated, shot, and finally hanged Neal in the courthouse square. Not only did local authorities fail to protect the victim, one deputy sheriff reportedly declared that, "in my opinion the mob will not be bothered, either before or after the lynching." Since the press and radio advertised the lynching in advance,

NAACP investigators charged that Florida officials had ample time to react, had they chosen or been able to do so. In an eight-page pamphlet, *The Lynching of Claude Neal*, the Association summarized the prearranged intentions to lynch, the news media's contributions to inciting mob action, officials' awareness of the planned lynching, and the totally inadequate protection afforded the prisoner.[4]

Because the mob had seized Neal in Alabama and taken him across the state line into Florida, the Association tried to invoke federal jurisdiction under the so-called Lindbergh Kidnapping Act (passed in 1932 in the wake of national horror over the kidnap-murder of Anne Morrow and Charles Lindbergh's infant son). Only five months before Neal's death, Congress had amended the law to provide punishment in those cases where victims were "held for ransom or reward or otherwise." Accordingly, the NAACP urged Franklin Roosevelt and Homer Cummings to institute proceedings against Neal's lynchers. The staff also approached several legislators and legal scholars about the applicability of the act, as amended, and found that most, though not all, agreed with the Association's position.[5]

Under Cummings, however, the Justice Department would not move. On November 23, Eleanor Roosevelt informed White of her conversation with the president about the Claude Neal lynching: "He hoped very much to get the Costigan-Wagner Bill passed in the coming session." She wished the Justice Department would take a different stand on the legitimacy of federal authority in such matters, and said, "I think possibly they will." But five days later, the attorney general dashed such optimism in a memorandum to Assistant Solicitor General Angus MacLean. Noting the many appeals to the federal government in cases of mob violence, Cummings cautioned that an attempt at too wide application of existing federal laws would have little practical result and could, by evoking conservative reactions, impede the Department's overall program against crime. Cummings doubted that Congress had ever wanted the kidnapping statute applied to mob violence: "It must be remembered that the same Congress declined to pass a law dealing with the general subject of lynching. It is difficult for me to believe that the Congress inadvertently passed an anti-lynching statute where kidnapping and interstate commerce were involved." He subsequently warned the president about the political repercussions that might follow, if the Justice Department tried to prosecute lynchers.[6] Because New Dealers were wary of southern Democrats, citizen Claude Neal and other black Americans from the Deep South would have to find their justice in heaven or in hell, or in some less ethereal setting, like Florida or Alabama.

NAACP frustrations with the Justice Department did not end with the Neal case. Hearing that Cummings planned a National Conference on Crime (December 10–13), the Association requested in early October that lynching be included on the agenda and that Costigan or Wagner make a presentation. NAACP inquiries brought noncommittal replies; but less than two weeks before the start of the conference, the Justice Department ruled against lynching as a topic. White asked, through Eleanor Roosevelt, that the president discuss lynching in his address to the conferees. When the District of Columbia branch picketed the conference to protest the omission, officials arrested a group including Emmett Dorsey of Howard University, George Murphy, Jr., of the *Afro-American*, Washington attorney Edward Lovett, and assistant executive secretary Roy Wilkins.[7] As one man who later became a prominent member of the Association's national staff recalled, an amusing charade followed. Because the patrol wagon lacked accommodations for all the pickets, he and three others followed in a taxi to the station house. The police refused to arrest the "latecomers," but Wilkins was delighted with his arrest on alleged violations of the District's sign law and of its regulations against "parading" without a permit.[8]

The Association thereafter stationed about five dozen pickets across the street from the conference. To circumvent the law that prohibited signs twelve inches or larger, the pickets carried placards eleven inches wide; to avoid charges of parading, the pickets stood silent and stationary, about ten feet apart, with nooses about their necks. No further incidents marred the demonstration, although White later reported that the District police and a Justice Department official were visibly nettled by the new tactics. The performance produced some results when Cummings yielded and permitted the Washington Bar Association to send five accredited delegates (Charles Houston among them) to the conference, where they subsequently submitted a resolution on lynching.[9] Later that month, the NAACP sent its memorial to Roosevelt to ask high priority for the Costigan-Wagner bill in the new Congress. The document bore the signatures of nine governors or ex-governors, twenty-seven mayors, fifty-eight bishops and clergy, fifty-four college presidents and professors, and over one hundred lawyers, editors, writers, and jurists.[10] It was the elite addressing the elite.

Walter White had high expectations for the new session. Eleanor Roosevelt's assurances that the president was hoping for passage greatly encouraged the NAACP, as did the resounding endorsement that Roosevelt and the New Deal received in the 1934 elections. No president since the Civil War had seen his party's majority in Congress grow so strikingly in off-year returns, and White mistakenly took this as further indication that the times were right for such measures as the antilynching bill.[11] The NAACP national office issued a flier urging letters, telegrams, and direct appeals to the White House, to senators and representatives, and to Senate Majority Leader Joseph T. Robinson on behalf of the bill. In addition, national organizations cooperating with the Association designated the week of January 6 to mount a citizens' campaign for passage.[12] Trying for further leverage, White sent Eleanor Roosevelt an editorial from the *Amsterdam News* that warned against treating the administration with kid gloves in the antilynching fight. Seeing daylight where others might have sensed no more than a blurr, White explained to NAACP special counsel Charles Houston that the editorial had had its effects at the White House. He asked Houston to arrange a conference for him with Elizabeth Eastman, Selma Borchard (of the American Federation of Teachers), Mike Flynn (AFL lobbyist), and Association strategists Houston and William Hastie. Simultaneously, White prepared to see Senators Costigan, Wagner, and Frederick Van Nuys (D–Indiana), Secretary of the Interior Harold Ickes (formerly an officer in the NAACP Chicago branch), Congresswoman Caroline O'Day (D–New York), and two or three others.[13]

Among the very tangible and lasting benefits of White's fight (like his and Johnson's work of the 1920s) were the contacts that the NAACP nurtured among a wide range of liberal, reformist, civic, labor, church, and other national lobbying groups holding similar aims. Reassessing the bill's status in both houses at the end of January, White sent a memorandum to Costigan and Wagner noting that Mike Flynn had spent several days discussing the measure on the Hill. Flynn warned that the NAACP would face some difficulty in getting early House hearings because of opposition from chairman Hatton Sumners (D–Texas) and his fellow southerners on the Judiciary Committee. Accordingly, Flynn advised that if the NAACP chose to make a stand in the House, it would have to intensify its grass-roots pressures on individual legislators, get as many as sixty, seventy-five, or even one hundred antilynching bills introduced for massive impact, and at the proper psychological moment have several Democratic representatives call for a caucus and demand that an antilynching bill be discharged from the Judiciary Committee and brought to the floor for a vote.[14] Weighing alternatives, the Association and its supporters decided to make their big push in the Senate. Not until 1936 and 1937 did the Association institute an effort of comparable magnitude in the House of Representatives.

Meanwhile, the NAACP sponsored the famous Art Commentary on Lynching. Arranged through the cooperation of the College Art Association, the exhibit (initially scheduled for New York City from February 15 to March 2, 1935) had to be relocated when a few days before opening the designated gallery withdrew its facilities, allegedly because "political, economic and social pressures had been brought to bear." Several other dealers telephoned the national office to offer space, and from these the staff selected the Arthur U. Newton Galleries on East Fifty-seventh Street. The Association and the CAA planned to feature more than three dozen artists, Peggy Bacon, George Bellows, Thomas Hart Benton, Reginald Marsh, and Hale Woodruff, among them.[15] Pearl Buck addressed the show's opening and Sherwood Anderson joined Erskine Caldwell in writing forewords for the catalog. With his usual enthusiasm, White hailed the exhibit as a "phenomenal success" attended by more than two thousand people, and he added that the visitors' registration list yielded the names of some 800 people whom the staff hoped to interest further in the Association's work. He was especially pleased that Eleanor Roosevelt accepted his invitation to view the exhibit, although she did so without any of the notoriety that White had wanted.[16] The exhibit also fared well in its brief road tour, but the Association found that developing the extended cross-country showing it had wished was impossible. Charles Houston, for example, informed White from Washington that Elizabeth Eastman tried without success to get the Phillips Gallery; the management felt the show was too grisly. Houston added acidly that "lynchings should be nice and tidy." Nonetheless, the NAACP raised $263 from the Art Commentary during March, the Baltimore *Sun* praised the exhibit, and the New York *World-Telegram* exclaimed, "It . . . tears the heart and chills the blood. If it upsets your compacency on the subject, it will have been successful."[17]

Walter White's campaign to steer the Costigan-Wagner bill through the Senate in 1935 proved unsuccessful, but certainly not for lack of effort. Both Senate sponsors made a fifteen-minute radio presentation over the CBS network on the night of February 12; White again tried to arrange NBC network coverage of the committee hearings. He worked carefully to screen potential witnesses for the hearings, used introductions from prominent constituents whenever possible to obtain conferences with individual senators, and even attempted to get such conservative spokesmen as former presidential candidate John W. Davis and former Republican Solicitor General of the United States James M. Beck to testify on the wisdom and constitutionality of the proposed measure.[18]

NAACP endeavors to move southern white liberals into line proved as unavailing as in the past, although Jessie Daniel Ames of the Association of Southern Women for the Prevention of Lynching did acknowledge the campaign's merits. Writing to New York Congresswoman Caroline O'Day, who helped White lobby for the bill, Ames admitted that pressure for the bill "unquestionably helps to keep this crime alive in the minds of the southern people. Even though the bill should not pass, I feel sure it has rendered a great service." She expressed a similar sentiment to Costigan.[19]

Meanwhile, Will Alexander and other whites in the Commission on Interracial Cooperation remained as ambivalent as ever. White had written Alexander in mid-March to inquire if there was any chance the CIC might publicly support the antilynching bill, and Alexander promised to reopen the question with his directors at their meeting in late April. Lamenting the persistent refusal of state authorities to defend their prisoners and to prosecute and punish lynchers, Alexander acknowledged that the federal government must "take positive and vigorous steps to protect the lives of its citizens." Repeated instances of mob violence made it hard for southern congressmen to justify their opposition to a federal law. Nonetheless, after checking with the directors, Alexander was forced to tell Costigan that the

CIC had decided not to endorse the bill, because its leaders still felt the thrust of remedial action must come from the local level and from a re-educated citizenry. But then, with the troubled uncertainty that continued to plague southern white liberals, Alexander noted that local hysteria had so often prevented successful apprehension, prosecution, and conviction of lynchers that he and his colleagues were now advocating resort to the federal courts. They hoped, therefore, that some form of national legislation would enable federal agents and judicial officials to act more effectively against lynchers.[20] One can hardly blame White and his staff for their frustrations in dealing with well-intentioned southern liberals; friends in Atlanta seemed frequently to take two steps backward to move one step forward.

From late winter to the spring of 1935, frustrations persisted on a number of fronts. White spent much of his time in the capital, and sent periodic reports to his associates in New York City for their use in press releases and news stories in *The Crisis*; he also dispatched fresh directives to NAACP branches about grassroots pressure on individual lawmakers. Anticipating a favorable Judiciary subcommittee report in early March, he asked Roy Wilkins to rally all cooperating organizations and to have NAACP branches in Indiana applaud Senator Van Nuys' work as chairman ("He deserves this and needs such recognition in his state"). Meanwhile, Charles Houston argued that it was about time "to put the screws on Roosevelt." White agreed but admitted that the Association still had to determine if the President was "giving us the run around."[21] As it turned out, the secretary's attempts to get a commitment from the administration proved largely unsuccessful, despite repeated appeals to Eleanor Roosevelt.[22]

It was not that the NAACP got no help from the White House, but simply that it got far too little to push the bill through Congress. In his disappointment, White characterized Roosevelt's silence as "the greatest single handicap." Yet, the president had sent word through his wife that he was working privately on individual senators. "This was unquestionably true," White conceded, "otherwise Senator Robinson as majority leader would never have permitted the bill to be taken up at all." But the odds remained enormous. On March 25, Roosevelt's secretary, Marvin McIntyre (whom White suspected of short-circuiting his appeals to the president), sent Costigan a copy of a four-page memo from Attorney General Cummings to the president. It was a response to Roosevelt's query both about the recent lynching of A. B. Young at Slayden, Mississippi, and Walter White's telegram requesting the Justice Department to intervene. Cummings agreed that in the Neal and the Young cases the victims had been kidnapped and taken across state lines, but he still denied that the Lindbergh law applied, argued that such cross-state lynchings remained rare, and urged that the executive branch decline action without a clear-cut, statutory mandate from Congress. In transmitting these materials to

Costigan, McIntyre observed lamely that it might help "in pushing the other Bill" (NAACP allies were considering ways to amend the Lindbergh law specifically to cover lynching).[23] By any reasonable standard, administration cooperation proved meager, indirect, hesitant, and totally insufficient.

The Senate campaign against the bill was not conducted on a particularly high plane, and White observed that the filibuster in late April elicited a mixture of disgust and amusement from northern senators and from the crowded galleries. Despite such recent lynchings as those at Marianna, Slayden, and Franklinton, Louisiana, southern Democrats continued to maintain that the number of reported lynchings had declined; therefore, no federal action, an interference with states' rights, was needed. Trafficking in the ancient rape myth, "Cotton Ed" Smith of South Carolina declared that friends of the bill wanted to penalize the South without cause: "Certain acts committed are beyond the reach of any court or jury, in the opinion of any right-thinking man or woman." Josiah Bailey of North Carolina threatened a lengthy filibuster: "this bill is not going to pass. . . . We will be here all summer. . . . We will speak night and day." Hugo Black assured the Senate that "everyone here knows that the effort to bring the antilynching bill before the Senate is going to prove futile," and his fellow Alabaman, John Bankhead, admonished the bill's friends not to "give a low order of people the idea that the Government of the United States is going to protect them regardless of what sort of crime they may commit. Do not get that sort of idea into their minds." Expressing the South's self-confidence that it could counter any civil rights measures in the Senate, Kentucky's Marvel Logan warned Costigan that if he pursued the matter "we shall enter into an endurance test . . . and see who can last the longest during the hot days of July and August."[24]

Costigan had indeed tried to force a discussion and a vote on the antilynching bill. On April 22, he had written the president of his publicly announced intentions to move the measure as soon as the Bankhead farm tenancy bill cleared; such a step, the *New York Times* predicted, would produce a southern filibuster blocking all New Deal programs. Costigan assured Roosevelt that he did not want to play a disruptive role. He would welcome an opportunity to explore the matter, if Roosevelt wished, but must be in the Senate by 3:00 P.M. to make his motion.[25] It was a spirited if ineffectual ploy. Neither warnings nor threats induced the president to champion the bill in the face of southern opposition.

The administration had moved into that phase later classified as the second New Deal or "Second Hundred Days." The session from January to late August 1935 processed such important measures as the Emergency Relief Appropriation Act, which established the Works Progress Administration, the Resettlement Administration, the Rural Electrification Administration, the National Resources Committee, and the National Youth Administration; the Farm Mortgage Moratorium Act; and the tax provision Revenue Act. At just the time when the Costigan-Wagner bill was being strangled to death for the second consecutive year, New Deal forces were beginning to mobilize their own successful campaigns for the passage of four major laws: the Social Security Act, the National Labor Relations Act, the new Banking Act, and the Public Utilities Holding Company Act.[26] With such an array of landmark legislation confronting them, neither the White House nor a majority in Congress had any inclination to stall the business of the Senate indefinitely over the antilynching bill. No less than in the days of the Dyer bill, the Costigan-Wagner measure and its later counterparts suffered from southern intransigence and from the higher priorities that national leaders accorded to other aspects of America's domestic and foreign policies. In exasperation Walter White resigned as a member of the Advisory Council for the Government of the Virgin Islands on May 6:

> It is a matter of great disappointment that you as President did not see your way clear to make a public pronouncement . . . giving your open endorsement to the antilynching bill and your condemnation of the shameless filibuster by a wilful group of obstructionists. . . . in justice to the cause I serve I cannot continue to remain even a small part of your official family.[27]

Charles Houston applauded White's resignation, but the breach between the NAACP and the New Deal was hardly permanent.[28] How could it be? Where else could White and his associates turn if they were to continue to insist on transforming American race relations by working from the top down, by penetrating, or attempting to penetrate, the national power structure in Washington? To whom else might they look, moreover, with Roosevelt and his party so firmly entrenched in power? To the radical left, where the NAACP was viewed with suspicion, and vice versa? No. To struggling black nationalist elements in metropolitan centers? Not likely. To the Republican party of conservative National Committee chairman John Hamilton, of western progressive and self-styled constitutional authority William Borah, of Senate Minority Leader Charles McNary, the farm lobbyist from Oregon who had already made it clear that he would not, despite past performances, consent to cloture? Hardly. The NAACP had nowhere else to go in national politics, and that left it increasingly vulnerable. Besides, NAACP leaders could read the election returns. The fact that by the mid-1930s black voters had shown an accelerated shift into the Democratic column merely seemed another inducement for working with Roosevelt and his legislative leaders.[29]

The Association had expended enormous amounts of its staff time and resources in lobbying for the Costigan-Wagner bill. The June 1935 *Crisis* might boast that the campaign "accomplished more education against lynching than ten years of quiet work," but it certainly bit into an NAACP operating budget already strained by the national depression.[30] On several occasions, White had to forestall creditors with a recital of expenditures in the campaign against lynching.[31] Nor were outsiders alone inconvenienced. In the midst of the big spring drive for the Costigan-Wagner bill, White wired Roy Wilkins from the capital to request forty dollars. His colleague replied that he had no idea where the money would come from, especially since White had added to their burdens with a sizeable new charge for telegrams.[32] Not infrequently clerical and secretarial members of the staff, the working backbone of any successful organization, got their checks late.[33] When competing with well-financed organizations for the government's attention, the NAACP clearly operated at a disadvantage.

White's unwavering determination to pass the antilynching bill caused some uneasiness within the Association. Charles Houston, long based in Washington and familiar with personalities and events behind the scenes, and farther to the left than other NAACP officials, voiced concern on several occasions. In February 1935, he had told White that AFL lobbyist Mike Flynn wanted the NAACP to join with labor in fighting for an expanded social security bill. Houston pleaded that the secretary seize this chance to broaden the Association's activities and thereby attract "a lot of people who are somewhat lukewarm on the anti-lynching bill." He explained that

> lots of us feel that a fight for anti-lynching legislation without just as vigorous a battle for economic independence is to fight the manifestation of the evil and ignore its cause. Joining Labor in this fight would show we see the relation between economics and lynching, as *one* of its major causes. Think it over carefully; and if you decide to go into it, not only do it independently but it seems to me it would be good strategy to connect up economics and economic causes in such fashion with the anti-lynching hearings.[34]

Two weeks later Houston tried once more to nudge White: "You remember what I told you about not letting the whole program get too wrapped around the anti-lynching measure as its sole major objective in the first six months of 1935."[35]

It was not that Walter White discounted economic matters and their relationship to racism. He had devoted an entire chapter ("The Economic Foundations of Lynch-Law") to the question in *Rope and Faggot*. In April 1935, while complaining to Eleanor Roosevelt about the impoverishment of black farm workers caused by the reduction in cotton acreage, he quoted a study by the Rosenwald Fund that warned that economic dislocation might intensify racial antagonisms and lead to more lynchings.[36] And he did eventually (after the antilynching bill was lost for the session, and the annual meeting in St. Louis had endorsed the modified New Plan and Program) confer with chairman Connery of the House Labor Committee about a possible federal survey of the treatment accorded black people under New Deal programs.[37] But for all that, White stubbornly refused to let anything take precedence over or jeopardize the antilynching bill. Once, for example, when exploring with Costigan what could be done about the exclusion of black voters from southern Democratic primaries, he quickly assured the Coloradan that, "We are, of course, going to do nothing that will embarrass you in any way or interfere with the anti-lynching bill."[38] On another occasion, when considering a federal probe of New Deal projects, he asked Wagner and Costigan if such an investigation would "in any way interfere with the Anti-Lynching Bill?" They responded with divided counsel. Wagner favored an investigation, while Costigan explained that his support of such an inquiry might lead opponents of the antilynching bill to charge him with a general animus against the South. Though White demurred, he probably welcomed Costigan's cautionary mood. How much emphasis the Association should give to an antilynching bill was not exclusively Walter White's to decide. However, with Du Bois gone, with the American Fund projects moving but slowed, with the Harris committee report revised by the NAACP national office to prevent any major, new adventures, with Board members generally inclined to honor White's judgment, his commitment to the fight against lynching took on added dimensions in the scheme of things.[39]

What White needed, and found, was an angel. In mid-October 1935, he wrote to Roy Wilkins from Boston that James Joseph Ryan, son of the millionaire Thomas Fortune Ryan, had taken an interest in the Association. Ryan wished to meet Senator Wagner and "to spend some real money and effort in the next session in pushing the Costigan-Wagner bill." White added, with his customary thoroughness, that Wilkins should dispatch a researcher to the Public Library to determine the amount and terms of Ryan's inheritance, "for our information and guidance."[40] When the NAACP Board met in early December, members learned that Ryan had given $5,000 to the NAACP, $4,750 to back the campaign for a federal antilynching bill and $250 for the Association's general expenses. The larger amount went into a special account administered by W. F. Illig, Ryan's attorney in Erie, Pennsylvania. There was good news, as well, for Charles Houston. The American Fund–NAACP Joint Committee had recommended an allotment of $10,000 for the Association's 1936–1937 legal campaign in education, with an additional $5,000 for publicity work. With obvious relief, Ovington remarked that these developments had resolved two major questions about the 1936 program. So, White had both a cause and a kitty, and he prepared to launch a new congressional antilynching drive.[41] It would, however, develop more obliquely than he preferred.

On January 2, 1936, the executive secretary spent thirty-five minutes with Franklin Roosevelt. Despite his resignation from the Virgin Islands Advisory Council eight months before, White knew he needed strong support from the White House. Facing his first re-election campaign in the fall, Roosevelt doubtless wished to attract black voters and avoid further ruptures with the NAACP. The president began with a generalized digression on the dangers of prejudice but frankly saw little hope that the Costigan-Wagner bill could pass in the new session. Instead, he proposed a Senate investigation of lawlessness, including lynching, and recommended a meeting between White and the attorney general on new legislation to guard the courts against interference from sensationalist reporting, community hysteria, and mob intimidation. When White observed that none of this would accomplish what the NAACP sought through the Costigan-Wagner bill, the president fell back on the therapeutic benefits of investigation and publicity. And there matters rested.

Whatever hesitations he felt, White could hardly ignore Roosevelt's suggestions. Worried about another Senate deadlock, his own Board had endorsed similar proposals just four weeks before. Senator Van Nuys of the Judiciary Committee had prepared a resolution that would launch the very type of federal inquiry mentioned by the president, and the Association had long tried to involve the Justice Department in the fight against lynching.[42] Franklin Roosevelt was not innovating, but simply reflecting some of what he knew about alternative actions that the Association, its congressional supporters, and influential southern liberals had already considered. It was all very good politics in a keenly political year.

Four days later, Van Nuys introduced Resolution No. 211 for a Senate investigation of lynchings that had occurred in 1935, after the filibuster of the Costigan-Wagner bill.[43] This would dramatize the fourteen incidents in question and further underscore the failure of the states to prevent mob violence and punish lynchers. Anxious to make the best of developments he could not fully control, White conferred with Will Alexander and Arthur Raper of the Commission on Interracial Cooperation, which had investigated most of those killings.[44] The secretary's acquiescence to congressional investigations contrasted sharply with James Weldon Johnson's coolness toward a similar proposal by Senator Frelinghuysen in the early 1920s. With good reason, Johnson had feared a diversion of attention and resources from the Dyer bill. Facing a different social and political climate, White hoped the Van Nuys inquiries would be a step toward Senate passage. He had enjoyed success in two earlier Senate struggles. Why not a third? A master of public relations, he sensed the educational value in a formal Senate study of violence, especially when the findings could be publicized nationally through network radio on a scale not available to Johnson. A Senate inquiry would have subpoena powers, ample financial resources (if voted), and access to all sections of the country. Federal investigators guided by NAACP expertise in the field could accomplish far more than White and his associates with their limited resources. Moreover, the NAACP had to face the argument that the problem itself would soon disappear. The Association felt, rather, that lynching had acquired a new style in which small, designated groups quietly seized and executed victims without the usual notoriety and frenzy of mob action. Implementation of the Van Nuys resolution would provide the NAACP an open forum for confirming this analysis and thereby augment the drive for an antilynching law. Finally, the plan for a federal investigation had the blessings of a national administration that was sympathetic to the problem, even if it steadily refused to extend itself on the issue. That, too, induced White to accept what Johnson had declined.

With the Van Nuys resolution pending in the Senate, where, as White gleefully told Frances Williams of the YWCA, "Senator Ashurst let us name the sub-committee,"[45] White tried to act on Roosevelt's second proposal, a conference with Homer Cummings about new legislation. The interview on January 16 proved to be a charade. According to White, the attorney general seemed distracted and somewhat indifferent, and his attitude changed only with the reminder that White had come to see him at the president's suggestion. Even then, Cummings expressed doubt about the value of White's (Roosevelt's) latest idea. He said his department could do little unless Congress appropriated a substantial increase in funds, and he went on to rehearse reasons for the Department's backlog of cases. When asked about the application of an amended Lindbergh law, Cummings became evasive, and he proved little more responsive to the prospects of the Van Nuys resolution. He even turned to the *World Almanac* for lynching statistics since 1889 as a measure of the argument that lynching had decreased and would soon die out. It was little wonder that White left the interview with feelings of frustration and contempt. He sent the president a brief note to indicate his disappointment with the attorney general, and confided to Eleanor Roosevelt that, having conferred with Cummings, the NAACP would concentrate on the president's recommendation for a Senate investigation.[46]

If White found the attorney general less than helpful, he soon discovered outright obstruction in the Senate. Although the Judiciary Committee favorably reported the Van Nuys resolution on February 13, it languished for over a month thereafter in the Audit and Control Committee. There, chairman James Byrnes (D–South Carolina) and Nathan Bachman (D–Tennessee) delayed a meeting and thus prevented the appropriation of $7,500 to implement the investigation.[47] Van Nuys intervened with Byrnes, but as White explained to Eleanor Roosevelt, the entire picture seemed terribly bleak. He had heard rumors in the capital that the Democratic National Committee advised all senators and representatives to avoid controversial issues in a major election year. There seemed no likelihood of moving the Costigan-Wagner bill, the Justice Department (White had talked again with Cummings) still refused to respond to the Claude Neal case, and the Van Nuys resolution was immobilized. White protested that he and the NAACP had now come under fire for failing to get federal action against lynching, and quite possibly, having played into the hands of their Senate "*friends*" (emphasis in the original) who needed an alibi for inaction.[48]

Stymied on three fronts, the Association tried to force a response from the House of Representatives, where Joseph Gavagan (D–New York City) served as chief NAACP sponsor. But Hatton Sumners (D–Texas), chairman of the Judiciary Committee, declared that he would never permit favorable action on any antilynching measure. This left the NAACP with two alternatives: circulate a discharge petition that would take the antilynching bill from committee, or petition Democratic House leaders for a caucus to endorse the measure. At first, White discounted the former. Charges that Republican signatories meant only to embarrass the administration would detract from the integrity of the effort and further complicate matters. Besides, House rules required 218 signatures on a discharge petition, with a mandatory thirty-day waiting period—all of which might prevent action before adjournment. Consequently, the NAACP chose the second alternative, only to hear reports that Democratic leaders had brought pressure on individual representatives either not to sign for a caucus or to withdraw their names. Adding to the Association's dilemma was the news, conveyed by Eleanor Roosevelt, that the president refused to make the Costigan-Wagner bill a priority item in that session.[49]

As White moved about Washington consulting friendly members of Congress, their staffs, and reporters, trying to exert leverage on the president, and constantly sending dispatches to his New York office for use in press releases and bulletins to the branches, an endless number of small impediments surfaced.[50] Caucus leader Edward Taylor of Colorado was laid low with a "severe cold." When White secured a more than ample thirty-nine signatures for the caucus petition (it required twenty-five), certain Democrats charged irregularities which forced the NAACP to retrace its steps. Next, Taylor claimed he could not accept a petition from anyone but Gavagan, then absent in California. Some New Deal legislators feared that other party members might manipulate a caucus to alter administration plans for relief funds and agricultural measures. Finally, Congressman Ford, an assistant majority whip who was among the sixteen Democrats sponsoring antilynching bills in that session, and whom White trusted, admitted the pinch of conflicting pressures. When he asked White to drop the caucus and count instead on getting the bill passed in the next session, the executive secretary refused.[51] Liberals at both ends of Pennsylvania Avenue were once again proving themselves undependable at meeting black needs.

The much-awaited caucus met on Friday, May 22, but, on the excuse that the sixty-five members present did not constitute a quorum, nothing happened on the antilynching question. This failure, the general delay in calling the meeting, Congressman Taylor's oversight in not issuing the customary forty-eight-hour notice to all members, and certain other peculiarities outraged the NAACP. White and his staff sent letters to 224 northern and border-state Democrats, and tried once more in the Senate to force the Van Nuys resolution from committee. White wrote an angry letter to Franklin Roosevelt about the House Democratic caucus; the NAACP national office had already prepared a report for the branches on the conduct of individual congressmen.[52] Always prepared for one last effort, White even tried (unsuccessfully), through Eleanor Roosevelt, to arrange for a White House showing of *Fury*, the MGM film on lynching, to the Roosevelts and any Senate or House leaders they might wish to invite.[53]

The Seventy-fourth Congress adjourned on June 20, with the lynching issue unresolved. Although it appeared that the NAACP had failed again, enormously important consequences continued to flow from the Association's efforts in Washington and across the country. The NAACP had reaffirmed to national leaders its determination not to be turned aside in the fight for interracial justice. Moreover, the campaign had strengthened a civil rights–reformist network that would endure for decades to come, through the Association's contacts with a wide range of labor, church, peace, social justice, and women's organizations.[54] The NAACP drive against summary justice also shaped its relationships with the Commission on Interracial Cooperation, the Association of Southern Women for the Prevention of Lynching, and (in mid-December 1935) the newly created Scottsboro Defense Committee.[55]

From a different perspective, petitions submitted to the Seventy-fourth Congress revealed the extent of nationwide interest and support that the NAACP had generated for the antilynching bill. Resolutions in favor of the Costigan-Wagner measure came from the state legislatures in Illinois, Massachusetts, New Jersey, Nebraska, and Minnesota, and from civic groups in such varied locales as: Boston; the District of Columbia; New York City; Kokomo, Indiana; Portsmouth, New Hampshire; Sweetwater County, Wyoming; Hartford, Connecticut; St. Louis; Corona, New York; and Cleveland.[56] The three-year effort had produced an unprecedented national outcry against racial violence and thrust the NAACP to the center of public attention. Building upon this recognition and upon its contacts with other lobbying groups in the capital, the Association joined the struggle for a range of socio-economic legislation important to black and white people alike in the New Deal and Fair Deal years.[57] And, the fight against lynching offered the NAACP a ready means of appealing for new members and financial assistance. The staff made good use of the campaign among philanthropic individuals and foundations to attract funds for the antilynching drive and other NAACP activities.[58]

The antilynching drive also served as a useful way of identifying and measuring opponents. This was most certainly the case with William Borah of Idaho and his aspirations in 1936 for the Republican presidential nomination. Borah, of course, had stood against the Dyer bill in the early 1920s, and Walter White found him equally adamant on the Costigan-Wagner measure. Here was a score to settle, not in personal terms (although White derived no little satisfaction from unsettling the Idaho senator), but in the broader sense of rebuking a national politician who doubted the legitimacy of invoking federal protection for black lives.

Borah had publicly proclaimed his intention to vote against antilynching bills and to veto them should he ever gain the White House.[59] He had now become as unacceptable as Judge Parker. Accordingly, when Borah came to New York City in the winter of 1936, the NAACP was waiting for him. "You should be here tonight," White wrote Frances Williams,

> We are picketing Borah's meeting in Brooklyn where it is expected he will open his campaign for the Presidency . . . and great news appeared in the New York *Times* this morning to the effect that Borah has withdrawn his name from use in the Ohio primaries because his sponsors there "fear that the Senator's stand against the antilynching bill will cause the Negro vote to make him lose the state."

When the senator appeared that evening he found about fifty pickets with signs denouncing his stand against the antilynching bill. He exclaimed testily, "Is William E. Borah the only culprit?" Two weeks later, the NAACP Board of Directors voted to warn all delegates to the Republican national convention that black Americans bitterly opposed Borah's candidacy, and the staff planned to accompany each letter with a copy of Louis L. Redding's article in the March *Crisis*, "Borah—What *Does* He Stand For?"[60] En route to the YWCA convention in Colorado that spring, White paused to attend an NAACP "Beat Borah" rally in Cleveland of some 1,000 delegates from ten Ohio branches. He also contended that the Idahoan had lost the Illinois primary by his inability to attract the state's black voters.[61]

While the Association could attack politicians for opposing an antilynching law, others occasionally criticized the NAACP for its handling of the issue. The Communist party, for example, felt that the Costigan-Wagner bill was inadequate, because it provided no direct punishment for lynchers. Moreover, the party argued that the Association had misdirected its campaign by failing to address the underlying economic and political causes of oppression. When the NAACP first reopened its struggle for a federal antilynching law in the winter of 1934, the CP-USA denounced the effort. The *Daily Worker* charged the NAACP with using the bill to erode the gains that radical groups had made on behalf of the black community. James Ford, the CP-USA's black candidate for vice president, asserted that the "Wagner-Costigan bill itself is a part of the whole system of Jim Crowism and oppression," and he called upon "the masses, both white and Negro, to protest against White's contemptible attitude."[62]

The CP-USA tried to fashion its own parallel, counter-remedies. For example, in September 1935, after the Costigan-Wagner bill had failed for the second consecutive year in the Senate, Benjamin J. Davis, Jr., wrote to Carol King:

> The thing I want to raise the devil about is our Bill for Negro Rights and Suppression of Lynching. Over six weeks ago . . . [the] general

secretary of our organization, left the Bill with the I.J.A. It was to be redrafted so that it had at least the appearance of constitutionality and at the same time contain the kernel of our political line.

Davis explained that he wanted the proposal prepared, distributed, and popularized among the organizations scheduled to attend the forthcoming meeting of the National Negro Congress, so that the bill could receive serious consideration by the delegates. The bill in question addressed itself to a host of matters affecting black people and appears to have been, at that point, a broadly structured criticism of racist oppression rather than a tightly prepared piece of legislation.[63]

Meanwhile, in response to the Comintern's strategy of a "United Front" against fascism, the party softened its public attitudes toward the NAACP, the National Urban League, and other moderate, reformist groups. With this, the CP-USA slipped into line behind the Costigan-Wagner bill. In early April 1936, for example, the *Daily Worker* analyzed the measure and declared, without saying anything about NAACP sponsorship, that the bill had the backing of the CP-USA and of the recently established National Negro Congress.[64]

The NNC had been launched at a Chicago meeting in mid-February. From the beginning it posed nothing but trouble for the Association. The NAACP Board had asked Roy Wilkins to attend the conference, and he returned to New York with a great deal to say about the representative gathering of almost 1,000 delegates. A number of NAACP figures, including lawyer William Hastie, several branch officers, and Marion Cuthbert of the Board of Directors, also participated in the Chicago meeting, as did prominent black figures James W. Ford, Langston Hughes, Max Yergan, and John P. Davis. The conference addressed a wide range of issues, such as labor union discrimination, civil and political disabilities, disfranchisement, lynching, New Deal legislation, and economic deprivations. Wilkins reported that the new organization took its strength from grassroots support and a concern about socio-economic questions. He declared:

> There is a wide-spread feeling among great numbers of people that the Association is not a true representative of the aspirations of the race and is not attacking the problems as vigorously as they should be attacked; that its machinery is undemocratic and that much of its program is arranged from the top rather than being a response to the wishes of the people.

Wilkins confirmed Hastie's advice that the NAACP ought to affiliate itself with the NNC, because "it would be better for the Association to be participant in the machinery and procedure than to be on the outside and perhaps become the victim of attacks, sabotage, etc."[65]

As it turned out, the NAACP made no serious efforts to join the NNC, which had sprung very largely from the organizational energies of John P. Davis. White found himself no more enthusiastic about Davis's new creature and about some of the Communist elements he feared were involved than he had been about the socio-economic emphases of Davis's Joint Committee on National Recovery. Two weeks after the Chicago conference, White reported the event to Eleanor Roosevelt as a warning of the widespread dissatisfaction throughout the black community. He explained (somewhat disingenuously—Houston had provided him considerable information on Davis's plans) that the NAACP had declined to participate in the group "first, because we were not given sufficient information about its sponsorship, program or purposes, and, second, because there were too many rumors that it was being pushed in some respects by Communists and in others by Republicans." The following fall, he wrote warily to Joel Spingarn that despite professions of cooperation, Davis and the NNC intended to rival the NAACP.[66]

The National Negro Congress had far less impact on the course of events than its sponsors had hoped. By 1940 it lost much of its earlier support and came under the influence of the CP-USA.[67] The organization, however, did offer some alternatives to black men and women restless with the NAACP's legal-judicial approach, and it certainly kept pressure on Walter White and his staff to demonstrate their success in combating racism. The very existence of this new group, to say nothing of White's suspicions about its affiliations and purposes, served as added incentives to push his antilynching bill to a satisfactory conclusion.[68] And, the fact that the CP-USA, the NNC, and others tried to make lynching an issue on which to win allegiance within the black community showed that the NAACP had identified a problem of vital and continuing concern. When the Association launched its antilynching drive in the Seventy-fifth Congress (1937–1938), the effort occupied White and his colleagues for almost fifteen months and proved the most intensified campaign that they would ever head on behalf of this particular legislative goal.

7
At the Peak and Beyond, 1937-1940

The NAACP had learned some hard lessons in the years 1934-1936, and sought to apply them in the next round of lobbying. This time, the Association chose to concentrate on the House of Representatives, evidently in the hope that fresh political and public notoriety derived from House passage would add momentum to the Senate drive and force the White House to support the measure. NAACP staff members fully anticipated obstruction from Judiciary Committee chairman Hatton Sumners, but knew from their recent experiences that they could gather the necessary 218 signatures for a discharge petition that would take the bill out of committee hands and move it to the floor. In fact, by the end of 1936, Walter White and his colleagues had already amassed pledges of support from 251 representatives scheduled to sit in the new Congress.[1]

Looking ahead, White had outlined his fund-raising views in an August 1936 memo to the Committee on Administration, entitled "Tentative Plans for Legal Defense—Anti-Lynching Fund Campaign."[2] Linking the two tasks revealed the Association's awareness of their mutuality and confirmed the growing importance of projects undertaken by lawyers Charles Houston, William Hastie, and Thurgood Marshall. It also increased the likelihood of attracting contributions to a single fund-raising drive, even if individual donors had no enthusiasm for one of the two major tasks. From White's perspective, the combination also assured him, within the limits of normal organizational restraints, access to a sizeable kitty of discretionary funds on which to draw for the new anti-lynching campaign.

However, Houston's reaction again showed the existence among NAACP leaders of alternative priorities, even though this did not create a divisive challenge to White's authority. Houston recommended more grassroots efforts and a more deliberate use of black fund raisers than the secretary's stress on prominent whites and foundation grants suggested. Houston also reiterated his concern about the role of the antilynching campaign in the Association's overall program, a concern no doubt sharpened by his own immediate responsibilities for NAACP work through the courts. In disarming fashion, Houston asserted that the fight against lynching lay "at the basis of all our activity," because "physical security and freedom from fear of violence are necessary in order to get people to go into court." Nonetheless, he went on to argue, many supporters had tired of the singular emphasis on lynching. They ought to have the option of earmarking their donations for specific purposes—lynching investigations, litigation in state courts growing out of lynchings, the antilynching drive in Congress, legal defense against unfounded criminal charges, voting rights, educational opportunities, economic justice, general civil rights issues, and the like.[3]

Although White's ambitious fund-raising schemes never quite matured as he wished, he found another means for shoring up the 1937 fight in Congress: the sale and distribution of special antilynching buttons. Headed by the tireless field secretary, Daisy Lampkin, and designed to reach the average person (National Negro Congress supporters had used button-selling to help finance their Chicago meeting in mid-February 1936), the buttons read, "Stop lynching! N.A.A.C.P. Defense Fund." Lampkin planned to sell 150,000 buttons at ten cents each, and the staff was allotted 100,000 more for sale or distribution. Because the black community wanted lynching stopped, the branches responded enthusiastically. The idea took hold that winter, and by April 1937, White announced gross receipts of $9,378.[4] This was good news against a background of serious financial problems, for the depression still took its disproportionate toll among Afro-Americans. The Treasurer's Report for November 1936 had disclosed a deficit of $3,352 in the Legal Defense–Antilynching Fund, with a notation that the amount was due the general fund; the special Ryan Antilynching Fund had a November balance of but $250. Clearly, the NAACP needed every bit of help that the button campaign and the branches could provide, and even these would prove insufficient.[5] But White remained too committed to the antilynching bill to let the matter slide. With the backing or tacit acquiescence of most of his Board and staff members, he prepared to mount another assault on Congress. As Roy Wilkins put the matter years later, when asked about the struggle for the Costigan-Wagner bill: "All the main moves were made by Walter."[6]

There seemed a number of promising signs. The Association possessed a wealth of contacts and experience, the New Deal had won a rousing affirmation at the polls in 1936, and Roosevelt had agreed to meet with White and Joel Spingarn. The New York *World-Telegram* reported that the GOP planned a big push for an antilynching bill to recapture black voter support, but also that the Republicans might simply use the antilynching issue to obstruct administration programs in Congress.[7]

Meanwhile, the Association revised its antilynching bill to exclude violence involving gangsters or racketeers and riots incidental to labor disputes. The amended bill also sought to broaden the Lindbergh Law to cover cases of the Claude Neal type. Remembering Mike Flyn's suggestion two years before, the national office wrote to 190 members of Congress who had already expressed interest in the matter to request that they consider sponsoring the NAACP measure. By early March, White informed his Board that forty-one identical bills had been introduced as a demonstration of support. With Costigan's retirement from the Senate because of failing health, Van Nuys of Indiana joined Wagner as cosponsor in the Senate. And that index of organizational behavior, the proportion of monthly press releases on any single topic, showed just how deeply involved the Association had become: 15 of the 30 releases for January 1937 focused on some phase of the antilynching question; 16 of February's releases touched on the issue.[8]

On February 19, Democrat Joseph Gavagan of New York City opened the NAACP offensive on the House floor by introducing a resolution to make his bill, H.R. 1507 (the NAACP bill), a special order of business. In due time, he submitted a petition to discharge the resolution from the Rules Committee. At that point White's care to get representatives and representatives-elect on record for the bill began to pay dividends.[9] Gavagan had first won a congressional seat in 1929, in a special election against Hubert Delany, a black lawyer and future NAACP Board member. Their district included Harlem; once in office, Gavagan regularly introduced antilynching bills and was no stranger to the NAACP. He became a New Deal proponent and remained in the House through 1943, when he won election to the New York State Supreme Court, where he served until his death in 1968.[10]

Gavagan and the NAACP expected that the discharge petition would circumvent Hatton Sumners' obstructionism, but they discovered that he had an unwitting ally in the House's lone black member. On January 8, Arthur Mitchell (D–Chicago) had introduced his own antilynching bill, H.R. 2251, and Sumners decided to impede the NAACP measure by steering the weaker Mitchell bill to the floor. The Texas Democrat later admitted to White "quite frankly that he had not believed that . . . [the NAACP] would have the nerve to oppose passage of a bill introduced by the one Negro member of Congress."[11] A comparison of the two bills explains Sumners' tactics and the Association's apprehensions. The Mitchell bill applied only to victims seized from official custody; the Gavagan bill covered all instances of mob violence against life and person. For officials found guilty of conspiring or cooperating with the mob, the Mitchell bill proposed imprisonment from two to ten years; the Gavagan bill carried a term of from five to twenty-five years. While Mitchell's bill remained silent about initial federal jurisdiction, Gavagan's invoked action by the United States District Court thirty days after the crime, if state and local officials had failed to respond. The Mitchell bill provided only for a $2,000 to $10,000 fine on the county of death; Gavagan's version held both the county of abduction and the county of death liable. Finally, unlike Mitchell's the Gavagan bill explicitly exempted from creditors' claims any damages assessed against the county(s) on behalf of the victim's survivors.[12]

The Association warned Mitchell of Sumner's trap and wired Democratic House leaders and party chairman James Farley against Mitchell's "emasculated, ineffective, and virtually worthless" bill.[13] Protecting himself, Mitchell immediately went on the radio to say that he had already assured the NAACP of his readiness to vote for any antilynching measure that reached the floor. Nevertheless, Walter White must surely have noticed that the congressman's name was not among those on the Gavagan discharge petition when the list appeared in the *Congressional Record*.[14]

This was not the first time that the NAACP found itself at odds with Mitchell, whom some considered an Uncle Tom. Born in rural Alabama, Mitchell had worked his way through Tuskegee Institute as a farm hand and as an assistant in Booker T. Washington's office. By all reports, he was deeply impressed with Washington's racial philosophy, and that probably added to his later suspicion of the NAACP. Unseating Congressman Oscar De Priest in 1934, Mitchell had his own political fortunes to tend and seemed intent upon preserving a belligerent independence in race matters. In the summer of 1935, for example, White learned of an incident in which Mitchell had allegedly crossed Capitol Hill to congratulate Senator "Cotton Ed" Smith of South Carolina on his speeches against the Costigan-Wagner antilynching bill. Never one to take lightly what he considered treason to the black community (he and Johnson, after all, had soundly rebuked Perry Howard during the fight for the Dyer bill), White made special efforts to secure an affidavit regarding Mitchell's behavior. However, Lee Johnson, Costigan's secretary, cautioned that any such revelation of one legislator's remarks to another might be used on the floor against Costigan and the measures he supported. White yielded,[15] but informed his Board in early August that the NAACP had written senators Ashurst of Arizona and J. Hamilton Lewis of Illinois to oppose Mitchell's bill for an Industrial Commission on Negro Affairs. (Lewis had cosponsored the measure at the urging of his Illinois colleague). Mitchell reportedly fumed that "nearly everything the Association does is vicious."[16]

The bitterness persisted into 1936. Stymied on the Van Nuys resolution, White tried to neutralize Senate obstruction by forcing House Democrats to consider the antilynching question. He found Mitchell unwilling to support the caucus petition and raised the threat of political reprisal. This time it was Roy Wilkins' turn to admonish White against any public assault on Mitchell's personal or political reputation. The following spring, with Sumners' attempt to exploit the Mitchell bill and to dissuade his committee members from signing Gavagan's discharge petition, White felt less reason for restraint, especially since he believed that Mitchell had also urged several representatives not to sign.[17]

The attitudes and activities of southern white liberals, especially those in the Association of Southern Women for the Prevention of Lynching, continued to plague the NAACP, as well. Chairman Sumners and ASWPL leaders enjoyed very cordial personal and political relationships. In the late spring of 1937, for example, Jessie Daniel Ames wired the Texan about a meeting in Jackson, Mississippi, for which her group would stand his expenses and had made arrangements for hotel accommodations and entertainment. A month later Georgia May Martin of Louisville, chairwoman of the ASWPL's central council, wrote Sumners to thank him for the copy of his April 15 House speech on the Gavagan bill and to say "we southerners" find that "words such as yours come with comforting reassurance."[18] With "allies" of this sort—a black congressman who used, and let himself be used by, the Gavagan bill's chief House opponent, and an organization of southern liberals whose white leaders warmly applauded that same House opponent—White and the NAACP might understandably groan beneath the weight of their lobbying burden.

In the House, however, the Association had the needed resources. Gavagan succeeded with his discharge petition and moved his bill to the floor. Meanwhile, the House refused, by a vote of 257 to 123, to consider the Mitchell bill, even though the Judiciary Committee had given it a favorable report.[19] In the controlled debate that followed, each side had three hours to discuss the Gavagan proposal. White conceded that opponents generally treated the issue in forthright terms, although two Georgians digressed on the "honor of womanhood" and the rape myth, and John E. Miller of Arkansas declared, "I know the heat has been applied to you [supporters of the bill] by the greatest racketeering organization in the United States today, an organization that is preying upon the credulity of the colored race." More worried about unionization than race questions, Frank Hook (D-Michigan) deplored House attention to an antilynching bill and apparent disregard for what he deemed the lawless occupation of private property by sit-down strikers. Representative John M. Robsion (R-Kentucky) befriended the measure and cited the NAACP's endorsement. Now Mitchell and Maury Maverick (Democratic liberal from San Antonio) both favored the bill. Put to a vote, it passed, 277 to 120.[20] White and the Association had achieved a major objective, and they sought at once to determine its impact on the Senate and the other end of Pennsylvania Avenue.

Just as the House had moved to the Gavagan bill, the question took on a horribly vivid reality with the news of a double lynching, involving acetylene torches, at Duck Hill, Mississippi. White asked to make a firsthand investigation on grounds that his testimony before the Senate Judiciary Committee would give added impetus to the bill, but the Board feared the trip was too hazardous. Rather, the Association turned, as it had on other occasions, to Howard Kester of the Southern Tenant Farmers Union; and the national office sent copies of his report, with an appeal for the antilynching bill, to members of the Senate.[21] To add to the momentum, Gavagan volunteered to speak in certain key cities, and asked the executive secretary to accompany him. The itinerary included Newark, Cleveland, Pittsburgh, Louisville, Indianapolis, Chicago, Kansas City, Los Angeles, Boston, New York, Philadelphia, Baltimore, and Denver, and was highly reminiscent of Dyer's circuit in the 1920s. Along the way, White and Gavagan conferred with newspaper editors, public officials, and representatives of various organizations; gross returns from the tour exceeded $1,000. While in Indiana, they met with Ludwell Denny, editor of the Indianapolis *Times*, and others, for the specific purpose of encouraging Van Nuys to fight more vigorously for Senate passage of the Gavagan bill.[22]

Two factors in the Seventy-fifth Congress affected the bill far beyond the commitment of any individual sponsor, however. First, there developed a steady erosion of Roosevelt's influence on Capitol Hill, despite his impressive re-election. The "Court packing" issue of 1937, reactions to proposals for executive reorganization, the protracted controversy over fair labor standards, and debates on tax revision and relief spending in the tense, recession atmosphere of 1937 all reflected the president's dilemma. Second, the attendant shifting of political alignments, the breakdown and reshuffling of loyalties, and the uncertainties of voter reactions in the off-year elections of 1938 all worked against any clear-cut, sustained action on the antilynching bill.[23]

In addition, there were the inevitable rumors and sometimes conflicting data that any successful lobbyist had constantly to gather through a network of informants and then assess. In mid-May one friend in the capital warned White, "Orders are [to] go after your bill . . . . [which] they are trying to kill . . . by compromise." Meanwhile, Van Nuys hinted that southern forces were themselves predicting passage without lengthy obstructions.[24] Senator Josiah W. Bailey (D–North Carolina) assured Wagner that he would not filibuster but would simply make a brief statement on constitutionality and states' rights. Bailey also claimed that Hugo Black might actually vote for the bill. Understandably, White remained wary, constantly alert to signs of bad news; he had been at this business too long to act otherwise. He and Joel Spingarn still found it impossible to get their long-promised meeting with the president, even though Eleanor Roosevelt assured them of her husband's interest. He was, she explained, swamped with the Court matter. Meanwhile, she continued to send whatever inside information she could gather from White House and other capital sources.[25] On May 20, Van Nuys responded to White's prodding with the promise of an affirmative report from the Judiciary Committee within a week or ten days, but by June 9, the secretary could only perceive "some inexplicable delay." Finally on June 15, the Committee had *Report No. 793* in hand, and one week later Van Nuys reported the measure favorably on the floor.[26]

Still, a vote remained painfully elusive. White spent almost the entire month of July and two weeks of August in Washington to lobby, but the measure kept losing ground to, or getting entangled with, other matters. Senator Wagner possessed impeccable antilynching credentials but seemed torn in two directions. The Association suspected that the New Yorker had for the moment got caught up with his housing bill and feared that the antilynching question would drive Senate support away from that priority measure.[27] Even the death of Majority Leader Joseph Robinson promised difficulties. He had driven the Senate through the hot summer for the president's Supreme Court bill, and now all sides talked of dropping the matter and heading for home. After the Senate on July 22 had buried the Court bill, floor leaders still ignored the antilynching measure in their push for one or two other items before adjournment. Then, somewhat unexpectedly, the Association's bill surfaced on July 27, when Royal S. Copeland (D–New York) moved to attach it as an amendment to the length-of-freight-train bill. White suspected that Copeland wished to defeat the train bill and woo black voters in a contemplated bid for the New York City mayoralty. Certainly the ploy angered the four railway brotherhoods sponsoring the train bill. When the motion lost by a mere seven votes, Copeland next suggested affixing the antilynching bill to the wages-and-hours measure, but Wagner and Van Nuys quickly discouraged that. They felt, and White agreed, that the antilynching bill deserved a test on its own merits in a recorded vote that would preserve the option of political reprisal. Furthermore, they were anxious to avoid any further appearance of working at cross purposes with organized labor.[28]

No amount of effort on White's part could suffice. He heard indirectly that the new Senate majority leader, Alben W. Barkley of Kentucky, who had his own goals to meet in assuming Robinson's duties, resented insistent demands to bring the bill to the floor.[29] At the same time, pressures mounted on the Association, whose friends around the country became increasingly restless with, and critical of, White's inability to win passage.[30] This set the stage for a little fast parliamentary footwork by Wagner in early August. Although Senate leaders had arranged for William King of Utah to move consideration of the District of Columbia airport bill, Wagner secured the floor on behalf of the antilynching measure. This jeopardized carefully laid plans for an orderly adjournment free of controversy, and threw the chamber into a mild furor. After several maneuvers and no end of harsh commentary, the Senate recessed for the day.[31]

White learned of activity overnight designed to untangle the situation and postpone action on the bill, but Wagner was determined not to yield without extracting some advantage. Consequently, Barkley consented to make the antilynching bill a special order of business at the next regular session. After consulting White, who had been advised by Senators La Follette, Capper, and Clark to accept the arrangement, Wagner and Van Nuys agreed. White assured his colleagues in New York that the bill would be the second item taken up in the regular session or perhaps in any special session that might develop.³² Surely the Association hoped to get help in the future from those who had come to its defense that summer: Democrats Bennett Champ Clark of Missouri, Robert L. Bulkley of Ohio, William Ashurst of Arizona, Homer Bone of Washington, Sherman Minton of Indiana, J. Hamilton Lewis of Illinois, and Republican Arthur Capper of Kansas. Clark even went so far as to display pictures from Duck Hill on the Senate bulletin board. To the anger of southern members, the caption explained: "There Have Been *No* Arrests, *No* Indictments, and *No* Convictions of Any One of the Lynchers. This was *NOT* a rape case."³³

Agreeing to the postponement, the NAACP laid itself open to further criticisms. But it had rather small choice. White and Wagner recognized the hazards in attempting to break a filibuster at the end, rather than at the start, of a session. The New York Democrat confided: "I am absolutely convinced that this victory [the Senate commitment to make the measure an item of unfinished business] means the passage of the bill early next winter."³⁴ In any event, the Association had no way of forcing a vote and had ultimately to depend upon the good faith of elected representatives. Those lukewarm to the bill enjoyed the best of both worlds. They could assure the NAACP of their interest, but escape any personal responsibility for obstruction and delay by southern Democrats. Furthermore, whatever advantages black voters possessed in northern and midwestern metropolitan centers when lobbying in the House were effectively cancelled by the more traditional, statewide constituencies with whom senators had to deal. Afro-American political leverage was an emerging but still limited force.

Even in the liberal atmosphere of the 1930s, the black community lacked allies willing to sacrifice and perhaps suffer a little politically on its behalf. Wagner, Gavagan, Costigan, and a handful of others on occasion might properly be excepted. Certainly the Association had come tantalizingly close to its goal. That fall, for example, two southern Democrats, Senator Byron (Pat) Harrison of Mississippi and Congressman Samuel McReynolds of Tennessee, reportedly declared that the momentum for the antilynching bill had reached such proportions that southerners could no longer stem the tide; the measure would pass when the Senate reconvened. Perhaps such assertions were meant to pacify constituents in the event of enactment, but they revealed a great deal more. They showed that the NAACP had created a groundswell, if only reputed sympathizers—White counted seventy senators in favor, should the measure come to a vote—were willing to see the fight through to the end.³⁵ As it turned out, these alleged supporters proved inadequate to the task.

The bill's status evoked fresh concern on all sides when the recession forced the White House to call a special session of Congress for November 15. The NAACP wondered about the mid-August agreement with politicians who now faced such questions as crop control, wage-and-hour legislation, government reorganization, regional planning, taxation, and a review of antitrust legislation.[36] White feared congressional leaders might delay all "controversial" items until the regular session in January, and urged the branches and all friends of the measure to impress on their senators the need to reject any rule that might displace or postpone the Wagner–Van Nuys–Gavagan bill. To counter lawmakers who had attacked or who might attack the measure as unconstitutional, the NAACP legal staff prepared a list of various laws since 1907 for which those same legislators had voted and which the Supreme Court had later declared unconstitutional. When the special session opened and seemed ready to work on government reorganization (the first business on the calendar, the crop control bill, was not yet ready), White wired all senators pledged to the antilynching bill to honor the sense of the August resolution and take up the Association's measure at once. But, when Wagner moved consideration of H.R. 1507, Tom Connally (D–Texas), coordinator of the southern forces, rose in opposition.[37]

Connally presented a lengthy reading of past remarks against the antilynching bill by former Senator Hugo Black, a recent appointee to the United States Supreme Court. Restless with the Senate's inability to consider the administration's program, Majority Leader Barkley pleaded, "Mr. President, . . . is this a speech with a rubber terminal that lengthens as it goes?" "Apparently it lengthens as it goes," Bennett Clark replied disconsolately from the chair. Intermittently, Connally reminded Wagner that time spent on H.R. 1507 would hinder the execution of the president's relief program,[38] and he made barbed references to Walter White. Commenting on a meeting by members of the Judiciary Committee in his absence, Senator Connally announced,

> I understand they had this colored man in the meeting; I had no objection to his being a colored man. I am not prejudiced against colored men. I protect them in my State. . . . I cannot say what I heard [laughter], but there was a colored man up there, a fellow named White. He runs the Association for the Advancement of Colored People. I do not know what happened; I cannot say what happened because I was not there.[39]

Furthermore, Connally demanded to know who had displayed pictures of lynched black men in the Senate chamber; he resented it. Clark acknowledged his responsibility and declared: "I can very readily understand how it may be irksome to the Senator from Texas to have these exhibits presented. It may cause some faint flurry of that conscience for which the Senator from Texas used to be renowned, but which his conduct this week has led most of us to believe has become calloused." The placard, Clark chided, seemed already to have served its purpose. Of course it had, retorted Connally, who became so infuriated that he violated Senate rules with his language. He charged that the purpose lay in a search for headlines and protested "against the Senate being made a sewer for the vaporings of the Senator from Missouri."[40]

With the long-awaited farm bill ready at last, Barkley asked Wagner to abide by the August agreement and postpone H.R. 1507. On November 23, the New York Democrat received assurances from the chair that he could return to the question once the farm legislation had cleared. On that basis, he withdrew his motion for the antilynching bill, and the Senate turned to the president's program.[41] However, the bill's status remained in doubt. On December 11, White asked Wagner if opponents might try to move consideration of amendments to the housing act and thus forestall, once again, any work on the antilynching measure. The NAACP did not welcome the embarrassment of having accepted postponements in August and again in late November only to see the question put off once more. Unable to accomplish any of the administration's major objectives in the special session, Congress adjourned just before Christmas; but before doing so, the Senate (on Barkley's initiative) made H.R. 1507 a matter of designated business for the fourth day of the new session, January 6, 1938.[42] Friends and enemies alike, therefore, had a specific target date; and the struggle moved toward its dramatic climax.

The fight for an antilynching law had generated considerable attention. For example, as Table 5 indicates, two Gallup polls conducted by the American Institute of Public Opinion showed a predominantly affirmative response to the question, "should Congress enact a law which would make lynching a federal crime?"[43]

Table 5. Gallup Polls on Lynching Legislation, by Region and Group, 1937

Category	January 1937		November 1937	
	% Yes	% No	% Yes	% No
Regions				
Nation	70	30	72	28
New England	75	25	75	25
Middle Atlantic	72	28	79	21
East Central	77	23	77	23
West Central	70	30	78	22
South	65	35	57	43
Mountain	65	35	75	25
Pacific Coast	59	41	65	35
Groups				
Women	75	25	Not reported	
Young persons	77	23	Not reported	
Reliefers	72	28	Not reported	
Farmers	69	31	Not reported	
Small towns	75	25	Not reported	
Urban	70	30	Not reported	

Only the South, perhaps sensing the likelihood of passage, had cooled a bit toward the bill by the end of 1937. Still, it endorsed the measure. Moreover, the NAACP had drawn support from several of the major media. During the special session, Dorothy Dunbar Bromley (whose syndicated column appeared daily in the Scripps-Howard chain) criticized the recently appointed senator from Alabama, Dixie Bibb Graves, for her opposition to the bill in floor debate. On December 4, 130 women from all parts of the country sent the senator an open letter protesting her speech. And while the Senate wrestled with the question, the following articles appeared: "Dixie Rejects Lynching," by Virginius Dabney, in *The Nation* of November 27; "They Lynched the Wrong Man," by Will Irwin, in the December 4 issue of *Liberty* magazine; and an editorial, "Does Senator Connally Favor Lynching?" from the New York *Daily News* of November 24. White assured his Board that the national staff made excellent use of these pieces with members of the Senate.[44]

There was momentum. Even Jessie Daniel Ames of the Association of Southern Women for the Prevention of Lynching conceded, however reluctantly, that passage was imminent. Ames reported talk of disbanding the ASWPL once a federal law went into effect, although she personally thought it better that the group reassess its program "to make the law effective." An address prepared for the 1938 ASWPL meeting in Atlanta revealed the expectations of the moment:

> The passage of the anti-lynching law must not be considered as an isolated act and when accomplished will become a closed subject. It is the entering wedge to the whole legal status of Negroes in the South. The political balance of power held by Negroes in the two party states give [sic] to this race an effective leverage with which to pry loose other conditions which react both unfavorably and undemocratically on this minority group. . . . Two of these conditions are the disfranchisement of Negroes and the discrimination in our public educational system from primary thro [sic] graduate school. Fear which has been the motivation in lynching is increasing. With overt attacks on disfranchisement and education, this fear will be increased.[45]

Whatever their differences over priorities and procedures, the ASWPL and the NAACP realized that the fight for a federal antilynching law served a major purpose in the total scheme of improved race relations.

Despite signs of progress, troubles mounted as the new session unfolded. To White's alarm, Senator Borah proposed the elimination of the section penalizing counties.[46] As always, that remained a ready target for the opposition. But Borah did not stop there. When Vice President Garner announced consideration of the antilynching bill on January 6, the Idaho Republican and William King (D–Utah) joined fifteen southern Democrats in launching a six-week filibuster that exhibited a mixture of constitutional traditionalism, political expediency, and outright racist slurs.[47]

In "recognition" of his work, White came under direct attack when Senator Byrnes of South Carolina warned members:

> One Negro, whose name has heretofore been mentioned in the debate—Walter White, secretary of the Association for the Advancement of Colored People—has ordered this bill to pass. If a majority can bring about a vote, the bill will pass. . . .
> What legislation will he next demand of the Congress of the United States? I do not know. Will he demand that Congress will enact legislation to punish officials of a State who fail to protect Negroes in the right to stop at hotels where white persons are entertained . . . ? Will he demand the enactment of laws providing for the supervision of elections within the States? I do not know; but I know he will make other demands.

Whether or not he thought back to Walter White when the Civil Rights Acts of 1957, 1960, 1964, 1965, and 1968 went into effect, the South Carolinian was clearly worried about the future in 1938. His Mississippi counterpart, Theodore Bilbo, more typically looked to an earlier age of political rhetoric when he fulminated,

> Mr. President, I may inquire, what Senator . . . will not understand that the underlying motive of the Ethiopian who has inspired this proposed legislation, the antilynching bill, and desires its enactment into law with a zeal and frenzy equal if not paramount to the lust and lasciviousness of the rape fiend in his diabolical effort to despoil the womanhood of the Caucasian race, is to realize the consummation of his dream and ever-abiding hope and most fervent prayer to become socially and politically equal to the white man.[48]

As the filibuster unfolded and opponents continued to control the tone, substance, and direction of debate, dismay prevailed at the NAACP. On January 15, Roy Wilkins confided to Houston the uneasiness that he and others felt over "the one-sided harangue which is going on in Washington." The New York *Daily News*, which had once endorsed the measure, now reversed itself in deference to southern arguments and suggested dropping the bill. And George Norris of Nebraska, who acknowledged the noble purpose of the legislation, reportedly worried that the racial bitterness raised in the debate might prove a greater price than the Senate wished to pay. Wilkins saw nothing but disaster in these developments: "we have plenty of friends in the Senate who are willing to argue at length and effectively on the question. . . . we have few men who are willing to go down the line in a nasty discussion involving the race question."[49]

On the basis of conversations with a liberal academician recently back from an extended southern visit, Joel Spingarn reported opposition to the antilynching bill among southern reformers. Apparently, they feared it would hinder liberalism's acceptance and progress in the region. According to Spingarn's informant, the fact that some twenty southern newspapers had responded favorably to the bill hardly outweighed overall sentiments in the area. Spingarn added matter-of-factly, "perhaps it might depress Walter too much to tell him."[50] In addition, Wilkins sent a lengthy letter to Board member Charles Edward Russell, which expressed the gloom hanging over the national office. Friends in both parties, with concurrence from the White House, had let the South dominate debate. Wilkins charged betrayal in a "gentlemen's agreement" that allowed supporters of the bill to avoid the embarrassment of a showdown vote. Van Nuys had failed the cause and even Wagner seemed to falter. Only Matthew Neely (D–West Virginia) had thus far gotten the floor to deliver a speech in support of the measure.[51] Northern as well as southern liberals were still long on words and hope, but decidedly short on deeds.

Wilkins had referred to a plan to let the filibusterers talk themselves out before the Senate majority took the floor and passed the bill, but after three weeks, it was clearly time for more aggressive and forthright action. On January 27, the bill's supporters tried for cloture, the parliamentary technique to limit debate. Under Rule 22, adopted in 1917, that required a two-thirds consent of members present and voting. The Senate, however, rejected this first of two cloture moves, 37 to 51. When the Majority Leader asked about the bill's future in the face of new and pressing legislative business, Wagner replied evasively, "I shall stand firmly for the passage of this measure, which I regard as important, and in which I believe, so long as a majority of the Senators who likewise believe in it will stand with me."[52]

Ill during early phases of the debate, Wagner took the floor on February 3 in a lengthy, comprehensive defense of the antilynching bill, a defense that exhibited the NAACP's care in providing legislative friends with essential materials.[53] There was little, though, that Wagner and others could do at this point to lift the Association's spirits—short of an open, sustained effort to break the filibuster and win passage. But that did not materialize. The following weekend, White felt the need to get away from Washington, and he returned to New York to confer with colleagues at the national office. By this time, hope and despair were simply matters of degree. Wilkins observed that while the secretary "is not optimistic enough to believe that we can pass this bill except through some miracle, he is by no means as discouraged as he was a week ago."[54]

From the capital, another and somewhat larger problem now imperiled the campaign. On February 10, the White House issued its relief message calling for an emergency appropriation of $250 million to ease the strain of recession unemployment. The urban communities of the North and West, where the strongest political endorsement for antilynching legislation originated, also comprised the areas most anxious for relief appropriations. As a result, White and his associates once again, as in the summer and late fall of 1937, found themselves both unable to overcome southern obstructionism and simultaneously put in the awkward position of seeming, by any further stubbornness, to obstruct "larger" programs deemed important to the administration and the national economy.[55]

Since delays might risk widespread alienation among nominal supporters of the antilynching bill, who, for the most part, had yet to display their commitment through overt action, Wagner submitted a second cloture petition to the chair in mid-February. No Republicans signed Wagner's appeal, but Robert M. La Follette (Progressive-Wisconsin) and sixteen Democrats, including Van Nuys, Truman of Missouri, and future Supreme Court Justice Sherman Minton of Indiana, did.[56] Their effort, however, failed: on February 16, the Senate rejected cloture by a vote of 42 to 46. The antilynching bill was in truly desperate straits. By unanimous consent, members allowed Louisiana's Allen Ellender to yield without losing the floor, and the Senate turned to other matters.[57]

Facing a crisis that threatened to erase completely its achievements in the Seventy-fifth Congress (the defeat of the Mitchell Bill, the discharge petition, and House passage of the Gavagan bill; the assignment of the antilynching bill as a special order of business and its centrality during six long weeks of Senate filibuster), the Association sought anxiously to determine if anything could save the measure and bring it to a vote. White sent urgent messages to Barkley and to Roosevelt on February 18; he implored them to set a day on which the Senate could reconsider the bill.[58] Eager to keep the drive going, White sought emergency funds from William Rosenwald and the officers of seven major branches.[59] On Saturday the nineteenth, Wagner met with White and Houston in Arthur Spingarn's office to plan their next move, but pressures of the national economy intervened. White learned from WPA authorities in Washington that unless the $250 million was immediately appropriated, some 500,000 persons needing relief could not be placed on the agency's rolls, and, in addition, some 445,000 others would be dropped between March 1 and June 1. Hoping to protect the integrity of both the antilynching bill and the relief measures, White and Houston requested the majority leader to designate March 28 for resumption of debate on the antilynching bill. At first Barkley seemed amenable, but he later reported to Wagner that Connally, Bilbo, and several others threatened to filibuster just as vigorously against this procedure as they had against any attempt to bring the antilynching bill to the floor. Evidently these southerners did not "give a damn" about the general legislative situation, since their section would receive a much smaller share of relief money than the major industrial cities.[60]

On February 21, Barkley took the floor to lament the Senate's inability to terminate debate and bring questions to a vote. However, since other bills needed attention and cloture appeared impossible, he asked that the Senate move on to vote relief appropriations. When Wagner sought to amend by reserving March 28 for debate on the antilynching bill, the vice president sustained Senator Connally's point of order in objection. After a lively exchange between Wagner and certain southern members, and a clash between Barkley and McNary over whose party had done more damage to the bill, the chamber voted 58 to 22 to sustain the Barkley motion. The antilynching bill had been displaced and, in effect, buried. Even Wagner and Van Nuys conceded: 2 of the 58 yeas were theirs.[61] A major climax in the NAACP's determined fight for a federal law had come, and had gone. Nothing in subsequent campaigns would ever again equal it.

The failure to enact the bill, however, did not imply defeat for the Association's campaign against mob violence or for its broader goals of equal justice. Over four years of intensive efforts had forced the American people to confront the most brutal aspects of racism. The lesson, however painful to acknowledge and absorb, helped in significant ways to prepare the national conscience for reforms that would follow in the next quarter century. This relentless process of education was desperately needed at a time of domestic economic collapse and mounting international crises, when the black community might very well have found itself totally written off the agenda of national affairs. Probing, exposing, hammering away incessantly to keep the plight of black people visible in the press and political arena proved inestimably valuable. If the lesson was poorly learned or badly applied, the fault lay with the nation and not with the NAACP.

The campaign against lynching had brought the Association itself to a new level of national attention. Walter White's picture on the cover of *Time* magazine's January 24, 1938, issue and the accompanying feature story on the antilynching struggle demonstrated that. And as Wilkins reminded the Board at its monthly meeting in April:

> . . . everyone recognizes that the Association, as well as the campaign against lynching received unparalleled publicity. As a consequence . . . the prestige of the NAACP has been increased tremendously. . . . It now remains for us to take the fullest advantage of the prestige and publicity in order to secure more members and to build a more effective Association.

NAACP leaders hoped that their forthcoming annual conference would provide the "means through which we will consolidate the gains of the antilynching fight and strengthen our machinery."[62] Nonetheless, there still remained the dilemma of what to do in the wake of the Senate defeat.

White asked the Board about introducing a federal voting-rights bill and about the possible consequences of such a move for the antilynching measure. The national office had issued a press release on March 4 about the need for black citizens to register and vote, a proposal that the *Afro-American* championed in print the next day.[63] Writing from the Virgin Islands, where he served as judge of the federal District Court, William Hastie urged fresh NAACP initiative with bipartisan sponsorship of a voting bill that would catch Association opponents off stride and not preclude the possibility of attaching the antilynching bill as a rider to some other measure. White thought such a move might induce southern senators "to yield on the anti-lynching bill as the lesser of two evils" but recognized the reluctance of Houston and others at headquarters to launch another congressional campaign so soon after the filibuster.[64]

When the Board met in April, the Committee on Administration put forth a seven-point program: action on President Roosevelt's suggestion (at his March 22 press conference) for lynching inquiries by the Federal Bureau of Investigation; continuation of the campaign for the Wagner–Van Nuys–Gavagan antilynching bill; introduction of a voting bill, or one or more years of preparation before sponsoring such a measure; continuation of the struggle against educational inequalities; continuation of the fight for equal rights on public projects; protection for black workers in civil service opportunities; and efforts for the just treatment of black people in school textbooks. Although the Board adopted these recommendations, members knew the problems beyond their immediate control. The antilynching bill had failed. Roosevelt's proposal might prove a mere diversionary tactic; the Association had often feared as much in years past, and had no ready assurance that FBI and Justice Department agents in the South represented a dependable counterweight to racism.[65] The introduction of a meaningful voting-rights measure required extensive preparations, while the black community continued to suffer damaging economic discriminations in both public and private employment. The Board finally chose to stress equal rights in publicly sponsored projects and in the civil service.[66] The decision seemed more a weary statement of intent than a vigorous plan for action.

On Capitol Hill, the fight for the antilynching bill strained relations rather badly between White and Senate Minority Leader Charles McNary. Despite reminders that he and several Republicans had voted for cloture on other measures in the past, the senator bristled at the Association's public rebuke of him and certain party members for refusing to do so on the Wagner-Gavagan bill. He pleaded that a beleaguered senatorial minority must always protect itself by endorsing the principle of unlimited debate and promised thereafter to withhold any help for antilynching bills so long as Walter White had direct involvement with them.[67] Seeking to mollify a disappointed black community, John Hamilton, chairman of the Republican National Committee, defended the concept of unlimited debate, and suggested that the NAACP level its anger at the White House and the huge (76 to 16) Democratic majority in the Senate.[68]

Apparently the southern filibuster had caused some political uneasiness among leading Democrats. A spokesman for James Farley, for example, assured representatives of the black press in mid-February that the president was not indifferent to the measure. And, in the aftermath of controversy and recriminations over the bill's defeat, Roosevelt did publicly propose an alternative whereby the government would investigate all lynchings and make reports to the administration, the Congress, and the nation at large.[69] Although skeptical, since friends in Washington found no evidence of Roosevelt's having discussed the matter with anybody in either house, the NAACP viewed the idea as evidence of administration concern over political reprisals. That seemed a reasonable interpretation, especially when Walter White's telegram asking a special conference with the president brought a return phone call from White House secretary Marvin McIntyre within a mere hour after the wire had been sent.[70] Shortly thereafter, Roosevelt received an all-black delegation headed by White, and composed of Frances Williams (of the national board of the YWCA), Charlotte Hawkins Brown (president of the Palmer Memorial Institute of Sedalia, North Carolina), George E. Haynes (of the Federal Council of Churches), A. Philip Randolph (of the Brotherhood of Sleeping Car Porters, and the National Negro Congress), and editor Carl Murphy (of the *Afro-American*) to talk about the antilynching bill. As usual, the session produced no tangible results. But Roosevelt acknowledged the antilynching campaign's significance to black people, and White concluded that the meeting had also underscored the importance of the black vote in future elections.[71]

The black community rallied to the antilynching fight. It made black men and women in the South more politically conscious, and stirred demands for equal rights nationally. White got requests to speak before black groups in Atlanta, Birmingham, New Orleans, Mobile, Richmond, and even Senator Ellender's home town in Louisiana. White took these and invitations from several smaller communities in the Deep South as a measure of the black community's courage to mobilize openly in the wake of the campaign. Elsewhere, he addressed overflow crowds in Cleveland, Detroit, and Toledo.[72] James Weldon Johnson's tragic death in an auto-train collision in early summer of 1938 further intensified public awareness, especially because in commenting on his many-sided career reporters and columnists re-examined his role in leading the drive for the Dyer bill.[73] Certainly one incident in June 1938 graphically confirmed the significance of Johnson's and White's efforts. According to press reports, some 3,000 armed black people formed a cordon around the jail in Coatesville, Pennsylvania, to prevent the rumored abduction and lynching of a twenty-year-old black man charged with attacking a white woman. As it turned out, the victim and her companion subsequently testified to the prisoner's innocence. But the prompt, determined, successful stand of the black community contrasted sharply with the frightful lynching of Zach Walker in the same town twenty-seven years before—an event that had mobilized the NAACP against mob violence. The *Afro-American* praised the black people of Coatesville and tied the decline in lynching to the struggle for the antilynching bill. In a companion column, Kelly Miller identified Walter White as an authentic moral hero for his relentless fight against lynching.[74]

Meanwhile, John P. Davis and the National Negro Congress

responded to the antilynching campaign in ways that further signaled its importance. The NNC made strenuous efforts to hold rallies, conferences, and fund-raising drives to revive the issue in Congress. Always suspicious of Davis and his group, White believed that they wished to capitalize on the publicity and momentum generated by the NAACP. During and after the filibuster, Davis called for strategy meetings on the antilynching bill, the wages-and-hours measure, and other progressive legislation, but several organizations joined the Association in refusing to participate. Nonetheless, Davis went ahead on March 19. Conferees endorsed resolutions to establish a nationwide antilynching committee with local units, a special antilynching fund, and mass demonstrations on behalf of the antilynching bill and the Scottsboro defendants; and pledged themselves to bring pressure on the NAACP, the CIO, the AFL, the Federal Council of Churches, and labor's Non-Partisan League for immediate cooperation with the National Negro Congress. The *Daily Worker* and the ILD supported Davis, and the New York committee of the Communist party announced plans for a mass demonstration in Union Square on April 9 to urge immediate enactment of the antilynching bill.[75] While genuine cooperation between them remained unlikely, the NNC and the NAACP each recognized the significance of the campaign against lynching and its impact on black Americans.

From their own perspectives, southern conservatives and reformers watched and maneuvered. Tom Connally was no liberal on race matters. Though he had often backed the president before the 1937 Court battle, the big Texan with the black string tie and broad-brimmed hat paid his respects to powerful oil and financial interests back home and proved an able, imaginative foe of the NAACP's antilynching bill. Southern senators followed his lead against civil rights measures, and he took the "honor" seriously. Arming for the task, Connally gathered extensive data on lynching from such diverse sources as Senate colleagues, Texas sheriffs, southern governors, and the U.S. Census Bureau; he was at the hub of a lively communications network committed to defeating the Wagner-Gavagan bills whenever they surfaced in the upper house.[76] In late January 1938, for example, Jessie Daniel Ames of the Association of Southern Women for the Prevention of Lynching wrote him. An advocate of local initiative against mob violence, Ames expressed gratification at the bill's troubles in the Senate, but warned that the South was now, more than ever, compelled to stop lynching. As if to reassure her, Connally replied that during the filibuster Senator McKellar of Tennessee had sent telegrams to the governors asking them to prevent lynching through the full use of existing state authority, and he hoped for ASWPL backing in such a drive.[77] Ames exchanged several detailed and cordial letters with Connally, as she had done with Hatton Sumners in days past. She thanked the senator for his willingness to help in the apprehension and punishment of mob members, if any more lynchings occurred in the South that year—an expression of intent he never implemented. She also enclosed a copy of an ASWPL committee report that urged six steps against violence: an extensive campaign of public education, direct local action, a detailed study of any federal antilynching law that might pass, an expansion of gubernatorial powers against lynching, a change of venue in lynching trials, and a wider use of radio contact among highway patrol cars to hasten preventive reactions.[78]

Not long after, Ames added another item to her list of remedies, a law permitting federal investigations of mob violence. Roosevelt had publicly endorsed the idea in the spring, and she tried (apparently without success) to interest Connally in the matter. Ames wrote in mid-July to remind him that he had not responded to the proposal, and she wished now to press him on the need for federal investigations. She reported her conversation with Senator Walter George (D–Georgia), who agreed that a bill of that sort should be introduced by a southern member of the upper house. It might deter lynchings by strengthening the position and the determination of southern sheriffs.[79] Connally was not much impressed. Whether Jessie Daniel Ames and her associates in the ASWPL and in the Commission on Interracial Cooperation responded on their own to Roosevelt's proposal for federal investigations, or whether he used them to promote the idea from within the South, is uncertain. Surely the president, especially with his frequent visits to the polio treatment center in Warm Springs, Georgia, and his friendships with George Foster Peabody, Will Alexander, and Aubrey Williams, among others, had ample opportunity for encouraging southern whites to back his recommendation as an alternative to the Wagner-Gavagan measure. The president was deeply involved in trying to effect changes in the South. He had consulted Clark Foreman and other southern liberals about the National Economic Council's "Report on the Economic Conditions of the South," delivered to the White House on July 25, 1938. And following an introduction by Eleanor Roosevelt, the president had also encouraged Alabaman Joseph Gelders in June to launch a campaign from within the South against the poll tax. Gelders organized the interracial Southern Conference for Human Welfare, whose first convention met in Birmingham that fall.[80]

Meanwhile, Southern liberals found themselves caught in the backwash of Roosevelt's efforts to influence the 1938 congressional primaries and elections. The attempt to replace conservative obstructionists with liberal, New Deal Democrats failed. Perhaps the president mistook his general popularity in the region as a measure of political influence at the local level; perhaps he too easily misread the primary victories of Alabama's Lister Hill in January and Florida's Claude Pepper in May as signs of revitalized southern liberalism. In any event, Roosevelt failed to dislodge Walter George of Georgia, "Cotton Ed" Smith of South Carolina, or Millard Tydings of Maryland—even though he succeeded nearer to home in displacing John J. O'Connor of New York, who chaired the powerful House Rules Committee.[81] The abortive purge evoked considerable resentment among those the White House sought to rally. In late August, for example, Jessie Daniel Ames wrote to her ASWPL colleague, Bertha Newell, that Georgia had split into two distinct political groups, conservative and liberal. She felt compelled to back Walter George over the New Deal candidate, Lawrence Camp, even though Senator George regularly had the support of forces she detested. But now, thanks to Roosevelt, Georgians would be voting not for Camp or for George, but on the question of outside interference.[82]

Disillusionment with New Deal politics hurt the drive for any federal antilynching law that originated with the NAACP and the northern-based civil rights forces. Ames and her friends persisted in their determination to combat mob violence in their own way. For example, she wrote to Connally in September: "This job of stopping lynching without a federal law such as the ones which were under consideration is my indulgence in the way of an avocation." She pursued that pastime resolutely. Two years later, after the NAACP had once again driven the Gavagan bill through the House but failed to bring it to a vote in the Senate, Ames and her associates still lobbied the Texas Democrat to endorse measures that would provide federal investigations of lynching and the presentation of evidence to grand juries.[83] But Connally remained unresponsive.

During the two-year period from mid-1938 to the summer of 1940, the NAACP renewed its efforts to secure a federal antilynching law, although the campaign lacked its former primacy in the Association's overall programs. From a recent high of twenty in 1935, the number of reported lynchings had dropped to eight each in 1936 and 1937, six in 1938, three in 1939, and five in 1940.[84] The need for protection against lynchings continued; the chances of convincing the federal government to undertake corrective steps receded. In mid-July 1938, for example, Senator Wagner asked the attorney general to probe the lynchings at Rolling Fork, Mississippi, and Arabi, Georgia, but Cummings stubbornly maintained that the Department of Justice could not act without statutory authorization.[85] In September the *Afro-American* ran stories on two lynchings that had escaped notice in the national press; the editors had already charged that the South deliberately withheld information about recent lynchings, because it feared the consequences of a renewed drive in Congress.[86] With the problem of violence unresolved and the black community still vulnerable to physical attack, the NAACP proceeded with plans for the Seventy-sixth Congress. By mid-November White informed his Board that William Hastie had completed a fresh draft of the antilynching bill.[87]

Of course, any hopes for success in Washington depended upon the Association's ability to mobilize a dedicated support among ranking members of both parties, a task it seemed increasingly unable to accomplish. Rather than the NAACP manipulating the politicians, the politicians manipulated the NAACP. Washington, after all, has always been a center of differential power relationships, a city in which influence, not justice, regularly dominates. For nearly three decades the NAACP had demonstrated how the voice of organized black protest could work effectively, on specific issues, with its political, labor, church, civic, and liberal-reformist counterparts. The Association operated on the belief that direct contacts with leadership figures and real or alleged public support would facilitate change. Neither the most satisfactory personal relationships nor a general consensus, however, nor both together, could assure the passage of items distasteful to a powerfully entrenched political minority.

The NAACP moved at the center of national politics; such people as Frank Murphy and Felix Frankfurter served on the NAACP legal committee, Harold Ickes had once been an officer of the Chicago branch, and Walter White became fast friends with Justice Hugo Black, New Deal administrators Aubrey Williams and Oscar Chapman, and Eleanor Roosevelt, among others.[88] But the Association had very few tangible rewards to distribute in a city that thrived on "benefits bestowed" for "value received." The NAACP undoubtedly had justice, but not influence, on its side, it had contacts but not power, appeals but not pay-off. It played the lobbying game in an energetic, straightforward, and thoroughly honest fashion but continuously had to sacrifice portions of its objectives in the game of trade-off, and repeatedly saw its interests simply discounted by those who had more leverage or, by their own definition, more pressing needs. That, of course, had always been the lot of the lobbyist, but when that lobbyist was black and represented an oppressed minority, the difficulties mounted many times over.

That his trouble persisted during a liberal presidency, no less than in those of Harding, Coolidge, and Hoover, galled Walter White. By the late 1930s the NAACP had worked its way into the New Deal coalition. In doing so, the Association became a captive of that coalition and found itself assigned a rather distant back seat on the New Deal bus. The diminished success of the Democratic party in the off-year congressional elections of 1938, and the president's failure to "purge" the Seventy-sixth Congress, even on a selective basis, heightened the black community's vulnerability, especially since it lacked reasonable political alternatives outside the Roosevelt coalition. Shortly after the November election, White wrote John Hamilton of the Republican National Committee about information that the party had decided against any further efforts to woo black voters, and would make a bid instead for white southerners. The secretary protested that whatever resentments Afro-Americans harbored toward the GOP stemmed from its indifference to the needs of black people and not from any expedient commitment on their part to New Deal programs. He warned, moreover, that rumors of an impending anti-New Deal coalition between Republicans and southern Democrats would have damaging consequences for American race relations.[89]

The retirement of Homer Cummings and the appointment of Frank Murphy (former governor of Michigan, mayor of Detroit, and trial judge during the second Sweet case) as attorney general early in 1939 did relatively little to resolve the Association's dilemmas. In late January, White wrote to Murphy to applaud the latter's proposal for a new Justice Department unit charged with the preservation of civil liberties and to offer NAACP assistance.[90] Nonetheless, just how active or effective such an office might be remained a mystery in the weeks that followed. In March, when an issue of *KEN* magazine reported that Murphy would investigate all lynchings and submit his findings to Congress, White wrote the Justice Department to ascertain the accuracy of the article. The uncertainty persisted. When planning a program for 1940, the Association's Committee on Administration recommended a number of items, among them "Legislation, including the Anti-Lynching Bill—*depending in large measure upon what the federal government will do on the reported plan of the Department of Justice to investigate all lynchings.*"[91] Once again the NAACP found itself in the awkward position of waiting for a clarification of federal policies before setting its own course, and hopes for swift government action proved highly premature. In April 1939, W. F. Caldwell, Associated Press news editor in Atlanta, wrote R. B. Eleazer of the Commission on Interracial Cooperation that early reports from Washington suggesting Murphy's civil liberties unit would probe all lynchings seemed unfounded; he had checked with a Justice Department aide and learned that plans for the new unit were by no means so comprehensive.[92]

On the Hill, Congress proved no more anxious than the Justice Department to undertake a vigorous fight against mob violence. Members diverted their attention from racist violence at home by concerning themselves with impending and actual violence abroad. The Seventy-sixth Congress met in three sessions consuming a total of 625 days from January 3, 1939, to January 3, 1941. During that period Germany seized Czechoslovakia, the Molotov–Von Ribbentrop pact was sealed, Poland was invaded, France fell, the Battle of Britain took place, Japanese aggression in Asia intensified, and the Axis partnership of Germany, Italy, and Japan was formalized. Congress revised American neutrality legislation by repealing the arms embargo and authorizing a "cash and carry" system, accelerated the nation's own preparedness measures, acquiesced in the president's exchange of fifty destroyers for the use of British naval and air bases in the Western Hemisphere, passed the Smith Act for internal security purposes, and legislated the country's first peacetime draft. And, it watched with mixed emotions as Franklin Roosevelt won an unprecedented third election to the White House. Such an array of extraordinary events hardly represented a setting in which the Congress would forthrightly address itself to racial injustices, especially since it had so persistently declined to do so under more tranquil domestic circumstances.[93]

In January 1939, congressman Gavagan again introduced the Association's antilynching bill, while Wagner, Van Nuys, and Capper acted as cosponsors in the Senate. Although the NAACP had agreed to make the opening fight in the upper house, delays in appointing a Judiciary subcommittee and in setting a date for hearings interfered. Meanwhile, Gavagan reported impatience among a number of House members anxious to consider the bill immediately. Forced to respond, the Association scrapped its plan and wrote to 326 representatives to ask that they sign Gavagan's discharge petition.[94] Suddenly, partisan enthusiasms, and perhaps speculation about the black vote in 1940, surfaced to complicate matters further. *Two* discharge petitions appeared on the Speaker's desk, one sponsored by Democrat Gavagan and the other by Republican Hamilton Fish of New York. By May 3, the former contained ninety-five signatures and the latter forty, but House rules did not allow a cumulative count. Accordingly, White asked House Minority Leader Joseph Martin, Jr., if he could persuade signers of the Fish petition to transfer their support to Gavagan's list. Martin agreed, though he doubted action on the bill in the current session. Fish and Gavagan finally combined their petitions, and by late July the measure had the necessary 218 signatures.[95] But Congress adjourned shortly thereafter with no vote on the bill. Seven months had elasped without passage in either house.

When the special session opened in late September, things were no better. Several Washington correspondents claimed that the antilynching bill might be used to forestall changes in the neutrality laws. The NAACP immediately wired Roosevelt and issued a statement declaring that if the president wished the session to confine its attentions to war-related matters, antilynching campaigners would cooperate by waiting until the regular session in January. If, however, Congress should deal with domestic questions, then friends of the bill would not willingly sacrifice its status in the House.[96]

While indifference, expediency, and competing issues impaired the antilynching measure in political circles, the Association's concern with other matters increasingly jeopardized the bill's standing within the NAACP. After the failure to surmount the filibuster in the Seventy-fifth Congress, several NAACP staff members had swung around to Houston's view. They advised White that there were just too many other demands facing the Association to continue the congressional antilynching drive at its past levels of intensity. Some colleagues doubted the bill could ever be rammed through the Senate. No one wanted to drop the fight against violence; it simply had to be reconciled with the organization's current tasks.[97] Accordingly, near the end of 1939, White reported and the Board endorsed an ambitious list of activities for the months ahead. These included amendments to Wagner's federal aid-to-health bill to insure an equitable distribution of money in those states having separate facilities for black people, changes in the federal aid-to-education bill, renewed pursuit of a federal antilynching law, further work in the campaign for educational equality, maintenance of legal defense activities to the extent permitted by available funds, continued efforts to secure justice for black workers in federally financed projects, a study of discrimination in labor unions, continuation of the campaign against anti-black propaganda in school textbooks and current literature, a fresh drive to raise funds for the antilynching and legal defense work through the sale of "Stop Lynching" buttons, and improved coordination between the branches and the national office.[98] This broad range of projects and the impending international crisis, which raised anew the issue of black people's roles in defense-related industries and the military services, would eventually induce the NAACP to curtail the time and energies spent on the antilynching bill. Yet, for the moment, it held its place among major priorities, pending developments in Congress.

In late November, Arthur Spingarn, White, and Thurgood Marshall met with Hamilton Fish and Joseph Gavagan at the latter's New York office to plan a bipartisan effort. Not long after, on January 10, 1940, the bill passed the House of Representatives (for the second time in three years, the third time in eighteen years, and the last time ever)[99] by a margin of 252 to 131. Again, however, the Senate proved unyielding, once committee hearings had ended in mid-March.[100] During those hearings, Association witnesses offered little that was different from previous years, except for an overt effort to relate lynching and racism to contemporary world problems, an approach sanctioned by the NAACP Board since, at least, the end of 1938. White declared that antidemocratic forces on the right and the left opposed the antilynching bill because they hoped black people would withhold their allegiance from American society.[101] In his testimony, Arthur Spingarn invoked the international theme with references to newspaper articles from Italy, Japan, the Soviet Union, and parts of South America that dealt with race and mob violence in the United States. He specifically cited a piece from the January 28, 1938, issue of *Voelkischer Beobachter*, the Nazi party organ, which characterized American treatment of black people as less humane than Germany's own conduct toward Jews. The argument that America must reform its racial customs to improve its image abroad was still taking root.[102] The concept would, of course, have wider currency during the war against Nazi Germany and wider endorsement still in the era of cold war tensions and Third World decolonization after 1945.

Simultaneously, NAACP executives renewed their efforts at the White House, where secretary Edwin M. Watson sought to keep them at arms length from a busy president. Finally, on February 7, White and Arthur Spingarn met with Roosevelt, but the results were disappointing.

When the chief executive again suggested a bill empowering the FBI to investigate mob violence, Spingarn bluntly told him that such a step, at that point, would do little good and would fail to win approval among those pressing for the antilynching bill. There was even a rumor in the capital that Vice President Garner hoped to advance his chances for a presidential nomination by steering to a vote a Senate bill of his own allowing FBI investigations of lynching cases, but that did not materialize.[103]

Maintaining an alert public response proved difficult. Many people by the late 1930s were prepared to accept southern arguments that lynchings were, or would soon be, a thing of the past. Accordingly, the NAACP had to convince America that racist brutality, intimidation, and death persisted, even if the number of reported lynchings indicated a drop in frequency. As usual, finances remained a problem. David Dubinsky of the International Ladies Garment Workers Union promised to increase his group's contribution of $200, if the Amalgamated Clothing Workers and the CIO would also contribute; the ACW's Sidney Hillman told White he would poll his Board about the money. By February, the latest "Stop Lynching" button sales had yielded only $2,319, and the special antilynching fund had a deficit of $3,141; two months later the button revenue reached only $3,657, while the fund deficit remained $2,779.[104]

The Association knew that its capacity to raise money depended in no small measure on the public's sense of urgency. "We face, frankly, the fact that there have been no considerable number of horrible lynchings to make the public—even the Negro public—lynching conscious," White confessed to Daisy Lampkin late in November 1939. But he hoped that Howard Kester's findings, about the work of small committees chosen to kill black victims secretly, might quicken national awareness. The fact that Kester believed there had been twenty such lynchings in Mississippi alone during the previous year helped to explain White's dogged determination to secure a federal statute. Trying to promote the cause, Senators Neely and Wagner agreed (Senators McNary and Democrat A. B. Chandler of Kentucky declined) to participate in a coast-to-coast broadcast explaining the need for a Senate vote. On the night of April 29, Arthur Spingarn, Wagner, Capper, and Neely discussed the antilynching bill over the NBC blue network.[105]

With the bill languishing in the Senate, relations grew tense between the NAACP and Majority Leader Alben Barkley. On April 2, the Association sent him a sharp letter about frequent Washington reports that a filibuster would prevail because no honest efforts would be made to force a floor vote. Barkley's lengthy and rather testy reply accused the NAACP of understating his cooperation and attempting to incite his constituents through the use of the Louisville *Defender*. White responded immediately with a detailed five-page letter that left no doubt about the NAACP's distress with the Senate leadership's failure to utilize every available tactic for cloture.[106]

In July, the NAACP commended Barkley for his alleged assurances to black delegates at the Democratic national convention in Chicago that the antilynching bill would get to a vote before the session ended. When the majority leader denied any such promise, the Association obtained a stenographic report of his remarks and circulated excerpts to the public:

> It [the antilynching bill] has now been reported by committee, and the reason why we haven't taken it up is because we have been concerned with our national defense, but I can say this—that this bill will be brought up and it would not surprise me, in fact, it is my opinion, that the bill may be voted upon before this Congress shall have adjourned.[107]

Although differences existed in its dealings with each, the NAACP found itself over the years unable to reach agreement with the Lodges, the Borahs, the McNarys, and the Barkleys on what they had or had not said, had or had not done, would or would not do about the antilynching bill. Evidently politicians remained unwilling to risk their reputations or working relationships within the "World's Greatest Club" in a direct commitment to black people's needs. Republican Senator Arthur Vandenberg of Michigan summed up the situation accurately when he asserted that Senate friends of the antilynching bill had never tried to break a filibuster with the main weapon at their disposal, round-the-clock sessions with a quorum intact.[108] Whether or not Senate leaders and sponsors could have forced a vote remains an intriguing historical question; the point is that they failed to make a genuine effort to do so.

By the fall of 1940, the full Senate had done nothing about the antilynching bill, even though the Judiciary Committee had reported the measure favorably on March 25.[109] For a full half year nothing had happened. In October, Warren Barbour of New Jersey read the Senate a letter from Walter White that urged action before adjournment and referred to "the seven lynchings" that had occurred that year.[110] When Barbour asked consideration of the bill, Barkley demurred. Current legislative complexities, past experiences with filibusters, and repeated failures to obtain cloture made the whole business impracticable, he declared. Barkley acknowledged the NAACP's urgent efforts to obtain a vote, and gratuitously chided the Association for its "insistent and sometimes peremptory demands that, regardless of anything else, the antilynching bill be brought forward for consideration in the Senate." Expressing hope that it might come up early in the next session, Barkley confessed that he and Minority Leader McNary had polled their colleagues and found little enthusiasm for the measure under existing circumstances. With that, the Senate moved into executive session and laid the antilynching bill to rest.[111]

The question of federal protections for black citizens continued to have too little priority at both ends of Pennsylvania Avenue. Democrats had no intention of risking party unity, especially in a presidential election year. Republicans had no inclination to jeopardize their ties with conservative Democrats, whose cooperation they welcomed against other liberal-reformist measures. The death of the antilynching bill in October seemed all the more curious in view of McNary's reported assurance to White on May 10 that a majority of GOP senators would vote for cloture if necessary to break the filibuster, an encouraging prediction that White had then shared with Barkley.[112] That both major parties could dismiss the bill only a month before Franklin Roosevelt's bid for an unprecedented third term underscored the prevailing assumption that, come what may, black voters would heavily favor the Democrats.[113] There would occur one more sustained push for a federal antilynching law, in the years 1947 to 1950, but the most intensive phase had ended. From 1882 to 1933, 61 antilynching bills were introduced in Congress; from 1934 to 1940, 130; from 1941 to 1951, 66.[114] When the Seventy-seventh Congress opened in 1941, six members (Gavagan of New York, Arthur Mitchell of Illinois, U. S. Guyer of Kansas, Lee E. Geyer of California, Bartlett Jonkman of Michigan, and Louis Ludlow of Indiana) sponsored antilynching measures, but nothing came of them. No antilynching bill was successfully reported from committee in either 1941 or 1942.[115] It was an idea whose time had gone.

8

Expanded Programs of War and Postwar Years, 1941-1947

With the expansion of NAACP activities in the 1940s, the antilynching bill ceased to be the organization's primary legislative objective. Nonetheless, whatever protest momentum, political contacts, public visibility, community support, and staff competence the Association could boast were owed, in part, to the antilynching campaigns. Not surprisingly, Walter White continued to argue that mob terror and physical intimidation formed an inextricable part of any problem at hand, whether it was illiteracy, disfranchisement, job discrimination, housing segregation, or Jim Crow transportation. Years later a former colleague would chuckle when recalling that, "regardless of the topic, Walter would eventually steer it around to the fight against lynching."[1]

One effort that had coexisted with the antilynching drive and come to a prominence of its own in the late 1930s was the fight against discrimination in education. The bulk of that work fell to Charles Houston, occasionally William Hastie, and eventually Thurgood Marshall, and drew upon monies from the American Fund for Public Service and any other foundations that the Association could importune. By 1938, the organization was engaged in a number of public school cases around the country, including those in Maryland, Virginia, Florida, and Oklahoma. Beyond mandamus action at the state level, the NAACP also sought injunctions and damage suits in federal courts for the equalization of educational opportunities and teachers' salaries.[2] In December 1938, Association lawyers won a major victory before the United States Supreme Court in *Missouri ex rel. Gaines* v. *Canada*, which barred racial discrimination in public institutions of higher learning.[3]

Pressed, meanwhile, by a revised ruling from the Internal Revenue Service that declared contributions to the NAACP no longer tax-deductible, the Association filed papers of incorporation in New York State for a separate but collateral unit, the NAACP Legal Defense and Educational Fund, Inc.[4] Known as the Inc. Fund, this new office protected contributors, which made it easier for the Association to raise money for non-political purposes; the fund conferred a special status on the legal work in education, transportation, housing, voting, jury service, general defense, and other emerging areas.[5] Although the incorporators and officers were mostly the same individuals who directed affairs at the parent body, the Inc. Fund eventually (certainly by the early 1950s) made NAACP lawyers semi-autonomous from the older Board and secretariat headed by White. One can only guess about the extent to which this arrangement made him, the non-lawyer but master lobbyist, more determined than ever to win clear-cut victories for racial justice at both ends of Pennsylvania Avenue and in the various federal agencies that dotted the landscape of downtown Washington.

For civil rights lobbyists, there was no lack of causes at the start of the war years. The most important included campaigns to outlaw the poll tax, to end segregation and discrimination in the Armed Forces, and to secure state and federal guarantees of fair employment practices. Such matters increasingly occupied White, Wilkins, and their staffs during the 1940s, even when the NAACP itself had not initiated the drive. The Southern Conference for Human Welfare championed the federal anti-poll tax bill, and SCHW organizer Joseph Gelders worked with Representative Lee Geyer (D-California) for the introduction of such a measure in September 1939. The idea attracted the same sort of broad, coalition support among civil rights, liberal, labor, church, and reformist groups that White's fight against mob violence had generated. In the spring of 1940, the NAACP Board voted to endorse the Geyer bill, to contribute a modest $25, and to publicize SCHW fund-raising efforts in NAACP press releases.[6] There evolved a National Committee to Abolish the Poll Tax, and a bill to outlaw the tax in federal elections passed the House of Representatives in 1942, 1943, 1945, 1947, and 1949. However, Senate opponents killed the measure each time.[7]

Most dramatic of all the issues to which the NAACP swung its attentions in the early 1940s was the fight for equal employment opportunities in national defense industries and the related drive for nondiscriminatory treatment in the Armed Forces. Throughout the summer of 1940, the Association lobbied for equal treatment in military service.[8] At the next annual meeting, in early January, NAACP delegates sent a resolution to the White House and to the War and Navy departments against discrimination in the Armed Forces, governmental agencies, and job training projects. The Board agreed to seek a Senate investigation of conditions facing black men and women in the national defense program. Shortly thereafter, the branches held protest meetings in twenty-five states to dramatize the black community's determination to resist inequities in defense-related employment.[9]

By temperament and experience, Walter White was ideally suited for this new Senate drive. Displaying his usual vigor, the secretary turned to former allies in the fight against lynching. Accordingly, on February 19,

Senators Barbour of New Jersey, Wagner of New York, Brown of Michigan, and Capper of Kansas jointly introduced Senate Resolution No. 75, which called for an investigation of the treatment given black people in national defense matters.[10] But the Senate refused to cooperate,[11] although an Education and Labor subcommittee approved the resolution in the spring and the NAACP begged help from Roosevelt. Several senators proposed turning the matter over to the Special Committee Investigating the National Defense Program, but neither White nor Committee chairman Harry Truman took kindly to that suggestion. The former wanted an autonomous body to give its full attention to investigating racism, while the latter argued that his group already had too few resources to meet its objectives.[12]

Far beyond the confines of Capitol Hill, however, an amazing development had thrust the question of wartime discrimination to the very center of political affairs when A. Philip Randolph boldly launched the March on Washington Movement. In late January 1941, Randolph proposed nationwide, mass demonstrations to denounce racist policies in the defense effort, and his union newspaper, *The Black Worker*, published a call to march on the capital. By late spring, no one holding public office and no one exercising or aspiring to community leadership could ignore the idea.[13] Though distant at first, White and his staff kept in touch with Randolph and with the groundswell he generated. At its mid-April meeting, the NAACP Board took official recognition of Randolph's proposal, now seconded by C. A. Franklin of the Kansas City *Call*, and voted a $100 contribution.[14] By early May, the momentum had increased appreciably, especially after Randolph's March committee publicized July 1 as the date to converge on Washington. The NAACP Board voted an additional $100. By mid-June, anxious administration officials, including Franklin Roosevelt himself, were meeting with Randolph and White in hopes of heading off the march.[15] In this highly charged atmosphere, the president issued Executive Order 8802 on June 25. It established a Committee on Fair Employment Practice (FEPC) within the Office of Production Management.[16]

Reactions varied, but whatever satisfactions black people found in Randolph's success were tempered by subsequent realities. The executive order left intact the racist arrangements afflicting black personnel in the military services. The White House had promised reforms in employment, but No. 8802 lacked enforcement powers and penalties for noncompliance. FEPC was a paper tiger, as its supporters and opponents quickly discovered. Moreover, the order had been wrested under pressure from an administration that had increasingly to worry about mounting Axis aggression abroad; the Nazis, for example, had invaded the Soviet Union on June 22. Roosevelt's action, therefore, stemmed from broad national considerations rather than any direct concern with the rights of black people themselves, and in that sense it paralleled Woodrow Wilson's reluctant denunciation of violence in the summer of 1918.[17] Conservative Republicans and southern Democrats disliked the agency from the start, and Roosevelt weakened the FEPC in mid-1942 by placing it under the jurisdiction of Paul McNutt's War Manpower Commission. The following January, McNutt succumbed to pressure from business and political interests to "postpone" scheduled hearings into discriminatory employment practices in railroading, which evoked a drive among black leaders in the winter and spring of 1943 to "save" the FEPC. That seemed all the more essential, because the off-year, congressional elections of 1942 had exhibited a conservative trend and encouraged a right-of-center assault upon federal solutions to social problems.[18]

Out of wartime problems and opportunities, then, the Association became deeply involved with such issues as anti-poll tax legislation, military desegregation, and FEPC. Although the antilynching campaign had lost priority standing, and though none of the organization's legislative measures made much headway in wartime Congresses, the NAACP never relinquished its fundamental concern for statutory protection against racist violence. White even tried to revive the Spingarn-Hornblower tactic of 1918. Claiming it a federal offense to jeopardize manpower reserves during a national emergency, the secretary hoped to win the essence of an antilynching law without mentioning lynching. Under such a scheme, the president would request Congress to pass an emergency measure protecting civil liberties against hysteria and mob violence emanating from wartime conditions.[19] This failed to attract sufficient support, however.

The NAACP did seek federal action in cases of physical violence and intimidation against black soldiers, especially though not exclusively in the South. As early as September 1941, the Board of Directors discussed the prospects of securing a federal investigation into violence among civilian and military personnel, with particular attention to the relationship between violence and racism in the service. In the spring of 1943, White testified before the Senate Military Affairs Committee about the government's failure to protect black soldiers from harassment, physical intimidation, and (occasionally) death at the hands of white racists. Citing the November 1942 murder of an on-duty black MP by a Louisiana state policeman, White explained that such unpunished occurrences made it impossible for the NAACP to endorse legislation for compulsory military service that the committee had under consideration.[20] Similarly, White, Mary McLeod Bethune (of the National Council of Negro Women, and a presidential advisor on minorities), and Channing H. Tobias (of the NAACP and the YMCA) met with the president on September 30, 1944, to ask that he help secure passage of two measures: S. 2048, to make FEPC a permanent governmental agency, and S. 1227, to provide federal protection "from assault or killing of persons in the uniform of the government."[21] Neither bill passed.

In January 1942, the NAACP responded to the lynching of civilian Cleo Wright in Sikeston, Missouri, by once more urging Franklin Roosevelt to champion federal action. And, when NAACP records showed six lynching victims for 1942, White wrote to Senator Wagner of the need to reopen the drive for a federal statute. Of course, the secretary realized the improbability of winning congressional approval. He toyed, therefore, with the idea of combining an antilynching bill with anti–poll tax legislation in ways that would underscore the implications of southern racism for a nation fighting fascist intolerance on a global scale.[22] Nor was the NAACP alone. In the summer of 1942, Randolph's March on Washington Movement denounced lynching, the execution of Virginia sharecropper Odell Waller, and the brutal assault on vocalist Roland Hayes by three white policemen in Rome, Georgia.[23] In the fall, George Murphy of the National Negro Congress wrote Harlem's Adam Clayton Powell, Jr., to say that he, Congressman Vito Marcantonio, and Max Yergan of the NNC wanted Powell to participate in an antilynching rally sponsored jointly by the NNC and the National Emergency Committee to Stop Lynching. Simultaneously, Yergan wired Roosevelt to protest lynchings in Mississippi and to ask that the federal government employ its wartime powers against mob terror.[24]

The black community, despite its many other needs and goals, was not about to disregard the issue of violence. White was not, and in mid-1943, he revived an earlier tactic by circularizing some 380 members of Congress to obtain signatures on a discharge petition for the Gavagan antilynching bill, H.R. 51. And, under NAACP coordination, some two dozen organizations helped prepare a 1944 "Declaration by Negro Voters" aimed at both major parties in a presidential election year. The statement contained "six minimum demands": the right to vote in every state, unrestricted by poll taxes, white primaries, lily-white party conventions, gerrymandered districts, or other devices designed to disfranchise black and other voters; abolition of the poll tax by act of Congress; federal antilynching legislation; unsegregated integration of black personnel into the Armed Forces; establishment of a permanent FEPC; and a foreign policy of international cooperation. Democrats responded with a general endorsement of equal opportunity, but the GOP platform distinguished itself with explicit references to a federal antilynching law, a constitutional amendment to end the poll tax, an FEPC, and an equal rights amendment.[25] The following January, with NAACP approval, Congressman David Lane Powers (R–New Jersey) introduced an antilynching bill (H.R. 1689) to provide federal protection against the lynching of black troops upon their return to civilian life.[26]

One other phenomenon, urban race riots, distressed the NAACP and its supporters. They remembered the bloodshed of 1919, and watched with alarm the events of 1943. These included the so-called "zoot suit" incidents in which white servicemen and civilians attacked minority-group members in Los Angeles and Philadelphia in late spring, the Detroit riot in late June, and its Harlem counterpart in early August. Confronted with these manifestations of racism, not in isolated, rural counties of the South but in major urban settings across the nation, the Association was more anxious than ever to invoke federal protections against violence and for voting, employment, housing, military, and educational opportunities.[27]

The Association could afford to pursue an aggressive role. America's war on fascism and early involvement in the United Nations raised prospects for domestic racial reform, as well.[28] Moreover, the NAACP was itself a vastly strengthened organization; membership reached new highs of 205,000 in 1943, 325,000 in 1944, 351,000 in 1945, and 395,000 in 1946.[29] Aware of the implications for justice at home in the emerging decolonization abroad, the Board rehired W. E. B. Du Bois in 1944, this time as Director of Special Research, and he and other staff members soon entered into a series of activities affirming the Association's prestige and expanded horizons.[30] For example, in late February 1945, Du Bois represented the NAACP at a meeting of 106 organizations gathered in Washington to discuss international monetary stabilization and economic development plans formulated at the Bretton Woods conference the previous summer. In April Du Bois, Walter White, and Mary McLeod Bethune attended the founding conference of the United Nations Organization in San Francisco, and did so as the NAACP personnel invited by the secretary of state to consult with the official American delegation.[31] That contrasted rather sharply with Du Bois' and Trotter's inability to get a hearing at Versailles twenty-six years before. White met with President Truman for a half hour in late spring to protest, among other things, the government's support of the British and French, instead of the Soviet and Chinese, position on colonial independence. The secretary testified at Senate hearings on full-employment legislation, and that autumn he had a hand in negotiations ending the United Automobile Workers strike against General Motors. Staff member Gloster Current attended the World Youth Conference in London, and Du Bois helped organize the fifth Pan-African Congress, which met in England during October 1945.[32] All this complemented and built upon the Association's earlier work and reflected an atmosphere of impending social change.

Still, change remained elusive, especially in the inability to pass an anti-poll tax law, establish a permanent FEPC, or check racial violence against black people. By the mid-1940s the poll tax, rather than lynching, had become the legislative issue most anxiously pursued by civil rights coalition forces. Through use of a discharge petition, the anti-poll tax bill had again reached the House floor, where it passed on June 12, 1945, in a 251-105 roll-call vote. It died in the Senate over thirteen months later for lack of cloture.[33]

Developments surrounding FEPC proved equally disheartening, despite the enactment of state laws against job discrimination in New York,

New Jersey, Indiana, and Wisconsin.[34] In 1943, A. Philip Randolph had spearheaded the drive to establish a multi-organizational National Council for a Permanent FEPC, and the movement assumed serious proportions the following January when over 125 delegates from 21 states representing 45 groups attended the Council's Washington meeting.[35] Thanks especially to heavy pressures on candidates during the election year, FEPC seemed a viable issue when the Seventy-ninth Congress convened in early 1945.[36] But opponents rather than friends of the measure prevailed. In the Senate, Robert A. Taft (R-Ohio) drained support from the Chavez bill, which had Randolph's backing, by sponsoring his own FEPC limited simply to investigative and advisory functions; an ineffectual effort to stop a filibuster against the Chavez bill in February 1946 ended the push for Senate passage in that Congress. Across the Hill, Mississippi Democrat John Rankin of the House Committee on Un-American Activities charged that Communists were behind the FEPC drive. A coalition of southern Democrats and conservative Republicans, abetted by lethargic northern liberals in both parties, prevented Mary T. Norton (D-New Jersey) from getting a strong FEPC measure to the House floor in 1945 and 1946.[37]

Nor did Congress limit itself to blocking FEPC legislation. It also terminated the FEP Committee, as of June 30, 1946.[38] Perhaps most painful of all, because he had openly endorsed FEPC in the spring and fall, was President Truman's directive of late November 1945 that the Committee not issue its findings against the Washington, D.C., Capital Transit Company for discriminatory employment practices. White House handling of the matter so angered Charles Houston, then a member of the president's FEPC, that he resigned in protest.[39]

Amid these disappointments in Congress and the White House, there occurred a series of mob attacks on black people. The excesses at Columbia, Tennessee, especially, induced the NAACP to revive and revise its campaign for a federal antilynching law. Columbia lay in the middle of the state, some forty-three miles south of Nashville. A small community of 3,000 blacks and 8,000 whites, it had a history of tense race relations. At least three lynchings had occurred in the area, and that of Cordi Cheek in 1933 had left the black community particularly angry and determined that no such murder would recur.[40] On February 25, 1946, a black woman and her son got into an argument with a white radio repairman who was pushed or fell through a plate glass window, and was badly cut. Rumors spread quickly of an impending lynching. When the town's eight white policemen entered the black district of Mink Slide to arrest the woman and her son, a black crowd gathered, and shots were exchanged. The state highway patrol instituted a house-to-house search—without warrants, according to NAACP reports—during which they fired indiscriminately into any buildings whose occupants did not open their doors on command. With the arrival of four hundred Tennessee National Guard troops that night, state police charged a dozen black men with attempted murder. There were other blacks arrested; but of the white mob members who roamed black neighborhoods during the police raids, only two were detained and these merely on charges of "disorderly conduct." Despite NAACP appeals that federal and state authorities restore order and protect the embattled black community, White had to telegraph President Truman three days after the initial incident to report a horrible development: state troopers had machine-gunned two black prisoners to death in the Columbia jail.[41]

Throughout the rest of 1946, the Association championed the Columbia defendants and made them a *cause célèbre*. Under NAACP pressure the Justice Department convened a federal grand jury to investigate. Thurgood Marshall and other NAACP lawyers handled the case personally, while White and his staff mobilized a coalition to secure federal action against mob violence generally. In Tennessee itself, however, federal involvement proved ineffectual, and the atmosphere remained so tense that White feared for the safety of his associates.

The federal grand jury, by late June, declined any action against the state and local officials involved. In separate state action, Tennessee prosecuted twenty-seven of the black prisoners. Two, initially found guilty in Columbia's charged setting, had their convictions overturned on appeal; one of these was convicted anew in December. The other twenty-five obtained a change of venue to Lawrenceburg fifty miles away, near the Alabama border, where each eventually won freedom, but not until they and their NAACP lawyers had been subjected to frightening doses of Jim Crow harassment. The closing episode of the Columbia incident nearly witnessed the lynching of Thurgood Marshall, when four white men spirited him away on false charges of drunk driving. Very likely the good sense shown by his colleagues in following the "arrest" vehicle closely, as it maneuvered along secondary country roads, saved Marshall from a beating or death.[42] In the macabre world of American race relations, events at Columbia looked simultaneously in two directions: the courtroom scenes were reminiscent of the Phillips County, Arkansas, trial of 1919; the Thurgood Marshall abduction was a dreadful portent of early 1960s civil rights experiences in the Deep South.

By mid-spring 1946, the Association had established the National Committee for Justice in Columbia, Tennessee, with Roger Baldwin, James B. Carey, Helen Gahagan and Melvyn Douglas, Marshall Field, Frank P. Graham, Langston Hughes, Freda Kirchwey, Joe Louis, Wayne L. Morse, David O. Selznick, and Lillian Smith, among other members. Gathering prominent figures into an ad hoc protest group was an old tactic for the NAACP. However, it had particular meaning in 1946, because it helped reawaken a national concern about mob violence and lent momentum to a rather different drive for federal action. By early August, the Association had also organized the National Emergency Committee Against Mob Violence; it included a variety of labor, religious, civic, professional, women's, interracial, and social justice groups whose combined energies provided an impressive breadth to postwar, civil rights crusades. In many instances, these were the same organizations the NAACP had rallied in years past in its campaigns against lynching.[43]

Southern apologists long declared that the region had solved the problem of lynching, and many indifferent northern and western whites eagerly grasped those reassurances. Columbia, Tennessee, dispelled that illusion early in the postwar era, and so too did a number of other southern communities where whites assaulted black men and women with unrelenting brutality. For instance, on July 25, 1946, two black men and their wives were lynched in Walton County, Georgia. The NAACP investigated immediately and turned its findings over to the FBI. White urged that Truman reconvene Congress to enact a federal antilynching law, and the Association announced rewards totaling $10,000 for information leading to the arrest and conviction of the lynchers. Near Gordon, Georgia, black worker John J. Gilbert was shot to death on August 3, apparently because of the white enemies he had made through his participation in a unionizing drive at the local chalk mines. In Athens, Tennessee, a black man was shot in the back for attempting to vote. There were assaults on black veterans in Alabama, where whites seemed determined that ex-service personnel "must not expect or demand any change in their status from that which existed before they went overseas." On August 7, a black veteran, John C. Jones, was lynched near Minden, Louisiana; left for dead, his seventeen-year-old companion, Albert Harris, escaped to share details of the incident with NAACP officials in New York and the Justice Department in Washington. Finally, there was the internationally reported case of Isaac Woodward, a young black veteran who, three hours after his discharge at a military demobilization center, was taken from a bus at Batesburg, South Carolina, and brutally assaulted by two white policemen. As he lay on the ground, they gouged out both his eyes with the blunt end of a blackjack and later threw him into a jail cell to suffer through the night without medical attention.[44] Using press releases, interviews, radio announcements, conferences with federal officials, branch communiques, and other information outlets, the NAACP brought these matters to national attention and made plans to reopen its campaign for an antilynching law. The events of 1946 made it clear that a very old question had not, in fact, been resolved.

Senator Wagner assured the Association that he would sponsor the antilynching measure and make no concessions to a filibuster. White conferred once more with Attorney General Tom Clark, and a follow-up report in *Newsweek* announced that the Justice Department was preparing a new civil rights bill. Although no legislation ensued, the national response to the summer's violence was growing. Assistant Attorney General Theron Lamar Caudle addressed the North Carolina Bar Association on August 3, and called for a federal law to punish lynchers, while the August 24 issue of the *Saturday Evening Post* editorialized that the wave of renewed racial violence might indeed make it necessary to enact federal legislation. Orson Welles used information supplied by the NAACP on several of his weekly radio broadcasts to denounce the attack on Isaac Woodard. By late summer, the special NAACP trust fund for Woodard reached almost $4,000.[45]

In the early months of his presidency, Harry Truman had little enthusiasm for Walter White's pleadings, and the Association, for its part, was uncertain about Truman's commitment to interracial change. However, a surge of postwar conservatism soon enough presented them both with a common enemy. In addition, Truman's performance in office increasingly drew fire from dissatisfied New Deal liberals; he badly needed opportunities to display effective leadership. Taking all this into consideration, the NAACP staff, by mid-1946, revived its hopes for executive action in the field of civil rights. When White asked the president to send a special statement to the Association's annual conference that summer, the White House responded with a message that incorporated all the points suggested.[46] Meanwhile, the secretary developed cordial, working relationships within the administration and found ways to keep the president and his advisors well informed of NAACP objectives. White had spent almost three decades lobbying in Washington, and he knew how to capitalize on a political climate that would increasingly throw him and the chief executive into each others arms.

On September 10, he approached the White House for what proved to be an historic meeting, one which helped to alter the entire public dialogue about race relations. White explained that representatives of some forty-two labor, church, management, fraternal, educational, and other organizations had formed the National Emergency Committee Against Mob Violence. He asked that Truman receive a small delegation to discuss "specific steps of arousing public opinion and of securing more adequate legislation and machinery to stop this wave of violence."[47] This simple, direct request, triggered by concern over mob terror, served as the catalyst that transformed the civil rights drive of the late 1940s and involved the president with the movement in totally unprecedented ways. The antilynching crusade was about to return enormous dividends.

Truman met with a group headed by White on September 19. As the discussions unfolded, White House assistant for minority problems David Niles suggested the appointment of a special presidential committee to investigate lynching and mob violence. Since Niles and Truman had agreed on this beforehand, the president readily concurred. Following through, Truman appointed the President's Committee on Civil Rights, in December of that year.[48] When the PCCR submitted its report, *To Secure These Rights*, in the fall of 1947, it became thereafter the American civil rights agenda at all levels: for the president, as dramatized in his special message to Congress on February 2, 1948; for Democratic reformers, as written into the civil rights plank of the 1948 party platform; and for the

NAACP, the civil rights coalition, and the nation at large, as formulated in the Truman civil rights "package" of 1949 and later resurrected, refined, and implemented, piece by piece, in the civil rights laws from 1957 to 1968. In very real terms, the NAACP's four-decade struggle against lynching was inseparably linked with the emerging, civil rights campaign of the late 1940s and with the subsequent transformation of campaign objectives into working realities for a quarter of a century thereafter.

The fight to end mob violence came sharply into focus during the thirty-five minute conference with Truman on September 19. As organizer of and spokesman for the group, White urged executive action against the rising tide of mob terror victimizing the black community. He described the blinding of Isaac Woodward and commented on NAACP evidence submitted to the Justice Department on the quadruple lynching in Walton County, Georgia, and the blow-torch and meat-cleaver lynching in Louisiana. He also discussed the plight of the Columbia, Tennessee, defendants and their counsel in the tension-ridden courtroom at Lawrenceburg.

Other members of the delegation sustained and elaborated on White's appeal. Channing Tobias told the president that in London and throughout Africa he found the publicized reports of lynchings doing great damage to America's image. Labor leader Boris Shishkin observed that AFL veterans had been beaten by mobs in Georgia, Tennessee, and Mississippi. Dr. Reissig of the Federal Council of Churches affirmed his group's wish that the federal government take a strong stand against racial violence. Both Tobias and James Carey underscored the need for White House leadership.[49] The meeting also illustrated a shift in emphasis. In the late 1930s the NAACP had tried to set the oppression of Afro-Americans into a worldwide context by arguing that the United States should dissociate its conduct from the racism afflicting central Europe. In the cold war era of impending decolonization, the Association urged that the United States make itself a model of racial justice to enhance its own reputation abroad and simultaneously diminish Soviet appeal in emerging Third World areas.

Race had become an issue that the White House could not ignore. In early September, 1946, Mayor Edward J. Jeffries, Jr., of Detroit had written the president to decry the recent wave of lynchings and to ask for a federal law. On the very day that White led the delegation to see Truman, black activist and artist Paul Robeson wired David Niles the names of those who would accompany him to see the president four days later. These included John Sengstacke of the Chicago *Defender*, Aubrey Williams, Max Yergan, and Bishop William Jernagin. Earlier that month Robeson had telegraphed the White House a lengthy list of those who endorsed his plans to launch an antilynching crusade in Washington on September 23. The names revealed an interracial mixture of publicists, actors, labor leaders, educators, and authors, and Niles's staff must have noticed the leftist leanings of several, including Robeson, Yergan, Benjamin J. Davis, Jr., and George Marshall.[50] While the cold war had not reached the intense levels of 1947 and 1948, there were few in White House circles enthusiastic about domestic radicals. Neither the Robeson group nor its plans induced Truman to appoint the PCCR, but he and his advisors doubtless felt such a step would deflect leftist momentum. It was always more comfortable for liberals and aspiring liberals, in the White House or across the country, to deal with the NAACP than with the CP-USA, the National Negro Congress, or its postwar counterpart, the Civil Rights Congress. So once again, White and the Association got an incremental boost as a result of contemporary leftist efforts.

Nor could Truman discount the persistent matter of the Columbia, Tennessee, trials. The Lawrenceburg drama unfolded in late summer and early fall. It received rather widespread coverage, thanks in part to NAACP success in attracting attention from the Associated Press and United Press (neither of which was at first responsive), the Pittsburgh *Courier*, Chicago *Defender, Afro-American*, and Norfolk *Journal and Guide*. White arranged to have Vincent Sheean attend the trial to write special articles for syndication in the New York *Herald Tribune*, Washington *Post*, St. Louis *Post-Dispatch*, and several other major newspapers. Beyond that, the Chicago *Tribune*, the New York *Post*, the *New York Times*, and the *Daily Worker* also had reporters present. By late September, the National Committee for Justice in Columbia, Tennessee, had raised over $17,000, and by early October, the Association had expended nearly $22,000 on the defendants' behalf.[51]

Truman's decision to establish the PCCR sprang from a number of considerations that intersected in the second half of 1946: the realities of mob violence and a growing public reaction against terrorism, the NAACP's initiative, and his own political dilemmas. Following the historic conference on September 19, Walter White wrote to Truman to express both appreciation and a hope that the proposed committee would not become a substitute for effective legislation or an excuse for congressional inaction. After all, the NAACP had worried about that in years past. But now there was less reason to fret. Invited to identify those who might serve, White submitted a list of names to Niles on September 26, from which four (Frank P. Graham, Franklin D. Roosevelt, Jr., Dorothy Tilly, and Channing Tobias) were chosen for the fifteen-person committee. PCCR members Sadie T. Alexander and Morris L. Ernst were friends of the NAACP, as well.[52] Consequently, the Association was assured that its perspectives on race and reform would penetrate to the very core of the group's deliberations.

White had wanted the PCCR established in early autumn,[53] but the president waited until the disastrous November elections had passed and the publicity accompanying them had subsided before announcing his appointees. Hard-pressed by GOP critics, by strikes, commodity shortages, and rising prices, and by some New Dealers' anger over his dismissal of Henry Wallace, Truman had his needs. Accordingly, his timing of the PCCR selections showed an adroit hand. Throughout the fall, he mollified black activists by assuring them of his plan to institute the special committee. Then, in early December, he seized the initiative, stole the headlines, and threw new burdens on the incoming, Republican-controlled Eightieth Congress.[54] Executive Order 9808 established the PCCR, and the accompanying presidential statement gave frank acknowledgement to the fears and realities of mob violence: "In some places from time to time the local enforcement of law and order has broken down and individuals, sometimes ex-servicemen and even women, have been killed, maimed or intimidated." Moreover, the order declared, "the Constitution's guarantees of individual liberty and of equal protection under the law, clearly placed on the federal government the duty to act when local or state authority abridged or failed to protect these Constitutional rights." Moorfield Storey, James Weldon Johnson, Joel Spingarn, and Louis Marshall, cold in their graves, might have written the draft. Fully aware of the Association's role, the White House made certain that the NAACP got an advance copy of the presidential release.[55]

White and Truman needed each other, and a recognition of their mutual interests intensified as the decade unfolded. The focal point of this reciprocity was the PCCR and the White House civil rights program (the "package") that the two men helped to fashion. Given the interplay of political forces in Washington, the NAACP became increasingly dependent upon Harry Truman the man, the party politician, and the national leader. If he proved sincere and effective, the Association might achieve several of its long-sought goals. If his commitment were merely expedient, or if he failed outright, then the NAACP might grievously jeopardize its own credibility among blacks, its prestige as a major reformist organization, and its ability to convince others that the tactics of lobbying, litigation, and high-level negotiation could improve the lives of black people and other oppressed minorities. As it turned out, close working relationships between White and Truman, and between the NAACP and the federal government, did not produce a single, substantive, civil rights statute. In less unsettled times, that might have triggered an immediate and widespread rejection of the NAACP and its tactics, but the liberal rhetoric and hopes of the time held fast. Cold war fears, domestic Red-baiting, Truman's 1948 Executive Order (No. 9981) desegregating the Armed Forces, the Korean emergency, and the NAACP's accomplishments in the federal courts (capped by the *Brown* decision in 1954), all combined to temper criticism of the Association and its methods.[56]

White had made his point with Truman in the fall of 1946, and he turned next to Republicans who would organize the new Eightieth Congress. On November 11, for example, he urged Senator Wallace White of Maine, a close and influential friend of Taft's,[57] to accord high priority to NAACP objectives when GOP leaders gathered to map their strategies three days later. He listed the antilynching bill first, but quickly added that a change of Senate cloture rules (a suggestion of Oregon's Republican Wayne Morse) was integrally linked to the bill's prospects. The secretary called for the establishment of a federal Fair Employment Practice Commission as pledged in the 1944 Republican platform, for the enactment of a federal anti–poll tax law, and for expanded Justice Department authority to protect basic civil liberties. And he asked for GOP support in the fight to deny a Senate seat to Mississippi's Theodore G. Bilbo, because of his open advocacy of mob violence against black people and his alleged violation of federal statutes covering the acceptance and use of campaign funds. Reflecting the socio-economic concerns that formed a basic part of the Association's postwar goals, White closed with an appeal for federal legislation that would provide aid to education and housing and an extension of social security benefits.[58] Similar requests went to House leaders Joseph Martin and Carroll Reece, but the party showed little interest in such matters.

Meanwhile, the NAACP set out to make the most of the new PCCR. On January 14, 1947, White asked each branch immediately to send him local and regional information on lynching, police brutality, interference with voting rights, and discrimination in employment, housing, transportation, recreation, education, and health facilities. That same evening in the capital, NAACP bureau chief Leslie Perry and several other staff members met with three PCCR appointees, Sadie T. Alexander, NAACP Board member Channing Tobias, and Morris Ernst of the Association's national legal committee. It was but one of numerous ways in which the organization exchanged information with PCCR personnel. Perry came away so optimistic about prospective PCCR recommendations that he suggested the NAACP national office temporarily "suspend its efforts on the anti-lynching legislative front" until more was known about the Committee's plans.[59] However, neither White's temperament nor the chilling realities of racism would permit indefinite delays. In mid-February, White dispatched a lengthy letter with appended materials to Robert K. Carr, the Dartmouth College political scientist who served as PCCR executive secretary. He pleaded that the PCCR complete its work as swiftly as possible, especially in light of "the lynching at Greenville, South Carolina this morning about which I have just telegraphed you."[60]

The PCCR had begun both to assemble and to attract substantial evidence about minority rights and mob violence. On January 15, the Civil Rights Section of the Justice Department submitted a twenty-six-page statement outlining the existing federal statutes that could be employed for the protection of civil rights and civil liberties. Not long after, Section chief Turner L. Smith informed the PCCR that well over half the complaints on racial matters received by his office in the previous twelve months had to do with lynching. The public was obviously troubled about this matter, he commented. On February 21, Carr himself sent PCCR members a memo on the Willie Earle lynching at Greenville. Accused of fatally stabbing a cab driver, young Earle was taken from jail by a mob who beat and shot him to death. The incident was to haunt the Committee's deliberations for the next several months. Carr distributed other items on the case and used confidential Justice Department materials in early March to explain why the federal government had recently failed to secure a single conviction of the Minden, Louisiana, lynchers.[61]

The issue of violence continually intruded on the PCCR's work. *The Christian Science Monitor* reported that the Southern Regional Council (chartered in 1944, the SRC replaced the older Commission on Interracial Cooperation) had discussed the possibilities of reactivating the Association of Southern Women for the Prevention of Lynching. Dorothy Tilly, SRC field secretary and a member of the PCCR, would play a central role in any such revival, the *Monitor* suggested. Similarly, throughout the spring and early summer various black newspapers emphasized the problems of lynching and mob violence. Periodically Carr would gather and circulate press clippings on these topics to PCCR members.[62] And a significant number of letters that denounced lynching and endorsed a federal law to curb violence were sent to the Committee.[63]

With the question of terrorism affecting PCCR and public perceptions, the NAACP prepared to make its formal presentations to the Committee. White pressed his associates at the national office and at the NAACP Washington bureau for suggestions, and they responded with a range of topics.[64] Among them, lynching and mob violence were recurrent themes. Madison Jones and White wanted to press for "a Civil Rights act, an anti-lynching law, an anti-poll tax law and the white primary proposition."[65] Robert Carter argued that the PCCR, if it wished to get more than an academic understanding of racism, should visit Greenville to learn firsthand about public attitudes and the causes of violence. Leslie Perry agreed but warned against a study of lynchings in the recent past alone. Just as the Association had argued for years, Perry held that "a lynching has a lasting effect on the Negro community. Undoubtedly, it colors their [sic] whole thinking at election time, in connection with the organization of unions, protests against discrimination, and particularly when there are race tensions in the area."[66]

NAACP witnesses, however, were not the first to discuss violence against the black community. J. Edgar Hoover, director of the Federal Bureau of Investigation, and Attorney General Tom Clark appeared before the PCCR on March 20 and April 3, respectively. Hoover discussed the government's recent failure to secure convictions of two deputy sheriffs and three private citizens in the Minden, Louisiana, lynching. He noted that Louisiana Congressman Overton Brooks had used the incident to criticize the FBI for interfering in local matters at the instigation of northern black organizations. Should Congress pass a federal antilynching law, Hoover, who had to work with police around the country, preferred that it cover all persons responsible for a lynching and not delinquent officials alone. Moreover, he argued for the power to intervene immediately, since speedy action in kidnapping cases had illustrated the importance of a prompt federal response. Hoover made one point that clashed sharply with the NAACP's position: he wanted any federal statute to extend only to victims charged with a crime and already in custody or out on bail. From many agonizing years of experience, the Association knew that hundreds of black victims had died without there being any formal charges against them and that local officials could easily circumvent the legal conveniences in Hoover's definition.

In his testimony, Clark countered the FBI's concern for speed and argued instead the need for Justice Department clearance before the Bureau could intervene. He did, however, agree that under certain circumstances individual mob members, rather than just delinquent officials, should be liable to federal prosecution, a proposition that the NAACP enthusiastically supported in the late 1940s. A quarter of a century before, the Association had had to delete mob members in order to pacify constitutional critics of its antilynching bills. Now the concept had resurfaced with high-level endorsements—which attested alike to the expansion of federal powers in the New Deal–Fair Deal years and to the NAACP's success in making lynching an issue of national concern.[67]

White and Thurgood Marshall came before the Committee on April 17. Not surprisingly, White used the opportunity to urge that the Committee investigate and support a broad range of NAACP objectives, including a federal antilynching statute; an anti–poll tax law; an FEPC with enforcement powers; executive action against segregation and discrimination in federal employment; governmental measures in the field of housing, health, education, and interstate travel on a nondiscriminatory basis; desegregation in military service and in the federally-controlled District of Columbia; and Senate rules changes to limit obstructive filibusters. White dramatized his testimony by referring to the acquittal of the Minden, Louisiana, lynchers and of the Batesburg, South Carolina, officials who had blinded Isaac Woodard. Marshall reinforced White's appeal for specific pieces of federal legislation. He particularly commented on the limitations of sections 51 and 52 of Title 18 of the U.S. Code, the key statutes under which the government could protect minority groups. Since federal initiative seemed further hobbled by the Supreme Court's recent *Screws* decision, congressional remedies were more essential than ever.[68] The next day, Committee staff member Frances Williams wrote to White and Marshall to applaud their presentations. A former NAACP Board member, and a YWCA official who had cooperated with White in earlier lobbying campaigns, Williams occasionally provided more than commendations alone. For example, she had written Board chairman Louis T.

Wright on March 14 to share information about PCCR subcommittee activities.[69] Relatively few of the Committee's inner workings seem to have escaped White and his colleagues.

If the NAACP took some satisfaction in PCCR developments during the spring and summer of 1947, it discovered rather little to celebrate in Congress. The conservative, Republican Eightieth Congress neither intended, nor proved, to be a reformist body; Taft-Hartley was its domestic legacy. Moreover, considerable amounts of energy, at both ends of Pennsylvania Avenue, went into cold war activities that left little time and fewer resources for civil rights. Throughout 1947, the NAACP found key congressional leaders willing to talk but unwilling or unable to act. Walter White wrote to Senate Majority Leader Wallace H. White and his Democratic counterpart, Alben Barkley, in early April to urge new cloture procedures by a majority rather than a two-thirds vote. A week later Speaker Joseph Martin of Massachusetts informed Madison Jones that the anti–poll tax bill would probably be the first among civil rights items considered by the House, once it completed debate on the labor and foreign loan bills. In the early summer, twenty-five delegates from the Association's annual conference met with John McCormack of Massachusetts (Democratic House whip) and with Ohio's Robert Taft (chairman of the GOP Policy Committee) to impress upon them the need for civil rights legislation. McCormack noted that his party remained split on labor questions and that its southern wing continued to oppose an antilynching bill and the FEPC. Taft remarked that the first of the three major items (antilynching, anti–poll tax, and FEPC) to get through the House would receive Senate action. However, anticipating time-consuming southern obstructions, he warned that only one of the measures could be pursued in the upper house. He admitted a preference for the antilynching bill. On the following day, Martin and House Majority Leader Charles Halleck of Indiana assured these same NAACP delegates that the House would pass the anti–poll tax bill that session. It did so on July 21.[70]

Such conferences and promises represented the constant dilemmas facing civil rights advocates in the Eightieth Congress: legislators' generalized, verbal endorsement of reformist goals; attention to civil rights once other matters had been resolved; insistence in one house that the issues be cleared first in the opposite chamber; a frank intention of limiting the range of items to be considered; and, finally, lack of agreement about priorities. Beyond that, reformists still faced the eternal problem of dealing with the heads of key committees and subcommittees in charge of the various proposals.

One of these was Earl C. Michener (R–Michigan), chairman of the House Judiciary Committee, who came under considerable pressure throughout 1947 to move the antilynching bill through committee and on to the floor. Michener was not an obstructionist in the style of southern chairmen with whom the NAACP had dealt in the past; he was neither a Hatten Sumners nor a James Byrnes. Nor did he oppose civil rights measures on carefully conceived, strongly held constitutional grounds, as had Borah of Idaho. Michener's behavior probably stemmed from general indifference, age and placidity, the complexities facing Republicans in organizing and controlling the House for the first time since 1931, and the fact that major GOP leaders, like Robert Taft, were not fully enthusiastic about the measures advocated by civil rights coalition forces. Taft, for example, would not accept an FEPC with enforcement powers, he disliked an antilynching bill that carried financial penalties for the county or counties involved, and he seemed to prefer a constitutional amendment rather than a simple statutory elimination of the poll tax.[71] "Mr. Republican" posed a formidable impediment.

In response to NAACP appeals for the antilynching bill, Michener wrote Roy Wilkins in late May 1947 that his committee was already swamped with work (over 1,700 bills) and that the Association should turn to the Senate to expedite matters. Prompt House action would follow. Wilkins replied that the Association saw no reason for House delays in deference to Senate action, but the congressman would not yield.[72] Everyone, including Michener and Wilkins, knew the prospects of Senate passage were slight, so long as filibuster and cloture rules remained unchanged. Michener told Democrat Emanuel Celler of New York City, who had also encouraged him to move the antilynching bill along, that the measure "stands little chance of passing the Senate," and that (unlike Celler), "*I do not believe that we can at this time afford to be so impractical as to spend time in considering legislation which it [sic] would be impossible to put through the Senate.*" A month later, Michener advised Congressman John Blatnik (D–Minnesota) that favorable Senate action on the antilynching bill "would be highly questionable."[73] In other words, the committee chairman who had the power to control the progress of the antilynching and of several other civil rights measures in the House was advising supporters of those bills to take steps which, as he confided to his congressional associates, he deemed utterly worthless. Little wonder that the Association's Washington bureau could report in some distress that Michener "practically refuses" to take up the antilynching bill. And yet, there was strong evidence of support for the measure among those writing to Michener's committee.[74]

Such political duplicity was not Michener's alone. Despite their 1944 party platform pledges, GOP congressional leaders gave no evidence of wishing to launch a major civil rights program. The GOP and southern Democrats cooperated to stall certain socio-economic measures that smacked of New Deal–Fair Deal reformist origins. Talk of a Republican–southern Democratic coalition might have been exaggerated, and performances did vary with issues.[75] Still, on questions affecting what each group considered vital to its own privileges and power, or those of its major supporters, there were ample incentives to collaborate. For southern Democrats, race held priority; for most Republicans, it was taxation, management-labor, and social-welfare issues. Both groups welcomed situations in which their connivance might embarrass liberal opponents without serious repercussions to themselves. Civil rights fit that definition. Consequently, on December 13 Michener wrote to New York Democrat Adam Clayton Powell, Jr., one of only two black congressmen and a sponsor of several civil rights measures, that antilynching advocates should turn first to the Senate, and then the House would act quickly. "This matter has been discussed by the leadership on numerous occasions and this course decided upon," Michener averred. These bills, he added, would be disposed of when "compatible with the program."[76] Evidently Michener had not taken the Senate-first position totally on his own.

Although Congressional leaders may not have had a sense of urgency, civil rights activists and the public did. Their anger had been fired anew in late May with the acquittal of Willie Earle's twenty-eight self-confessed killers. Wilkins immediately wired Truman that the "SHOCKING VERDICT IN SOUTH CAROLINA LYNCHING TRIAL REITERATES NECESSITY OF FEDERAL ANTILYNCHING LEGISLATION," while the *Afro-American* declared that without federal protection "the only alternative is that colored people, like whites, take the law in their own hands."[77] The *Afro-American* also listed papers that expressed their disbelief over the outcome at Greenville: The London *Daily Mail*, the Memphis *Commercial Appeal*, the Richmond *Times Dispatch*, the Raleigh *News and Observer*, the Atlanta *Journal*, the Charlotte, North Carolina, *News*, the Baltimore *Evening Sun*, and the Birmingham *Age-Herald*. They all asserted that the failure to convict would intensify pressures for federal antilynching legislation. An emergency session in Atlanta of the Negro Newspapers Publishers' Association board of directors sent telegrams to Truman, Attorney General Clark, and Democratic and Republican party leaders demanding passage of a federal statute. Letters to the White House confirmed the widespread sentiment for such action and, on June 4, the executive committee of the National Emergency Committee Against Mob Violence gathered at the NAACP offices to plot strategy.[78]

Meanwhile, civil rights proponents got an unprecedented dividend when Truman agreed to deliver a personal address at the Lincoln Memorial to delegates attending the NAACP's annual conference in late June. Network executives consented to the use of air time to explain the NAACP's functions and goals while introducing the chief executive. Walter White could hardly contain his glee: "As there may be 30 to 40 million radio listeners in addition to a crowd of 75,000 to 100,000 if it is a good day, this offers the greatest opportunity we have ever had to sell the NAACP to the country." White's enthusiasm had led him to overestimate the crowd size; about 10,000 actually attended.[79] But it was still a dream come true, if nearly forty years in the making, for the Association. And, like so many civil rights triumphs, small and large, the recurrent phenomenon of racist violence had helped to make it possible.

The PCCR worked hard to confront the realities of that violence. To facilitate matters, Carr had divided the Committee into three groups: subcommittee number one examined federal legislation and sought to recommend new statutes; number two explored discrimination against minorities in employment, community services, education, housing, and the Armed Forces; and number three considered ways of dealing with organized groups trafficking in bigotry and intolerance.[80] By mid-April, subcommittee number one had reviewed federal civil rights laws and found them wanting. Noting the defects of sections 51 and 52, Title 18 of the U.S. Code, the group recommended legislation for the prosecution of both private citizens and public officials in police brutality and lynching cases. Moreover, it advocated enlarged federal, statutory powers in elections and suffrage cases, in the fight against peonage, in civil rights protections within the District of Columbia, and in interstate travel.[81] Carr later transmitted to all PCCR members a detailed, thirty-one-page study, "Background Notes on the Lynching Problem," that he and staff member Nancy Wechsler had prepared; and staff member John L. Vandegrift gave Carr a sixteen-page resumé of antilynching legislation proposed in Congress since the early 1890s.[82] When the full Committee discussed mob violence on June 30, members well understood that their very existence as a group stemmed from presidential and public concern over the issue.[83]

In recommending a federal law against lynching, the Committee had four elements to weigh. A statute might provide penalties for (*a*) delinquent public officials, (*b*) mob members, (*c*) communities in which lynchings occurred, and (*d*) kidnappers who transported lynching victims across state lines. There were ample models at hand. The NAACP had long argued the need for three of these, and by the mid- and late 1940s had also advocated the federal prosecution of mob members. As recently as May 15, Clifford Case (R–New Jersey) introduced H.R. 3488, and on May 27, Robert Wagner and Republican Wayne Morse of Oregon cosponsored S.1352, almost identical antilynching bills incorporating the NAACP objectives. By June 30, there were a dozen antilynching bills pending in Congress, thanks to such legislators as Emanuel Celler, Adam Clayton Powell, Jr., Everett Dirksen (R–Illinois), William Dawson (D–Illinois), and Helen Gahagan Douglas (D–California) in the House, and Albert W. Hawkes (R–New Jersey) in the Senate.[84] PCCR members agreed on the need for federal action but could not reconcile their differences over the controversial county-liability scheme. That provision had often come under fire from those who wished to discredit federal intervention, and the question now plagued the PCCR's deliberations. Fearful, in part, that support of community fines might raise political storm waves and impede the passage of effective antilynching bills, the Committee finally avoided the matter. In its official report to the president in late October, *To Secure These Rights*, the PCCR remained silent on that point and skirted the question of kidnap-lynchings. But to the Association's delight, it endorsed a strong federal law that would hold public officials and private individuals liable in lynching cases.[85]

The President's Committee on Civil Rights had provided the NAACP and the entire civil rights coalition with a unique opportunity to argue the need for interracial reform before an impartial body of national standing, and they made the most of it. PCCR findings echoed objectives sought by the Association over the previous three decades. Moreover, the PCCR recommendations served as a checklist of civil rights goals for the next quarter of a century. These included: expansion of the Justice Department's Civil Rights Section to divisional status; establishment of a permanent Commission on Civil Rights; new statutes to supplement sections 51 and 52 of Title 18 of the U.S. Code; termination of the poll tax; local self-government and congressional representation for the District of Columbia; an end to discrimination and segregation in the Armed Forces; enactment of a federal FEPC; federal legislation for equal treatment in interstate travel; state action for equal access to places of public accommodation; and the prevention of discrimination in education, housing, and health services within the states.[86] The year 1947 could hardly have ended on a more exciting note for the NAACP staff. Violence had evoked a federal response; that response must now be used to end violence and secure other essential protections. With an exhilarated and determined air, White and his colleagues set about to transform PCCR proposals into legal realities. They suffered no delusions that it would be an easy task.

9

The Last Great Drive, 1948-1950

The NAACP would have preferred action on the recommendations of the President's Committee on Civil Rights without the complications of political partisanship. However, that proved impossible, especially in the election campaigns of 1948. On its own, the Association undertook a widespread distribution of the PCCR's report. Where the recipient was a national political figure, or likely to become one, the NAACP asked for reactions and inquired which measures the person would support. It also urged all branches to mobilize grassroots backing for the PCCR's findings.[1] White, meanwhile, collaborated with Roger Baldwin of the American Civil Liberties Union, Louis Wirth of the Chicago-based American Council on Race Relations, and an ad hoc coalition group known as the Steering Committee on the Civil Rights Program, in a vain effort to win implementation of the PCCR's proposals. Both parties in Congress remained cool to the idea, and Truman was too distracted by Democratic divisions to undertake a sustained fight for such a program, even if he wished to do so.[2]

The president had very real problems. Southerners resented his stance on civil rights, his appointment of the PCCR, and his unprecedented special message to Congress on February 2, 1948, endorsing legislative action on most of the PCCR's recommendations. Governor Fielding L. Wright of Mississippi had already assailed the PCCR on January 20, and throughout the late winter and spring he fostered a movement of "Dixiecrats" around conservative racial and economic objectives. On July 17, at Birmingham, they nominated South Carolina governor J. Strom Thurmond for president and Wright for vice president on the States' Rights ticket.[3] A second split among Democrats involved the presidential candidacy of Henry A. Wallace, New Deal secretary of agriculture and vice president during Roosevelt's third term. Displaced from the national ticket in 1944, Wallace was dismissed as secretary of commerce for his September 1946 Madison Square Garden speech on the emerging cold war. On December 29, 1947, Wallace announced in Chicago that he would run for the presidency on the Progressive ticket, and in mid-January he and the

Progressive Citizens of America issued a seventy-four-point program that included demands for antilynching, anti–poll tax, and FEPC legislation.[4]

If Wright and Thurmond threatened Truman on the right, and Wallace did so from the left, a third challenge jeopardized his renomination. By late winter, certain powerful forces within the Democratic party had focused their hopes for success in November on the extraordinary scheme of running Dwight D. Eisenhower instead of their own president. Before this venture had run its course and Truman had secured renomination in July, the Eisenhower backers included such big city bosses as Jacob Arvey of Chicago, Frank Hague of Jersey City, and Mayor William O'Dwyer of New York; liberals Leon Henderson, Wilson Wyatt, and Franklin D. Roosevelt, Jr. (each affiliated with the Americans for Democratic Action); Alabama Senators John Sparkman and Lister Hill; Claude Pepper of Florida; Richard Russell of Georgia; Kentuckian A. B. "Happy" Chandler; Connecticut's John Bailey and Chester Bowles; senatorial candidate Paul Douglas of Illinois; Mayor Hubert H. Humphrey of Minneapolis; and, it appeared, Walter Reuther of the United Automobile Workers, and the CIO's Philip Murray and Jack Kroll. Moreover, some of those who doubted Truman's leadership capacities and his ability to win in November also promoted the candidacy of Supreme Court Justice William O. Douglas. Like Eisenhower, though, Douglas, too, declined to run.[5]

Facing such divisiveness within his own party, Truman was unlikely to risk further controversy by going beyond his February 2 civil rights message. So long as the prospects of effective interracial change rose and fell with the conduct and fortunes of the president, the NAACP found itself in double jeopardy. It needed, as always, to lobby for reform, without having the power to accomplish its goals fully. If the Democratic party and the nation discredited Truman, the PCCR sponsor, the benefits the Association hoped to derive from the exceptional work of a presidential committee might disappear totally. And, quite apart from executive and congressional reluctance to act on civil rights, the coalition forces with whom the NAACP worked lacked among themselves any clear-cut unanimity about tactics and priorities. In November 1947, the NAACP Board of Directors had endorsed a drive to revise Senate cloture rules in order to secure passage of anti–poll tax, antilynching, and especially FEPC legislation. This not only indicated the Association's determination to attack the filibuster, but it also responded to the mounting pressures on the NAACP to throw its weight behind one or two from among several goals. Still, throughout the winter, White and his colleagues refused to issue any statement of priorities. They feared it would jeopardize major components of their program, alienate members of the coalition who might feel slighted by any arbitrary ranking of objectives, and simply play into the hands of opportunistic politicians without improving the prospects of any civil rights enactments at all.[6]

NAACP leaders were wise to worry about the political manipulation of civil rights issues, especially in a national election year. Coalition forces had rammed the anti–poll tax bill (H.R. 29, sponsored by Ohio Republican George H. Bender) through the House on July 21, 1947, by suspending the rules and invoking a roll call vote. However, the Senate leadership of both parties persistently ignored the measure. Bender's January 1948 appeal to Robert Taft elicited an evasive answer that revealed the tenuous status of all civil rights matters in the Eightieth Congress. He reminded Bender of the three issues involved, antilynching, anti–poll tax, and FEPC, and of the likelihood that the South would filibuster against each. Cloture had never occurred on a civil rights measure of any kind (it would not until the passage of the 1964 Civil Rights Act). Taft admitted uncertainty about which of the three questions the GOP majority would tackle first and with what enthusiasm.

Anti–poll tax sponsors learned soon enough how little the Senate was prepared to do for them. H.R. 29 did not reach the floor until late July, when Congress had reconvened—reluctantly and at Truman's insistence—for a truncated, thirteen-day meeting between the close of the national conventions and the start of the campaign. The bill had little chance, especially with sentiment growing to avoid a statutory fight by shifting to a constitutional amendment banning the poll tax. On July 28, Bender wrote Taft in some distress that the amendment proposal was a "meaningless gesture" and a "shabby device to evade the issue." On August 2, the entire question was laid to rest when Arthur Vandenberg (R–Michigan), the Senate's president pro tem, rejected a cloture petition aimed at opening debate on the anti–poll tax bill. In a procedural matter that would return to perplex the Eighty-first and subsequent Congresses, Vandenberg ruled that cloture, under the Senate's 1917 definition, applied only to bills and not to a motion to consider a bill. That, and the haste to adjourn, killed the anti-poll tax measure once more, even though it had passed the House in four successive Congresses.[7]

In the intricate political maneuverings of 1948, the NAACP discovered no less intrigue surrounding FEPC as a major statutory objective. Although the Association had cooperated actively with various groups for passage of an anti–poll tax bill and even made that goal its own, it had a deeper, more intimate relationship with the fair employment coalition. By early 1948, for example, the National Council for a Permanent Fair Employment Practice Committee listed the following personnel, among others: Roy Wilkins as chairman of the executive committee; Allan Knight Chalmers and A. Philip Randolph (both of whom had served as NAACP Board members) as National Council cochairmen; and antilynching advocates Robert Wagner of New York and Arthur Capper of Kansas (for years an NAACP vice president) as honorary chairmen. Beyond that, the National Council's board included a number of persons involved, directly or indirectly, with Association activities: Roger Baldwin, Earl Dickerson, Alfred Baker Lewis, and Walter White himself, to say nothing of Edwin Embree of the Rosenwald Fund, Lester Granger of the National Urban League, Hubert Humphrey of the Americans for Democratic Action, and Willard Townsend of the United Transport Service Employees.[8] Indeed, its very closeness to the National Council occasionally limited the NAACP's options and pushed it, if slightly, toward statements and tactics not necessarily of its own choosing. This heightened White's caution against any premature announcement of NAACP priorities. It also left the antilynching bill, viewed by some civil rights activists as desirable but obsolescent, vulnerable as never before.

White had no power to restrain others from selecting and publicizing their aims. But he could complain, as he did in late February 1948, of Chalmers' and Randolph's error in asking senators to accord FEPC priority over other civil rights bills. Meanwhile, Robert R. Church, Jr., the prominent black Republican who also served as a Board member of the National Council for a Permanent FEPC, asked Taft on February 23 for full-party support of S. 984, the pending FEPC bill sponsored by Irving M. Ives (R–New York) and Congressman James Fulton (R–Pennsylvania). Church argued that the bill was essential to future Republican hopes at the polls and added that the antilynching and anti–poll tax bills, though important, were secondary to the question of equal job opportunities. Arnold Aronson of the American Council on Race Relations, Paul Sifton of the National Council, and Church sent Taft a memo that claimed that the NAACP and the National Council would support S. 984, even if the enforcement provisions were deleted.[9] Taft, of course, had already sponsored an FEPC bill without enforcement powers, and he believed that that was the only proper approach for federal law.[10] What sort of agreement Aronson, Sifton, and Church had, or thought they had, from the NAACP remains a mystery, because the Association never consented to bargain away enforcement provisions. The incident illustrated the difficulties that White faced with coalition forces over which he had no direct control.

Even Roy Wilkins, when acting as executive committee chairman for the National Council rather than as NAACP assistant executive secretary, occasionally distressed White. For example, by the mid-spring of 1948, GOP Senate leaders sought to resolve their own political dilemmas by announcing priority for the antilynching over the FEPC and anti–poll tax measures. Wilkins told Ives on May 20 that he hoped, with the antilynching bill stalled in committee, that the senator would press Taft and other Republicans to move to S. 984 rather than Bender's measure (even though both had cleared committee). Aronson and Sifton had also encouraged Wilkins to issue a National Council press release charging Republicans with cynical manipulation in dropping the FEPC and anti–poll tax items in favor of an antilynching bill that appeared the "most innocuous" of the three. That earned Wilkins a stiff rebuke from Walter White, in light of the

NAACP Board's refusal "to permit the Republicans to make us make the decision on these three bills."[11] In other words, exactly the type of divisiveness that White feared would hurt all civil rights objectives was well underway.

In this unstable setting—abortive hopes for implementing PCCR recommendations, fragmentation within the President's own party, congressional indifference, political expediencies, and conflicting strategies among civil rights activists—prospects for the antilynching bill seemed quite uncertain. Beyond that, another factor clouded all reformist issues in the late 1940s: the backwash of anti-Communist hysteria. In March 1947, Truman established a loyalty review program for federal employees (Executive Order 9835). The following year the Department of Justice secured indictments under the Smith Act against eleven Communist party leaders; their 1949 convictions were upheld two years later by the Supreme Court. Congress kept busy through the House Committee on Un-American Activities, which launched an assault against the Southern Conference for Human Welfare in June of 1947, investigated the movie industry that fall, and took Whitaker Chambers' testimony against Alger Hiss in the summer of 1948.[12] These highly publicized events reflected a national mood that discredited dissent, intimidated reformers, and widened the already existing divisions within and among liberal, left-of-center, and radical groups. The anti-Communist, national security crusade created anything but a hospitable atmosphere in which to pursue meaningful interracial change.

Fears of guilt by association and attack by innuendo hounded non-Communist reformers. In reacting, the lines between courage and foolhardiness, principle and expediency, prudence and cowardice were easily blurred. Under such circumstances, the NAACP and other civil rights activists long committed to working within a traditional, legal framework tried to protect their reputations and save their programs by espousing the "American Way" and guarding against bad companions.[13] Others sought to salvage their integrity by adopting a low profile, but Walter White was never one to "hunker down." Instead, he ventured out to fasten alliances in respectable anti-Communist circles, among ADA liberals, Truman Democrats, and the like. With them, the NAACP might be safe from the witch hunters and still advance its program.[14] The president in turn, with Clark Clifford, Charles Murphy, Oscar J. Ewing, and others anxiously charting his renomination and reelection, welcomed the NAACP and cultivated its black constituency. The Justice Department, for example, filed an *amicus curiae* brief in the *Shelley* v. *Kraemer* housing case.[15]

Bent on maintaining credibility, the White House prepared model civil rights bills for introduction in Congress. To help matters along, Murphy and John R. Steelman induced Treasury Secretary John W. Snyder to lend them the services of Stephen J. Spingarn, Arthur Spingarn's nephew and the son of the NAACP's late president, Joel Spingarn.[16] However, administration personnel differed over the best tactics to follow in substantive as well as political terms. The White House staff favored a comprehensive, or omnibus, bill, but Attorney General Clark felt that that presented more problems than advantages. Perhaps administration consultants should design separate bills that complemented measures pending on the Hill and leave to Truman's discretion any endorsement of those already introduced. Moreover, Justice Department personnel worried about antilynching prosecutions of delinquent public officials; the Department preferred unspecified procedures for dealing with local officials on an ad hoc basis.[17] And, as it had the year before in PCCR circles, the county-liability provision troubled some White House advisors as they drafted the antilynching components of an omnibus bill.[18] If the trick was to protect black lives while pacifying local sensibilities, the latter continued to surface as a consideration.

In any event, the White House felt some political confidence in sponsoring a civil rights program in the winter of 1948. A National Opinion Research Center study published in mid-February showed, for example, that 69 percent of the entire population and 56 percent in the South favored federal initiative against lynching, if the states persisted in their inaction. That same month the Southern Regional Council meeting in Atlanta endorsed a federal antilynching law, FEPC, an end to the poll tax, desegregation of graduate and professional school programs, non-discriminatory jury service, and special training for police officers in handling civil rights matters. The SRC also urged Truman to revoke his executive order on loyalty investigations in federal service.[19]

Meanwhile, the NAACP pursued its own goals within this complex political setting. After months of indifference and delay, both the Senate and House Judiciary committees bowed to the realities of an election year with hearings on the antilynching bills during the opening weeks of 1948. On January 19, Charles Houston, chairman of the NAACP's national legal committee, testified before a Senate subcommittee in support of the Morse-Wagner bill (S. 1352). He explained that other pending measures, such as S. 42 (sponsored by Senator Hawkes), lacked the necessary coverage, especially in their insistence on proving conspiracy between a local official and mob members. Houston pointed to the outrageous quadruple killing at Monroe, Georgia, in July 1946 as an example of how murderers relieved the sheriff of responsibility, in this case, simply by lynching two black men and two black women *after* one of them had been released on bail. And, unlike the Dyer bills of the 1920s, adequate federal legislation at mid-century had to provide liability for mob members rather than delinquent officials alone, Houston maintained. He cited PCCR findings of at least forty-three lynchings from 1936 to 1947, in which there were no state prosecutions, in the majority of cases, and no use whatsoever of the death penalty against lynchers.[20]

In the House, the NAACP favored the Clifford Case antilynching bill. Accordingly, Leslie Perry offered a list of suggestions that Walter White might use at those subcommittee hearings in early February. Because of the recent PCCR report and numerous civil rights proposals pending in Washington, Perry urged that White stress the relationships between lynching and other forms of oppression. That is, lynching offered whites an instrument of intimidation with which to prevent political participation, to discourage unionization and various means of collective behavior among black voters, and to remind returning black veterans that they must not seek to exercise in peacetime the rights they fought to preserve in war. Perry wanted White to underscore the use of terror to perpetuate among black people the crippling effects of "illiteracy, poor housing, ill health, low wages, slave farm conditions," all antithetical to "the 'fundamental human rights' agreed on by international groups and authorities."[21] Several groups with whom the NAACP worked also testified in support of federal action.[22] But not everyone found it easy to get on the witness list. The subcommittee seemed reluctant, perhaps because of cold war tensions, to take oral testimony from Clark Foreman of the Southern Conference for Human Welfare or from representatives of the CP-USA's Civil Rights Congress.[23]

Whatever gratifications the NAACP took from the hearings, it still had to fear the gutting of the Morse-Wagner-Case bills and election-year manipulations of the antilynching issue. Such fears were far from groundless. In late March a badly divided House Committee on the Judiciary reported an antilynching bill that closely approximated the Case measure. It retained the customary penalties for delinquent officers, empowered the federal government to investigate when states had failed to act, and, to the Association's pleasure, contained provisions for punishing individual mob members, for county liability, and for invoking federal action in the event of kidnapping across state lines. The committee majority affirmed that the threat of lynching persisted and asserted, with an eye to the cold war, that the "strength of our moral leadership in world affairs will be seriously impaired if, as a nation, we continue to condone lynching and mob violence."[24] However, a minority of eight committee members would have none of it. Citing press statements and editorials that the South must resolve the problem for itself and challenging the bill as a "vote-catching venture," the minority also denounced the county-liability scheme as unconstitutional.[25]

Senate developments were disastrous, with subcommittee efforts to eliminate liabilities against political subdivisions. And the NAACP found that it was powerless to reverse this process.[26] Although the Republican caucus had agreed on April 9 to give antilynching legislation priority among the various civil rights measures, the bill that emerged from the Judiciary committee in mid-June was, according to Walter White, "little more than a pious denunciation of lynching which, based on the NAACP's

39 year experience with the question, will do virtually nothing to stop that crime." The committee's insertion of a stipulation that would require legal proof of conspiracy between a lynch mob and derelict officials made the bill a worthless gesture.[27]

Facing congressional maneuvers that could only damage its objectives and possibly discredit the PCCR recommendations, the NAACP sought to rally coalition forces to a counter offensive. On March 27, some twenty national black organizations sent delegates to a meeting at Freedom House, 20 West Fortieth Street, where the Association now had its national headquarters. Representing over six million members, they hammered out a "Declaration of Negro Voters" to mobilize "the balance of power . . . [black voters] hold in at least seventeen states with 295 electoral votes." The group pledged support to those candidates endorsing the President's Committee on Civil Rights and urged Congress to pass FEPC legislation, a federal antilynching measure, and an anti–poll tax bill. The conferees called for an end to segregation and discrimination in military service and established a "continuations committee" through which to coordinate common efforts. By late spring, platform committees for both the Democratic and Republican conventions agreed to receive recommendations for a civil rights plank from these black representatives.[28]

Walter White took special care to make the civil rights coalition's presence felt at the Democratic national convention in Philadelphia. In doing so, he utilized all the competence, finesse, experience, and personal contacts he had developed in thirty years with the NAACP, years largely defined by his campaigns against lynching. Reacting to press reports of a last minute effort to deny Truman the nomination (a move that would discredit the PCCR and the president's February 2 recommendations), White sent northern and western liberals an angry telegram warning against collaboration with those who displayed an "UNALTERABLE OPPOSITION TO THE FREE BALLOT, FAIR EMPLOYMENT PRACTICES, THE SUPPRESSION OF LYNCHING, AND ABOLITION OF SEGREGATION IN THE ARMED SERVICES, EDUCATION AND TRANSPORTATION."[29] As an added touch, he circulated informational packets to selected party leaders to stiffen their stand on a strong civil rights plank.[30]

White had appeared before the platform committee on July 8 to argue the party's need for effective civil rights proposals,[31] including an endorsement of the PCCR and of Senate cloture by a majority vote. He rejected any simple restatement of the 1944 plank, and reminded the committee of black voting power in a dozen crucial states (Ohio, Indiana, New York, New Jersey, Pennsylvania, Illinois, Michigan, Missouri, Delaware, Maryland, West Virginia, and Kentucky) with a combined total of 228 electoral college votes. He also noted the pivotal nature of black ballots in some seventy-five congressional districts spread across seventeen border and northern states.[32]

For a majority of the platform committee, White's appeal fell on deaf ears. Taking their cues from White House strategists, platform committee chairman Francis Myers of Pennsylvania and most of his colleagues preferred to avoid a controversial civil rights plank and to seek, instead, reconciliation with southern and border-state conservatives. Truman's managers even tried, without success, to "clear" their version with the NAACP just before the convention opened.[33] Meanwhile, a minority on the committee, reflecting sentiments held by the Americans for Democratic Action, rallied around Hubert Humphrey of Minnesota, Andrew J. Biemiller of Wisconsin, Hugh B. Mitchell of Washington, and Esther Murray of California to insist, even at the price of a floor fight, on a vigorous civil rights stand.[34] They strengthened White's hand and eventually carried the day.

On Sunday, July 11, the day before the convention opened, White sent a "Verification of Delivery" telegram to three men close to the president: Rhode Island Senator J. Howard McGrath, chairman of the Democratic National Committee; Francis Myers; and Oscar Ewing, head of the Federal Security Agency. He urged them to resist the conservatives and force the civil rights question to the convention floor if necessary. Next, he went to work on New York State chairman Paul E. Fitzpatrick with the political threat that no voter could endorse a party "which does not fight to the utmost" against discrimination, lynching, and segregation. And on the morning of July 14, with the platform scheduled to go before the full convention, White talked on the telephone to an apparently distraught Emanuel Celler. The New York congressman declared that Esther Murray had mistakenly accused him in a platform committee meeting of having "sold out Negroes." According to White's memo on the conversation, he asked the NAACP to "protect" him. Celler explained that he had not joined with Humphrey to force the inclusion of specific items in the platform (antilynching, anti–poll tax, the FEPC, desegregation in military service), because he had devoted his energies to fighting the states' rights plank. Now he pledged his commitment to the Humphrey minority report and promised immediately to see Fitzpatrick about bringing the New York delegation in line, as well. To close the circle, White turned to Will Maslow of the American Jewish Congress, with whom the NAACP had cooperated on a number of issues. Maslow agreed to get in touch with Celler, Fitzpatrick, and Bronx Democratic boss, Ed Flynn, in the name of the AJC and to urge their endorsement of the Humphrey report.[35]

Simultaneously, platform minority and ADA delegates had been negotiating with northern and western party leaders, several of whom decided that, regardless of Truman's fate, they would desperately need black votes in the fall. One of the first bosses to come over on the fourteenth was Ed Flynn of the Bronx, who then proceeded to confer with Chicago's Jacob Arvey, Jersey City's Frank Hague, and Pennsylvania's David Lawrence on behalf of the minority plank. Before the close of that night's session, the convention had rejected three southern, conservative planks and repudiated the platform committee's (i.e., Truman's) moderate civil rights statements in favor of the Humphrey, et al., provisions. With Illinois, Indiana, Kansas, Massachusetts, Michigan, Minnesota, New Jersey, New York, and Pennsylvania falling in line, the minority civil rights plank passed by a floor vote of 651 1/2 to 582 1/2, whereupon thirteen Alabama and all twenty-three Mississippi delegates bolted.[36] Walter White expressed his gratitude to those responsible. Then, looking to November rather than the events of the past ten days, he put on a straight face and wired Harry Truman congratulations on the "vindication of your civil rights stand."[37]

White, after all, felt that the NAACP had few alternatives in this campaign. A repudiation of Truman at the polls might very well impede constructive action in the years ahead. Thurmond's candidacy had no redeeming features. The Progressives had little prospects of victory and seemingly too much involvement from Communist party members.[38] And the GOP still brought to mind Lodge's half-hearted conduct toward the Dyer bill in the 1920s, McNary's reluctance to support cloture in the late 1930s, and Republican indifference to civil rights in the Eightieth Congress.

That indifference hurt Thomas Dewey and the GOP ticket in November. As governor of New York, Dewey's civil rights record was not altogether unsatisfactory. He shared credit for a law in 1945 that established the State Commission Against Discrimination, and had appointed a number of Afro-Americans to public office. Dewey, however, had a problem in the presidential race. An energetic campaign on civil rights would further publicize the failings of his party in the Eightieth Congress and antagonize GOP congressional leaders and conservatives; and relative silence meant that he could not compete with Truman for vital blocs of black and liberal voters in northern and western states.[39]

White and the coalition forces had not totally ignored the Republican convention that assembled in Philadelphia in mid-June, but their approach to the GOP platform committee on the eighteenth had an accusatory tone. Emphasizing the crucial role of black voters in seventeen key states, White underscored the party's refusal to amend Senate cloture rules, to provide civil rights protections in the Selective Service bill, or to support legislation for the extension of social security benefits and public housing. He especially pointed to an "emasculated anti-lynching bill, whose worthlessness is attested to by the fact that the most reactionary and anti-Negro Southern Democratic Senators do not disapprove it." Although the Republican convention did adopt a civil rights plank endorsing a federal antilynching law, federal legislation for equal employment opportunities, an end to the poll tax (without specifying how that might be accomplished), and a generalized disavowal of racial segregation in the Armed Forces, those declarations remained less inclusive than Truman's special message of February 2, and did little to counter long-standing suspicions among black and white reformers.[40]

If the NAACP continued to view the GOP as an unlikely instrument of interracial reform, White felt an outright aversion toward the Progressive Citizens of America and Henry Wallace's candidacy. The executive secretary had taken the initiative for giving testimony before the Republican and Democratic platform committees but had no such enthusiasm for a presentation to the Progressives. In mid-June, he sent a perfunctory letter to Rexford Tugwell, chairman of the Progressive platform committee, acknowledging an invitation to address the committee and to provide for an NAACP delegation at the convention. He hedged on both counts. White had a much deserved reputation for prompt action, but not until July 12—almost four weeks later and then only in response to Tugwell's follow-up inquiry of July 7—did he reply substantively. Begging lamely that his trips to Kansas City and to California had prevented his writing, White rejected any convention role for the NAACP but agreed to address the platform committee on behalf of the coalition's continuations committee. The opportunity came ten days later, but unlike the detailed appeal to the Democrats or the critical challenge to the Republicans, the statement of objectives laid before the Progressives was curt and almost unfriendly. Alive to the charges and to some evidence of Communist involvement in the Wallace candidacy, White and most of his colleagues kept as much distance as possible between themselves and the New Party, as it was sometimes called. Indeed, when Du Bois insisted on supporting Wallace, it helped precipitate his dismissal from the NAACP that fall.[41]

Truman had given himself and reformers a lift by announcing in his acceptance speech that he would call Congress back from recess on July 27 to enact legislation on prices, housing, aid to education, medical care, civil rights, and minimum wages.[42] It was grand political theater, and left Republicans out-flanked and fuming. The NAACP staff began at once to lay plans for a coordinative meeting of labor, liberal, church, civic, and civil rights organizations. On July 16, Leslie Perry advised White how they might proceed. His proposals indicated the fragile status of the antilynching bill within a complex package of legislative objectives. They showed, too, how the measure had fallen prey to political manipulation. Perry thought that the coalition should avoid any drive for an omnibus civil rights bill, because it would cause too great delay. The anti–poll tax bill had priority; already passed by the House and placed on the Senate calendar, it was the civil rights measure farthest along in the parliamentary process. Far too optimistic about the FEPC, he thought it might slip through the Senate with a successful liberal effort to break a filibuster against the poll tax.

Perry warned, however, against attempting any antilynching action. The Senate Judiciary Committee had turned aside the Morse-Wagner bill and reported out a much weaker measure. Even if the House should enact the Case bill without crippling amendments, according to Perry, "we might be sold out in Conference and have to spend the next ten years trying to get the law amended." In other words, the NAACP would not waver from its commitment to strong civil rights legislation. As for other objectives, Perry believed that military desegregation should be handled by a White House executive order, now that the draft law had passed without the inclusion of major civil rights provisions. He expressed serious misgivings about the aid-to-education and the housing bills, because they also lacked protections against racial segregation.[43]

The coalition conference of July 22 attracted delegates from nineteen participant and two observer organizations. The group called on Truman to issue an executive order abolishing segregation and discrimination in federal agencies and the armed forces. It then urged that Congress pass S. 984 to establish a permanent FEPC; enact Bender's anti-poll tax bill, H.R. 29; approve the Powell bill to end segregation in interstate travel; reject the gutted antilynching bill and pass instead the Case-Morse-Wagner version; and amend the Displaced Persons Act to increase to 400,000 the number of admissible refugees without provisions that would discriminate against Jews and Catholics.[44] The NAACP staff sent materials to each of the Association's 1,691 branches, youth councils, and college chapters, encouraging them to get behind the coalition drive.[45]

On Monday, July 26, Truman issued two Executive Orders, No. 9980 to end discrimination in federal employment, and No. 9981 to establish equal opportunity in the Armed Services. Both had been under White House study for several months, and threats by A. Philip Randolph and Grant Reynolds to launch a black boycott of Jim Crow military duty no doubt facilitated Truman's timing.[46] But the NAACP and coalition forces could find gratification in having helped to create an atmosphere for presidential initiative. They took no comfort from developments on the Hill, however, where Congress displayed a petulant mood toward reform legislation before recessing on August 7. Stymied once again, civil rights, labor, and coalition forces therefore decided to press for cloture reform in the Senate and procedural changes in the House Rules Committee at the start of the new Congress in January.[47] For the moment they had only expressions of dissatisfaction and the task of electing a responsive Congress and president.

Harry Truman and liberal Democrats from the North and West fully understood the importance of the black vote in November. Although Henry Wallace threatened to cut into the president's base, black leaders like Walter White helped to neutralize that prospect by emphasizing that a vote for a third-party candidate with no hope of winning would simply strengthen the enemies of reform. Meanwhile, Truman had means of his own. Aware that Congress had done nothing in civil rights to enhance the party's appeal, on September 18, he moved to implement his executive order on military desegregation by appointing the seven-member President's Committee on Equality of Treatment and Opportunity in the Armed Services. Headed by Charles Fahy, former solicitor general of the

United States, the group included two prominent black men in Lester Granger and John H. Sengstacke. Executive secretary of the National Urban League, Granger had worked closely with civilian and naval authorities in 1945 to plan desegregation procedures. As publisher of the Chicago *Defender*, Sengstacke headed the only major black newspaper to support Truman in 1948.

For at least two reasons, the establishment of the Fahy Committee caused less stir than might otherwise have occurred. It seemed to some a mere political gesture in a heated election campaign, especially since most experts confidently predicted Truman's defeat; moreover, the army had long shown itself unenthusiastic about desegregation, and many felt that the ultimate battle had to be waged in military, not presidential, circles.[48] Aside from appointments policies, Truman also had the campaign trail, which he utilized far more effectively than his opponents. Making a final drive for black votes in northern metropolitan areas, Truman visited Harlem on October 29, the first president ever to do so. Well received by 65,000 people, he reminded his audience of his own PCCR, of the refusal by Congress to follow his lead in civil rights, and of his two executive orders of late July.[49]

Four days later the nation re-elected Harry Truman. His recognition of the new State of Israel helped him with Jewish voters in northern and midwestern metropolitan areas; and his over-all cold war leadership attracted or held millions of votes to the Democratic column. Meanwhile, Fair Deal domestic proposals, and the lack of viable alternatives from his opponents, further encouraged workers, farmers, veterans, professionals, and Afro-Americans to send Truman back to the White House. Voters also provided him with Democratic majorities in both houses of the Eighty-first Congress, 263 to 171 in the House, 54 to 42 in the Senate.[50] It remained for White and the civil rights coalition to discover whether the Democratic president and Congress would implement in practice and in law the egalitarian assertions of the postwar years. The PCCR had charted a public course, which the party's platform had then endorsed. The 1948 presidential campaign had dramatized and legitimized the issue of civil rights on a nationwide basis as never before; it served as a vast educational laboratory for America.[51] Now Truman's conduct and that of the Eighty-first Congress would reveal how much or how little real learning had occurred.

Walter White lost no time getting in touch with Truman and his staff after the election. White House correspondence files indicate that the NAACP secretary enjoyed a ready access to presidential circles, and he was asked to prepare a checklist of objectives in the new Congress. Meanwhile, the Association made plans for a special conference of civil rights coalition forces in Washington after the first of the year. The special committee on legislation of the NAACP Board of Directors met on December 14 to establish the organization's priorities, and the full Board approved the list shortly thereafter: a change in Senate Rule 22 to provide cloture for motions as well as bills, by a simple majority of senators present and voting; bipartisan sponsorship once again for an FEPC bill in the Senate; an antilynching law; an anti–poll tax statute; a legislative prohibition against segregation in interstate travel; and civil rights legislation for the District of Columbia. In two other areas, the Board anticipated administration initiative: presidential desegregation of the military, and Justice Department preparation of an omnibus measure to amend and strengthen existing civil rights laws.[52]

Events of the past two years had induced the civil rights coalition to press the Senate for new cloture rules; all other objectives would rise or fall on the outcome of that struggle. Beyond that, labor members of the coalition were most concerned with the FEPC, and the anti–poll tax bill had a recent congressional momentum of its own that could not be disregarded. All these developments meant that the antilynching bill had slipped far back among the coalition's goals. The NAACP understood and acceded. Following the Columbia, Tennessee, riot and the six reported lynchings of 1946, the number of lynchings declined to one in 1947, and two in 1948. The worst seemed over (there would be three in 1949, two in 1950, one in 1951, and none at all reported for the next three years).[53] Beyond the statistics, however, the Association was concerned that opponents of civil rights would try once more to use a token antilynching bill to divide coalition members and divert public attention from other reforms. White and his colleagues were not about to pay so high a price for the questionable pleasure of seeing an ineffectual law passed.

Civil rights was a predominant theme during the first two and a half months of the Eighty-first Congress. Journalists and national commentators watched the struggle with intense interest but remained skeptical about the outcome. For example, the January 1949 issue of *Kiplinger Magazine: The Changing Times* predicted that "Truman's honeymoon" with Capitol Hill hinged on the fate of the civil rights package. More interested in financial and business matters than minority-group rights, the magazine observed that administration efforts to undercut southern conservatives would drive non-Dixiecrat southerners into a regional coalition against the president. That would imperil other parts of Truman's program. Consequently, both sides were privately searching for workable compromises in which the passage of anti–poll tax and antilynching bills would head off enactment of an FEPC law with enforcement powers.[54] Conservatives in both parties would fight adamantly to prevent major rules changes and employment legislation, because those developments would hit simultaneously at southern sensibilities and business-management prerogatives. Because of the seniority-and-committee systems, these conservative forces held congressional power far beyond their numerical strength. They would negotiate to a point, but beyond that they had no need to yield and would not. Civil rights activists, always laboring under the difficulties of a coalition effort, eager to capitalize on their 1948 election gains before they slipped away, and having very little to bargain with in any event, could not readily compromise. As it turned out, then, the Eighty-first Congress became a graveyard for the items in the civil rights package and the resting place for the NAACP's thirty-two-year-drive toward a federal antilynching law.

There were ample signs of trouble. In December, for example, Washington bureau chief Leslie Perry had reported disconsolately to the national office that he could not predict who might come forward to champion civil rights measures in the new Congress, because even the "Democrats, particularly in the Senate, have manifested only the slightest interest in introducing and working for any of these bills."[55] Moreover, not all liberals and moderates, in or out of Congress, were ready to fight for change in ways the Association wished. Howard Odum of the University of North Carolina, scholar, southern moderate, and civil libertarian, wrote to presidential assistant John Steelman in mid-January to argue that the administration's number one objective should be to bring the South into line with the rest of the nation. He expressed admiration for Truman's domestic program, but thought it best to drop the FEPC as a strategically unwise measure in the South.[56]

Yet, black publicists expressed optimism over the administration's intentions and capabilities. The *Afro-American* anticipated "improved political alignments in Congress which should bring passage of antilynching and anti-poll tax legislation and we must hold to their pledges those whom we have helped to put in high office." Similarly, in an *Afro-American* article, Jesse O. Thomas anticipated that Truman would push for the repeal of Taft-Hartley, and for FEPC, antilynching, anti-poll tax, federal housing, improved social security, and federal aid-to-education legislation. Three weeks later the *Pittsburgh Courier* praised the inaugural address and declared that "Negro Americans feel that the man in the White House is their special champion and their patron saint."[57] Of course, as the year unfolded and those glowing expectations proved groundless, and people remembered that the NAACP had favored Truman's re-election, the Association itself became increasingly liable to criticism.

By the time the NAACP-sponsored conference of coalition organizations met on February 5, the dilemma was fully apparent. Responding to NAACP pressure and White House encouragement, Democratic whip Francis Myers of Pennsylvania had introduced Senate Resolution 11, which called for an end to filibusters by a majority of those present and voting. Closely in touch with the Association, Wayne Morse of Oregon sponsored an identical resolution. However, Democrats Carl Hayden of Arizona and Claude Pepper of Florida joined Massachusetts Republican Leverett Saltonstall in a different resolution that would retain the requirement of two thirds present and voting, but extend cloture to motions, as well as to substantive measures. Alarmingly, the Democratic

Senate Policy Committee actually voted, in early February, to delay entirely the question of cloture changes. This brought an angry rebuke from the NAACP's coalition conference, several of whose members feared that filibusters would jeopardize not only civil rights but a number of other bills vital to them. Meanwhile, House liberals successfully curtailed the power of the Rules Committee to obstruct reformist measures. The Senate filibuster, therefore, remained the ultimate weapon with which southern Democrats and conservative Republicans could guard against civil rights and socio-economic reforms they deemed objectionable.[58]

There were four basic alternatives for dealing with cloture. The most liberal permitted a simple majority of those present and voting to end debate. The NAACP and the president endorsed this. The second required a constitutional majority, a minimum of forty-nine, regardless of the number present and voting. The third alternative had been in existence since the Senate first devised a cloture system in 1917, a two-thirds concurrence of those present and voting. The fourth, which the Senate finally adopted in 1949, required two-thirds of the entire membership—a formidable sixty-four votes. At the same time, there was disagreement over a substantive aspect, and all sides used it as a lever for compromise. This involved the application of cloture to motions as well as to bills.[59] The wrangle over rules changes lasted until March 17, so that throughout the first ten weeks of the Eighty-first Congress all major civil rights measures were left in a state of uncertainty. Worst of all from the administration's standpoint and from that of organized labor to whom the president owed a major debt for his re-election, the promised repeal of Taft-Hartley also suffered. Just as a demand from its coalition friends for new relief appropriations had induced the NAACP to relent on its drive to break a filibuster against the antilynching bill in March of 1938, the NAACP now sensed a growing uneasiness among its associates in the labor movement over fears that a lengthy cloture fight might impair a Taft-Hartley repeal.[60] Increasingly, the Association felt pressed by allies, as well as enemies.

Fully aware of what an extended fight on rules would mean to the president's legislative program, Senate Majority Leader Scott Lucas of Illinois preferred to keep the issue off the floor. Public criticism, however, especially evident in the black press, and the need for some action two full months into the session finally forced the White House to confront the matter squarely. On February 28, therefore, Truman advised Lucas to proceed, and that afternoon the senator moved consideration of Senate Resolution 15, known as the Hayden-Wherry proposal. It would apply cloture to bills and motions alike with the consent of two-thirds of those present and voting. When this evoked an anticipated southern filibuster, administration forces submitted a cloture petition to the chair and thereby set the stage for a pivotal decision by Vice President Alben Barkley. A fascinating but deadly parliamentary game ensued.[61]

Taking a position different from Vandenberg's the previous summer,

Barkley ruled the cloture petition legitimate, although everyone knew that opposition forces would challenge his ruling in a vote of the full Senate. If the body upheld Barkley by a majority vote, Lucas (and thus the administration and the NAACP) would be greatly strengthened in debating and voting the cloture petition itself. Success at that point would open the way for subsequent cloture and a possible vote on changing Rule 22. If, however, a majority of the Senate reversed Barkley's ruling, no further cloture petitions could be introduced to sustain any motion whatever, and the prospects of debating and changing Rule 22, to say nothing of enacting any substantive civil rights measures, would be seriously dimmed. Otherwise extraneous factors now played into the hands of civil rights opponents. With the issue squarely before the Senate, Truman publicly endorsed, foolishly some charged, a new cloture procedure by a mere simple majority, while the much-respected Vandenberg reiterated his objection to Barkley's ruling, but advised his colleagues to follow their own consciences. This "reasonable" stance bore a striking resemblance to Borah's position on the Dyer bill in 1922. White House critics asserted that Truman's statement had cut the ground out from under Senate moderates, and White later declared that Vandenberg's speech "cost us a minimum of five votes and perhaps seven votes and was the speech that defeated our efforts to sustain the Barkley ruling." In the crucial test on March 11, Truman and the civil rights forces suffered a grievous blow when the Senate voted 46 to 41 to override Barkley's ruling. Senate Minority Leader Kenneth Wherry of Nebraska and Vandenberg himself were among the 23 Republicans who voted with 23 Democrats against Barkley; Ohio's Robert Taft, California's William Knowland, and 14 other Republicans joined 25 Democrats supporting the vice president.[62]

From that point forward, everything else concerning civil rights in the Eighty-first Congress was a mere anticlimax. Whatever meaning Truman's re-election held for civil rights now paled before a revived coalition of southern Democrats and conservative Republicans, who worked fast to consolidate their gains. Hayden and Wherry lent their names to a new bipartisan proposal endorsed by Georgia's Richard Russell, for the South, and William Knowland for the GOP. This would apply cloture to both motions and bills, but to pacify southerners it exempted debate on rules changes from cloture and required a two-thirds vote of the full Senate membership. Majority Leader Lucas prophesied that it meant "goodbye to the anti-lynching, anti–poll tax and fair employment practices bills."[63] He was, of course, correct, and civil rights opponents knew it. Two days later, on March 17, the Senate settled the cloture question in a way that left no doubts about who controlled the body. A proposal by Francis Myers to apply cloture by constitutional majority lost 69 to 17; Wayne Morse's recommendation for cloture by simple majority was defeated 80 to 7; the newly constructed Wherry-Hayden "compromise" then passed solidly, 63 to 23. Of the Republicans, 34 supported the measure, 8 opposed. No further changes occurred in cloture provisions until 1959, when the Senate reestablished cloture by two-thirds of those present and voting.[64]

It did little good for Henry Wallace to denounce the action and declare that the "real fight against Jim Crow and lynch law must begin now," or for freshman Senator Paul Douglas (D–Illinois) to lament that the Senate was giving "to a comparatively small minority the power to prevent the great majority of the American people from carrying their will into law," or for Arthur Vandenberg to assure his colleagues that two-thirds of the Senate would certainly apply the new cloture ruling to the antilynching bill.[65] Prominent white men, it seemed, were forever promising, denouncing, and predicting. It remained for Langston Hughes' Simple to express the reactions of the black community. Noting that the federal government could find the means to pass espionage and security legislation, Simple declared that it "yet cannot and will not and won't pass no bill to keep me from getting lynched if I ever look cross-eyed at a white man when I go down south. That is one reason I am not going down South no more."[66]

Tempers exploded in the wake of the cloture setback. White and Senator McGrath, chairman of the Democratic National Committee, found themselves in a heated public exchange over where to place blame for the disaster. It was a replay of the frustrations felt by Johnson toward Lodge in 1922, and by White toward McNary in 1938, and Barkley in 1940. And, like the angry political cartoons in the black press of 1922–1923, the Chicago *Defender* ran a sketch of "Justice" standing helplessly amidst a crowd marked "Mob Rule." It expressed the sentiments of editors and readers alike.[67] Of course, Walter White also came under attack for not having discovered sooner "that all this Truman campaign hooey about civil rights was in fact so much eyewash, that it was strictly a vote-getting campaign measure."[68] Meanwhile, the NAACP's official response to the situation was fairly typical. On March 31, Leslie Perry sent a lengthy memorandum to all Association branches, youth councils, and college chapters explaining the outcome of the cloture fight, laying responsibility at the doorstep of the Dixiecrat-Republican coalition, and vowing a renewed drive for FEPC, antilynching, anti–poll tax, and antisegregation laws. Bent on achieving political reprisals if possible, Perry included a detailed list of senators who had voted against the Barkley ruling on March 11, and for the Wherry-Hayden cloture rule on March 17, with a special designation of those up for re-election in 1950.[69]

With the cloture issue resolved, however disastrously, the NAACP squared its shoulders and set out to pursue its substantive legislative goals. Acting on behalf of himself, Robert Wagner, and Wayne Morse, Hubert Humphrey on March 25 introduced the NAACP's antilynching bill, S. 1404. This was the first measure that the freshman senator handled as a principal sponsor, and he declared that "without it all other civil rights become academic . . . . [because] we consider anti-lynching legislation to represent the heart and core of the civil-rights program and respectfully suggest that it have priority."[70] In asking such priority, however, Humphrey spoke merely for himself, or at most for himself, Wagner, and Morse. At long last the NAACP stood ready openly to rank another objective ahead of the antilynching measure.

There were several reasons. The steady decline in reported lynchings reflected the Association's success in making the issue one of national concern and, with the threat of a federal law, a practice that the South could no longer pursue indiscriminately. Even though the physical intimidation and murder of black people did not cease, the phenomenon of mob-dominated lynchings had fallen out of favor. This further encouraged southern apologists and indifferent, non-southern politicians to discount the problem and, thereby, to take much of the steam out of any antilynching campaign in Washington. Second, for Americans generally, civil rights had "matured" as a viable, public topic with the findings of the PCCR and the election drives of 1948; it had even acquired a certain momentum among the nation's cold war imperatives. Consequently, the Association could and had to move beyond the antilynching bill in pursuit of other civil rights and socio-economic measures. Third, the frustrating experiences of the previous two and a half months—cloture's failure, and restlessness among its liberal and labor friends in the coalition—forced the NAACP to declare priority for a goal on which most reformers could agree and concentrate. Not to do so would possibly have isolated the Association. Fourth, NAACP officials once again sensed an attempt in the capital to exploit the antilynching campaign in ways that would impair other civil rights items. Republicans planned to bring up either a weak antilynching bill or a measure to end the poll tax through constitutional amendment. Across the aisle, Majority Leader Lucas announced his intention of calling up an FEPC bill to demonstrate that the recent cloture revision had lessened, rather than improved, prospects for breaking a filibuster. It was now time to be counted. Although they had disavowed any announcement of preferences the year before, White recommended and the Board agreed on April 11 that the Association "now indicate priority for FEPC over other civil rights legislation." As Roy Wilkins explained, the passage of weak civil rights laws would damage the entire reform movement; but even the defeat of a strong FEPC that enjoyed united backing would keep pressure on Congress.[71]

While determined to block the FEPC, civil rights opponents had made gestures of compliance elsewhere. The Chicago *Defender* reported in mid-March that two southern legislatures apparently hoped to forestall federal action by adopting their own state regulations. Arkansas had antilynching and anti-poll tax measures pending, while South Carolina had a referendum on the poll tax under consideration. In his regular *Defender* column, White quoted Drew Pearson to the effect that southern and northern Democrats would strike a compromise by endorsing some form of antilynching, anti-poll tax, increased minimum wage, and amended labor legislation in return for dropping the FEPC, which southern conservatives absolutely refused to accept.[72] These rumors took on special substance because of a separate civil rights package proposed by Democratic Congressman Brooks Hays of Arkansas, who as early as mid-February urged that all sides settle on alternative versions for each of the main civil rights bills. Hays recommended a limited antilynching bill that would invoke federal authority only after state action had proved insufficient, a constitutional amendment rather than statutory abolition of the poll tax, and an FEPC law with advisory rather than mandatory federal powers. Such a compromise solution paralleled earlier suggestions from the Republican leadership in the Eightieth Congress, and even Georgia's Richard Russell sanctioned the Hays plan as a basis for negotiations. The NAACP found the idea unacceptable, however, and the White House rejected the scheme, as well.[73]

The administration had drafts of its own civil rights bills for introduction in Congress. The package consisted of four separate measures: anti-poll tax, antilynching, FEPC, and the so-called omnibus bill. The last would create a civil rights unit in the executive branch of government, raise the civil rights section of the Justice Department to divisional status, establish a joint congressional committee on civil rights, amend and strengthen sections 51 and 52 of Title 18 of the U.S. Code, protect the right to vote from violence and intimidation, and prohibit segregation in interstate travel.[74] Truman's sponsorship was an unprecedented step for an American president, and he hoped thereby to honor his commitments to the civil rights coalition forces. On April 28, Senator McGrath introduced each of the administration's bills (S. 1725, the omnibus bill; S. 1726, the antilynching bill; S. 1727, the anti-poll tax measure; and S. 1728, for the FEPC). Chief House sponsorship was carried by Emanuel Celler (the omnibus civil rights bill, H.R. 4682; and the antilynching bill, H.R. 4683; both on May 16), by New Jersey's Mary Norton (the anti-poll tax bill, H.R. 3199, on March 3), and by Adam Clayton Powell, Jr. (the FEPC bill, H.R. 4453, on April 29).[75]

Although generally pleased, the NAACP objected to an administration antilynching bill that contained no county liability provision. It also resented the lack of White House initiative on behalf of the Humphrey-Morse-Wagner version. There were over a dozen pending measures directed at mob violence, but the one receiving most favorable committee treatment was that sponsored by Homer Ferguson (R-Michigan). S. 91 carried no civil sanction against counties and, even worse, required proof of conspiracy in order to prosecute mob members. Less than six months after November's election triumphs, therefore, the Association had seen cloture procedures tightened rather than relaxed and found itself confronting two antilynching bills it deemed defective—one from a friendly administration, another from an indifferent congressional minority. And, as Leslie Perry observed in analyzing the Truman bill, the lack of civil liabilities further reduced NAACP options, "since we could probably agree to drop that section as a compromise for keeping . . . individual liability."[76] It was a sorry turn of events when White and his colleagues had to consider eliminating a provision they had fought three decades to preserve. Now, the PCCR's reluctance to sanction county liability had come back to haunt advocates of a strong antilynching law.

Nor were matters destined to improve, as many little things got out of hand, beyond the Association's ability to control or even contest. Extensive rumors circulated about vote swapping among Republicans and Democrats on civil rights measures. Perry reported a nascent arrangement between midwestern senators (like Ferguson and Alexander Wiley of Wisconsin) on oleomargarine legislation and southern Democrats anxious to forestall an effective antilynching measure.[77] White complained to his Board that a Senate Judiciary subcommittee scheduled antilynching hearings to begin at 2:30 on May 25, but that interested persons, organizations, and even congressional sponsors were not notified until noon that day. When the full committee finally made its report in early June, it approved the Ferguson version, which the NAACP found totally unacceptable.[78] A rather pathetic and little-noticed incident in late June actually marked the end of the Association's thirty-two-year drive for a federal antilynching law. While temporarily presiding, Senator Guy Gillette (D–Iowa) called up the measure; it might have passed, because none of its opponents responded. Suddenly Florida's Spressard Holland got the floor, objected, and the effort collapsed.[79] That proved to be the somewhat comic high point for antilynching legislation in the Eighty-first Congress. The Senate declined to consider the question throughout the rest of 1949 and 1950, and House committees reported no such bill to the floor in either session.[80]

As if to symbolize not merely the loss of the bill but the climax of a three-decade crusade, the Association temporarily lost the services of Walter White, beginning in the summer of 1949. Personal needs and plans, rather than events in Congress, explained his departure. Plagued by a heart ailment that would claim his life six years later, White had submitted his resignation that spring. But the Board insisted that he yield his duties to Wilkins and take, instead, a year's leave of absence. There followed more explosive news, however, which stunned and sharply divided White's family, friends, and associates in the NAACP. He had asked his wife of twenty-seven years, Gladys Powell-White, for a divorce. Upon securing it, he promptly married a well-known food consultant and author, Poppy Cannon, on July 6, 1949. In the atmosphere of the late 1940s, this seemed an imprudent and, to some, a disloyal, move for so visible a paragon of black middle-class standards, all the more in the eyes of certain friends and enemies, because Poppy Cannon was a white woman.[81] Walter White's personal life had no direct bearing on the larger issue of national civil rights legislation. But it seemed somehow oddly fitting that he should have made this dramatic change in life style just as the antilynching bill, for which he had sacrificed so much, was undergoing its last major test in Congress.

In the late spring of 1949, advocates for black rights faced bad news on every front, and pessimism abounded. Rumor had it that the administration planned to abandon civil rights legislation for the remainder of the first session, although Scott Lucas tried to reassure Wilkins that such reports were inaccurate.[82] Meanwhile, he and Walter White attended a small dinner conference in Washington. Other participants included Shad Polier and a Mr. Edelberg representing several Jewish organizations, James B. Carey and George Weaver of the CIO, Lou Hines and Nelson Cruikshank of the AFL, Joseph Rauh of the Americans for Democratic Action, Senator Humphrey, and Clark Clifford of the White House staff. At first Humphrey spoke in favor of bringing up the omnibus civil rights bill, because full opposition had not yet crystalized against it. However, the lobbyists unanimously voted the FEPC the first order of business. A follow-up meeting took place on July 7, with Senators Lucas, Myers, and McGrath. Wilkins informed the NAACP Board that although Democratic leaders were disturbed over criticisms of their civil rights failures and over threats of political retaliation in 1950, they were "not disturbed enough to take forthright action on civil rights legislation."[83]

The Eighty-first Congress would not be moved, and the tactic of concentrating on the FEPC proved abortive. The Powell version, H.R. 4453, was favorably reported on August 2 by the House Education and Labor Committee, but supporters failed to get the measure on the floor during the first session, either by clearing the Rules Committee or by utilizing the new twenty-one-day rule. When the FEPC finally reached the floor in 1950, it was stripped of its enforcement powers, but passed on February 23. Meanwhile, the situation was no more promising in the Senate, where the chairman of Labor and Public Welfare reportedly informed Clark Clifford that he would not bring up the measure in committee, because the bill would antagonize southern senators and thereby jeopardize the administration's overall program. Later, the committee did report S. 1728, but without recommendation; no floor action followed. Civil rights forces had no success during the second session; two cloture votes, May 19 and July 12, 1950, failed to get the FEPC bill on the Senate floor.[84]

Of the three major legislative goals held by civil rights advocates throughout the 1940s, only the anti-poll tax continued to demonstrate the resiliency and support needed to win passage in at least one house without being gutted. The House Rules Committee refused to clear Congresswoman Mary Norton's measure, but she succeeded in forcing it to the floor by invoking, for the first time in the session, the twenty-one-day rule. On July 26, 1949, her bill passed, 273 to 116. However, it failed to reach the Senate floor in either session of the Eighty-first Congress, although a Judiciary subcommittee on May 23, 1949, did approve a resolution to abolish the poll tax by constitutional amendment.[85]

The Eighty-first Congress simply smothered, then buried, most civil rights objectives—despite the momentum generated in the postwar years by a forceful coalition, widespread concern over mob violence, the work of the President's Committee on Civil Rights, Truman's unprecedented special message in early February 1948, the drama over a civil rights plank at the Democratic convention, the promises in the 1944 and 1948 GOP platforms, and the election of Truman and a Democratic Congress with the help of black voters and civil rights issues. This backdrop of events notwithstanding, reformers still failed to alter sufficiently the power structure and procedures within Congress or to weaken sufficiently the working arrangements invoked selectively among southern Democrats and conservative Republicans. Moreover, no combination of efforts by civil rights forces could surmount the backwash of domestic, anti-Communist hysteria or of international cold war tensions reflected in the loyalty programs and witch hunts of the period, the Truman Doctrine of 1947, the Berlin blockade of 1948–1949, the establishment of NATO in 1949, and the diplomatic and military developments on the China mainland and in Korea in 1949 and 1950, respectively. Such issues at home and abroad robbed the American public and its leaders of valuable time, energy, and resources that might otherwise have gone to a more open, thorough search for civil rights solutions, had the will to do so been strong enough. Moreover, attempts by some reformers to promote better race relations on grounds that it would improve America's image and strengthen its posture abroad also proved insufficient to counterbalance the debilitating effects of cold war attitudes.

Overall, then, the late 1940s turned out to be far less conducive to civil rights than contemporaries hoped and assumed. Quite possibly the tradition and extent of American racism itself militated against any fundamental improvements, regardless of political promises and prospects, wide-ranging cooperation among civil rights activists, and fresh avowals for "tolerance" and "human rights." Though high on the agenda for discussion, minority-group rights continued to have but marginal status when it came to corrective action. As the lead item in the black community's ongoing drive against terrorism, the antilynching bill, like the black victims it sought to protect, stood little chance of survival. The endless accusations thrown back and forth across the aisles of Congress, from one end of Pennsylvania Avenue to the other, look in retrospect, as they must have seemed to Johnson, White, and Wilkins at the time, no more convincing than the bland findings of the countless coroner's juries who claimed that the death of lynching victims had come "at the hands of parties unknown."

10

In the Hands of Parties Yet Unknown

A gruesome instrument of social control, lynching exposed white America's contempt for black people and its disregard for duly constituted legal procedures. The mob exercised a ruthless, indiscriminate sovereignty over all black lives, and racism was never more blatantly displayed than when a gang of lynchers roused themselves to fury against a defenseless victim whose ultimate crime was being black in a white world.

But lynching was more than a sadistic ritual reenforcing the conventions of racial solidarity. It also tested the values of those whites who would never indulge directly in such brutality but refused, nonetheless, to put an end to the practice. Anxious to deny personal responsibility, they sought refuge in indifference, feigned ignorance, racial myths, expressions of regret, constitutional niceties, and recitations of stock platitudes. Yet, even the most detached or naive had eventually to realize that lynching as a recurring phenomenon jeopardized everything that Americans professed to honor—individualism, fair play, justice, law and order, the Judeo-Christian ethic, the right of personal security, democracy itself. Beginning in 1909, the National Association for the Advancement of Colored People set out to shatter the public's complacency and to challenge the inconsistencies in its values and behavior.

Called into existence by America's failure to end discrimination in general and violence in particular, the NAACP invoked every possible constitutional guarantee against racial injustice. The Association used investigations and exposés to insist that society acknowledge and remedy the malicious cycle of racism that victimized the minority and left the majority callous and inert. Through conferences, publications, negotiations, lobbying, and litigation, the NAACP sought to change public attitudes, stir politicians to corrective action, and generally redefine the settled contours of American race relations. By campaigns against mob violence, the Association placed itself in the vanguard of black activism, and earned the thanks of Afro-Americans who knew full well what the constant threat of physical assault meant to them, their families, and their friends.

Moreover, the Association profited by, and learned from, its antilynching work. These lessons it applied in other areas of civil rights reform. The crusade against violence kept opponents at bay and attracted supporters from disparate sources. It deflected criticism from Garveyites, the Communist party, and other radical elements, while it pulled together an assortment of civic, reform, labor, liberal, women's, and church groups that, by the 1930s, formed the inner core of an unfolding twentieth-century civil rights movement. Thanks to the struggle against mobbism, the NAACP gained new members, financial assistance, and vital experience for its staff, who learned to cope on a regular basis with national issues and negotiate with influential journalists and well-placed public figures. Just as much, then, as lynching was a central factor in race relations throughout the late nineteenth and early twentieth centuries, the drive against it proved an integral part of the Association's emerging status as a leading advocate of human rights.

The NAACP faced numerous obstacles from the start. It had limited resources and was forced to rely upon a membership scattered throughout metropolitan centers in the North and Midwest. Among blacks, many potential supporters hesitated at first, because Booker T. Washington's powerful Tuskegee machine resisted all challenges to his Alabama-based system of accommodation. Across America, Jim Crow assumptions prevailed by law or by custom, and there was no quick or easy way to change them. And a revived Ku Klux Klan promised to outdistance any gains that a fledgling civil rights group might make. Clearly, the task of launching and maintaining a new, national organization to fight for black rights was an enormous undertaking. But three developments coincided in the Association's favor: a climate for change, a national emergency of unprecedented proportions, and the availability of vigorous staff talent. A generation of Progressive reformers had already learned the techniques for combatting social evils; those who could not overlook or countenance racism in general and lynching in particular brought considerable skills to the struggle. The enormous expansion of governmental initiatives during the First World War made it much easier to argue that national problems required solutions at the federal level. And, with the appointments of James Weldon Johnson in 1916 and Walter White in 1918, the NAACP acquired two gifted black activists who could neither disregard their experiences with lynching and Jim Crow nor temper their opposition to them.

At the outset, the NAACP identified a range of disabilities that afflicted Afro-Americans; insisting on nothing less than equal justice, it was determined to end them all. In 1915, for example, Moorfield Storey helped convince the United States Supreme Court to overturn the Oklahoma "grandfather clause." That same year, W. E. B. Du Bois denounced the agrarian peonage and industrial exploitation that plagued black workers in the South and North, respectively. He called, as well, for federal aid to public schools as a means of relieving black students from the impoverishments of Jim Crow classrooms.[1] During World War I, the Association sought decent treatment for blacks in the national defense program,[2] and in the spring of 1920, the Board of Directors set a list of objectives that included suffrage, fair court trials, access to jury duty, equal service on public carriers, and nondiscriminatory educational and employment opportunities.[3] As it turned out, of course, these efforts brought very few fundamental changes in American race relations. They were, however, harbingers of what the civil rights movement would someday accomplish, once it had established a national base of recognition and support and learned how to deal with entrenched sources of power. To all of that, the antilynching campaigns made inestimable contributions in the years from 1909 to 1950.

Initially, the NAACP tried to work with state and local officials to end lynching, but this produced minimal results. Elected leaders throughout the South felt no obligation to honor appeals from a black constituency denied access to the polls. They felt even less inclined to deal with reformers based in New York City. Even in Pennsylvania, the NAACP spent many fruitless months trying to bring Zach Walker's killers to justice. Early hopes of coordinating an antilynching campaign with southern liberals also proved fanciful. The NAACP's famous 1919 conference failed to attract a sizeable endorsement from that quarter, and the assault on secretary John Shillady shortly thereafter convinced the most sanguine advocates of regional cooperation that justice could not be achieved on a local or state basis.

This strengthened the arguments by Johnson and White that the Association should seek redress in Washington. Despite the hesitation of such respected constitutional advisors as Moorfield Story, Louis Marshall, and George W. Wickersham, Johnson and White persisted. Joel E. Spingarn, Mary White Ovington, and Albert E. Pillsbury provided support, Storey fell in line, and the NAACP launched a determined three-decade drive for a federal antilynching law. The high points of this campaign occurred from 1918 to 1923, 1934 to 1940, and 1946 to 1950. The House passed the measure in 1922, 1937, and 1940, but no antilynching bill was ever brought to a vote in the United States Senate.

Difficulties abounded in Washington, where the Association lacked the means to surmount them. Constitutional traditionalists and southern conservatives argued that lynching was murder and must be left to the jurisdiction of the separate states. Beyond that, congressional opponents employed every possible parliamentary device—stalling the legislation in committee, quorum calls and motions to adjourn, objections to the minutes, weakening amendments, outright political deals, and Senate filibusters—to impede consideration and passage. For their part, liberals and moderates on Capitol Hill and in the White House not infrequently urged patience, accepted delays, sought compromises, and treated the antilynching bills with considerably less priority than they accorded to partisan harmony, bipartisan collegiality, and pieces of favored legislation.

The NAACP's antilynching bills were regularly sacrificed to politicians' definitions of "larger" public necessities, such as the GOP's legislative agenda for 1922-1923, New Deal relief measures in 1937 and 1938, and innumerable cold war issues to which Washington experts surrendered their energies in the late 1940s. On a regional basis, the Commission on Interracial Cooperation of the 1920s and the Association of Southern Women for the Prevention of Lynching, throughout the 1930s, remained more concerned about white sensibilities and sectional autonomy than about black people's needs. Even the modernizing tendencies of New Deal programs failed to shake southern loyalties to home-based remedies for lynching. The 1940s promised better, but anti-Communist campaigns and their own hesitations impeded reformers associated with the Southern Conference for Human Welfare and the Southern Regional Council.[4] Overall, there existed no greater index to the inelasticity of twentieth-century American liberalism than the unwillingness of its adherents to stand and make a fight for black people's security against unchecked mobs or select committees sworn to execute their victims without public notoriety. When it came to the protection of black rights, most liberals, North and South, scored higher on professions of concern than they did on actual performance.

Although the NAACP was never alone in its condemnation of lynching, it did lead the attack with a perseverance and intensity unmatched by any other element in American society. In doing so, the Association played a singularly important role in redirecting public attitudes and policies toward Afro-Americans. Some have argued that fundamental demographic, political, and economic factors—more than NAACP campaigns—explained lynching's decline.[5] Certainly mass migrations of black people from the rural South during the first half of the century and their growing participation in urban and national politics, plus the expansion of viable, nonagricultural, economic bases within the South, helped to create national and regional atmospheres inhospitable to the lynching bee. But NAACP leaders had no assurances from 1909 to 1950, or beyond, that the dominant majority had rid itself of the temptations to lynch, as the incidents at Duck Hill, Mississippi in 1937, and at Greenville, South Carolina in 1947, or the murders of Emmett Till in 1955 and of Mack Parker in 1959 dramatically revealed.[6] Besides, the NAACP was intent upon ending more than lynching in its classic forms. Johnson, White, Wilkins, and their colleagues resisted all forms of violence, whether the victims were Arkansas sharecroppers in 1919, residents of Columbia, Tennessee, in 1946, or four young girls in a Birmingham, Alabama, church in 1963.[7]

By the late 1940s, the decline in lynching signalled the opportunity to shift attention to other matters, such as voting rights, desegregation in military service, employment, education, housing, and a variety of issues that increasingly demanded the energies of the civil rights coalition. Although a federal law against lynching remained an objective, it was now but one of several essential goals.[8] Indeed, the 1947 report of the President's Committee on Civil Rights, an unprecedented federal inquest that derived from the NAACP's appeals against postwar violence, announced an enlarged agenda of interracial reforms that America would struggle to implement during the next two decades.

NAACP campaigns against mob violence constituted a story with innumerable subplots, some with international ramifications. For example, America's professed dedication to interracial justice after World War II was quickened by a revulsion against Nazi racial doctrines and sharpened by the need to attract cold war support for the West among newly emerging nations of the Third World. All of this worked to the Association's advantage. On the domestic front, the northern wing of the Democratic party had preempted the civil rights issue ever since the early 1930s. Although this presented White and his associates with powerful allies in Congress and the administration, it left them no place to turn politically when entrenched southern Democrats, especially in the Senate, refused to yield. With mounting cold war hysteria during the late 1940s and early 1950s threatening to isolate, undermine, or discredit civil rights activists and other political dissenters, NAACP leaders, like most anti-Communist liberals of the day, sought shelter in respectable quarters. These the Association found in the White House, a precarious refuge at best, wherein the cause of civil rights rose and fell with Truman's political priorities, fortunes, and popularity. Once the Senate had refused in March 1949 to relax its cloture rules, the prospects for passing any strongly worded civil rights legislation faded. All that remained was the possibility of a face-saving gesture, such as the Ferguson antilynching bill, which the NAACP found wholly unacceptable. That some lawmakers imagined the Association could be bought off so cheaply was a sad commentary on their attitudes toward the black community and its needs.

The Association's crusade against lynching made considerable contributions to interracial justice. It influenced the public's perceptions of race relations, stimulated opportunities for cohesive protest action within the black community, and strengthened the NAACP in organizational terms. But that crusade alone could not permanently transform white America's long-ingrained racist tendencies. In retrospect, the shortcomings, as well as the successes, of the antilynching campaigns prove highly instructive. What the Association had accomplished was necessary but not sufficient.

Social change is, at the very least, dependent on the interaction of three key variables: values, behavior, and institutional structure. The

NAACP sought to alter all three. It affected values to the extent that it forced most whites to reassess the indifference or endorsement that they usually exhibited toward lynch mobs. As the NAACP and others hammered away at the senseless nature of mob rule, northern whites discovered their opposition to violence and southern whites became less enthusiastic, even embarrassed, about its recurrence. Under pressure from a national crusade and with the threat of federal intervention, southern whites did shift their behavior from the lynching bee to other means of control in a biracial setting. These new behavioral forms were perhaps no less racist, but certainly they were less extreme.

Institutional arrangements remained the least maleable. The antilynching bill did not pass, and no legal, constitutional, or structural changes occurred in relationships between the races. Whites still exercised a monopoly on power—in economics, politics, and even raw, physical force—and controlled the authority of the law. In a federal system of multiple jurisdictions, southern Democrats continued to benefit from one-party rule. This preserved their seniority in Congress and enabled them to maintain a collective opposition to reform measures. So long as northern liberals were unwilling to risk all on behalf of civil rights measures, and so long as Dixiecrats could rely upon selective cooperation from conservative Republicans, the filibuster prevailed as the ultimate weapon to frustrate the hopes for change.

When a later generation of civil rights advocates by-passed the legal-judicial techniques perfected by the NAACP, when they chose, instead, the path of non-violent, participatory, direct action that took them into the streets, they were expressing their intellectual and visceral judgments on the limitations of the Association's approach. They forced certain institutional changes that the NAACP had not achieved. These civil rights activists were, nonetheless, heirs who built upon a foundation laid by the Association; their initiatives prompted the enactment of five civil rights laws and two constitutional amendments in the years from 1957 to 1968.[9] This new phase of the civil rights movement generated enormous momentum, and no one should discount its importance. However, the gains of the sixties would have been impossible if the NAACP had not persisted for forty years in its commitment to the right of personal security and forced the nation to reconsider its dependence on lynching as an instrument of interracial policy. Violence had not disappeared, of course, but it was no longer condoned. One example is helpful. In 1940, Texas Congressman Lyndon B. Johnson opposed the antilynching bill.[10] In 1964, he negotiated the Omnibus Civil Rights bill into law and turned loose the federal forces at his disposal to locate the bodies of three missing civil rights workers in Mississippi.[11] For most people, the connection between those presidential actions and the work of James Weldon Johnson and Walter White is not direct or readily perceived; but it is, nevertheless, quite real.

For four decades the malignancy of mob violence plagued the

NAACP and threatened the black men and women it was created to serve. A vicious reality that could not be ignored, lynching absorbed inordinate amounts of the Association's time, energies, resources, and emotional capital. If we understand how much a part of black life this problem was, and if we appreciate how the NAACP's attack on violence fashioned a national response to race relations, then we can grasp the nature of the twentieth-century civil rights movement. Though lynching per se has gone out of style, it has left layers of raw scar tissue on the body politic; these may never be healed in our lifetime. The NAACP long practiced what therapies it could, and there are men and women eager to continue that work. Unfortunately, in today's atmosphere of political skepticism and economic uncertainties, many Americans seem reluctant to extend themselves in the continuing search for interracial justice. Healing remedies and future prognoses, therefore, may well depend upon socio-economic changes formulated now but brought to maturity by a more humane generation of parties yet unknown.

Notes

Abbreviations

AAF	*Afro-American* Files on Lynching, Baltimore, Md.
ABS	Arthur B. Spingarn Papers, Library of Congress, Washington, D.C.
AFPS	American Fund for Public Service Collection, New York City Public Library
Bd. Min.	Minutes of the Board of Directors of the NAACP, Papers of the National Association for the Advancement of Colored People, National Office, New York City, and Library of Congress, Washington, D.C.
BSCP	Brotherhood of Sleeping Car Porters and Maids Papers, Library of Congress, Washington, D.C.
BTW	Booker T. Washington Papers, Library of Congress, Washington, D.C.
CBO	Carrie Burton Overton Papers, Archives of Labor History and Urban Affairs, Wayne State University, Detroit, Mich.
CC	Calvin Coolidge Papers, Library of Congress, Washington, D.C.
CCl	Clark Clifford Papers, Harry S. Truman Presidential Library, Independence, Mo.
CER	Charles Edward Russell Papers, Library of Congress, Washington, D.C.
CIC	Commission on Interracial Cooperation Papers, Atlanta University Library
Cong. Rec.	U.S. Congress, *Congressional Record*, Washington, D.C.
CRC	Civil Rights Congress of Michigan Papers, Archives of Labor History and Urban Affairs, Wayne State University, Detroit, Mich.
DuB	W. E. B. Du Bois Papers, Herbert Aptheker Files, New York City
DuBF	W. E. B. Du Bois Papers, Fisk University Library, Nashville, Tenn.
EPC	Edward P. Costigan Papers, Microfilm (reels in the possession of the author), University of Colorado Library
ER	Eleanor Roosevelt Papers, Franklin D. Roosevelt Library, Hyde Park, N.Y.
FDR	Franklin D. Roosevelt Papers, Franklin D. Roosevelt Library, Hyde Park, N.Y.
Gav	Statement of Joseph Gavagan, Columbia University Oral History Project, New York City
HAK	Howard A. Kester Papers, Microfilm, University of Akron Library (originals at the Southern Historical Collection, University of North Carolina Library, Chapel Hill)

218   Notes

Has	William Hastie's Personal Files, Philadelphia, Pa.
HCL	Henry Cabot Lodge Papers, Massachusetts Historical Society, Boston, Mass.
HST	Harry S. Truman Papers, Harry S. Truman Library, Independence, Mo.
JD	Josephus Daniels Papers, Library of Congress, Washington, D.C.
JDA	Jessie Daniel Ames Papers, University of North Carolina Library, Chapel Hill, N.C.
JDF	Justice Department Files, National Archives and Records Service, Washington, D.C.
JES	Joel E. Spingarn Papers, Moorland Collection, Howard University, Washington, D.C.
JHM	J. Howard McGrath Papers, Harry S. Truman Presidential Library, Independence, Mo.
JWJ	James Weldon Johnson Collection, Yale University, New Haven, Conn.
McAd	William G. McAdoo Papers, Library of Congress, Washington, D.C.
MCT	Mary Church Terrell Papers, Library of Congress, Washington, D.C.
MSP	Moorfield Storey Papers, Library of Congress, Washington, D.C.
MWO	Mary White Ovington Papers, Archives of Labor History and Urban Affairs, Wayne State University, Detroit, Mich.
NAACP-LC	Papers of the National Association for the Advancement of Colored People (used by the author since 1965), Library of Congress, Washington, D.C.
NAACP-NY	Papers of the National Association for the Advancement of Colored People, National Office, New York City (used by the author during the years 1958 to 1965)
NARS	National Archives and Records Service, Washington, D.C.
NNC	National Negro Congress Papers, Schomburg Collection, New York City Public Library
NUL	National Urban League Papers, Library of Congress, Washington, D.C.
OC	Oscar Chapman Papers, Harry S. Truman Presidential Library, Independence, Mo.
OGV	Oswald Garrison Villard Papers, Houghton Library, Harvard University, Cambridge, Mass.
PCCR	Files of the President's Committee on Civil Rights, Harry S. Truman Presidential Library, Independence, Mo.
PN	Philleo Nash Papers, Harry S. Truman Presidential Library, Independence, Mo.
RAT	Robert A. Taft, Sr. Papers, Library of Congress, Washington, D.C.
RFW	Robert F. Wagner Papers, Georgetown University, Washington, D.C.
RW	Statement of Roy Wilkins, Columbia University Oral History Project, New York City
Schom	Schomburg Collection, New York City Public Library
Sec. Rep.	Monthly reports of the Secretary to the Board of Directors, NAACP
SJS	Stephen J. Spingarn Papers, Harry S. Truman Presidential Library, Independence, Mo.
STFU	Southern Tenant Farmers Union Papers, microfilm, University

	of Akron Library (originals at Southern Historical Collection, University of North Carolina Library, Chapel Hill)
TC	Tom Connally Papers, Library of Congress, Washington, D.C.
WA	Statement of Dr. Will Alexander, Columbia University Oral History Project, New York City
WEB	William E. Borah Papers, Library of Congress, Washington, D.C.
Wils	William Wilson, Secretary of Labor, Private File, General Records of the Department of Labor, RG 174, National Archives and Records Service, Washington, D.C.
Wood	Woodrow Wilson Papers, Library of Congress, Washington, D.C.
WW	Walter White Papers, James Weldon Johnson Collection, Yale University Library, New Haven, Conn.

Chapter 1

1. James Elbert Cutler, *Lynch-Law: An Investigation into the History of Lynching in the United States* (Montclair, N.J., 1969), chaps. 2-6. See also Richard Gambino, *Vendetta: A True Story of the Worst Lynching in America, the Mass Murder of Italian-Americans in New Orleans in 1891, the Vicious Motivations behind It, and the Tragic Repercussions That Linger to This Day* (Garden City, N.Y., 1977), chaps. 13 and 19; and Frank Shay, *Judge Lynch: His First Hundred Years* (Montclair, N.J., 1969), chaps. 2 and 3 and pp. 221-45.

2. James M. McPherson, *The Abolitionist Legacy: From Reconstruction to the NAACP* (Princeton, N.J., 1975), pp. 299-304; C. Vann Woodward, *Origins of the New South, 1877-1913* (Baton Rouge, 1966), pp. 351-52; George M. Fredrickson, *The Black Image in the White Mind: The Debate on Afro-American Character and Destiny, 1817-1914* (New York, 1971), chaps. 8-10; Walter White, *Rope and Faggot: A Biography of Judge Lynch* (New York, 1929), chap. 2; Richard Maxwell Brown, *Strain of Violence: Historical Studies of American Violence and Vigilantism* (New York, 1977), pp. 217-18. Also, personal interview, H. L. Mitchell, Akron, Ohio, Nov. 27-28, 1978.

3. Jessie Daniel Ames, *The Changing Character of Lynching* (Atlanta, Ga., 1942), pp. 1-21. See also John Shelton Reed, "A Note on the Control of Lynching," *Public Opinion Quarterly* 33 (Summer 1969): 268-71. See also Walter White to Daisy E. Lampkin, Nov. 30, 1939 (copy), box C-80, NAACP-LC.

4. Arthur F. Raper, *The Tragedy of Lynching* (Chapel Hill, 1933), pp. 46-47; and Gunnar Myrdal, *An American Dilemma*, 2 vols. (New York, 1964), 2. p. 566.

5. George Sinkler, *The Racial Attitudes of American Presidents: From Abraham Lincoln to Theodore Roosevelt* (Garden City, N.Y., 1972), pp. 430-34; and *New York Times*, Aug. 10, 1903, 1:7; White, *Rope and Faggot*, p. 227.

6. Ida B. Wells-Barnett, "Lynching and the Excuse for It," *The Independent* 53 (May 16, 1901): 1133-36; Ida B. Wells-Barnett, "A Red Record," rpt. in her *On Lynchings: Southern Horrors, a Red Record, Mob Rule in New Orleans* (New York, 1969), chaps. 1 and 6; Jacquelyn Dowd Hall, "Revolt against Chivalry: Jessie Daniel Ames and the Women's Campaign against Lynching" (Ph.D. diss., Columbia University, 1974), pp. 271-306; White, *Rope and Faggot*, pp. 251-69.

7. For illustrations of this phenomenon, see Raper, *The Tragedy of Lynching*, pp. 13-19; White, *Rope and Faggot*, pp. 29-33; and NAACP, *Thirty Years of Lynching in the United States, 1889-1918* (New York, 1919), pp. 12-19.

8. Brown, *Strain of Violence*, pp. 208-13, 324-25; Joseph Boskin, ed., *Urban Racial Violence in the Twentieth Century* (2d ed.; Beverly Hills, Calif.,

1976), chaps. 1 and 2; William Ivy Hair, *Carnival of Fury: Robert Charles and the New Orleans Race Riot of 1900* (Baton Rouge, 1976), passim; David A. Gerber, "Lynching and Law and Order: Origin and Passage of the Ohio Anti-lynching Law of 1896," *Ohio History* 83 (Winter 1974): 46–50; James Weldon Johnson, *Along This Way* (New York, 1933), pp. 341–44. See also Allen D. Grimshaw, "A Study in Social Violence" (Ph.D. diss., University of Pennsylvania, 1959), pp. 177–80.

9. Allison Davis, Burleigh B. Gardner, and Mary R. Gardner, *Deep South: A Social Anthropological Study of Caste and Class* (Chicago, 1941), chap. 18; Hadley Cantril, *The Psychology of Social Movements* (New York, 1941), pp. 83–85; Raper, *The Tragedy of Lynching*, pp. 25–31; Alexander Mintz, "A Reexamination of Correlations between Lynchings and Economic Indices," *Journal of Abnormal and Social Psychology* 41 (April 1946): 154–60; Erle Fiske Young, "The Relation of Lynching to the Size of Political Areas," *Sociology and Social Research* 12 (March-April 1928): 348–53; John Shelton Reed, "Percent Black and Lynching: A Test of Blalock's Theory," *Social Forces* 50 (March 1972); 356–60.

10. See, for example, Asa Philip Randolph, *The Truth about Lynching: Its Causes and Effects*, with Owen, *The Remedy* (pub. in 1 vol.; New York, [1917]); Robert Minor, *Lynching and Frame-up in Tennessee* (New York, 1946); and William L. Patterson, ed., *We Charge Genocide: The Historic Petition to the United Nations for Relief from a Crime of the United States Government against the Negro People* (New York, 1951), pp. 3–7.

11. W. J. Cash, *The Mind of the South* (New York, 1941), pp. 43–46; Hortense Powdermaker, *After Freedom: A Cultural Study in the Deep South* (New York, 1939), pp. 52–55. For a theoretical discussion of these patterns, see Robin M. Williams, Jr., *The Reduction of Intergroup Tensions: A Survey of Research on Problems of Ethnic, Racial, and Religious Group Relations* (New York, 1947), pp. 41–60.

12. John Dollard, *Caste and Class in a Southern Town* (3d ed.; Garden City, N.Y., 1949; orig. pub. 1937), chap. 15; Myrdal, *American Dilemma*, vol. 2, chaps. 27 and 31.

13. Allen D. Grimshaw, "Lawlessness and Violence in America and Their Special Manifestations in Changing Negro-White Relationships," *Journal of Negro History* 44 (Jan. 1959): 52–72; "Factors Contributing to Colour Violence in the United States and Britain," *Race* 3 (1962): 3–19; and "Three Major Cases of Colour Violence in the United States," ibid. 5 (1963); 76–86.

14. James M. Inverarity, "Populism and Lynching in Louisiana, 1889–1896: A Test of Erikson's Theory of the Relationship between Boundary Crises and Repressive Justice," *American Sociological Review* 41 (April 1976): 262–80; Ira M. Wasserman, "Southern Violence and the Political Process," ibid. 42 (April 1977): 359–62; and Whitney Pope and Charles Ragin, "Mechanical Solidarity, Repressive Justice, and Lynchings in Louisiana," ibid. 42 (April 1977): 363–68.

15. Hall, "Revolt Against Chivalry," pp. 198–213; Pete Daniel, "The Metamorphosis of Slavery, 1865–1900," *Journal of American History* 66 (June 1979): 88–99.

16. *Survey* 36 (May 20, 1916):196; Cantril, *Psychology of Social Movements*, pp. 93–122; White, *Rope and Faggot*, chap. 4; Davis et al., *Deep South*, pp. 24–49; Florette Henri, *Black Migration: Movement North, 1900–1920* (Garden City, N.Y., 1976), pp. 43–46; John Dittmer, *Black Georgia in the Progressive Era, 1900–1920* (Urbana, 1977), p. 137. See also Susan Brownmiller, *Against Our Will: Men, Women and Rape* (New York, 1975), chap. 7.

17. Neil J. Smelser, *Theory of Collective Behavior* (New York, 1963), chaps. 4, 5, and 8; Roger Brown, *Social Psychology* (New York, 1965), pp. 744–60.

18. White, *Rope and Faggot*, passim.

19. Byron de la Beckwith was tried twice for the Evers killing but not convicted; in 1975 he was found guilty in federal court of transporting a bomb to New Orleans (*New York Times*, Aug. 2, 1975, 26:1); James Earl Ray is serving a ninety-nine-year sentence for Dr. King's murder, although the question of accomplices, if any, remains a matter of debate (ibid., March 11, 1969, 1:8; March 12, 1969, 1:2; Jan. 27, 1978, 15:5; Nov. 9, 1978, 17:6; Nov. 11, 1978, 8:6); Deputy Sheriff Cecil Ray Price and six others were sent to prison for their part in the 1964 lynching of three civil rights workers in Mississippi (ibid., Oct. 21, 1967, 1:8). An Alabama grand jury indicted Gary Thomas Rowe, Jr., a former FBI informant, for his role in the 1965 murder of civil rights worker Viola Liuzzo (ibid., Nov. 6, 1978, 53:2; July 5, 1979, 11:1).

20. Myrdal, *American Dilemma*, 2. p. 565.

21. Reed, "A Note on the Control of Lynching," pp. 268–71. For further indications of how economic patterns affected forms of social control, see Jonathan M. Weiner, "Class Structure and Economic Development in the American South, 1865–1955," *American Historical Review* 84 (October 1979): 970–92.

22. Hall, "Revolt Against Chivalry," pp. 77–88, 166–84, 350–54. See also Henry E. Barber, "The Association of Southern Women for the Prevention of Lynching, 1930–1942," *Phylon* 34 (Dec. 1973): 378–89.

23. Raper, *Tragedy of Lynching*, p. 484.

24. William Pickens, *The New Negro: His Political, Civil and Mental Status and Related Essays* (New York, 1969), pp. 190–91; Walter White, *How Far the Promised Land?* (New York, 1955), pp. 229–31; Powdermaker, *After Freedom*, p. 55; and Myrdal, *American Dilemma*, 2. p. 565.

25. Cash, *Mind of the South*, pp. 306–18; and Dan Lacy, *The White Use of Blacks in America* (New York, 1972), chap. 7.

26. Charles S. Johnson, Edwin R. Embree, and Will W. Alexander, *The Collapse of Cotton Tenancy* (Chapel Hill, 1935), pp. 48–61; Leslie H. Fishel, Jr., "The Negro in the New Deal Era," *Wisconsin Magazine of History* 48 (Winter 1964–1965): 111–23; John B. Kirby, "The Roosevelt Administration and Blacks: An Ambivalent Legacy," in Barton J. Bernstein and Allen J. Matusow, eds., *Twentieth-Century America: Recent Interpretations* (2d ed.; New York, 1972), pp. 265–88; and Lacy, *White Use of Blacks*, chap. 9.

27. Morton Sosna, *In Search of the Silent South: Southern Liberals and the Race Issue* (New York, 1977), chap. 10.

28. Emma Lou Thornbrough, *T. Thomas Fortune: Militant Journalist* (Chicago, 1972), pp. 106–16, 124–25; Fortune's address to the Afro-American League is presented in John H. Bracey, Jr., August Meier, and Elliott Rudwick, eds., *Black Nationalism in America* (Indianapolis, 1970), pp. 211–22; and Donald L. Grant, *The Anti-lynching Movement: 1883–1932* (San Francisco, 1975), pp. 26–28, 32, and 104–05.

29. Frederick Douglass, *Why is the Negro Lynched?* (Bridgwater, England, 1895), pp. 4–7, and 12–13. Frederick Douglass, "Lynch Law in the South," *North American Review* 155 (July 1892): 117–24.

30. Alfreda M. Duster, ed., *Crusade for Justice: The Autobiography of Ida B. Wells* (Chicago, 1970), pp. 61–71, and 87–200; David M. Tucker, "Miss Ida B. Wells and Memphis Lynching," *Phylon* 32 (Summer 1971): 112–22; and Gerda Lerner, "Early Community Work of Black Club Women," *Journal of Negro History* 59 (April 1974): 160–61.

31. Duster, *Crusade for Justice*, pp. 252–62; Mary Frances Berry, *Black Resistance/White Law: A History of Constitutional Racism in America* (New York, 1971), pp. 116–17.

32. Grant, *Anti-lynching Movement*, chaps. 5 and 6; and August Meier, *Negro Thought in America, 1880-1915: Racial Ideologies in the Age of Booker T. Washington* (Ann Arbor, 1966), pp. 224-33. See, for example, Francis J. Grimké, *The Lynching of Negroes in the South: Its Causes and Remedy* (Washington, D.C., 1899), passim; and Gerber, "Lynching and Law and Order," pp. 45-48.

33. Meier, *Negro Thought in America*, chap. 10; Robert L. Factor, *The Black Response to America: Men, Ideals, and Organization from Frederick Douglass to the NAACP* (Reading, Mass., 1970), chap. 24; and Booker T. Washington to Oswald Garrison Villard, Nov. 16, 1904, OGV.

34. On the Niagara Movement and the Atlanta riot, see W. E. B. Du Bois to Mary White Ovington, Sept. 28, 1906, ser. 2, box 1, MWO. In *Dusk of Dawn: An Essay Toward an Autobiography of a Race Concept* (New York, 1968), pp. 86-93, Du Bois recalled the growing resentment to Washington but confused the sequence of events. See also Charles Crowe, "Racial Massacre in Atlanta, Sept. 22, 1906," *Journal of Negro History* 54 (April 1969): 150-73. On Brownsville, see Richard B. Sherman, *The Republican Party and Black America: From McKinley to Hoover, 1896-1933* (Charlottesville, 1973), pp. 56-63; and Emma Lou Thornbrough, "The Brownsville Episode and the Negro Vote," *Mississippi Valley Historical Review* 44 (Dec. 1957): 469-93.

35. Variations on these themes are discussed in Andrew Sledd, "The Negro: Another View," *Atlantic Monthly* 90 (July 1902): 65-73; and Clarence H. Poe, "Lynching: A Southern View," ibid. 93 (Feb. 1904): 155-65.

36. *New York Times*, Aug. 10, 1903, 1:7; March 28, 1906, 1:2; Dec. 4, 1912, 1:3; and Dec. 7, 1912, 1:1. See also James Wilford Garner, "Lynching and the Criminal Law," *South Atlantic Quarterly* 5 (Oct. 1906): 333-41; and Robert Strange, "Some Thoughts on Lynching," ibid. 5 (Oct. 1906): 349-51.

37. Cutler, *Lynch-Law*, chap. 8; James Harmon Chadbourn, *Lynching and the Law* (Chapel Hill, 1933), chap. 4; Shay, *Judge Lynch*, chap. 7; Charles S. Mangum, Jr., *The Legal Status of the Negro* (Chapel Hill, 1940), chap. 11; and Gerber, "Lynching and Law and Order," pp. 33-50.

38. *New York Times*, Nov. 22, 1902, 2:3; Winfield T. Durbin, "The Mob and the Law," *The Independent* 55 (July 30, 1903): 1790-93; His Eminence, Cardinal Gibbons, "Lynch Law: Its Causes and Remedy," *North American Review* 181 (Oct. 1905): 502-9; Charles B. Galloway, "Some Thoughts on Lynching," *South Atlantic Quarterly*, 5 (Oct. 1906): 351-53; *Survey* 36 (May 20, 1916): 196; W. D. Weatherford, *The Negro from Africa to America* (New York, 1969), pp. 360-64; and Edgar Gardner Murphy, *Problems of the Present South: A Discussion of Certain of the Educational, Industrial and Political Issues in the Southern States* (New York, 1916), pp. 176-82.

39. Otto H. Olsen, *Carpetbagger's Crusade: The Life of Albion Winegar Tourgée* (Baltimore, 1965), chap. 24; and McPherson, *Abolitionist Legacy*, pp. 317 and 386.

40. Frederic S. Monroe, secretary of the Union League, to congressman William S. Green, November 23, 1899, RG 233, Committee on the Judiciary, HR 56, "Legislation against Lynching, Dec. 4, 1899-Jan. 20, 1900" folder, NARS. For illustrations, see *The Nation* 77 (July 2, 1903): 4; 87 (Nov. 5, 1908): 428-29; 96 (April 13, 1913): 326-27; and *The Independent* 51 (Dec. 7, 1899): 3286-87; 52 (March 29, 1900): 783-84; 60 (March 8, 1906): 582-84; 61 (Oct. 11, 1906): 889; 62 (Jan. 31, 1907): 278-79; 65 (Aug. 27, 1908): 456; and 66 (Feb. 11, 1909): 330.

41. 109 U.S. 3, 163 U.S. 537, and 203 U.S. 1, respectively.

42. John L. Vandegrift to Robert K. Carr, June 27, 1947, PCCR; *Gambino Vendetta*, passim.; Sinkler, *Racial Attitudes of American Presidents*, pp. 324-27, 360-62, 430-34; "Lynching and Law and Order," pp. 47-48; Charles Flint

Kellogg, *NAACP: A History of the National Association for the Advancement of Colored People*, vol. 1: *1909-1920* (Baltimore, 1967), p. 211.

43. McPherson, *Abolitionist Legacy*, pp. 128-37; Daniel W. Crofts, "The Black Response to the Blair Education Bill," *Journal of Southern History* 37 (Feb. 1971): 41-65.

44. *Cong. Rec.*, 48th Cong., 1st sess., index, pp. 82, 535; 53d Cong., 2d sess., pp. 8182, 8206, (Aug. 3, 1894).

45. Ibid., 51st Cong., 1st sess., p. 1715, (Feb. 26, 1890); 52d Cong., 1st sess., p. 5272 (June 15, 1892), and p. 5821 (July 6, 1892); 53d Cong., 3d sess., p. 15, (Dec. 4, 1894), p. 477 (Dec. 19, 1894), and p. 1051 (Jan. 16, 1895).

46. Ibid., 56th Cong., 1st sess., pp. 846-47 (Jan. 16, 1900), and p. 1021 (Jan. 20, 1900).

47. Ibid., 57th Cong., 1st sess., p. 51 (Dec. 2, 1901); p. 212 (Dec. 9, 1901); p. 248 (Dec. 10, 1901); and p. 5286 (May 12, 1902). See also Albert E. Pillsbury, "A Brief Inquiry into a Federal Remedy for Lynching," *Harvard Law Review* 15 (May 1902): 707-13; and Eugene Levy, *James Weldon Johnson: Black Leader, Black Voice* (Chicago, 1973), pp. 240-41.

48. *Cong. Rec.*, 57th Cong., 1st sess., pp. 5902-05 (May 26, 1902); p. 636 (Jan. 13, 1902); 59th Cong., 1st sess., p. 112 (Dec. 5, 1905); and 60th Cong., 1st sess., p. 308 (Dec. 12, 1907).

49. Ibid., 63d Cong., 1st sess., p. 2013 (June 13, 1913); p. 1985 (June 10, 1913); 63d Cong., 2d sess., p. 3814 (Feb. 23, 1914); p. 11278 (June 27, 1914); and 64th Cong., 1st sess., pp. 11717 (July 27, 1916).

50. Maurine Christopher, *Black Americans in Congress* (2d ed.; New York, 1976), pp. 309-10 and 114-17. See also *Cong. Rec.*, 44th Cong., 1st sess., pp. 2100-04 (March 31, 1876).

51. RG 233, Committee on the Judiciary, HR 56, "Legislation against Lynching, Dec. 4, 1899-Jan. 20, 1900" folder, NARS.

52. Jesse Woodland Reeder, "Federal Efforts to Control Lynching" (Ph.D. diss., Cornell University, 1952), passim.

53. Mary White Ovington, *How the National Association for the Advancement of Colored People Began* (New York, 1914), pp. 1-7.

54. The literature on the nature of the Progressive movement is enormous, and there is no need to recapitulate it here. However, by way of illustration, see Robert H. Wiebe, *The Search for Order, 1877-1920* (New York, 1967), chap. 5. On NAACP organizers, see Wilson Record, "Negro Intellectual Leadership in the National Association for the Advancement of Colored People: 1910-1940," *Phylon* 17 (4th qtr., 1956): 375-89; and Kellogg, *NAACP*, chaps. 2 and 3, and pp. 297-308.

55. John Haynes Holmes, *I Speak for Myself* (New York, 1959), pp. 197-98.

56. Albert P. Blaustein and Robert L. Zangrando, eds., *Civil Rights and the Black American: A Documentary History* (New York, 1970), pp. 227-41, 359-72, and 582-89. *To Secure These Rights: The Report of the President's Committee on Civil Rights* (Washington, D.C., 1947), pp. 114-25.

57. National Archives, 82 *Statutes at Large* (April 11, 1968), pp. 73-75; Berry, *Black Resistance / White Law*, pp. 246-50.

58. For example, Slaughter-House Cases, 16 Wall. 36 (1873); United States v. Cruikshank, 92 U.S. 542 (1876); and Hodges v. United States, 203 U.S. 1 (1906).

59. See, for example, William B. Hixson, Jr., *Moorfield Storey and the Abolitionist Tradition* (New York, 1972), pp. 163-68; and Levy, *James Weldon Johnson*, pp. 238-44.

60. Mangum, *Legal Status of the Negro*, pp. 294-304; and Gerber, "Lynching and Law and Order," pp. 44-48.

Chapter 2

1. "The So-Called Race Riot at Springfield, Illinois," rpt. from *Charities and the Commons* (Sept. 19, 1908), in Allen D. Grimshaw, ed., *Racial Violence in the United States* (Chicago, 1969), pp. 51–56.
2. William English Walling, "The Race War in the North," *The Independent* 65 (Sept. 3, 1908): 529–34.
3. Quoted in Mary White Ovington, *How the National Association for the Advancement of Colored People Began* (New York, 1914).
4. Mary White Ovington, *The Walls Came Tumbling Down* (New York, 1970), pp. 100–07.
5. The activities of the conference are preserved in *Proceedings of the National Negro Conference, 1909* (New York, 1969), especially pp. 174–79.
6. Ibid., pp. 222–25. William Monroe Trotter proposed that the formal resolutions should demand that lynching be made a federal crime, but the conferees (by a vote of 53 to 21) decided that the question was, for the moment, satisfactorily covered in the words "murdered with impunity" (p. 225).
7. Minutes of the Special Meeting of the National Negro Committee, Thursday, May 5, 1910, box A-1, NAACP-LC.
8. Gunnar Myrdal, *An American Dilemma*, 2 vols. (New York, 1964), 1, p. 48.
9. For data on the founding members, see Ovington, *How the NAACP Began*, pp. 4–5; Wilson Record, "Negro Intellectual Leadership in the National Association for the Advancement of Colored People: 1910–1940," *Phylon* 17 (4th qtr. 1956): 376–79; and Charles Flint Kellogg, *NAACP: A History of the National Association for the Advancement of Colored People, vol. 1:1909–1920* (Baltimore, 1967), chap. 1, and pp. 298–99. Nancy J. Weiss has examined the professional, middle class, and Progressive orientations of NAACP organizers in "From Black Separatism to Interracial Cooperation: The Origins of Organized Efforts for Racial Advancement, 1890–1920," in Barton J. Bernstein and Allen J. Matusow, eds., *Twentieth-Century America: Recent Interpretations*, 2d ed. (New York, 1972), pp. 52–87. She has discussed the NAACP and the Urban League in this regard in her book, *The National Urban League, 1910–1940* (New York, 1974), chap. 4.
10. Elliott M. Rudwick, *W. E. B. Du Bois: Propagandist of the Negro Protest* (New York, 1968), pp. 68–70.
11. W. E. B. Du Bois, *The Souls of Black Folk* (Greenwich, Conn., 1961), pp. 23, 41, 87.
12. Quoted in Kellogg, *NAACP*, p. 44.
13. M. A. DeWolfe Howe, *Portrait of an Independent: Moorfield Storey* (Boston, 1932), pp. 39, 151–61, 170, 191–98, 250–51. See also William B. Hixson, Jr., *Moorfield Storey and the Abolitionist Tradition* (New York, 1972), chaps. 1 and 2.
14. Peter G. Filene has properly warned us on that score in "An Obituary for 'the Progressive Movement,'" *American Quarterly* 22 (Spring 1970): 20–34. What makes NAACP personnel "Progressive" are the factors noted in my text. On some Progressive's shortcomings in racial matters see "W. E. B. Du Bois' Confrontation with White Liberalism during the Progressive Era: A *Phylon* Document," with an Introduction by William M. Tuttle, Jr., *Phylon* 35 (Sept. 1974): 241–58.
15. William B. Hixson, Jr., "Moorfield Storey and the Defense of the Dyer Anti-Lynching Bill," *New England Quarterly* 42 (March 1969): 68–73.
16. Quoted in Walter White, *Rope and Faggot: A Biography of Judge Lynch* (New York, 1929), pp. 219-20.
17. On the emergence of twentieth-century liberalism, see Charles Forcey, *The Crossroads of Liberalism: Croly, Weyl, Lippmann, and the Progressive Era*,

1900–1925 (New York, 1961), passim. On the failure of Progressivism to meet black people's needs, see Nathan Irvin Huggins, *Harlem Renaissance* (New York, 1973), pp. 26–29, 34–35, and 154–55.

    18.   See Table 2 on p. 6.

    19.   *New York Times*, Jan. 16, 1911, 1:4–5.

    20.   Ibid., April 21, 1911, 1:4; April 22, 1911, 12:5; and May 13, 1911, 1:4.

    21.   Bd. Min., May 2, 1911, box A-1, NAACP-LC. Also Kellogg, *NAACP*, pp. 210–11.

    22.   Bd. Min., June 6, 1911, box A-1, NAACP-LC.

    23.   *New York Times*, Aug. 14, 1911, 1:4; *Nation* 93 (Aug. 31, 1911): 183–84; *Montgomery [Alabama] Advertiser*, Aug. 15, 1911, as quoted in Ralph Ginzburg, *100 Years of Lynchings* (New York, 1962), p. 73.

    24.   Kellogg, *NAACP*, pp. 91–92 and 306.

    25.   For a discussion of the Coatesville affair, see Ovington, *The Walls Came Tumbling Down*, pp. 113–15; Bd. Min. Oct. 16, 1911, Nov. 14, 1911; and Minutes of the Annual Meeting, Jan. 4, 1912, box A-1, NAACP-LC. Also, *New York Times*, Nov. 16, 1911, 18:5.

    26.   *New York Times*, Sept. 10, 1911, 11:2; Oct. 6, 1911, 13:4; Oct. 11, 1911, 1:2; Oct. 13, 1911, 10:2; Feb. 6, 1912, 2:3; May 4, 1912, 7:3. See also *Nation* 93 (Oct. 26, 1911): 386.

    27.   Bd. Min., Nov. 12, 1912 and Nov. 30, 1912, financial statement, box A-1, NAACP-LC. May Childs Nerney to Joel E. Spingarn, May 27, 1913, JES.

    28.   NAACP, *Notes on Lynching in the United States* (New York, 1912), pp. 1–16.

    29.   *New York Times*, June 27, 1912, 1:2 and June 26, 1912, 5:6.

    30.   Ibid., Dec. 6, 1912, 1:3 and Dec. 7, 1912, 1:1.

    31.   As it did, for example, in cases of racial violence in South Carolina, Mississippi, and Maryland, in mid-1914. Bd. Min., Aug. 4, 1914, NAACP-NY.

    32.   Bd. Min., Oct. 6, 1914, box A-1, NAACP-LC.

    33.   See Table No. 2, p. 6; Leonard Dinnerstein, *The Leo Frank Case* (New York, 1968), chap. 9; Kellogg, *NAACP*, pp. 215–16; Frank v. Mangum, 237 U.S. 309 (1915). See also Eugene Levy, " 'Is the Jew a White Man?': Press Reaction to the Leo Frank Case, 1913–1915," *Phylon* 35 (June 1974): 212–22.

    34.   Bd. Min., March 13, 1916, box A-1, NAACP-LC.

    35.   For a full discussion of the report of the Committee on Anti-Lynching Programme, see Bd. Min., April 10, 1916, box A-1, NAACP-LC.

    36.   See the thirty-five page typescript, "Memorandum for Mr. Philip G. Peabody on Lynch-Law and the Practicability of a Successful Attack Thereon," with cover letter, Roy Nash to Storey, May 18, 1916, box 8, MSP.

    37.   Philip G. Peabody to Storey, May 29, 1916, box C-75, NAACP-LC.

    38.   Storey to Nash, May 31, 1916, box C-75, NAACP-LC.

    39.   The Weatherford pamphlet is available in the Vertical File, "Lynching" folder, Schom. For a discussion of southern Progressives and race, see Wilma Dykeman and James Stokely, *Seeds of Southern Change: The Life of Will Alexander* (Chicago, 1962), pp. 110–20; and Jack Temple Kirby, *Darkness at the Dawning: Race and Reform in the Progressive South* (Philadelphia, 1972), especially chaps. 6 and 8, and the epilogue.

    40.   Bd. Min., June 12, 1916, box A-1, NAACP-LC. For a report on Weatherford, see "A Growing Social Effort in the South," *Survey* 36 (May 20, 1916): 196.

    41.   *New York Times*, May 16, 1916, 4:3; Bd. Min., June 12, 1916, box A-1, NAACP-LC; Nash to Joel Spingarn, June 14, 1916, JES, and Bd. Min., July 10, 1916, box A-1, NAACP-LC.

    42.   Bd. Min., June 12, 1916, and Sept. 11, 1916, box A-1, NAACP-LC.

43. Roy Nash to all branch officers, July 1, 1916, "NAACP" folder, JWJ.

44. Roy Nash, "The Lynching of Anthony Crawford," *The Independent* 88 (Dec. 11, 1916): 456, 458, 460–62 (rpt., New York. 1916), "Lynching—Case Stories" folder, Schom.; and James Weldon Johnson, *Along This Way* (New York, 1933), p. 314.

45. Bd. Min., Sept. 11, 1916, Oct. 9, 1916, Nov. 13, 1916; and Jan. 8, 1917, box A-1, NAACP-LC; Kellogg, *NAACP*, pp. 106–07 and 217–18; and NAACP, *Eighth Annual Report* (New York, 1918), p. 14.

46. For an indication of the various uses to which antilynching funds were put, see the Bd. Min. of Nov. 13, and Dec. 11, 1916, box A-1, NAACP-LC. The expenditures for November, for example, included the printing and mailing of 100,000 antilynching campaign circulars, travel expenses to investigate the Gainesville, Fla., lynchings, and the like.

47. Bd. Min., Dec. 11, 1916, box A-1, NAACP-LC. Also, Mark Adkins of Paine College to the author, March 14, 1979.

48. William Monroe Trotter to Joel Spingarn, Aug. 16, and 23, 1916, and Du Bois to Joel Spingarn, n. d., but undoubtedly written in the summer of 1916, JES; and "The Amenia Conference," a tentative four-page printed schedule, box 2, MCT. See also B. Joyce Ross, *J. E. Spingarn and the Rise of the NAACP, 1911–1939* (New York, 1972), pp. 46–48.

49. Bd. Min., Feb. 13, 1917, box A-1, NAACP-LC. See also Kellogg, *NAACP*, pp. 216, 220–21.

50. Membership figures provided to the author with a letter from Muriel S. Outlaw, NAACP Assistant Secretary for Membership, Aug. 25, 1971; see also Bd. Min., June 12, 1916, box A-1, NAACP-LC.

51. Kellogg has outlined these tensions and difficulties in *NAACP*, chap. 5; so too has Ross, *Spingarn*, pp. 59–80. See also Oswald Garrison Villard to Joel Spingarn, March 20, 1913, April 16, 1914, and Nov. 3, 1915, JES; W. E. B. Du Bois, *The Autobiography of W. E. B. Du Bois* (New York, 1968), p. 257; and Nerney to Joel Spingarn, Jan. 6, 1916, JES.

52. Bd. Min., May 8, 1916, and Sept. 17, 1917, box A-1, NAACP-LC.

53. Committee Report, with the Bd. Min. of Dec. 13, 1915, box A-1, NAACP-LC.

54. Joel Spingarn to Johnson, Oct. 28, 1916, and Johnson to Joel Spingarn, Nov. 5, 1916, "Spingarn, J.E." folder, JWJ. Ovington to Joel Spingarn, Nov. 24, 1916, JES; and Bd. Min., Dec. 11, 1916, box A-1, NAACP-LC. Ovington to Joel Spingarn, Sept. 26, 1917, JES.

55. Eugene Levy, *James Weldon Johnson: Black Leader, Black Voice* (Chicago, 1973), pp. 215, 292–93, and 151–54.

56. Ibid., pp. 178–80; and Nash to Johnson, April 24, 1916, "NAACP" folder, JWJ.

57. Johnson, *Along This Way*, p. 308.

58. Ibid., pp. 128, 142–44, 190–91, 219–20, 223, 238–39, 306; Du Bois, *The Autobiography*, pp. 293–94; and Levy, *James Weldon Johnson*, pp. 263–64, 344–46. See also Bernard Eisenberg, "James Weldon Johnson and the National Association for the Advancement of Colored People, 1916–1934" (Ph.D. diss., Columbia University, 1968), p. 75.

59. Johnson, *Along This Way*, pp. 165–70.

60. For some indication of the energies and talents that Johnson brought to his work, see the Bd. Min. of July 9 and Sept. 17, 1917, box A-1, NAACP-LC.

61. Johnson, *Along This Way*, pp. 314–17; Walter White, *A Man Called White* (New York, 1948), pp. 33–37.

62. Levy, *James Weldon Johnson*, pp. 5–7, 29; White *A Man Called White*, pp. 3–22, 39–43; Robert L. Zangrando, "Walter Francis White," in John A. Garraty

and Jerome L. Sternstein, eds., *Encyclopedia of America Biography* (New York, 1974), pp. 1188–89.

63. August Meier and Elliott Rudwick, "The Rise of the Black Secretariat in the NAACP, 1909–1935," *The Crisis* 84 (Feb., 1977): 58–61, 64–68; also Meier and Rudwick, "Attorneys Black and White: A Case Study of Race Relations within the NAACP," *Journal of American History* 62 (March 1976): 913–46.

64. For a discussion of the founding and development of the twentieth-century Klan, see David M. Chalmers, *Hooded Americanism: The History of the Ku Klux Klan* (Chicago, 1968), especially chap. 4. Thomas Cripps has assessed the film's impact in "The Myth of the Southern Box Office: A Factor in Racial Stereotyping In American Movies, 1920–1940," in James C. Curtis and Lewis L. Gould, eds., *The Black Experience in America: Selected Essays* (Austin, 1970), p. 118.

65. *The Clansman* (New York, 1905); Thomas Cripps, *Slow Fade to Black: The Negro in American Film, 1900–1942* (New York, 1977), chap. 2.

66. W. E. B. Du Bois, *Dusk of Dawn: An Essay toward an Autobiography of a Race Concept* (New York, 1968), pp. 239–40.

67. The national office's reactions are indicated in Joel Spingarn to Nerney, March 17, 1915, box C-75, NAACP-LC. NAACP, *Fighting a Vicious Film* (Boston, 1915) is available in box 8, MSP. See also Thomas R. Cripps, "The Reaction of the Negro to the Motion Picture *Birth of a Nation*," *The Historian* 25 (May 1963): 344–62.

68. Storey to Nerney, May 8, 1915, box C-75, NAACP-LC. See also Ovington, *The Walls Came Tumbling Down*, pp. 127–31; and Kellogg, *NAACP*, pp. 142–45. Thomas Cripps has discussed early efforts by blacks to use the motion picture medium in constructive ways in "*The Birth of a Race* Company: An Early Stride toward a Black Cinema," *Journal of Negro History* 59 (Jan. 1974): 28–37.

69. Bd. Min., Oct. 14, 1918, box A-1, NAACP-LC.

70. For an examination of the 1919 riots in the context of the times, see Arthur I. Waskow, *From Race Riot to Sit-In, 1919 and the 1960s: A Study in The Connections between Conflict and Violence* (Garden City, N.Y., 1966), chaps. 1 and 2.

71. I. A. Newby, *Jim Crow's Defense: Anti-Negro Thought in America, 1900–30* (Baton Rouge, 1965), p. 162.

72. Emphasis added. W. E. B. Du Bois, "Of the Culture of White Folk," *Journal of Race Development* 7 (April 1917): 434–37.

73. Clipping from the New York *Tribune*, April 5, 1917, vol 5, CER; and Bd. Min., April 9, 1917, box A-1, NAACP-LC.

74. Johnson, *Along This Way*, pp. 317–18; and Bd. Min., July 9, 1917, box A-1, NAACP-LC.

75. Bd. Min., July 9, 1917, box A-1, NAACP-LC.

76. Data computed from *Historical Statistics of the United States* (1961), pp. 46–47. See also Emmett J. Scott, *Negro Migration during the War* (New York, 1969), chap. 2; T. Lynn Smith, "The Redistribution of the Negro Population of the United States, 1910–1960," *Journal of Negro History* 51 (July 1966): 155–73; and Secretary of Labor William Wilson's Private File, General Records of the Department of Labor, RG 174, box 185, NARS.

77. For a discussion of the various factors that provided a backdrop to racial tensions in the city, see Elliott M. Rudwick, *Race Riot at East St. Louis July 2, 1917* (New York, 1972), pp. 3–15. See also Joseph Boskin, ed., *Urban Racial Violence in the Twentieth Century* (2d ed.; Beverly Hills, Calif., 1976), pp. 39–45.

78. The background of the July riot is discussed in Rudwick, *Race Riot at East St. Louis*, chaps. 3 and 4.

79. For review of the varying reports on death and loss of property, see ibid., pp. 49–53.

80. *Cong. Rec.*, 65th Cong., 1st sess., p. 5774, (Aug. 3, 1917). It was under this resolution, referred to the Committee on Rules, that the congressional investigation took place. Congressman Leonidas Dyer, Republican of St. Louis, had earlier requested a joint Senate and House inquiry; his proposal, also referred to the Rules Committee, never received further action (ibid., Index, pp. 72, 138).

81. Ibid., 65th Cong., 2d sess., pp. 8826–34 (July 6, 1918). The committee reported that intimidation of black people had, indeed, hurt interstate commerce by interrupting railroad operations.

82. Kellogg, *NAACP*, p. 223.

83. Roi Ottley, *"New World A-coming"* (Boston, 1943), p. 37; Martha Gruening, "Democratic Massacres in East St. Louis," *Pearson's Magazine* 38 (Sept. 1917); 106–08; and *Crisis* 14 (Sept. 1917); 219–38.

84. Bd. Min., Sept. 17, 1917, box A-1, NAACP-LC; Kellogg, *NAACP*, pp. 224–25.

85. Rudwick, *East St. Louis*, pp. 58–73.

86. Johnson, *Along This Way*, pp. 320–21; and Bd. Min., Sept. 17, 1917, box A-1, NAACP-LC. In his autobiography, written in 1933, Johnson recalled that Oswald Garrison Villard had mentioned the idea of a silent parade at the 1916 Amenia conference (*Along This Way*, p. 308). Reforming activist that he was, Villard had some basis for the suggestion. In May 1911, as a member of the Men's League for Women Suffrage, he had walked in a similar demonstration. *See* Walter Lord, *The Good Years* (New York, 1962), pp. 260–61.

87. New York *Evening Post*, Aug. 1, 1917, clipping, "Lynching" folder, JWJ.

88. Robert V. Haynes, *A Night of Violence: The Houston Riot of 1917* (Baton Rouge, 1976), chaps. 4, 6, 9; Johnson, *Along This Way*, pp. 321–24; NAACP, "Chronology of a Crusade" (mimeograph), pp. 10–11, NAACP-NY; and Ovington, *The Walls Came Tumbling Down*, p. 137.

89. Bd. Min., March 11, 1918, box A-1, NAACP-LC; Johnson, *Along This Way*, pp. 321–26; and Kellogg, *NAACP*, pp. 260–62.

90. Sec. Rep., Dec. 6, 1923, June 4, 1924, Feb. 5, 1925, and Nov. 4, 1937, NAACP-NY.

91. Henry Blumenthal, "Woodrow Wilson and the Race Question," *Journal of Negro History* 48 (Jan. 1963): 10–15. See also John Hope Franklin, *From Slavery to Freedom: A History of Negro Americans* (3d ed.; New York, 1967), pp. 455–59.

92. *Survey* 40 (Aug. 3, 1918): 511–12.

93. Oswald Garrison Villard, *Fighting Years* (New York, 1939), pp. 236–40; and *Crisis* 4 (Aug. 1912): 180–81, and ibid., 5 (Nov. 1912): 29. Also, Moorfield Storey, "Letter to Colored Voters," Oct. 1912, box 8, MSP.

94. On appointments, see Kathleen L. Wolgemuth, "Woodrow Wilson's Appointment Policy and the Negro," *Journal of Southern History* 24 (Nov. 1958): 457–71. See also Josephus Daniels' Office Diary, April 11, 1913, pp. 7–9, box 1, JD; and the New York *Evening Post*, Oct. 21, 1913, 9:3. On the threats, see Nerney to Joel Spingarn, July 31, 1913, JES. The NAACP was still protesting over a year later (Villard to Joseph Tumulty, Nov. 23, 1914 [copy] OGV).

95. See, for example, Joel Spingarn to Edmund Platt, April 7, 1917; Nash to Joel Spingarn, telegram, April 11, 1917; Nash to C. H. Studin, April 12, 1917; and Martin Madden to Joel Spingarn, April 21, 1917, JES; and Bd. Min., May 14, 1917, box A-1, NAACP-LC; Du Bois, *Dusk of Dawn*, pp. 250–51.

96. NAACP, "Chronology of a Crusade," pp. 9–10; Kellogg, *NAACP*, pp. 114–15; personal interview with Arthur B. Spingarn, New York City, Dec. 9, 1960; Bd. Min., July 8, 1918, box A-1, NAACP-LC. For examples of Shillady's activities,

see Bd. Min., March 11, 1918, box A-1, NAACP-LC. See also Meier and Rudwick, "The Rise of the Black Secretariat," pp. 64–65.

97. Johnson, *Along This Way*, p. 329; NAACP, *Thirty Years of Lynching in the United States, 1889–1918* (New York, 1919); and NAACP, *Supplement to Thirty Years of Lynching in the United States, 1889–1918* (New York, yearly, 1919–1946), available at NAACP-NY.

98. Kellogg, *NAACP*, pp. 228–30; Ovington, *The Walls Came Tumbling Down*, p. 152. See also John R. Shillady to William English Walling, July 19, 1918 (copy), box C-74, NAACP-LC; and NAACP, *Thirty Years of Lynching*, p. 26–27. Kellogg cites eight lynching victims at Valdosta; White's report, published in *Thirty Years of Lynching*, lists ten.

99. Shillady to Ovington, July 16, 1918 (copy), box C-74, NAACP-LC; Sec. Rep., May 5, 1921, NAACP-NY.

100. Bd. Min., Dec. 10, 1917, box A-1, NAACP-LC.

101. Bd. Min., Feb. 11 and March 11, 1918, box A-1, NAACP-LC.

102. U.S. Congress, *U.S. Congressional Directory*, 65th Cong., 3d sess., p. 58 (Dec. 1918); ibid., 67th Cong., 2d sess., pp. 59, 496 (Dec. 1922). Lewis F. Thomas, *The Localization of Business Activities in Metropolitan St. Louis*, Washington University Studies, n.s. no. 1 (St. Louis, 1927), p. 12.

103. U.S., Congress, *Biographical Directory of the American Congress, 1774–1971*, Senate Document no. 92-8, 92d Cong., 1st sess. (Washington, D.C., 1971), p. 892; *Cong. Rec.*, 64th Cong., 2d. sess., p. 249 (Dec. 12, 1961); 65th Cong., 1st sess., p. 3025 (May 28, 1917); p. 501 (April 9, 1917).

104. *Cong. Rec.*, 65th Cong., 1st sess., p. 4879 (July 9, 1917); quoted in Johnson, *Along This Way*, pp. 319–20.

105. *Cong. Rec.*, 65th Cong., 2d sess., p. 8827 (July 6, 1918).

106. Bd. Min., March 11, 1918, box A-1, NAACP-LC.

107. On the provision, see *Cong. Rec.*, 65th Cong., 2d sess., p. 4821 (April 8, 1918); pp. 6176–77 (May 7, 1918). Moores' bill was H.R. 11554; ibid., p. 5362 (April 19, 1918). Dyer's and the NAACP's antilynching bills in the years immediately thereafter are noted in ibid., H.R. 259, 66th Cong., 1st sess., p. 17; (May 19, 1919); H.R. 14097, 66th Cong., 2d sess., p. 7188 (May 17, 1920); H.R. 13, 67th Cong., 1st sess., p. 87; (April 11, 1921); and H.R. 1, 68th Cong., 1st sess., p. 25 (Dec. 5, 1923). On Dyer's bill and Pillsbury, see Levy, *James Weldon Johnson*, pp. 240–41.

108. See the eight-page typescript, "Statement of Charles H. Houston before the Senate Judiciary Subcommittee, in Support of S. 1352, the Federal Anti-Lynching Bill, January 19, 1948," RG 46, 80th Congress, "S. 2860" folder, NARS.

109. NAACP, "Memorandum to the Anti-Lynching Committee on Federal Anti-Lynching Bills, May 17, 1918, box C-74, NAACP-LC.

110. Bd. Min., May 13, 1918, box A-1, NAACP-LC.

111. Storey to White, May 2, 1918, box C-75, NAACP-LC; and White to Merrill Moores, May 8, 1918 (copy), and White to Storey, May 8, 1918 (copy), box C-76, NAACP-LC. Storey explained his position more fully in Storey to White, July 11, 1918 (copy), box C-75, NAACP-LC. On some of the legal issues involved, see Mary Frances Berry, *Black Resistance / White Law: A History of Constitutional Racism in America* (New York, 1971), pp. 126–28; and Albert P. Blaustein and Robert L. Zangrando, eds., *Civil Rights and the Black American: A Documentary History* (New York, 1970), pp. 246–58, 268–81.

112. Hixson, "Moorfield Storey and the Defense of the Dyer Anti-lynching Bill," pp. 65–81.

113. U.S., Congress, House, House Committee on the Judiciary, *Hearings*, 65th Cong., 2d sess., H.R. 11279, pp. 3–4, 7, 9–10, and 14. (June 6, 1918). The

Hornblower brief appears in ibid. ser. 66-pt. 2. See also Kellogg, *NAACP*, pp. 231-32.

114. *Cong. Rec.*, 65th Cong., 2d sess., pp. 6176-77 (May 7, 1918).
115. Storey to White, July 11, 1918 (copy), box C-75, NAACP-LC.
116. Bd. Min., Sept. 9, 1918, box A-1, NAACP-LC.
117. NAACP, *Ninth Annual Report* (New York, 1919), pp. 33-34.
118. Kellogg, *NAACP*, pp. 228-31. Bd. Min., Feb. 11, 1918, box A-1, NAACP-LC; and Shillady to Ovington, July 16, 1918 (copy), box C-74, NAACP-LC. See also Bd. Min., Feb. 10, 1919, NAACP-NY.
119. NAACP, *Eighth Annual Report* (New York, 1918), p. 14; and NAACP, *Tenth Annual Report* (New York, 1920).
120. Bd. Min., Dec. 9, 1918, box A-1, NAACP-LC; Johnson to Julius Rosenwald, July 11, 1918 (copy), plus attached budget statements, box C-74 NAACP-LC.
121. Bd. Min., Dec. 9, 1918, and Dec. 11, 1916, box A-1, NAACP-LC.
122. The new facilities housed both *The Crisis* and the NAACP national staff; the League to Enforce Peace had been the previous occupant. See Bd. Min., Dec. 9, 1918, box A-1, NAACP-LC.
123. Johnson, *Along This Way*, p. 329; NAACP, *Thirty Years of Lynching in the United States*; and NAACP, "Chronology of a Crusade," pp. 12-13.
124. Storey to Shillady, March 29, 1919, box C-75, NAACP-LC.
125. Shillady to Storey, March 18, 1919 (copy), box C-74, NAACP-LC; Storey to Shillady, March 20, 1919, box C-75, NAACP-LC; Stephen R. Fox, *The Guardian of Boston: William Monroe Trotter* (New York, 1970), pp. 140-41, 222-23.
126. Shillady to Storey, March 21, 1919 (telegram copy), box C-74, NAACP-LC; and Madame C. J. Walker to Storey, March 24, 1919, box C-75, NAACP-LC.
127. This list is available at the Association's national offices in New York City and in the "Lynching—Legislation" folder, Schom.
128. For a discussion of the conference planning, implementation, and follow-up see NAACP, *Tenth Annual Report*, pp. 30-32; Ovington, *The Walls Came Tumbling Down*, p. 153; *Crisis* 18 (June 1919): 92; and Kellogg, the NAACP, pp. 232-35.
129. Typescript of "Address to the Nation" attached to letter from Shillady to Storey, June 9, 1919 (copy), box C-74, NAACP-LC.

Chapter 3

1. NAACP, *Tenth Annual Report* (New York, 1920), p. 23.
2. Storey to Ovington, Sept. 6, 1919, box C-75, NAACP-LC.
3. Shillady to Storey, Sept. 13, 1919 (copy), box C-74, NAACP-LC.
4. Mary White Ovington, *The Walls Came Tumbling Down* (New York, 1970), pp. 174-75; see also James Weldon Johnson, *Along This Way* (New York, 1933), p. 343; W. E. B. Du Bois, *Dusk of Dawn; An Essay Toward an Autobiography of a Race Concept* (New York, 1968), p. 264; NAACP, "Chronology of a Crusade" (mimeograph), NAACP-NY, p. 13, pt. 2, p. 1; personal interview with Arthur Spingarn, New York City, Dec. 9, 1960.
5. See Charles Flint Kellogg's resumé of officers, *NAACP: A History of the National Association for the Advancement of Colored People, vol. 1, 1909-1920* (Baltimore, 1967), p. 307. Kellogg dates Shillady's official resignation as August 1920. See ibid., p. 241; and W. E. B. Du Bois "Memorandum to the Chairman of the Board and the Committee on Secretary," June 28, 1920, box C-64, NAACP-LC.

6. Edmund David Cronon, *Black Moses: The Storey of Marcus Garvey and the Universal Negro Improvement Association* (Madison, 1955), pp. 204–07, 14–20; and see, for example, Amy Jacques-Garvey, ed., *Philosophy and Opinions of Marcus Garvey*, 2 vols. (New York, 1925), 1: 52–53, 63–64.

7. W. E. B. Du Bois, *The Autobiography of W. E. B. Du Bois* (New York, 1968), p. 271; Minutes of the Annual Meeting of the NAACP, Jan. 6, 1919, and Report of the Director of Research for the April 14, 1919 Meeting of the NAACP Board of Directors, NAACP-NY; see also Clarence G. Contee, "Du Bois, the NAACP, and the Pan-African Congress of 1919," *Journal of Negro History* 57 (Jan. 1972): 13–28.

8. Elliott M. Rudwick, *W. E. B. Du Bois: Propagandist of the Negro Protest* (New York, 1968), pp. 212–15; and Stephen R. Fox, *The Guardian of Boston: William Monroe Trotter* (New York, 1970), pp. 221–30.

9. W. E. B. Du Bois, "Opinion," *Crisis* 18 (May 1919): 13–14.

10. Elliott M. Rudwick, "W. E. B. Du Bois in the Role of *Crisis* Editor," *Journal of Negro History* 43 (July 1958): 229–31.

11. Robert K. Murray, *Red Scare: A Study of National Hysteria, 1919–1920* (New York, 1964), chaps. 4–6; and Bd. Min., May 12, 1919, NAACP-NY.

12. Table no. 2, p. 6. Arthur I. Waskow has discussed the major riots in *From Race Riot to Sit-In, 1919 and the 1960s* (Garden City, N.Y., 1966), chaps. 2–8. See also William M. Tuttle, Jr., *Race Riot: Chicago in the Red Summer of 1919* (New York, 1970), passim; and his article, "Labor Conflict and Racial Violence: The Black Worker in Chicago, 1894–1919," *Labor History* 10 (Summer 1969): 408–32.

13. Storey to Shillady, Oct. 1, 1919, box C-75, NAACP-LC. NAACP publicity director, Herbert J. Seligmann, discussed race riots in general and the Omaha riot in particular in his book, *The Negro Faces America* (New York, 1920), chap. 2. See also Allen D. Grimshaw, *Race Violence in the United States* (Chicago, 1969), pp. 92–94.

14. Shillady to Storey, Nov. 8, 1919 (copy), box C-75, NAACP-LC; and Johnson to Storey, Jan. 16, 1920, box 8, MSP. See also an NAACP flier on the Curtis Senate Resolution no. 189, box 3, MCT.

15. On Curtis, see U.S., Congress, *Biographical Directory of the American Congress, 1774–1971*, Senate Document no. 92-8, 92d Cong., 1st sess. (Washington, D.C., 1971), pp. 814–15; and *New York Times*, July 1, 1928, 9, 7: 1–4. On the NAACP's later attitudes, see pp. 132–33 below.

16. Field Secretary's Report to the Board of Directors, NAACP (hereafter Field Secretary's Report), Jan. 12, 1920, NAACP-NY.

17. Eugene Levy, *James Weldon Johnson: Black Leader, Black Voice* (Chicago, 1973), pp. 240–41; and A. E. Pillsbury to James Weldon Johnson, Jan. 22, 1920, box 8, MSP.

18. On Pillsbury, see Kellogg, *NAACP*, pp. 42, 51, 89, and 160, n. 20.

19. Field Secretary's Report, Feb. 9, 1920, NAACP-NY; *Cong. Rec.*, 67th Cong., 2d sess., pp. 1308–09 (Jan. 17, 1922).

20. Storey to William Paul Dillingham, Jan. 19, 1920 (copy), box C-75, NAACP-LC.

21. Sec. Rep., Dec. 8, 1920, NAACP-NY.

22. Bd. Min., Feb. 9, 1920, NAACP-NY. Six additional points dealt with discrimination, interstate travel, disfranchisement, the independence of Haiti, national aid to education, and racial discrimination in the military and civil services.

23. Field Secretary's Report, June 14, 1920, NAACP-NY; Kirk H. Porter

and Donald Bruce Johnson, eds., *National Party Platforms, 1840-1964* (3d ed.; Urbana, 1966), p. 236.

24. Report of the Field Secretary on Interview with Senator Warren G. Harding, Marion, Ohio, Aug. 9, 1920, box C-64, NAACP-NY. See also Bd. Min., Sept. 10, 1920, NAACP-NY.

25. Johnson, *Along This Way*, p. 360. Ovington also discusses Johnson's role in providing Harding with information on Haiti, *(The Walls Came Tumbling Down*, pp. 181-82). The *Nation* articles also appeared in a forty-eight-page pamphlet, James Weldon Johnson's *Self-Determining Haiti* (New York, 1920), ser. 9, box 10, MWO.

26. Report of the Secretary's Visit to Senator Harding, Jan. 15, 1921, box C-64, NAACP-LC.

27. Sec. Rep. April 6, 1921, and May 5, 1921, NAACP-NY; *New York Times*, April 13, 1921, 2:1.

28. U.S. Congress, *Congressional Directory*, 87th Cong., 2d sess., (Washington, D.C., 1962), p. 324. NAACP, "Chronology of a Crusade" (mimeograph), pt. 2, p. 3; and Sec. Rep., May 5, 1921, NAACP-NY.

29. Sec. Rep., May 5, 1921, NAACP-NY.

30. *National Cyclopaedia of American Biography* 18 (New York, 1922), 18. 356-57; Walter White, *A Man Called White* (New York, 1968), pp. 25-26.

31. Wilma Dykeman and James Stokely, *Seeds of Southern Change: The Life of Will Alexander* (Chicago, 1962), pp. 110-20, 131-41. See also Jack Temple Kirby, *Darkness at the Dawning, Race and Reform in the Progressive South* (Philadelphia, 1972), pp. 177-81.

32. NAACP, "Chronology of a Crusade," pt. 2, p. 3.

33. White to Storey, Feb. 25, 1921 (copy), box C-76, NAACP-LC.

34. White to Storey, April 26, 1921 (copy), box C-76, NAACP-LC; and Sec. Rep., June 9, 1921, and Aug. 15, 1921, NAACP-NY.

35. Sec. Rep., June 9, 1921, NAACP-NY.

36. On Storey, see William B. Hixson, Jr., *Moorfield Storey and the Abolitionist Tradition* (New York, 1972), pp. 163-75.

37. White to Storey, March 14, 1921 (copy), box C-76, NAACP-LC.

38. White to Storey, April 28, 1921 (copy), box C-76, NAACP-LC. The persistent problems of getting a constructive federal response is indicated in Mary Frances Berry, *Black Resistance / White Law: A History of Constitutional Racism in America* (New York, 1971), chaps. 10 and 11, and pp. 157-61. See also White to George Wickersham, April 28, 1921 (copy), box C-76, NAACP-LC.

39. White to Storey, May 12, 1921; and Johnson to Storey, Aug. 1, 1921, box 8, MSP. Storey's letter to Leonidas Dyer of Aug. 4, 1921 is quoted in Hixson, *Moorfield Storey*, p. 169.

40. Wickersham's remark is reported in Shillady to Storey, Nov. 8, 1919 (copy), box C-75, NAACP-LC. On Marshall, see *Who's Who in America*, vol. 11: *1920-1921* (Chicago, 1920), 11. 1837.

41. Sec. Rep., Aug. 15, 1921, NAACP-NY; Levy, *James Weldon Johnson*, pp. 242-44.

42. *New York Times*, Oct. 21, 1921, 18:4.

43. Sec. Rep., Nov. 10, 1921, NAACP-NY.

44. For the dates of congressional sessions, see the *Congressional Directory*, p. 324. Madden represented the Illinois First Congressional District from 1904 until his death in 1928, and he enjoyed the support of such powerful elements as William "Big Bill" Thompson (mayor and leader of Chicago's Republican machine) and Robert Abbott (editor of the Midwest's most influential black newspaper, the Chicago *Defender*). In fact, the *Defender*, regardless of its

reputation for militancy in certain matters affecting the black community, did not even advocate the election of a black congressman until after Madden had died. Privately wealthy, Madden liked spending his time and money on politics, and it was widely believed that he helped black job applicants through his earlier membership on the House Committee on Post Office and Post Roads. When he first entered Congress, Madden's district had but a small black bloc; by the mid-1920s, however, black voters comprised something near a majority of his constituents. See Harold F. Gosnell, *Negro Politicians* (Chicago, 1935), pp. 39, 78–80, 102, 307. For supportive and critical views of Madden, see Allan H. Spear, *Black Chicago: The Making of a Negro Ghetto, 1890–1920* (Chicago, 1967), pp. 124, 199.

45. Johnson to Storey, Oct. 28, 1921, Box 8, MSP. Also Sec. Rep., Nov. 10, 1921, NAACP-NY.

46. *Cong. Rec.*, 67th Cong., 1st sess., pp. 7060 and 7063; (Oct. 31, 1921); and U.S., Congress, House, House Judiciary Committee, *Anti-Lynching Bill, Report No. 452*, 67th Cong., 1st sess., p. 18 (Oct. 31, 1921).

47. Ibid., pp. 3, 5, 10, 13–14, 16–17.

48. Sec. Rep., Oct. 6, 1921, NAACP-NY; David M. Chalmers, *Hooded Americanism; The History of the Ku Klux Klan* (Chicago, 1968), pp. 35–38; and U.S. Congress, House, *Ku Klux Klan: Hearings before the Committee on Rules*, 67th Cong., 1st sess. (Oct. 11, 1921).

49. *Congressional Directory*, 67th Cong., 2d sess. pp. 129, 131 (Washington, D.C., 1922).

50. Henry Lincoln Johnson frequently served as liaison between black voters and Republican politicians in Chicago (Gosnell, *Negro Politicians*, p. 316). Perry Howard was then in his first of eight years' service as special assistant to the United States attorney general. In the mid-1920s he also became chairman of the Republican State Committee for his native Mississippi and a member of the Republican National Committee. See G. James Fleming and Christian E. Burckel, eds., *Who's Who in Colored America* (7th ed.; Yonkers-on-Hudson, N.Y., 1950), p. 273.

51. Special Report of the Secretary on Washington Trip, Nov. 18, 1921, box 8, MSP. For an indication of the Association's earlier concern about Dyer's motives, see Richard B. Sherman, *The Republican Party and Black America: From McKinley to Hoover, 1896–1933* (Charlottesville, 1973), p. 182.

52. White to Storey, Oct. 26, 1921. Each of the four involved the use of force (sometimes under color of public authority) by whites against black people. See also Ovington to Storey, Oct. 24, 1921, box 8, MSP.

53. Special Report of the Secretary on Washington Trip, Nov. 18, 1921, NAACP-NY.

54. *Cong. Rec.*, 67th Cong., 2d sess., pp. 541–62, (Dec. 19, 1921); and pp. 602–05 (Dec. 20, 1921); Sec. Rep., Jan. 6, 1922, NAACP-NY; and *New York Times*, Dec. 20, 1921, 10:2, and Dec. 21, 1921, 11:3.

55. Sec. Rep., Jan. 6, 1922, NAACP-NY. Robert Abbott's Chicago *Defender*, founded in 1905, had long favored a federal antilynching law. See, for example, Chicago *Defender*, Aug. 10, 1929, II, 2:1; Oct. 21, 1933, 14:1; Nov. 18, 1933, 14:1; and Nov. 25, 1933, 3:6–7. Also, *Cong. Rec.*, 67th Cong., 2d sess., pp. 1697–98 (Jan. 25, 1922).

56. Ibid., pp. 1699–1700, and 1706.

57. Ibid., pp. 1714 and 1716.

58. Ibid., p. 1721.

59. Sec. Rep., Feb. 1922, NAACP-NY.

60. *Afro-American*, Jan. 27, 1922, 1:1.

61. *Cong. Rec.*, 67th Cong., 2d sess., pp. 1773, 1794–95 (Jan. 26, 1922);

Sec. Rep., Feb. 1922, NAACP-NY; NAACP, *Thirteenth Annual Report* (New York, 1923), p. 9. While the vote exhibited a highly partisan division, 17 Republicans joined southern Democrats in opposition and 8 northern Democrats voted for passage. The *New York Times* asserted that many of the negative votes by Republicans stemmed from reservations about the bill's constitutionality (Jan. 27, 1922, 17:8).

62. Sec. Rep., March 9, 1922, NAACP-NY.
63. Bd. Min., May 8, 1922, NAACP-NY; and *Cong. Rec.*, 67th Cong., 2d sess., p. 6480 (May 6, 1922).
64. For a discussion of NAACP tactics, see Johnson to Storey, May 18, 1922, box 9, MSP; and Sec. Rep., Sept. 7, 1922, NAACP-NY.
65. Sec. Rep., May 22, 1922, and Sept. 7, 1922, NAACP-NY.
66. Bd. Min., March 13, 1922; and Sec. Rep., April 6, 1922, NAACP-NY.
67. James Weldon Johnson, Memorandum Regarding Secretary's Washington Trip, March 7-11, 1922, box 9, MSP. NAACP, *Thirteenth Annual Report*, p. 11; and "Brief of Herbert K. Stockton on the Dyer Anti-Lynching Bill," for the Senate Committee on the Judiciary, 67th Cong., 2d sess., pp. 1-8 (June 5, 1922), "Lynching—Legislation" folder, Schom.
68. William E. Borah to Storey, Feb. 9, 1922; Borah to Harry (sic) K. Stockton, May 10, 1922 (copy); Borah to Storey, June 1, 1922, box 9, MSP; and Borah to Edward H. Berg, June 27, 1922 (copy), box 218, WEB.
69. On Borah, see U.S., Congress, *Congressional Directory*, 68th Cong., 1st sess. (Washington, D.C., 1923), pp. 83-84; and *New York Times*, Dec. 3, 1922, 1:7; John A. Garraty, *Henry Cabot Lodge, A Biography* (New York, 1953), pp. 411-14; "The Official Facts About Senator Lodge," a nineteen-page carbon-copy typescript by Lynn Haines (n.d.); J. A. Hopkins to Borah, Aug. 11, 1922; and press release of the Committee of 48 Functioning as the Liberal Party, sent to Borah on Nov. 15, 1922 box 220, WEB.
70. Bd. Min., June 12, 1922; and Sec. Rep., July 8, 1922, NAACP-NY.
71. *Afro-American*, Dec. 9, 1921, editorial page: 2-3, and Jan. 20, 1922, 1:6. *Cong. Rec.*, 67th Cong., 2d sess., pp. 1308-09 (Jan. 17, 1922). The Henry Cabot Lodge Papers reveal a solid degree of public support for the Dyer bill. On Lodge's political response, see Sherman, *The Republican Party and Black America*, pp. 192-93. On the "Force Bill," see Garraty, *Henry Cabot Lodge*, pp. 117-21.
72. Lodge to Johnson, Feb. 18, 1922, and May 11, 1922, box C-69, NAACP-LC; and Lodge to Eben W. Burnstead, May 23, 1922 (copy), HCL.
73. *Afro-American*, May 19, 1922, 7:3; June 2, 1922, 7:3; and June 30, 1922, 1:6-7. The Association did not hesitate to bring direct pressure upon individual members of the Judiciary Committee, whenever it could do so. In early March, it revealed its intention to submit to the committee a charge it had made public that Senator Overman of North Carolina had "looked interestedly on" during the lynching of three black people taken from the Rowan County jail (ibid., March 10, 1922, 1:5).
74. Borah to Lodge, telegram, June 6, 1922, HCL.
75. Lodge to Johnson, June 23, 1922 (copy), HCL.
76. Absentees Henry Ashurst (D-Ariz.) and George Moses (R-N. H.) did not vote. Sec. Rep., July 8, 1922, NAACP-NY.
77. Johnson to Lodge, July 7, 1922; and Lodge to Butler Wilson, July 11, 1922, (copy), HCL. What particularly troubled Johnson was a Washington dispatch in the July 7 New York *Tribune*. Johnson to Storey, July 7, 1922, box 9, MSP.
78. Lodge to Johnson, Sept. 15, 1922 (copy) HCL.
79. White to Johnson, Aug. 24, 1922 (telegram, copy), box C-77, NAACP-LC.

80. White to Storey, July 15, 1922 (copy), box C-77, NAACP-LC.

81. Senator Calder wrote the Association on August 18 to say that the tariff bill would shortly pass and that in order to move the antilynching bill the Association should intensify its efforts, revisit a number of senators, and generate a letter-writing campaign by black voters throughout the nation. White to Johnson, Aug. 22, 1922, box C-77, NAACP-LC.

82. *Cong. Rec.*, 67th Cong., 2d sess., pp. 13075-79 (Sept. 21, 1922). For a complete transcript of Shortridge's other remarks that day, see pp. 13082-86. The Secretary's Report, Oct. 4, 1922, indicates Johnson's awareness that Shortridge was at least making an effort on behalf of the antilynching bill (NAACP-NY).

83. Sec. Rep., Oct. 4, 1922, NAACP-NY; see also *Cong. Rec.*, 67th Cong., 2d sess., pp. 13086-87 (Sept. 21, 1922).

84. Sec. Rep., Oct. 4, 1922, NAACP-NY. A comparison of various roll calls taken on the afternoon of Sept. 21, 1922 reveals the limited backing given the Dyer antilynching bill. Even though many legitimate causes force a senator's absence from the floor, eight, who might have been expected to befriend the measure, failed to answer at crucial moments in the chamber. Colt, Dillingham, Ernst, Frelinghuysen (R-New Jersey), LaFollette (Progressive Republican of Wisconsin), Lodge, Nelson, and Sterling. Senators Colt, Dillingham, Ernst, Nelson, and Sterling had been among those eight Republicans on the Judiciary Committee who voted to report the bill favorably. Borah and Thomas Du Pont (R-Del.) were also among those present earlier but absent from the final quorum call on the afternoon of Sept. 21. Sec. Rep., Oct. 4, 1922, and July 8, 1922, NAACP-NY.

85. Shortridge to Lodge, Oct. 6, 1922, HCL.

86. Lodge to Shortridge, Oct. 9, 1922 (copy). In mid-September, Lodge had written Charles Curtis from Nahant, Mass., to justify another Senate absence: "I ought to be here continuously now until election to look after my campaign, if the party wants me to be elected." See Lodge to Curtis, Sept. 15, 1922 (copy), HCL.

87. For a discussion of Trotter's efforts at this time, some of which paralleled, and some of which seemed to conflict with, the NAACP campaigns, see Fox, *The Guardian of Boston*, pp. 236-48; Lodge "To the President, The White House," Oct. 4, 1922 (copy), HCL.

88. W. M. Trotter to Lodge, Oct. 10, 1922, HCL. See also, *Afro-American*, Oct. 13, 1922, 1:3. Within two weeks Trotter wrote again to thank Lodge for a copy of his letter to Harding on the Dyer bill and to request another meeting. See Trotter to Lodge, Oct. 23, 1922, HCL.

89. White to Rosenwald, Oct. 20, 1922 (draft), box C-77, NAACP-LC.

90. U.S., Congress, *Congressional Directory*, 87th Cong., 2d sess. (Washington, D.C., 1962), p. 324.

91. Sec. Rep., Dec. 18, 1922; and Bd. Min., Dec. 11, 1922, NAACP-NY.

92. *Cong. Rec.*, 67th Cong., 3d sess., p. 288; (Nov. 27, 1922); pp. 332-39 (Nov. 28, 1922); pp. 393-409 (Nov. 29, 1922); p. 450 (Dec. 4, 1922). Sec. Rep., Dec. 18, 1922, NAACP-NY. See also *New York Times*, Dec. 3, 1922, 1:7. Johnson to Lodge, telegram, Dec. 3, 1922 HCL. Also, personal interview, Charles L. Watkins, parliamentarian of the U. S. Senate, Washington, D.C., Dec. 21, 1962.

93. Lodge to Johnson, Dec. 4, 1922 (copy), HCL.

94. Sec. Rep., Dec. 18, 1922, NAACP-NY.

95. Ibid.

96. Ibid.

97. *Congressional Directory*, 68th Cong., 1st sess., pp. 129, 131 (Dec. 1923); *Congressional Quarterly Guide to the Congress of the United States: Origins, History and Procedure* (Washington, D.C., 1971), pp. 81-83.

98. White to Johnson, Dec. 6, 1922 (telegram, copy), box C-77, NAACP-LC.

99. On the general coolness of liberal Republicans to issues vital to black Americans, see Sherman, *The Republican Party and Black America*, pp. 187, 191–92, 210, 212–13. Also Richard Lowitt, *George W. Norris: The Persistence of a Progressive, 1913–1933* (Urbana, 1971), pp. 327–29. Levy suggests some liberal Republicans endorsed the Dyer bill only when it fit their other political plans. *James Weldon Johnson*, pp. 257–58, 260–63.

100. See, for example, Richard B. Sherman, "The Harding Administration and the Negro: An Opportunity Lost," *Journal of Negro History* 49 (July 1964): 151–68.

Chapter 4

1. Emphasis added. White to Storey, Nov. 29, 1922 (copy), box C-77, NAACP-LC.

2. Robert Bagnall to Johnson, telegram, Dec. 3, 1922 box C-11, NAACP-LC.

3. See letters in the W. E. B. Du Bois Papers, under the care of historian Herbert Aptheker. Among them, replies from Bishop Robert E. Jones of the Methodist Episcopal church (n.d.); editor W. B. Andrews of the *Baltimore Herald-Commonwealth* (Dec. 26, 1922); Robert Vann (Dec. 21, 1922); and James Cobb, John Hurst, and P. A. Wallace. Kelly Miller was decidedly in the minority among the respondents by suggesting that the "Republican party, despite its apostacy from the ancient faith, is still the best existing instrument of racial service. The Negro is too helpless to practice vindictive politics" (Miller to Du Bois, Dec. 16, 1922).

4. "Tentative Draft of Proposed Activities of the N.A.A.C.P.," submitted to the NAACP Board of Directors on Feb. 5, 1923, NAACP-NY. A conference of the Women's Missionary Council and Conference, Social Service Superintendents of the Commission on Race Relations of the Women's Missionary Council, Methodist Episcopal Church, South, held in Atlanta, had condemned lynching and called upon officials, the press, and the pulpit for its suppression. Noting the defeat of the Dyer bill, the assembled women declared that the Senate had thereby placed the responsibility back upon each state and they asked authorities to "make good their claim proving their competency to abolish mob violence and lynching" (Norfolk *Journal and Guide*, Dec. 16, 1922, 1:2). In October 1923 R. W. Miles of the southern-liberal Commission on Interracial Cooperation wrote C. Bascom Slemp, secretary to President Calvin Coolidge, that "the greatest single menace to the South is the prevalence of lynching" (Miles to Slemp, Oct. 15, 1923, ser. 1, No. 93A, box 97, CC).

5. *Afro-American*, Feb. 3, 1922, 1:2, 4–5.

6. Ibid., April 14, 1922, 7:2; see also Richard B. Sherman, *The Republican Party and Black America; From McKinley to Hoover, 1896–1933* (Charlottesville, 1973), pp. 183–84; and Andrew Sinclair, *The Available Man: The Life Behind the Masks of Warren Gamaliel Harding* (Chicago, 1969), pp. 230–35. Robert Murray, in *The Harding Era: Warren G. Harding and His Administration* (Minneapolis, 1969), argues that Harding was more sympathetic to black rights than his critics recognized, pp. 398–403. Both Sinclair and Murray credit Harding with courage for advocating black people's political rights even though he acquiesced in social segregation.

7. *Afro-American*, April 7, 1922, 7:2; June 16, 1922, 7:2; and July 14, 1922, 7:8; clipping from an unidentified newspaper, but marked with the date July 9, 1922, box 9, MSP; and clipping from the *St. Louis Argus*, July 27, 1923, 1:1–2, ser. 1, no. 93, box 95, CC.

8. Sec. Rep., Nov. 8, 1922, NAACP-NY. See also U.S. Congress, *Congressional Directory*, 68th Cong., 1st sess., p. 48 (Dec. 1923).

9. Sec. Rep., Nov. 8, 1922, NAACP-NY; and *Afro-American*, Feb. 9, 1923, 1:2; and Dec. 29, 1922, 1:7–8.

10. Sec. Rep., Nov. 8, 1922, NAACP-NY; and *Afro-American*, Nov. 24, 1922, 9:6. Cooperation with the Association did not, however, guarantee political success. Senator Joseph I. France of Maryland, who had spoken at NAACP antilynching rallies and remained (along with eighteen other Republican senators) in the Senate chamber on September 21, 1922, to answer quorum calls in support of Shortridge's efforts for the Dyer bill, lost his seat in a tightly fought contest to his Democratic opponent, William Bruce, in November (Sec. Rep., Dec. 8, 1920, and Oct. 4, 1922, NAACP-NY; and *Afro-American*, Nov. 10, 1922, 1:5). On the congressmen and senators in question, see U.S., Congress, *Biographical Directory of the American Congress, 1774–1971*, Senate Document no. 92-8, 92d Cong., 1st sess. (Washington, D.C., 1971), passim,

11. Chicago *Defender*, Dec. 16, 1922, 12:2; and Dec. 30, 1922, editorial page; *Afro-American*, Dec. 15, 1922, 9:3–5; Norfolk *Journal and Guide*, Dec. 2, 1922, 1:6, and 4:1. For additional information on the NAACP and election campaigns, see Sherman, *The Republican Party and Black America*, pp. 192–94.

12. Norfolk *Journal and Guide*, Dec. 23, 1922, 4:1. For a report on Perry Howard's proposed changes in the Dyer bill the year before, see Special Report of the Secretary on Washington Trip, Nov. 18, 1921, box 8, MSP.

13. *Afro-American*, Dec. 29, 1922, 9:5–6. Reporter Morris Brown credited the NAACP with contributing to Senator Du Pont's defeat (Norfolk *Journal and Guide*, Dec. 23, 1922, 1:3–4).

14. White to Bagnall, Dec. 5, 1922 (copy), box C-11, NAACP-LC. See also White to Johnson, Dec. 5, 1922, box C-77, NAACP-LC; and Bagnall to White, Dec. 9, 1922, box C-11, NAACP-LC.

15. See, for example, the Norfolk *Journal and Guide*, Dec. 23, 1922, 4:1; and *Afro-American*, Dec. 29, 1922, 9:5–6. James Cobb to Johnson, Dec. 19, and Dec. 24, 1922, box C-63, NAACP-LC.

16. Perry Howard to Slemp, May 23, 1924, and Weeks to Slemp, May 26, 1924, ser. 1, no. 93, box 96, CC.

17. *Afro-American*, April 6, 1923, 1:2, 6:2, and 9:4–7; and Pittsburgh *Courier*, April 7, 1923, 13:5–6. A month later the *Afro-American* (May 18, 1923, 1:2) announced that Harding had issued an interim appointment to Walter Cohen as collector of the port in New Orleans, but in mid-February 1924 the Senate again refused to confirm Cohen's appointment. *Cong. Rec.*, 68th Cong., 1st sess. p. 2733 (Feb. 19, 1924), and index, p. 70.

18. Sec. Rep., June 7, 1923, NAACP-NY; and Pittsburgh *Courier*, June 2, 1923, 1:6, 14:3–4. *Afro-American*, Aug. 10, 1923, editorial page: 1–2. For a complete discussion of the embittered relations between the GOP and the black community at this time, see Richard B. Sherman, "The Harding Administration and the Negro: An Opportunity Lost," *Journal of Negro History* 49 (July 1964): 151–68.

19. R. R. Moton to Coolidge, Sept. 14, 1923, ser. 1, no. 93, box 95, CC; *Cong. Rec.*, 67th Cong., 2d sess., p. 1795 (Jan. 26, 1922); and Sec. Rep., Aug. 24, 1923, NAACP-NY. On voting patterns, see John M. Allswang, "The Chicago Negro Voter and the Democratic Consensus: A Case Study, 1918–1936, in Bernard Sternsher, ed., *The Negro in Depression and War: Prelude to Revolution, 1930–1945* (Chicago, 1969), pp. 234–57; and V. O. Key, Jr., "Secular Realignment and the Party System," *Journal of Politics* 21 (May 1959): 198–210.

20. *Afro-American*, Sept. 7, 1923, 1:7. In its racist antagonisms to black people, the Ku Klux Klan had encouraged both discrimination and intimidation in distorting the operations and intended purposes of the Veterans Administration

hospital at Tuskegee, Ala. Walter White, *A Man Called White* (New York, 1948), pp. 69–71.

21. James Weldon Johnson, *Along This Way* (New York, 1933), pp. 392, and 306–07, 358–60.

22. William H. Lewis to Slemp, Oct. 4, 1923; Lewis to Coolidge, Oct. 4, 1923; Lewis to Slemp, Oct. 30, 1923; and Lewis to Slemp, Nov. 14, 1923, ser. 1, no. 661, box 202, CC. On Lewis' defection from the GOP, see William C. Matthews to Coolidge, Oct. 31, 1924, ser. 1, no. 93, box 96, CC.

23. Note by Arthur G. Froe, Nov. 20, 1923; and Melvin J. Chisum to Slemp, Dec. 1, 1923, and July 28, 1924; see also a list of the eighteen most important black papers (*The Crisis* among them) prepared by the White House staff (dated Nov. 10, 1923), ser. 1, no. 93, box 96, CC.

24. As the black journalist Ted Poston later noted, every black reader understood the point, whenever Langston Hughes' Simple came upon a policeman and speculated about the unchecked force of authority that even such a lowly white official commanded within the black community (personal interview with Ted Poston, New York City, Dec. 13, 1962).

25. *Afro-American*, Feb. 10, 1922, 1:2–3. The fiery Dungee became a legend in his own right. Among the many lynchings he investigated, the one that occurred in northeastern Texas was the one he spoke most often of. Dungee stayed with a family whose daughter worked as a domestic for a white family. One evening when her employers attempted to drive her home, their auto was halted at a lynching in progress, and, fearful of the mob's temper, the couple advised the young woman to hide on the rear floor of the car. From her crouched position she heard the gruesome sounds of the lynching, which the mob capped with a rousing chorus of "Happy Days Are Here Again" (personal interview with Clarence Mitchell, Washington, D.C., Dec. 20, 1962).

26. Bd. Min., June 12, 1922, NAACP-NY; and *Afro-American*, June 16, 1922, 1:2.

27. Bd. Min., July 10, 1922, and Sept. 11, 1922, NAACP-NY.

28. See, for example, John Drake to Shortridge, July 3, 1922; G. Dorothy Pelham and Norman McGee to Shortridge, July 7, 1922; Charles Johnston to Shortridge, July 7, 1922; and S. W. Green and Butler R. Wilson to Shortridge, July 8, 1922, RG 45, 67th Cong., "H.R. 13" envelope, NARS.

29. *Afro-American*, Feb. 16, 1923, 9:6–8.

30. Chicago *Defender*, May 19, 1923, 1:7; and Sec. Rep., June 7, 1923, NAACP-NY. The *Defender* was so impressed with Dyer's work for antilynching legislation that it suggested he be nominated for the presidency (Chicago *Defender*, July 28, 1923, 12:2).

31. General letters distributed by Mary Church Terrell in her role as President of the Women's Republican League of the District of Columbia, in the late summer and fall of 1924, box 4, MCT.

32. *Afro-American*, Feb. 9, 1923, 5:3; Nov. 16, 1923, 16:7; and Oct. 12, 1923, 1:3.

33. See, for example, Jesse O. Thomas to Monroe N. Work, March 23, 1921 (copy); and Vivian L. Saunders (secretary to Jesse O. Thomas) to White, March 24, 1921 (copy), G. O. F., Box 6, NUL. See also the two-page report on NUL activities, by Jesse O. Thomas, NUL field secretary, June 12, 1920, G. O. F., box 2, NUL. Former executive director of the NUL Lester Granger agreed that the League always endorsed the NAACP's efforts to secure a federal law against lynching and mob violence (personal interview with Lester Granger, Sterling Forest near Tuxedo Park, N.Y., July 16, 1964). See also Nancy J. Weiss, *The National Urban League, 1910–1940* (New York, 1974), pp. 141–47, and 266–67 for later developments.

34. Burnstead to Lodge, July 10, 1922, HCL.

35. Sec. Rep., May 9, 1923, NAACP-NY; and Pittsburgh *Courier*, July 7, 1923, 4:1–2. From 1917 to 1932, fifteen other states had laws explicitly dealing with lynching, and nine of those provided for punishment of delinquent officials. Twenty-three more had regulations about mobs, riots, prisoners' safety, and so forth. While many of these laws predated the NAACP's campaigns, they helped to reinforce a growing national concern over lynching. See James Harmon Chadbourn, *Lynching and the Law* (Chapel Hill, 1933), appendix C.

36. Bd. Min., Sept. 10, 1923, NAACP-NY. At the Board meeting on July 9, Dr. George Cannon had reported that the Colored Republican Club of New Jersey would call the conference, and on his suggestion that the NAACP send a delegate, the Board voted that James Weldon Johnson attend. (ibid., July 9, 1923, NAACP-NY).

37. Chicago *Defender*, Dec. 16, 1922, 1:3. For indications of the *Defender's* stance, see St. Clair Drake and Horace R. Cayton, *Black Metropolis* (New York, 1945), pp. 58–61, and Roland E. Wolseley, *The Black Press, U.S.A.* (Ames, Iowa, 1971), pp. 35–39.

38. See, for example, Pittsburgh *Courier*, April 14, 1923, 14:1–4.

39. Tony Martin, *Race First: The Ideological and Organizational Struggles of Marcus Garvey and the Universal Negro Improvement Association* (Westport, Conn., 1976), pp. 276–77, and 322–26.

40. Johnson, *Along This Way*, p. 365.

41. Bd. Min., Jan. 3, 1922, and Jan. 2, 1923, NAACP-NY.

42. Ibid., March 12, 1923.

43. Ibid., Feb. 14, 1921; Report of Field Work, Feb. 9, and March 9, 1921; and Sec. Rep., March 8, 1921, NAACP-NY.

44. Report of Field Work, May 9, 1921, NAACP-NY; and *Afro-American*, May 5, 1922, 7:3.

45. *Afro-American*, Jan. 12, 1923, 1:2–3. Established in 1914 through Joel Spingarn's $20,000 gift, the Spingarn Medal is presented annually to the black American, male or female, judged by a special NAACP committee to have "made the highest achievement during the preceding year or years in any honorable field of human endeavor" (NAACP, *Fortieth Spingarn Medal* [New York, June 24, 1955], p. 3).

46. *Afro American*, Feb. 9, 1921, 1:3; Treasurer's Reports and Minutes of the Board Meetings, monthly for 1922, NAACP-NY.

47. By November 1923, both the staff and the Board of Directors showed acute concern over diminished income and slackened activity among the branches (Sec. Rep., Nov. 8, 1923; and Bd. Min., Nov. 12, 1923, NAACP-NY).

48. Emphasis his. Johnson, *Along This Way*, pp. 385–86; see also *New York Times*, April 13, 1924, 17:2. Garland's friend, Roger Baldwin of the American Civil Liberties Union, took charge of administering the American Fund.

49. Arthur Spingarn to the American Fund for Public Service, Sept. 19, 1922; Baldwin to Arthur Spingarn, Oct. 13, 1922; and Johnson to Norman Thomas, Dec. 12, 1922, *Gifts, 1922 / 27*, 9, sec. 3, AFPS. The effort to effect reformist action in Congress by running high-priced advertisements in newspapers throughout the country was a splendid example of the public relations tactics so much a part of Progressive reformers' style and strategy. Nevertheless, Perry Howard criticized the NAACP for ignoring the black press when it placed the ads, and the incident also brought a stinging rebuke from J. Finley Wilson, president of the National Negro Press Association, who regretted this inadvertent NAACP subsidy to white newspapers (*Afro-American*, Dec. 29, 1922, 9:5–6; Norfolk *Journal and Guide*, December 2, 1922, 1:6). See also the file memo on antilynching advertisements placed in major newspapers, DuB.

50. Pittsburgh *Courier*, Oct. 30, 1926, 1, 16; Resumé—"Appropriations

Voted by the American Fund for Public Service, Inc. for Negro Organizations," Jan. 24, 1928, *Gifts and Loans, 1934–38*, Vol. 8, sec. 2, AFPS. See also Board of Directors, Correspondence, 1923 / 33, Vol. 1, sec. 10; Bd. Min., July 10, 1922; Sec. Rep., Sept. 6, 1935, NAACP-NY; Morris Ernst, Lewis Gannett, and James Weldon Johnson (Committee on Negro Work), "Memorandum for the American Fund for Public Service," (n.d.), "American Fund for Public Service, Inc." folder, JWJ; Charles Houston, Report to the Joint Committee, Nov. 12, 1937, Gifts and Loans, 1934–38, Vol. 9, sec. 4, AFPS; *Afro-American*, Feb. 11, 1939, 2:6; and Bd. Min., Dec. 13, 1937, NAACP-NY.

51. Interview with Grace Nail Johnson, New York City, Oct. 16, 1962. Grace Johnson recalled that her husband carefully observed other organizations and movements of the period to see how they functioned. He belonged also to the National Committee of the American Civil Liberties Union (Johnson, *Along This Way*, pp. 385–86). For a general discussion of Johnson's activities in the 1920s, see Eugene Levy, *James Weldon Johnson: Black Leader, Black Voice* (Chicago, 1973), chaps. 12 and 13.

52. Hasia R. Diner, *In the Almost Promised Land: American Jews and Blacks, 1915–1935* (Westport, Conn., 1977), chap. 4.

53. Sec. Rep., July 9, 1923; and Bd. Min., Jan. 14, 1924, NAACP-NY. On Burton, see *The Crisis* 29 (March 1925): 210.

54. Sec. Rep., May 8, and June 4, 1924, NAACP-NY.

55. Ibid., April 9, 1924. Without elaborating, Du Bois asserted that the filibuster and the abject surrender of friends killed the Dyer bill. "It was not until years after," he added, "that I knew what killed that anti-lynching bill. It was a bargain between the South and the West. By this bargain, lynching was let to go on uncurbed by Federal law on condition that the Japanese be excluded from the United States." W. E. B. Du Bois, *Dusk of Dawn: An Essay Toward an Autobiography of a Race Concept* (New York, 1940), p. 266. While the failure of the Dyer bill was indeed hedged around with many political deals, Du Bois' particular explanation remains unique, and to my knowledge he offered no further explicit confirmation. My efforts to contact him in 1962, the year before his death, proved unavailing. However, the *New York Times* did report that Democratic floor leader Finis Garrett of Tennessee urged House members from the Pacific Coast to recognize their own perplexing race question and stand with opponents of the Dyer bill in preventing federal interference in state affairs (*New York Times*, Jan. 26, 1922, 6:1). The immigration law of 1924 excluded Japanese. See John Higham, *Strangers in the Land: Patterns of American Nativism, 1860–1925* (New York, 1963), p. 324.

56. For an indication of other issues of concern to NAACP Board members, see Louis L. Athey, "Florence Kelley and the Quest for Negro Equality," *Journal of Negro History* 56 (Oct. 1971); 249–61. Also, Bd. Min., Feb. 14, 1923, and Sec. Rep., Feb. 5, 1925, NAACP-NY; James Weldon Johnson to "Dear Friend," Nov. 16, 1925, R.G. 46, 76th Cong., "H.R. 801" folder, NARS; and *Crisis*, 31 (March 1926): 229–32.

57. U.S. Congress, Senate, Subcommittee of the Committee on the Judiciary, *Hearings on the Anti-Lynching Bill, (S.121)*, 69th Cong., 1st sess., pp. 7, 24, 29, 34–36 (Feb. 16, 1926); see also Warren F. St. James, *The National Association for the Advancement of Colored People: A Case Study in Pressure Groups* (New York, 1958), pp. 241–42.

58. Sec. Rep., April 8, 1926; Bd. Min., April 12, 1926, NAACP-NY.

59. Sec. Rep., Nov. 3, 1926, and Feb. 9, 1928, NAACP-NY.

60. White, *A Man Called White*, pp. 47–51. See also Ovington, *The Walls Came Tumbling Down*, pp. 154–64; St. James, *NAACP*, pp. 241–42; and *Crisis* 29 (April 1925): 272–73.

61. Moore v. Dempsey, 261 U.S. 86, 90–92 (1923). See also Ovington, *The Walls Came Tumbling Down*, pp. 160–62; and Bd. Min., Jan. 8, 1923, NAACP-NY.

62. Sec. Rep., Feb. 5, 1925, NAACP-NY.

63. Interview with Arthur Spingarn, New York City, Dec. 9, 1960.

64. Sec. Rep., Sept. 9, 1921, and March 9, 1923, NAACP-NY; and *Afro-American*, March 9, 1923, 9:6–7. Also, Sec. Rep., Nov. 10, 1932 NAACP-NY. See also Dan T. Carter, *Scottsboro: A Tragedy of the American South* (Baton Rouge, 1969), chap. 3; and White, *A Man Called White*, pp. 125–33 for discussions of the NAACP and CP-USA controversy in the Alabama case.

65. Ovington, *The Walls Came Tumbling Down*, p. 137; Johnson, *Along This Way*, pp. 322–23; NAACP, "Chronology of a Crusade," mimeograph, 1959, pp. 10–11, NAACP-NY; and Charles Flint Kellogg, *NAACP, A History of the National Association for the Advancement of Colored People*, vol. 1: *1909–1920* (Baltimore, 1967), pp. 260–62. The case is discussed above, pp. 39–40. See Sec. Rep., Dec. 6, 1923, June 4, 1924; Feb. 5, 1925, and Nov. 4, 1937, NAACP-NY. See also Langston Hughes, *Fight for Freedom: The Story of the NAACP* (New York, 1962), pp. 40–41.

66. Ovington, *The Walls Came Tumbling Down*, pp. 198–203. Ossian Sweet fully understood the implications of white violence. As a boy in a small Florida town he had seen the charred remains of a lynched black man, and the sight was "burned into his spirit." (ibid., p. 200).

67. Buchanan v. Warley, 245 U.S. 60 (1917); Sec. Rep., Oct. 8, 1925, NAACP-NY; and Corrigan v. Buckley, 271 U.S. 323 (1926). See also Clement E. Vose, *Caucasians Only: The Supreme Court, the NAACP, and the Restrictive Covenant Cases* (Berkeley, 1967), pp. 17–19; and Loren Miller, *The Petitioners: The Story of the Supreme Court of the United States and the Negro* (Cleveland, 1966), pp. 252–55.

68. The other areas demonstrated the national scope of the problem: Baltimore; Brooklyn; Cleveland; Denver; Detroit; Falls Church, Va.; Kansas City, Mo.; Los Angeles; New Orleans; Norfolk; Oakland; Pittsburgh; Roanoke; St. Louis; St. Paul; and Staten Island (Sec. Rep., Oct. 8, 1925, NAACP-NY).

69. Moorfield Storey to American Fund for Public Service, Oct. 22, 1925, Gifts, 1922 / 27, 9, sec. 6, AFPS. Ovington, *The Walls Came Tumbling Down*, pp. 203–05. Of the ten branches submitting the largest contributions by early December, Philadelphia's $2,300 more than doubled the amount of runner-up Cleveland (Sec. Rep., Dec. 8, 1925, NAACP-NY).

70. Johnson to Elizabeth Gurley Flynn, secretary of the AFPS, Jan. 5, 1926, Gifts, 1922 / 27, 9, sec. 6, AFPS. The NAACP director of branches, Robert Bagnall, informed the Board in December 1929 that branch contributions for each of the previous ten years had hit their peak in 1925 with a total of $66,301; 1921, one of the major Dyer bill years, and a recession year, ranked second with $45,835 (Department of Branches Report, Dec. 9, 1929, NAACP-NY).

71. Ovington, *The Walls Came Tumbling Down*, pp. 200–13. Johnson to Flynn, May 21, 1926, Gifts, 1922 / 27, 9. sec. 6, AFPS.

72. Sec. Rep., April 8, 1926, NAACP-NY; Frederick Lewis Allen, *Only Yesterday* (New York, 1959), pp. 142–43. Also Richard D. Lunt, *The High Ministry of Government: The Political Career of Frank Murphy* (Detroit, 1965), pp. 25–26, and chap. 6.

73. Information on these various cases has been drawn from the Board Minutes, Secretary's Reports, correspondence files, and *Annual Reports* of the NAACP for the years 1922–1933. For a discussion of these cases in more detail, see Robert L. Zangrando, "The Efforts of the National Association for the Advancement of Colored People to Secure Passage of a Federal Anti-Lynching

Law, 1920–1940" (Ph.D. diss., University of Pennsylvania, 1963), pp. 211–18. Nixon v. Herndon, 273 U.S. 536 (1927), and Nixon v. Condon, 286 U.S. 73 (1932).

74. For impressions of the NAACP staff officers and the Renaissance, I am indebted to the comments, in personal interviews, of the following: Grace Nail Johnson (New York City, Oct. 16, 1962); Daisy Lampkin (Morris Beach, N.J., Aug. 30, 1962); George Schuyler (New York City, Jan. 3, 1963); Arthur B. Spingarn (New York City, Dec. 9, 1960, and April 2, 1963); Carl Van Vechten (New York City, Oct. 29, 1962); and Gladys Powell-White (Mainz, Germany, April 22 and 23, 1978). See also James Weldon Johnson to Walter White, Sept. 26, Oct. 19, and Dec. 9, 1927 (copies), box C-77, NAACP-LC; and White, *A Man Called White*, p. 43.

75. James Weldon Johnson, *The Autobiography of an Ex-Coloured Man* (New York, 1976), pp. v–x, and 186–88. For a discussion of Johnson's literary activities during the Harlem Renaissance, see Johnson, *Along This Way*, pp. 374–83, and Levy, *James Weldon Johnson*, chap. 13.

76. For information on Grimké, I am indebted to the work of Carolyn Amonitti Stubbs, "Angelina Weld Grimké: Washington Poet and Playwright" (Ph. D. diss., George Washington University, 1978), pp. 13–16; 137–63, and 168–72. See also Richard Bardolph, *The Negro Vanguard* (New York, 1961), pp. 117, 206; and Harry A. Ploski, ed., *Reference Library of Black America*, bk. 3 (New York, 1971), p. 38.

77. On Georgia Douglas Johnson, see *Afro-American Encyclopedia*, vol. 5 (North Miami, Fla., 1974), pp. 1337–38; and Bardolph, *Negro Vanguard*, pp. 202–03, 208. I am indebted to Linda Berry of Skidmore College for her insights into Johnson's career, and for access to her copy of "Catalogue of Writings by Georgia Douglas Johnson," a typescript from the Trevor Arnett Library, Atlanta University.

78. Wayne F. Cooper, ed., *The Passion of Claude McKay: Selected Poetry and Prose, 1912–1948* (New York, 1973), pp. 122, 124; Claude McKay, *Harlem Shadows* (New York, 1922), p. 53. See also Bardolph, *Negro Vanguard*, pp. 204, 207; and James Weldon Johnson, *Black Manhattan* (New York, 1969), pp. 264–66.

79. Jean Toomer, *Cane* (New York, 1975), pp. 28–35.

80. White, *A Man Called White*, pp. 65–69 and 92–98. Charles F. Cooney, "Walter White and the Harlem Renaissance," *Journal of Negro History* 57 (July 1972): 231–40. See also Zangrando, "Walter Francis White," in John A. Garraty and Jerome L. Sternstein, eds., *Encyclopedia of American Biography* (New York, 1974), pp. 1188–89; and Edward E. Waldron, *Walter White and the Harlem Renaissance* (Port Washington, N.Y., 1978), chap. 3.

81. Cronon, *Black Moses*, pp. 15–20, 41–70. Duse Mohammed Ali to Du Bois, March 27, 1922; and Du Bois to Garvey, July 25, 1922 (copy); Garvey to William Pickens, July 10, 1922; and Pickens to Garvey, July 24, 1922 (mimeographed copies), DuB. See also James Weldon Johnson's discussion of the UNIA-NAACP confrontation in *Black Manhattan*, pp. 251–59.

82. Cronon, *Black Moses*, pp. 188–91; Amy Jacques-Garvey, *Garvey and Garveyism* (London, 1970), pp. 106–07; and Amy Jacques-Garvey, ed., *Philosophy and Opinions of Marcus Garvey*, 2 Vols. (New York, 1925), 2: 39.

83. On the role of NAACP personnel, see Martin, *Race First*, pp. 191–204, and 322–27.

84. David M. Chalmers, *Hooded Americanism: The History of the Ku Klux Klan* (Chicago, 1968), chaps. 3 and 4. See also, Charles Alexander, *The Ku Klux Klan and the Southwest* (Lexington, 1966), chaps. 1 and 2.

85. Bd. Min., Sept. 9, 1918, box A-1, NAACP-LC; Shillady to Storey, Jan. 14, 1919 (copy), box C-74, NAACP-LC; and NAACP, *Eleventh Annual Report* (New York, 1921), p. 47. See U.S., Congress, House, Committee on Rules, *Ku Klux*

Klan: Hearings before the Committee on Rules, 67th Cong., 1st sess. (Oct. 11, 1921). See also Sec. Rep., Sept. 9, 1921, NAACP-NY; NAACP, *Thirteenth Annual Report* (New York, 1923), p. 44; and NAACP, press release of June 2, 1922 box 9, MSP.

86. Sec. Rep., Nov. 3, 1926, and Dec. 8, 1926; and Bd. Min., Nov. 8, 1926, NAACP-NY; and White to Thomas G. McLeod, Oct. 28, 1926 (copy), Walter White file cabinet "M," JWJ.

87. NAACP, *The Recent Record of the Ku Klux Klan—As Set Forth by 2 Alabama Editors* (New York, n.d.), NAACP-NY.

88. Walter White, *Rope and Faggot: A Biography of Judge Lynch* (New York, 1929), pp. 121, 196, and 226. In November 1929 the Association's Committee on Administration instructed White to purchase twenty copies of *Rope and Faggot* "to be used only in cases of quite important individuals who seek exhaustive information on lynching" (Minutes of the Meeting of the Committee on Administration, Nov. 25, 1929, NAACP-NY).

89. Chalmers, *Hooded Americanism*, chap. 40. See also Table 2, p. 6.

90. NAACP press release, June 24, 1929, Board of Directors Correspondence, 1934–41, 2, pp. 12–20, AFPS.

91. *New York Times*, Aug. 24, 1931, 2:1–2. In December 1934, the NAACP tried again—also without much success—to get Attorney General Homer Cummings to place lynching on the agenda of the National Crime Conference. See NAACP, *Twenty-fifth Annual Report* (New York, 1935), p. 26; and *Crisis* 42 (Jan. 1935): 5, 26.

92. Wilson Record, *The Negro and the Communist Party* (Chapel Hill, 1951), p. 32. For a discussion of the party's origins, see Theodore Draper, *The Roots of American Communism* (New York, 1963), chaps. 11 and 16; on tensions between the CP-USA and the NAACP, see also Wilson Record, *Race and Radicalism: The NAACP and the Communist Party in Conflict* (Ithaca, N.Y. 1964), chaps. 2 and 3.

93. Ibid., p. 31; B. D. Amis, *Lynch Justice at Work* (n.p., n.d.), pp. 23–27, 30–31, "Lynching" folder, Schom.

94. Record, *The Negro and the Communist Party*, pp. 91, 33–36, 78–79; as quoted in the *Labor Defender* (June 1930); 126, "Lynching—Case Stories" folder, Schom; and Chicago *Defender*, May 24, 1930, 13:7–8. See also Robert Minor, "The Negro and His Judases," *The Communist* 10 (July 1931): 639; Cecil S. Hope, "The Flames of Lynch-Law Spread," *Labor Defender*, no vol. (Dec. 1931): 237 "Lynching—Statistics" folder, Schom.

95. The Association's work in 1920 for a reduction of southern representation in Congress because of black disfranchisement, its successful attack in 1915 on the Oklahoma "grandfather clause" (Guinn and Beal v. United States, 238 U.S. 347 [1915]), its victory in 1917 against residential segregation in Louisville (Buchanan v. Warley, 245 U.S. 60 [1917]), and its assault upon discrimination in southern primaries in 1927 (Nixon v. Herndon), each showed offensive intentions. See Bd. Min., Jan. 10, 1921, and "Tentative Draft of Proposed Activities of the N.A.A.C.P.," Feb. 5, 1923, NAACP-NY; also St. James, *NAACP*, pp. 236–39.

96. Ovington to Baldwin, June 18, 1923, Gifts, 1922 / 27, 9, sec. 6, AFPS.

97. Committee on Negro Work (Morris Ernst, Lewis Gannett, and James Weldon Johnson), "Memorandum for the American Fund for Public Service," (n.d.), "American Fund for Public Service, Inc." folder, JWJ.

98. Committee on Negro Work (Morris Ernst, Lewis Gannett, James Weldon Johnson), "Report of the Committee on Negro Work," Oct. 18, 1929, Board of Directors, Correspondence, 1934–41, 2, pp. 4–9, AFPS. Incidentally, no such AFPS fund against lynching was established.

244   Notes

99. Charles R. Lawrence, "Negro Organizations in Crisis: Depression, New Deal, W.W. II" (Ph.D. diss., Columbia University, 1953), pp. 157; and R[obert] W[.] D[unn] to NAACP, Oct. 2, 1931, Gifts and Loans, 1934–38, 8, sec. 3, AFPS.

100. There was an item of $9,000 for expenses due Nathan Margold, hired to implement the original $100,000 campaign. See White to Baldwin, Nov. 5, 1931, Gifts and Loans, 1934–38, 8, sec. 3, AFPS. See also White to Anna Marnitz, Feb. 19, 1932, Gifts and Loans, 1934–38, 8, sec. 5, AFPS. A[nna] M[arnitz] to White, June 6, 1932 (copy); and White to Dunn, June 17, 1932; and accompanying letters, Gifts and Loans, 1934–38, 8, sec. 2, 66–91, AFPS.

101. Personal interview with William Hastie, Philadelphia, July 25, 1962; resumé, Nov. 8, 1929, and Summary, March 1, 1933; White to American Fund, May 10, 1933; Marnitz to White, Nov. 5, 1934 (copy), Gifts and Loans, 1934–38, Vol. 8, sec. 2, 28; sec. 3, 113, 179, AFPS, Sec. Rep., April 6, 1933, and June 7, 1933; and Bd. Min., November 13, 1934, NAACP-NY. See also Lawrence, "Negro Organizations in Crisis," p. 157. Not all AFPS-NAACP personnel took seriously the Fund's statement of dire financial problems. One well-placed observer argued years later that Garland executives turned needlessly cautious in their distribution of money during the depression (confidential source.)

102. James Weldon Johnson's extended leave of absence and eventual resignation, and the assumption of his duties by Walter White, necessitated some adjustments at the national office (Minutes of the Meeting of the Committee on Administration, Dec. 15, 1930, NAACP-NY). Meanwhile from 1930 to 1934, the staff and legal advisors kept extremely busy with such matters as: (1) the defeat of Hoover's nominee to the Supreme Court, John J. Parker (Chicago *Defender*, May 3, 1930, 1:7–8, and May 10, 1930, 1:6–7; *Cong. Rec.*, 71st Cong., 2d sess., p. 8487 [May 7, 1930]); (2) campaigns to unseat those who, like Republican Rosco McCulloch of Ohio, had endorsed Parker's nomination (Report of the Meeting of the Committee on Administration, Oct. 20, 1930, NAACP-NY); (3) the Scottsboro affair (Sec. Rep., Aug. 15, 1932, NAACP-NY); (4) the Mississippi Valley Flood Control project, and discriminatory employment practices at the Hoover Dam, in various government work projects, and in government bureaus (Sec. Rep., Dec. 8, 1932, Sept. 6, 1933, NAACP-NY); (5) the question of voting rights (Sec. Rep., Dec. 8, 1932, NAACP-NY); (6) partial implementation of the program developed under the auspices of the American Fund-NAACP Joint Committee (Sec. Rep., June 7, 1933, NAACP-NY); (7) work on improving the general economic conditions of black people (Sec. Rep., Sept. 6, 1933, NAACP-NY); and (8) a seemingly endless number of individual cases involving violence, segregation, discrimination, and other forms of racial injustice.

Chapter 5

1. Sec. Rep., May 9, 1928, NAACP-NY. Unfortunately, hopes for a lynchless year were quickly dashed. In June, Johnson announced the occurrence of four lynchings since May 1: one in Texas, one in Missouri, and two in Louisiana. (Ibid., June 8, 1928, NAACP-NY). For lynching data, see Table No. 2, p. 6.

2. Walter White, *A Man Called White* (New York, 1948), chap. 13. See also Richard B. Sherman, *The Republican Party and Black America: From McKinley to Hoover, 1896–1933* (Charlottesville, 1973), pp. 224–33.

3. Emphasis added. Report of the Acting Secretary to the Committee on Administration, Jan. 13, 1930, NAACP-NY.

4. NAACP, *Twenty-first Annual Report* (New York, 1931), p. 4. Subsequent *Annual Reports* through the early 1940s showed no reactivation of the standing antilynching committee.

5. NAACP, *Twenty-second Annual Report* (New York, 1932).
6. See Table No. 2, p. 6.
7. On White's investigation of the double lynching see White to Marnitz, Aug. 1930, Gifts and Loans, 1934–38, vol. 9, sec. 5, pp. 150–51, AFPS; and NAACP, Minutes of the Meeting of the Committee on Administration, Aug. 11, 1930, NAACP-NY.
8. Minutes of the Meeting of the Committee on Administration, Sept. 15, 1930; and Report of the Meeting of the Committee on Administration, Oct. 20, 1930, NAACP-NY. Chicago *Defender*, May 3, 1930, 1:7; May 10, 1930, 1:7; May 17, 1930, 14:3–4; and May 24, 1930, 2:1–2. See also Sherman, *The Republican Party and Black America*, p. 249.
9. On the feud, see Grace M. Burnham to Baldwin, Jan. 20, 1930, Board of Directors Correspondence, 1934–41, Vol. 2, 28, AFPS. Burnham's stationery, that of the Labor Research Association, listed Robert W. Dunn (of the American Fund Board) as executive secretary. Also see, for example, Du Bois to Baldwin, March 27, 1930, and accompanying *Crisis* editorial, "Programs on Emancipation," ibid., 2, 51–52.
10. U.S., Congress, *Congressional Directory*, 71st Cong., 3rd sess., (Washington, D.C., 1931), p. 208. In January 1931, Hamilton Fish, Jr., submitted to the House *Report No. 2290*, on the topic of Communism. *Cong. Rec.*, 71st Cong., 3rd sess., p. 2526. (Jan. 17, 1931). See also Charles R. Lawrence, "Negro Organizations in Crisis: Depression, New Deal, W.W. II" (Ph.D. diss., Columbia University, 1953), p. 172; and White to Simon Guggenheim, Oct. 26, 1931, "White, Walter (1927–1933)" folder, JWJ. Also White to Herbert Hoover, Aug. 21, 1931 (copy), box C-77, NAACP-LC.
11. J. E. Spingarn to White, Jan. 27, 1932, box C-75, NAACP-LC.
12. H. Haywood and M. Howard, *Lynching* (New York, 1932), pp. 5, 12, vertical file, "Lynching" folder, Schom.; and Wilson Record, *The Negro and the Communist Party* (Chapel Hill, 1951), pp. 80–81.
13. Dan T. Carter, *Scottsboro: A Tragedy of the American South* (Baton Rouge, 1969), chaps. 1 and 2.
14. Personal interview with Arthur B. Spingarn, New York City, Apr. 2, 1963; White to Johnson, Jan. 15, 1932, "White, Walter (1927–1933)" folder, JWJ. For a full discussion of the extended attempts of both the NAACP and ILD to gain dominance in the case, see Carter, *Scottsboro*, chap. 3, and also Mary White Ovington, *The Walls Came Tumbling Down*, (New York, 1970), pp. 230–32.
15. For a penetrating analysis of the difficulties confronting the NAACP, see Carter, *Scottsboro*, pp. 68–9, 87–90, and 114–21. For a discussion of the Scottsboro affair that credits the CP–USA and the ILD with sincere and effective work, see Hugh T. Murray, Jr., "The NAACP versus the Communist Party: the Scottsboro Rape Cases, 1931–32," *Phylon* 28 (3d qtr. 1967): 276–87. One of the Scottsboro defendants, Haywood Patterson, has discussed the case in Patterson and Earl Conrad, *Scottsboro Boy* (New York, 1951), passim.
16. Nathan Glazer, *The Social Basis of American Communism* (New York, 1961), pp. 171–75.
17. ILD press release dated July 7, 1933, vertical file, "Lynching" folder, Schom.
18. George Maurer to Baldwin, April 20, 1931; G. Ackerman of the ILD to Marnitz, May 29, 1931; and R. W. D. (Robert W. Dunn?) to the ILD, June 6, 1931, Applications Favorably Acted Upon, Gifts and Loans, 1934–38, vol. 7, sec. 8, AFPS.
19. "Miscellaneous, Correspondence, 1922–41," 1, p. 156, AFPS. That single year's allotment to the ILD reflected a handsome increase in AFPS support,

if one notes that from Dec. 1927 to May 1930, the Garland Fund had given the ILD a total of $31,047. over the two and a half year period (Applications Favorably Acted Upon, Gifts, 1928–33, 4, "I," secs. 4–10, AFPS).

20. White's energy and vanity seem as evident as his thorough identification with interracial justice. In fact, these personality traits undoubtedly made immeasurable contributions to his work against racism. Friends, critics, and researchers have all recognized the man's vanity and need for success. His second wife, Poppy Cannon White, classified him as "meticulously neat, enduringly vain," and she added—perhaps with an unconscious double entendre—that "Walter always manages!" See Poppy Cannon, *A Gentle Knight* (New York, 1956), pp. 175, 179. His friend and associate, Ted Poston, smilingly recalled the pleasure White derived from working with influential people (personal interview with Ted Poston, New York City, Dec. 13, 1962). A former staff member, somewhat less enthusiastically, confirmed the vanity others recognized in Walter White (confidential source). Beyond White's personal pride and the organizational problems confronting the NAACP itself in the early 1930s, there remained the new executive secretary's need to demonstrate his ability to direct the Association. Hesitant to employ little-known black people, the Board had initially lacked enthusiasm about hiring White in the winter of 1918 (Nathaniel P. Tillman, "Walter Francis White: A Study in Interest Group Leadership" [Ph.D. diss., University of Wisconsin, 1961], pp. 102–05). Although White had demonstrated his worth by the early 1930s—especially in his timely, successful attack on Judge John J. Parker—he had still to show that he could lead the NAACP on a sustained basis. Moreover, he had had his troubles internally in winning the full support and loyalty of the staff, and the major black figure at the national office, W. E. B. Du Bois, found him "absolutely self-centered and egotistical" and not fully trustworthy (Du Bois, *The Autobiography of W. E. B. Du Bois* [New York, 1968], pp. 293–95). All of this, it seems reasonable to argue, provided White with further motivation for re-opening the antilynching campaign in Congress—a task for which his vigor, Washington contacts, investigative experiences, and previous efforts on behalf of the Dyer bill uniquely fit him.

21. Chicago *Defender*, Nov. 18, 1933, 14:1, and Nov. 25, 1933, 3:6–7.

22. For an assessment of the Washington atmosphere in mid-1933, see William E. Leuchtenburg, *Franklin D. Roosevelt and the New Deal, 1932–1940* (New York, 1963), p. 61.

23. Sec. Rep., Nov. 9, 1933, NAACP-NY.

24. Johnson to White, Oct. 30, 1933, "White, Walter (1927–33)" folder, JWJ. Johnson's reference was to the lynching of George Armwood in Princess Anne, Md., on Oct. 18, 1933 (*New York Times*, Oct. 19, 1933, 1:5).

25. Wilma Dykeman and James Stokely, *Seeds of Southern Change; The Life of Will Alexander* (Chicago, 1962), pp. 133–41. *The Tragedy of Lynching* (Chapel Hill, 1933) involved a distinguished team of scholars headed by Arthur F. Raper.

26. Statement of Dr. Will Alexander, Columbia University Oral History Project, New York City, pp. 258–9.

27. White to Johnson, Aug. 16, 1932, and White to Alexander, Aug. 16, 1932, "White, Walter (1927–1933)" folder, JWJ. See also Dykeman and Stokely, *Seeds of Southern Change*, pp. 123–24, 154–55.

28. Jessie Daniel Ames to My dear Friend, Aug. 11, 1932, box 4, folder no. 31, JDA.

29. Commission on Interracial Cooperation, *Mob Murder in America* (Atlanta, Ga., n.d.—late 1920s, early 1930s?); Commission on Interracial Cooperation, *The Cost of the Mob* (Atlanta, Ga., n.d.), a sermon by Dr. Henry M.

Edmonds (rpt. from the Birmingham *Age-Herald*, Oct. 8, 1933); and Association of Southern Women for the Prevention of Lynching, *A New Public Opinion on Lynching* (Atlanta, Ga., 1933), JWJ. See also Dykeman and Stokely, *Seeds of Southern Change*, chap. 6.

30. CIC findings are contained in George Fort Milton, *The Plight of Tuscaloosa: A Case Study of Conditions in Tuscaloosa County, Alabama, 1933* (Atlanta, Ga., 1933), pp. 3–39. For other reactions to the Tuscaloosa lynchings, see "Nullification–1933" (four-page, double-spaced typescript; n.d.), and the ILD news release, Aug. 19, 1933; and the article by R. B. Eleazer in the *Dunbar News*, Nov. 15, 1933, vertical file, "Lynching" folder, Schom; and "Memorandum from Mr. White Re Long Distance Telephone Conversation with Mr. Charles H. Houston," Nov. 1, 1933, and "Charlie" (Houston) to White, Oct. 30, 1933, box C-64, NAACP-LC. Incidentally, the ILD materials urged support for the Edmonds antilynching bill introduced in the spring of 1933.

31. *New York Times*, Oct. 19, 1933, 1:5; I. Amter to Franklin D. Roosevelt, Oct. 24, 1933, file 93, FDR; and Sec. Rep., Dec. 7, 1933, NAACP-NY.

32. *New York Times*, Dec. 1, 1933, 4:2.

33. Ibid., Dec. 1, 1933, 1:4; and Sec. Rep., Dec. 7, 1933, NAACP-NY.

34. *New York Times*, Dec. 1, 1933, 4:4, 4:5, and 4:6.

35. Ibid., Dec. 7, 1933, 1:8, and 2:4; "Memorandum Re Requests Made by the N.A.A.C.P. of President Franklin D. Roosevelt, file X-36, box 3, NAACP-LC. On December 3, the NAACP asked Roosevelt to include a recommendation for antilynching legislation in his forthcoming message to the Congress, and the presidential message of January 3, 1934 did contain an oblique reference to lynching (ibid.).

36. On the reinforcement, see James Weldon Johnson, "The Practice of Lynching," *Century* 115 (Nov. 1927): 66; *The Crisis* 41 (Jan. 1934); 66; Robert M. Miller, "The Protestant Churches and Lynching, 1919–1939," *Journal of Negro History* 42 (April 1957): 118–31.

37. Alexander to Edwin R. Embree, Dec. 6, 1933 (copy), CIC.

38. Typescript copy of the Atlanta *Constitution* editorial of Dec. 9, 1933, "As a Federal Offense," and Alexander to Douglas S. Freeman, Dec. 19, 1933 (copy), CIC.

39. See, for example, Alexander to the Members of the Commission on Interracial Cooperation, Inc., Dec. 19, 1933; and letters to Alexander from: Jackson Davis of the General Education Board, Jan. 2, 1933; George Fort Milton of the Chattanooga *News*, Dec. 13, 1933; W. W. Ball of the Charleston, S. C. *News and Courier*, Dec. 21, 1933; Harry M. Ayers of the Anniston, Ala. *Star*, Dec. 22, 1933; Mark Ethridge, then of the *Washington Post*, Dec. 22, 1933; Robert Lathan of the Asheville, N.C. *Citizen-Times*, Dec. 22, 1933; Jonathan Daniels of the Raleigh, N.C. *News and Observer*, Dec. 23, 1933; Douglas S. Freeman of the Richmond, Va. *News Leader*, Dec. 23, 1933; G. B. Dealey of the Dallas *News*. Dec. 28, 1933; and P. H. Callahan of Louisville, Jan. 3, 1934; the Rev. Theodore D. Bratton of Jackson, Miss., Dec. 28, 1933; Mary McLeod Bethune of Bethune-Cookman College, Dec. 31, 1933; B. G. Alexander of Louisville, Jan. 1, 1934; and John W. Abercrombie of the Alabama Department of Education, Dec. 28, 1933, CIC.

40. Harry M. Ayers to Alexandria (sic), Dec. 22, 1933, and D. S. Freeman to Alexander, Dec. 23, 1933, ibid.

41. M. H. McIntyre to Mrs. Atwood Reading Martin, Jan. 26, 1934 (copy), plus a three-page "Statement" and a one-page "Resolution" of the ASWPL, file 93a, FDR; Jacquelyn Dowd Hall, "Revolt Against Chivalry: Jessie Daniel Ames and the Women's Campaign Against Lynching" (Ph. D. diss., Columbia

University, 1974), pp. 323-31. See also White to Eleanor Roosevelt, May 13, 1935, and an attached two-page typescript copy of an editorial from the Chattanooga *News*, May 4, 1935, file 100, ER.

42. Personal interview, Arthur Spingarn, New York City, April 2, 1963. See also Ovington, *The Walls Came Tumbling Down*, pp. 251-52; Warren F. St. James, *The National Association for the Advancement of Colored People: A Case Study in Pressure Groups* (New York, 1958), pp. 123-24; Edwin R. Embree, *13 Against the Odds* (New York, 1945), p. 90; Tillman, "Walter Francis White," pp. 86-89; *New York Times*, May 8, 1930, 1:8; and Chicago *Defender*, May 10, 1930, 1:6-7. Although no direct relationship existed between the vote on Judge Parker and the antilynching bills, both matters concerned the NAACP vitally. Therefore, the positions of certain senators at least bears comment. Among those who at one time had expressed interest in or actively worked for the Dyer bill, Senators Gillett, Watson, and Shortridge voted for Parker and consequently against the NAACP. Meanwhile, those opposed to the antilynching bills but voting against Parker included Borah, Hugo Black (D-Ala.), Tom Connally (D-Tex.), Kenneth McKellar (D-Tenn.), and Joseph Robinson (D-Ark.). Only Arthur Capper (R-Kan.) and Robert Wagner (D-N.Y.) stood out among those who sustained the Association's position on both the Parker affair and the antilynching bills. The entire Parker question was complicated by pressures from organized labor, the growing impact of black urban voting strength, political animosities among Republicans and Democrats, personal and ideological antagonisms within the Republican party, and the peculiar implications of sectional strife made worse by the possibility of having a southern Republican elevated to the Court. For a resumé of Senate votes on the Parker nomination, see *Cong. Rec.*, 71st Cong., 2d sess., p. 8487 (May 7, 1930).

43. St. James, *NAACP*, p. 126. Ovington offers an interesting first-hand account of the Parker incident in *The Walls Came Tumbling Down*, pp. 251-57.

44. Tillman, "Walter Francis White," pp. 94, 97-100. Tillman, however, discounted black claims of defeating certain senators in the early 1930s; that, he argued, merely reflected deeper voting patterns of the depression (ibid., pp. 95-96).

45. Quoted in St. James, *NAACP*, pp. 126-27. See also Henry L. Moon, *Balance of Power: The Negro Vote* (Garden City, N.Y., 1949), p. 112. As late as 1960, Arthur Spingarn still designated the Parker affair as the Association's single most important incident for attracting widespread public and press attention (personal interview with Arthur Spingarn, New York City, Dec. 9, 1960).

46. See Sherman, *The Republican Party and Black America*, pp. 225-29. See also Pete Daniel *Deep'n as It Come: The 1927 Mississippi River Flood* (New York, 1977), passim.

47. *Cong. Rec.*, 72nd Cong., 2d sess, pp. 4691-92 (Feb. 22, 1933). See also Supplementary Secretary's Report, Sept. 12, 1932; Bd. Min., Sept. 12, 1932; Sec. Rep., Dec. 8, 1932, and March 9, 1933; and Minutes of the Twenty-fourth Annual Meeting of the NAACP, Jan. 9, 1933, NAACP-NY. See also, Ovington, *The Walls Came Tumbling Down*, pp. 245-50; and Lawrence, "Negro Organizations in Crisis," pp. 159-62.

48. The War Department, under pressure from the NAACP and the Wagner resolution, had ruled that workers should receive not less than forty cents an hour or work more than thirty hours per week, which meant that some 30,000 would take a weekly pay increase of between $75,000 and $90,000. NAACP investigations were funded through the generosity of Mother M. Katherine and her Sisters of the Blessed Sacrament at Cornwells Heights, Penn. and of her sister, Louise Drexel Morrell Sec. Rep., Dec. 8, 1934; and Bd. Min., Oct. 9, 1933, NAACP-NY.

49. "Memorandum to the Spelman Fund from the NAACP," copy attached to a letter from White to Johnson, Oct. 13, 1932, "White, Walter (1927-1933)" folder, JWJ. White to Johnson, Nov. 13, 1933 (copy), box C-78, NAACP-LC.

50. Bd. Min., Nov. 13, 1933, NAACP-NY.

51. On staff tensions, see Raymond Wolters, *Negroes and the Great Depression: The Problem of Economic Recovery* (Westport, Conn., 1970), pp. 266-71; and B. Joyce Ross, *J. E. Spingarn and the Rise of the NAACP, 1911-1939* (New York, 1972), pp. 130-38.

52. Although White had assigned the assistant executive secretary, Roy Wilkins, to the project (see Sec. Rep., July 7, 1932, NAACP-NY), rumor had it, though he denied it, that White was not keen on the proposal. See Elliott M. Rudwick, *W. E. B. Du Bois: Propagandist of the Negro Protest* (New York, 1968), p. 272. On the resignation, see J. E. Spingarn "To the Board of Directors of the National Association for the Advancement of Colored People," March 6, 1933, box C-75, NAACP-LC.

53. White to Joel Spingarn, March 14, 1933 (copy); White to Johnson, March 22, 1933 (copy); and White to Johnson, March 29, 1933 (copy), box C-78, NAACP-LC. White to Johnson, April 3, 1933, "White, Walter (1927-1933)" folder, JWJ.

54. See, for example, White to Johnson, June 1 (?), 1933 (copy), box C-78, NAACP-LC; Bd. Min., June 12, 1933, NAACP-NY; Joel Spingarn to Johnson, June 26, 1933, "Spingarn, J. E." folder, JWJ. For a discussion of the issues involved in Spingarn's resignation, see Ross, *J. E. Spingarn*, pp. 168-78.

55. Du Bois, *The Autobiography*, pp. 294-95. See also Tillman, "Walter Francis White," pp. 237-41.

56. See Rudwick, *W. E. B. Du Bois*, pp. 266-71; and Ross, *J. E. Spingarn*, pp. 139-43. See also Bd. Min., Nov. 13, 1933, NAACP-NY.

57. *Crisis* 41 (Jan. 1934). 20. For a full analysis of the controversy over black economic autonomy and Du Bois's resignation from the NAACP in June 1934, see Francis L. Broderick, *W. E. B. Du Bois: Negro Leader in a Time of Crisis* (Stanford, Calif., 1966), pp. 169-79; see also Rudwick, *W. E. B. Du Bois*, pp. 272-85. Du Bois told Abram Harris in mid-January that his difficulties stemmed from White's opportunism and from the Spingarns' outmoded economic theories (Du Bois to Harris, Jan. 16, 1934 [copy], DuB).

58. *Crisis* 41 (April 1934): 115-17; Bd. Min., May (14), 1934, NAACP-NY.

59. Minutes of the Meeting of the Committee on Administration, June 21, 1934, box A-26, NAACP-LC; Du Bois to George Streator, June 26, 1934 (copy), DuB; Du Bois to the Board of Directors, June 26, 1934 (copy), with the Bd. Min., July 9, 1934, NAACP-NY. For a brief commentary on the issues involved, see also Elliott Rudwick, "W. E. B. Du Bois in the Role of *Crisis* editor," *Journal of Negro History* 43 (July 1958); 237-40.

60. Ovington to Joel Spingarn, Nov. 7, 1914, JES; and Ovington to Villard, July 22, 1934, OGV. For a detailed discussion of the controversies between Du Bois and the NAACP over the issues of segregation and control of the *Crisis*, see Wolters, *Negroes and the Great Depression*, pp. 270-94, and Ross, *J. E. Spingarn*, chap. 7.

61. Personal interview with William Hastie, Philadelphia, July 25, 1962.

62. Roy Wilkins to Arthur Spingarn, Jan. 16, 1933 (copy), box C-78, NAACP-LC; and Ovington to Villard, July 22, 1934, OGV.

63. W. E. B. Du Bois, *Dusk of Dawn: An Essay toward an Autobiography of a Race Concept* (New York, 1968), pp. 299-301. Du Bois expressed genuine disappointment over the fact that the conferees would not unite behind his concept

of an autonomous black economy. For a discussion of other particpants' reactions to the conference, see Ross, *J. E. Spingarn*, pp. 178–85.

64. See, for example, Charles Houston's mixed reactions to the work of the conferees (Houston to Joel Spingarn, Sept. [?] 13, 1933, JES).

65. Wilkins to White, Aug. 14, 1933 (copy); and White to Johnson, Nov. 13, 1933 (copy), box C-78, NAACP-LC.

66. See Ross, *J. E. Spingarn*, pp. 218–41; Bd. Min., June 11, 1934, Minutes of the Special Meeting of the Board of Directors, Sept. 25, 1934, and Bd. Min., Oct. 8, 1934, NAACP-NY. Sterling D. Spero and Harris had co-authored *The Black Worker: The Negro and the Labor Movement* (New York, 1931).

67. White to Ovington, Oct. 1, 1934; (copy); and White to Charles Houston, Sept. 21, 1934 (copy), box C-78, NAACP-LC. See also White to Houston, Oct. 9, 1934 (copy), box C-78, NAACP-LC, for a further indication of White's reservations about having Davis and the JCNR take the initiative.

68. Houston to White, Feb. 17, 1935, Feb. 23, 1935, and Nov. 5, 1934, box C-64, NAACP-LC.

69. Sec. Rep., Nov. 9, 1933, NAACP-NY; and White's memorandum to the Board of Directors, April 9, 1934, box A-26, NAACP-LC. When NAACP officials appealed to the Horace and Mary Rackham Fund for a $100,000 grant, they cited four key projects on July 24, 1934: adult education, antilynching, economic justice under the New Deal, and a more unified legal defense campaign (Sec. Rep., Sept. 5, 1934, NAACP-NY).

70. For a revealing discussion of how the NAACP Board and staff reworked the Harris committee's recommendations, so that the proposals were sharply emasculated before presentation to and adoption by the Twenty-sixth Annual Conference in St. Louis in late June 1935, see Ross, *J. E. Spingarn*, pp. 238–41. On implementation, see Sec. Rep., July 5, 1935, Aug. 2, 1935, and Sept. 6, 1935, NAACP-NY.

71. Wolters, *Negroes and the Great Depression*, pp. 337–42.

72. "Memorandum for Conference at Mr. Spingarn's Tomorrow," Oct. 21, 1933, box C-78, NAACP-LC; and Sec. Rep., Nov. 9, 1933, NAACP-NY. See also "Memorandum Re Requests Made by the NAACP of President Franklin D. Roosevelt," file X-36, box 3; NAACP-LC; and Sec. Rep., Dec. 7, 1933, NAACP-NY.

73. See for example, White to Charles West, Jan. 10, 1934 (copy), and Lee F. Johnson (Secretary to Senator Costigan) to White, Jan. 13, 1934 (copy), EPC.

74. Robert F. Wagner to White, Dec. 27, 1933 (copy), "Lynching" folder, Schom. For a discussion of Wagner's key role as a New Deal reform senator, see J. Joseph Huthmacher, *Senator Robert F. Wagner and the Rise of Urban Liberalism* (New York, 1968), chap. 8.

75. George Creel, Foreword to *Public Ownership of Government: The Collected Papers of Edward P. Costigan* (New York, 1940), pp. v–xiii. I am also indebted to insights derived from Professor Fred Greenbaum's *Fighting Progressive: A Biography of Edward P. Costigan* (Washington, D.C., 1971).

76. *Cong. Rec.*, 74th Cong., 1st sess., p. 6295 (April 24, 1935). White had written to Costigan on November 27, 1933 to ask if the Coloradan would sponsor the NAACP-prepared antilynching bill in the next session of Congress, and within a week Costigan had his staff gathering data on federal and state laws and those of other countries that would throw light on the question of preventing mob violence (White to Costigan, Nov. 27, 1933; and H. H. B. Meyer, director of the Legislative Reference Service, Library of Congress, to Costigan, Dec. 5, 1933, EPC).

77. White to Johnson, Dec. 1, 1933; see also form telegram of Lewis Gannett, Benjamin Stolberg, Helen Woodward, and Walter White, Dec. 1, 1933, "White, Walter (1927–1933)" folder, JWJ.

78. List of the Writers' League Against Lynching, and the attached Sec. Rep., Dec. 7, 1933, NAACP-NY. For an indication of the controversies that sometimes evolved from the Association's use of ad hoc groups, see clippings from the New York *World-Telegram*, identified as Dec. 13, 15, and 20, 1933, and accompanied by an undated compilation of statements titled "Views of Mr. (Westbrook) Pegler and the San Jose Lynching," "Lynching" folder, JWJ.

79. Copy available, JES.

80. "Memorandum Re Requests Made by the N.A.A.C.P. of President Franklin D. Roosevelt," file X-36, box 3, NAACP-LC. See also White's telegram to Franklin D. Roosevelt, Jan. 4, 1933 (copy); White to Joel Spingarn, Jan. 13, 1933 (copy); and White to Franklin D. Roosevelt, March 24, 1933 (copy), box C-78, NAACP-LC. The Association also sought to arrange a meeting with the president by working through Senators Wagner and Costigan (White to Wagner, Jan. 10, 1934, RFW).

81. Quotation from the *New York Times*, Jan. 4, 1934, 2:5.

82. Alexander to Embree, Dec. 6, 1933 (copy); Mark Ethridge to Alexander (n.d., but bearing the pencilled notation "showed to J.D.A., 1/24/34"); and Alexander to Mark Ethridge, Jan. 26, 1934 (copy), CIC.

83. Alexander to George Foster Peabody, Feb. 5, 1934 (copy); White to Alexander, Nov. 19, and Nov. 28, 1934; and Eleanor Roosevelt to White, Nov. 23, 1934 (copy), CIC.

84. As governor and later as president, Franklin Roosevelt took full advantage of Eleanor Roosevelt's competence as observer, advisor, and source of information. On these matters I wish to acknowledge the illuminating comments of Morris Ernst in a personal interview, New York City, Nov. 20, 1962. See also Tamara Hareven, *Eleanor Roosevelt: An American Conscience* (Chicago, 1968), chap. 2. Eleanor Roosevelt not only made herself available to White's lobbying, she also entertained his family. See White to Eleanor Roosevelt, Aug. 28, 1934, file 100, box 1325, ER.

85. "Memorandum of Conference of the Secretary with Mrs. Eleanor Roosevelt at her New York home," March 1, 1934, box C-73, NAACP-LC. The Arthurdale project is discussed at length in Joseph P. Lash, *Eleanor and Franklin* (New York, 1973), chap. 37.

86. White to Eleanor Roosevelt, April 20, 1934; and White's "Memorandum to Mrs. Eleanor Roosevelt," April 20, 1934, file 100, box 1325, ER.

87. See White to Franklin D. Roosevelt, May 9, 1934 (copy); White to Daisy E. Lampkin, May 11, 1934 (copy), box C-78, NAACP-LC; and White to Eleanor Roosevelt, May 29, 1934, file 100, box 1325, ER.

88. *Cong. Rec.*, 73rd Cong., 2d sess., pp. 1820–21 (Feb. 2, 1934).

89. James W. Ford in the *Daily Worker* of Feb. 20, 1934, asserted that the lack of the death penalty in the Costigan-Wagner bill was simply a ruse by the NAACP to fool the families of lynching victims into believing that it was leading an effective fight on their behalf. See clipping, vertical file, "Lynching" folder, Schom. Even southerners liberal on the race issue, such as Jessie Daniel Ames, objected to the proposed fine on county governments (White to Eleanor Roosevelt, April 20, 1934 [copy], box C-78, NAACP-LC).

90. George Fort Milton, *Lynchings and What They Mean: General Findings of the Southern Commission on the Study of Lynching* (Atlanta, Ga., 1931), p. 49.

91. For a statement of the NAACP's position throughout the decade, see White's testimony in U.S., Congress, Senate, Subcommittee of the Committee on the Judiciary, *Hearings (H.R. 801)*, 76th Cong., 3d sess., pp. 68–70 (Feb. 6, 7, and March 5, 12, 13, 1940).

92. Ovington had expressed these assumptions in her assessment of the jury

in the Sweet trial. See *The Walls Came Tumbling Down*, p. 205. On Progressive perspectives of this sort, see David P. Thelen, *Robert M. La Follette and the Insurgent Spirit* (Boston, 1976), pp. 21-26.

93. White to Charles West, Jan. 10, 1934 (copy); Thomas F. Ford to White, Jan. 11, 1934 (copy); White to Leon Keyserling, Jan. 10, 1934; Keyserling to White, Jan. 13, 1934 (copy), White to Lee F. Johnson, Jan. 13, 1934 (copy); White to Charles West, Jan. 13, 1934 (copy), White to Thomas F. Ford, Jan. 13, 1934 (copy); White to Robert F. Wagner, Jan. 18, 1934; and Wagner to White, Jan. 22, 1934 (copy) RFW. In April 1933, De Priest had asked the NAACP for data on lynchings "as a basis for a speech I expect to make in the near future on the floor" (Oscar De Priest to White, April 11, 1933, box C-64, NAACP-LC). On De Priest, see U.S. Congress, *Biographical Directory of the American Congress, 1774-1971*, Senate Document no. 92-8, 92d Cong., 1st sess. (Washington, D.C., 1971), p. 851.

94. White to Alexander, Feb. 8, 1934; Alexander to George Fort Milton, Feb. 7, 1934 (copy); Alexander to Milton, Feb. 8, 1934 (copy); Douglas S. Freeman to Milton, Feb. 9, 1934 (copy); and Milton to Alexander, Feb. 12, 1934, CIC. Apparently, White had gotten a bit ahead of himself. See, for example, White to Leon Keyserling, Feb. 1, 1934, and three attached lists, RFW.

95. M. T. Van Hecke (Dean of the Law School, University of North Carolina, Chapel Hill) to Alexander, Jan. 4, 1934; Alexander to Van Hecke, Jan. 12, 1934 (copy); Alexander to Van Hecke and to Dr. W. C. Jackson, Jan. 31, 1934 (copy); Alexander to Milton, Dr. W. C. Jackson, and Van Hecke, Feb. 6, 1934 (copy); and Van Hecke to Alexander, Feb. 15, 1934, CIC. The matter of state laws dealing with mob violence was later reviewed by Charles S. Mangum, Jr., *The Legal Status of the Negro* (Chapel Hill, 1940), especially chap. 11.

96. On Alexander, see Alexander to Albert E. Barnett, Jan. 15, 1934 (copy), CIC. On the splinter group, see Jessie Daniel Ames to Mrs. W. A. Newell, Jan. 30, 1934, box 3, folder 27, JDA. See also a letter from Mary McLeod Bethune, Charlotte Hawkins Brown, Mrs. John Hope, Fannie Williams, Nannie Burroughs, Mrs. George Long, Mrs. H. A. Hunt, Cordelia Winn, Mrs. W. J. Johnson, and Mrs. H. L. McClorey (black women affiliated with the CIC) to the editor of the *New York Times*, Jan. 11, 1934 (copy), CIC.

97. Mrs. R. P. Neblett to Alexander, Nov. 1, 1934; Alexander to Mrs. R. P. Neblett, Nov. 16, 1934 (copy); and White to Alexander, Jan. 2, 1934, ibid.

98. White to H. L. Mencken, Jan. 17, 1934, and Feb. 5, 1934 (copies), box C-78, NAACP-LC. H. L. Mencken to "Dear Henry" (not otherwise identified), Feb. 6, 1934; and H. L. Mencken to White, Feb. 6, 1934 (copy), RFW.

99. White to Wagner, Feb. 7, 1934; Wagner to White, Feb. 14, 1934 (copy); and Keyserling to White, Feb. 9, 1934 (copy), ibid. In mid-April, White was able to write Mencken that the hearings were a great success although "the Senate Committee, despite our urging, did not follow through and yank out of the Eastern Shore the lynchers that [Maryland's] Attorney General Lane named." He added, "the hearings were broadcast in a coast-to-coast hook-up" (White to H. L. Mencken, April 17, 1934 [copy], box C-78, NAACP-LC).

100. U.S., Congress, Senate, Subcommittee of the Committee on the Judiciary, *Hearings (S. 1978)*, 73rd Cong., 2d sess., pp. 9-20, (Feb. 20, 21, 1934).

101. The persistent problem among students of lynching about what incidents legitimately constituted a "lynching," as contrasted with "murder," "manslaughter," and other forms of violent death, resulted in somewhat differing data for any year or set of years. In an effort to rectify this semantic dilemma, a meeting was held at Tuskegee Institute in late 1940, and White attended (Report of the Department of Branches, Jan. 6, 1941, NAACP-NY). I am also indebted to the recollections of the late journalist, Ralph McGill, in a personal interview in Philadelphia, April 4, 1963.

102. Senate, Subcommittee of the Committee on the Judiciary, *Hearings (S. 1978)*, pp. 62-67, 93-102. An alphabetical list of witnesses scheduled to appear at the Senate Judiciary subcommittee hearings on Feb. 20, 21, 1934 is available in RG 46, 73rd Cong., S. 1978 folder, NARS. Also, personal interview with Clarence Mitchell, Washington, D.C., Dec. 20, 1962. See also Sec. Rep., Feb. 1934, and Nov. 9, 1933, NAACP-NY.
103. U.S., Congress, Senate, Report No. 710 (*S. 1978*), 73rd Cong., 2d sess., pp. 1-3, 6-7, (March 28, 1934). White to Franklin D. Roosevelt, May 9, 1934 (copy), box C-78, NAACP-LC.
104. White to Lampkin, April 14, 1934 (copy); and White to Marvin McIntyre, April 14, 1934 (copy), box C-78, NAACP-LC.
105. Eleanor Roosevelt to White, May 2, 1934 (copy), box 1325, file 100, ER.
106. White to Lampkin, May 11, 1934 (copy), box C-78, NAACP-LC.
107. White to Franklin D. Roosevelt, May 9, 1934 (copy), box C-78, NAACP-LC; White to Costigan, May 8, 1934, EPC; and Sec. Rep., May 1934, NAACP-NY.
108. White to Eleanor Roosevelt, May 14, 1934 (copy), box C-78, NAACP-LC.
109. Sec. Rep., June 1934, NAACP-NY; and White to Eleanor Roosevelt, May 29, 1934 (copy), box C-78, NAACP-LC.
110. Costigan to Joseph T. Robinson, June 11, 1934 (copy), RFW; and White to Costigan, June 8, 1934, EPC.
111. Costigan to White, June 15, 1934 (telegram, copy), EPC. For an indication of Costigan's efforts, and of representative Joseph Gavagan's remarks at the end of the session, see *Cong. Rec.*, 73rd Cong., 2d sess., p. 11941 (June 16, 1934), and p. 12607 (June 18, 1934).
112. White to Franklin D. Roosevelt, June 13, 1934 (copy), RFW. White to Eleanor Roosevelt, May 29, 1934 (copy), box C-78, NAACP-LC. Costigan to White, June 19, 1934 (telegram, copy), and White to Costigan, June 18, 1934, EPC.
113. White to Lowell Thomas and Gabriel Heatter, Nov. 29, 1933 (handwritten copies of telegrams), box C-41, NAACP-LC; and Sec. Rep., March 9, 1934, and Bd. Min., February 1934, NAACP-NY.
114. L. C. Dyer to White, Jan. 28, 1935 (copy), file 100, ER.
115. *Congressional Quarterly Guide to the Congress of the United States: Origins, History and Procedure* (Washington, D.C., 1971), pp. 85, 92-93, and 117.
116. Eleanor Roosevelt to White, March 19, 1936 (copy), file 100, ER.
117. Stephen Early to Malvina Scheider, Aug. 5, 1935, file 100, ER. On the general disinclination of White House staff members to champion the antilynching bill, see Marvin McIntyre to Malvina Scheider, March 14, 1935, and White to Eleanor Roosevelt, June 24, 1937, ibid.

Chapter 6

1. Wagner to White, June 20, 1934 (copy); White to Wagner, telegram, Oct. 27, 1934; and Wagner to White, Oct. 27, 1934 (telegram, copy), RFW; Sec. Rep., Sept. 1934, NAACP-NY. See also White to Costigan, Aug. 21, 1934, EPC.
2. With NAACP assistance, black voters had twice surmounted the all-white primary, in Nixon v. Herndon (273 U.S. 536) in 1927 and Nixon v. Condon (286 U.S. 73) in 1932. To circumvent these rulings, Texas changed its laws and empowered the political parties themselves to handle the matter. This was at issue in the fall of 1934. In 1935 the Supreme Court (Grovey v. Townsend, 295 U.S. 45 [1935]) upheld the validity of a Democratic state convention resolution restricting primary voting to whites. However, the NAACP persisted, and white primary

devices were finally struck down in Smith v. Allwright (321 U.S. 649) in 1944 and in Terry v. Adams (345 U.S. 461) in 1953.

3. Sec. Rep., Oct. 1934, NAACP-NY.

4. NAACP, *The Lynching of Claude Neal* (New York, 1934), pp. 1-8. See also U.S., Congress, Senate, Subcommittee of the Committee on the Judiciary, *Hearings (S. 24)*, 74th Cong., 1st sess., pp. 42-52 (Feb. 14, 1935).

5. White to Franklin D. Roosevelt, Nov. 20, 1934 and White to Homer S. Cummings, Jan. 18, 1935, RG-60, box 1230XC and box 1231, respectively, JDF; Roscoe Pound to White, Nov. 27, 1934 (copy), RFW. A southern white liberal, Howard "Buck" Kester, executive secretary of the Committee on Economic and Racial Justice (with headquarters in Baltimore) and later active in the Southern Tenant Farmers Union, investigated the Claude Neal lynching for the NAACP (Sec. Rep., Nov. 1934, NAACP-NY). In 1936, Kester reported on the STFU in his book, *Revolt among the Sharecroppers* (New York, 1936), for which White helped to arrange publication. See Walter White to Frances Williams, Jan. 29, 1936 (copy), box C-79, NAACP-LC.

6. Eleanor Roosevelt to White, Nov. 23, 1934 (copy), EPC; Cummings to Angus MacLean, Nov. 28, 1934, quoted in Carl Brent Swisher, ed., *Selected Papers of Homer Cummings* (New York, 1939), pp. 38-39; White to Eleanor Roosevelt, Nov. 27, 1934 (copy), box C-78, NAACP-LC; and Cummings to Franklin D. Roosevelt, March 20, 1935 (copy), RG-60, box 1231, JDF.

7. White to Costigan, Oct. 9, 1934, EPC; White to Eleanor Roosevelt, Dec. 3, 1934 (copy), box C-78, NAACP-LC.

8. Confidential source. See also White to William Pickens, Dec. 11, 1934, box C-78, NAACP-LC.

9. NAACP, *Twenty-fifth Annual Report* (New York, 1935), p. 26; and *The Crisis* 42 (Jan. 1935): 5, 26. See also Walter White, "U.S. Department of (White) Justice" ibid. 42 (Oct. 1935): 309-10.

10. *New York Times*, Dec. 30, 1934, 4:2.

11. See, for example, Eleanor Roosevelt to White, Jan. 8, 1935 (copy), file 100, box 1362, ER. The only previous presidential administration since the Civil War to gain seats in an off-year election had been that of Theodore Roosevelt in 1902 (U.S., Bureau of the Census, *Historical Statistics of the United States, Colonial Times to 1957* [Washington, D.C., 1961], p. 691).

12. One-sheet NAACP flyer (n.d., prepared for distribution in Dec. 1934), vertical file, "Lynching" folder, Schom.

13. White to Eleanor Roosevelt, Jan. 12, 1935, file 100, box 1362, ER; and White to Houston, Jan. 25, 1935 (copy), box C-78, NAACP-LC.

14. White memorandum to Costigan and Wagner, Jan. 30, 1935, EPC. According to White's memorandum, eight antilynching bills were introduced in the House early in the session by Joseph Gavagan, Emanuel Celler, W. F. Brunner, U.S. Guyer, Thomas F. Ford, Louis Ludlow, James Mead, and Arthur W. Mitchell (the black Chicago Democrat who had won Oscar De Priest's seat in the 1934 elections).

15. Bd. Min., Feb. 11, 1935, NAACP-NY. Incidentally, the original Thomas Hart Benton painting never appeared. Left, out of season, in his country cottage, it suffered the effects of inclement weather and a leaky cottage roof and was damaged beyond repair (letter to the author from Thomas Hart Benton, March [n.d.], 1963).

16. *Crisis* 42 (April 1935): 106; Sec. Rep., March 7, 1935, NAACP-NY; "An Art Commentary on Lynching," the program from the exhibit at the Arthur U. Newton Galleries, "Lynching" folder, Schom.; White to Houston Feb. 26, 1935 (copy), box C-78, NAACP-LC; and Eleanor Roosevelt to White, Feb. 20, 1935 (copy), file 100, box 1362, ER. In recalling her remarks at the exhibit's opening,

author Carl Van Vechten remembered that they had helped to make and to seal his friendship with Pearl Buck (personal interview with Van Vechten, New York City, Oct. 29, 1962). See also Lash, *Eleanor and Franklin*, pp. 674–75.

17. Sec. Rep., April 4, 1935; and Bd. Min., June 10, 1935, NAACP-NY; *Crisis* 42 (April 1935); 106; Houston to White, Feb. 23, 1935, box 64, NAACP-LC; NAACP Treasurer's Report for March 1935, NAACP-NY; an unidentified newspaper article by Gerald W. Johnson, "Comment on Lynching," "Lynching" folder, JWJ. The drawing by E. Simms Campbell, "I Passed along This Way," hung for years in the chambers of New York State Supreme Court Justice Joseph A. Gavagan (personal interview with Joseph Gavagan, New York City, Jan. 17, 1963).

18. Typescripts of Costigan and Wagner's remarks during their Feb. 12, 1935 CBS broadcast are in EPC; see also White to John F. Royal of NBC, Feb. 6, 1935 (copy); White to Senator William Dieterich of Illinois, March 9, 1935 (copy); White to Costigan, Feb. 7, and Feb. 6, 1935, EPC; and Houston to White, Feb. 7, 1935, box C-64, NAACP-LC.

19. See Caroline O'Day to Jessie Daniel Ames, March 16, 1935; Ames to O'Day, March 23, 1935 (copy), CIC; and Ames to Costigan, May 8, 1935, EPC. See also Keri Halpin (?), secretary to Lady Kathleen Simon, to "Miss Ames," March 6, 1935, and Lady Simon to Ames, Jan. 22, 1935, CIC.

20. White to Alexander, March 20, 1935; Alexander to White, April 8, 1935 (copy); and Alexander to Costigan, April 26, 1935 (copy), CIC. White to Eleanor Roosevelt, May 13, 1935, and attached two-page typescript of an editorial from the Chattanooga *News*, May 4, 1935, file 100, ER.

21. White to Wilkins, (n.d., but stamped with office in-date of March 8, 1935), box C-78, NAACP-LC; Houston to White, March 11, 1935, Box C-64, NAACP-LC; and White to Houston, March 12, 1935 (copy), box C-78, NAACP-LC.

22. White to Eleanor Roosevelt, April 10, 1935, file 100, box 1362, ER; and White to Eleanor Roosevelt, April 20, 1935 (copy), box C-78, NAACP-LC. In preparing his autobiography thirteen years later, White recalled a meeting he had with Franklin, Eleanor, and Sara Delano Roosevelt at the White House in the spring of 1935. Since no evidence exists in the NAACP files of this meeting that year, and since the description coincides perfectly with a session that White did attend on May 6, 1934, one can assume that the executive secretary's memoirs reflect a lapse of memory. See Walter White, *A Man Called White* (New York, 1948), pp. 168–70. According to Selma Borchard of the American Federation of Teachers, both Majority Leader Joe Robinson and Georgia Senator Richard Russell could be induced by the White House to temper their attacks on the antilynching bill by political favors from the president. Robinson hoped for appointment to the Supreme Court and Russell needed administration backing against Eugene Talmadge (Houston to White, March 19, 1935, and April 10, 1935, box C-64, NAACP-LC). For an analysis of "Roosevelt's Civil Rights Dilemma," see Frank Freidel, *F. D. R. and the South* (Baton Rouge, 1965), chap. 3.

23. Report of the Secretary to Board of Directors on the Costigan-Wagner Anti-Lynching Bill, May 6, 1935, NAACP-NY. See also Marvin McIntyre, "Memorandum for Senator Costigan," March 25, 1935; copy of the Attorney General's four-page memo to President Roosevelt, dated March 20, 1935, EPC. In late April, Cummings informed Costigan that he could use the attorney general's memo to the president as he saw fit (Cummings to Costigan, April 22, 1935, EPC). White House secretaries Stephen Early and Marvin McIntyre both objected to vigorous presidential action in race matters. See Lash, *Eleanor and Franklin*, pp. 675–77.

24. "Memo to Mr. Schuyler from W[alter]. W[hite]. for Press Release on 3 May," May 2, 1935, box C-78, NAACP-LC; and *Cong. Rec.*, 74th Cong., 1st sess.,

p. 5749 (April 16, 1935); ibid., pp. 6366-67, 6369 (April 25, 1935); ibid., p. 6534 (April 29, 1935); ibid., pp. 6622, 6625 (April 30, 1935); ibid., p. 6676 (May 1, 1935).

25. Costigan to Franklin D. Roosevelt, April 22, 1935 (copy), EPC.

26. For a discussion of the New Deal's legislative thrust in the 1935 session, see William E. Leuchtenburg, *Franklin D. Roosevelt and the New Deal: 1932-1940* (New York, 1963), chap. 7. On efforts to reconcile the antilynching bill's status and the administration's legislative program, see the memo on Costigan to Franklin D. Roosevelt, April 26, 1935, 93-A, FDR.

27. White to Franklin Roosevelt, May 6, 1935 (copy),box C-78, NAACP-LC. Having failed to break the filibuster, the NAACP national staff thought about attaching the antilynching bill as a rider to another measure, but lawyers Houston and Hastie warned against the tactic. They proposed a specifically worded amendment, perhaps to the Bankhead farm tenancy bill, but neither Costigan nor Wagner approved. See Houston to White, May 7, 1935, box C-64, NAACP-LC; "Memorandum on the Secretary's Trip to Washington," July 26, 1935, box C-79, NAACP-LC; and Sec. Rep., June 7, 1935, Aug. 2, 1935, and Sept. 6, 1935, NAACP-NY.

28. Houston to White, May 7, 1935, box C-64, NAACP-LC.

29. Hanes Walton, Jr., *Black Politics: A Theoretical and Structural Analysis* (Philadelphia, 1972), chap. 7. See also John M. Allswang, "The Chicago Negro Voter and the Democratic Consensus: A Case Study, 1918-1936," in Bernard Sternsher, ed., *The Negro in Depression and War: Prelude to Revolution, 1930-1945* (Chicago, 1969), pp. 234-57.

30. *Crisis* 42 (June 1935): 177. For Walter White's own evaluations of the campaign see "Report of the Secretary to the Board of Directors on the Costigan-Wagner Anti-Lynching bill," May 6, 1935, NAACP-NY.

31. White to Du Bois, March 18, 1935 (copy), box C-78, NAACP-LC; Houston to White, Feb. 23, 1935, box C-64, NAACP-LC; and White to Houston, February 28, 1935 (copy), box C-78, NAACP-LC.

32. White to Wilkins, April 15, 1935 (wire), and Wilkins to White, April 15, 1935 (copy), box C-78, NAACP-LC.

33. Personal interview with Richetta Randolph (a secretary at the NAACP national offices from the early days of the organization until her retirement, on a part-time basis, in the late 1940s), New York City, Oct. 16, 1962. In May, 1935, the Budget Committee reported a bleak financial picture and the need to cut expenses (Bd. Min., May 13, 1935, NAACP-NY).

34. Houston to White, Feb. 9, 1935, box C-64, NAACP-LC.

35. Houston to White, Feb. 23, 1935, box C-64, NAACP-LC.

36. White to Eleanor Roosevelt, April 10, 1935 (copy), box C-78, NAACP-LC.

37. "Memorandum of the Secretary's Trip to Washington," July 26, 1935, box C-79, NAACP-LC.

38. White to Costigan, Aug. 19, 1935, EPC.

39. White to Wagner, March 27, 1935; and Wagner to White, March 29, 1935 (copy), RFW; and Costigan to White, March 29, 1935 (copy, wire), and White to Costigan, April 1, 1935, EPC. For an indication of White's influence within NAACP leadership circles, see August Meier and Elliott Rudwick, "The Rise of the Black Secretariat in the NAACP, 1909-1935," *Crisis* 84 (Feb. 1977): 67.

40. White to Wilkins, October 16 [1935] and see White to Joel Spingarn, Oct. 22, 1935 (copy), box C-79, NAACP-LC. Early in 1937, White suggested to Arthur Spingarn that Victor Ridder, WPA administrator and the person "who steered Jim Ryan into my clutches," would make a fine addition to the NAACP Board of Directors (White to Arthur Spingarn, Jan. 30, 1937 [copy], box C-79, NAACP-LC).

41. Bd. Min., Dec. 9, 1935, NAACP-NY. In some ways, the allotment from Ryan had more immediate impact than the larger sum from the AFPS, because the American Fund often gave its grants on the condition that the recipient raise an equal amount from other sources. Such a tactic had both constructive and negative effects. It stimulated the organization to renewed activity and made it easier to convince other potential donors of the need to act; but, as Morris Ernst (who had sat with the Joint Committee and was also an NAACP Board member) has pointed out, the practice too often impeded an organization's regular substantive functions by sending its staff members off on a frenetic search for matching contributions (personal interview with Morris Ernst, New York City, Nov. 20, 1962).

42. "Memorandum of Interview of the Secretary of N.A.A.C.P. with the President at the White House on January 2, 1936, From 12:15 to 12:50 pm," Jan. 3, 1936, EPS. See also Bd. Min., Dec. 9, 1935, NAACP-NY.

43. *Cong. Rec.*, 74th Cong., 2d sess., pp. 48–49, (Jan. 6, 1936).

44. White to Wilkins, Oct. 16 [1935], box C-79, NAACP-LC; Sec. Rep., Feb. 6, 1936, NAACP-NY; White to Costigan, January 22, 1936, EPC.

45. White to Frances Williams, Jan. 29, 1936 (copy), box C-79, NAACP-LC.

46. "Memorandum of Conference of the Secretary with the Attorney General, Department of Justice, Washington, D.C.," Jan. 16, 1936; and White to Franklin Roosevelt, Jan. 20, 1936 (copy), box C-79, NAACP-LC; and White to Eleanor Roosevelt, Jan. 28, 1936, file 100, box 1411, ER.

47. On the delay, *Cong. Rec.*, 74th Cong., 2d sess. (Feb. 13, 1936), p. 1951. See also U.S., Congress, Senate, *Report No. 1561*, 74th Cong., 2d sess. (1936); and White to Franklin Roosevelt, Feb. 17, 1936 (telegram, copy), box C-79, NAACP-LC. On the delay, Sec. Rep., March 5, 1936, and April 9, 1936, NAACP-NY.

48. White to Eleanor Roosevelt, Feb. 28, 1936, file 100, box 1411, ER; and White to Franklin Roosevelt, Feb. 4, 1936 (copy), box C-79, NAACP-LC. See also Sec. Rep., Feb. 6, 1936, and March 5, 1936, NAACP-NY.

49. White identified House whip Patrick Boland (Pa.), Rules Committee chairman John J. O'Connor (N.Y.), and Speaker Joseph W. Byrns (Tenn.) in his charges (White to Eleanor Roosevelt, April 5, 1936 [wire, copy], box C-79, NAACP-LC). See also F. D. R. typescript "Memorandum for E. R.," March 9, 1936, and Eleanor Roosevelt to White, March 16, 1936 (copy), file 100, ER.

50. See, for example, White to Wilkins, March 19, 1936, box C-79, NAACP-LC. Among the legislators whom White identified as helpful in these emergencies were: Van Nuys, Costigan, Wagner, Arthur Capper (R–Kan., who also held an honorary post as an NAACP vice president), Charles McNary (R–Ore.), and Robert La Follette, Jr. (Indep.–Wis.) in the Senate, and House Democrats Thomas Ford (Calif.), Joseph Gavagan (N.Y.), Louis Ludlow (Ind.), Herman Kopplemann (Conn.), Caroline O'Day (N.Y.), William Granfield (Mass.), Edward Kenney (N.J.), Byron Scott (Calif.), Thomas C. Hennings, Jr. (Mo.), Fred Hildebrandt (S. D.), William Connery, Jr. (Mass.), and John Tolan (Calif.). White also indicated that several southerners favored the bill but could not support it openly for fear of political repercussions at home. Among these were Frank Boykin (D–Ala.) and Maury Maverick (D–Tex.). In January 1937, Maverick announced his support for the antilynching bill; in March of 1940, he appeared as a witness for the Southern Conference for Human Welfare at House hearings to endorse the Geyer anti–poll tax bill. See Richard B. Henderson, *Maury Maverick: A Political Biography* (Austin, 1970), pp. 110–12, 140–41, and 220–24.

51. White to Wilkins, April 24, 1936; and White to Franklin D. Roosevelt, April 24, 1936 (copy), box C-79, NAACP-LC. See also confidential memorandum, White to Costigan, April 2, 1936, EPC.

52. Sec. Rep., May 4, 1936, June 8, 1936, NAACP-NY; White to Lampkin,

May 27, 1936, (copy); White to Franklin D. Roosevelt, May 23, 1936 (copy); and White to Wilkins, March 19, 1936, box C-79, NAACP-LC.

53. White to Eleanor Roosevelt, June 1, 1936 (copy); and "Memorandum Telephone Conversation from Mr. White in Washington with Mr. Wilkins," June 5, 1936, box C-79, NAACP-LC.

54. U.S., Congress, *Congressional Directory*, 87th Cong., 2d sess., (Washington, D.C., 1962), p. 325. Among the groups were the American Civil Liberties Union, National Urban League, Women's Peace Society, National Committee for the Defense of Political Prisoners, Young Women's Christian Association, American Federation of Labor, Federal Council of Churches, Women's International League for Peace and Freedom, American Federation of Teachers, National Association of Colored Women, Society of Friends, League for Industrial Democracy, Women's Missionary Council of the Methodist Episcopal Church, South, American Jewish Committee, and National Federation of Temple Sisterhoods. See Charles R. Lawrence, "Negro Organizations in Crisis: Depression, New Deal, W.W. II" (Ph.D. diss., Columbia University, 1953), p. 231; Report of the Department of Branches, Feb. 13, 1934, and White to members of the Board, Dec. 29, 1934, NAACP-NY; National Public Affairs Committee of Young Women's Christian Association, Bulletin no. III, Public Affairs News Service, Dec. 14, 1936, pp. 2-4; *Applications Favorably Acted upon, Gifts and Loans, 1934-38*, Vol. 9, sec. 4, 7-18, AFPS; *New York Times*, Feb. 5, 1936, 21:3; T. Arnold Hill to Atlanta Field Director [Jesse O.] Thomas, Feb. 21, 1934, GOF no. 44, NUL; and vertical file, "Lynching" folder, Schom.

55. Dan T. Carter, *Scottsboro, A Tragedy of the American South* (Baton Rouge, 1969), pp. 334-35; and Minutes of the Special Meeting of the Board of Directors, Dec. 16, 1935, Bd. Min., Jan. 6, 1936, and Minutes of the Special Meeting of the Board of Directors, Jan. 18, 1936, NAACP-NY.

56. RG 46, 74th Cong., S. 24 folder, NARS. Always anxious to develop maximum publicity against lynching, White assured his Board in April 1936 that "the item of the Association's work which received most space in the newspapers during March was the continued fight for the consideration of the anti-lynching bill" (Sec. Rep., April 9, 1936, NAACP-NY).

57. See, for example, Bd. Min., June 10, 1935, and Oct. 14, 1935, and Sec. Rep., July 5, 1935, and Oct. 5, 1933, NAACP-NY; ILD press release, Dec. 30, 1935, "Lynching—Causes" folder, Schom; Bd. Min., Sept. 14, 1936, and Dec. 14, 1936, and Sec. Rep., Feb. 4, 1937, March 8, 1937, and Sept. 1, 1938, NAACP-NY; White to Elisabeth Gilman, Jan. 7, 1936, reel 2, HAK; and White to Howard Kester, Nov. 3, 1937, reel 3, ibid.

58. For examples of the manner in which the fight against lynching fit into the NAACP's general organizational, membership, and contributions drives, and of the way in which contacts and relationships established in one area had reciprocal effects on other issues, see the following: White to Lampkin, Sept. 17, 1935 (copy), and White to William Rosenwald, Nov. 26, 1935 (copy), box C-79, NAACP-LC; White to Rosenwald, Feb. 24, 1930 (copy), box C-77, NAACP-LC; White to Jacob Billikopf, Jan. 9, 1936 (copy) and White to Lampkin, May 27, 1936 (copy), box C-79, NAACP-LC; White to Herbert H. Lehman, Jan. 9, 1934 (copy), box C-78, NAACP-LC; Bd. Min., July 8, 1935, NAACP-NY; White to Joel Spingarn, Oct. 22, 1935 (copy), box C-79, NAACP-LC.

59. White to Borah, July 19, 1935, (copy), and Borah to White, Nov. 23, 1935 (copy), EPC.

60. White to Frances Williams, Jan. 29, 1936 (copy), box C-79, NAACP-LC; Sec. Rep., Feb. 6, 1936, and Bd. Min., Feb. 10, 1936, NAACP-NY. For an indication of the opposition against Borah on the antilynching issue, see editorial cartoon "A Sock in the Eye," *Amsterdam News*, Jan. 11, 1936, 8:4-6.

61. "Notes to R[oy]. W[ilkins]. from W. W. on 'Beat Borah' meeting, April 26th, Cleveland at Antioch Baptist Church," April 27 [1936], box C-79, NAACP-LC. For further indications of Borah's adamant stand on the antilynching bill, see Borah to C. Franklin Ward, Feb. 22, 1936 (copy), Borah to George F. Robinson, March 17, 1936 (copy), and Borah to W. C. Thomas, March 25, 1936 (copy), box 396, WEB. White's Illinois figures made good public relations material, but he failed to say how many of the 226,000 black voters would have backed any GOP aspirant by 1936. See White to Borah, May 18, 1936 (copy), file 100, ER.

62. *Daily Worker*, Feb. 21, 1934, 1, 2. Ford had seen his grandfather lynched by a mob because of a dispute over the ownership of a pig (Roi Ottley, "*New World A-Coming*" (Boston, 1943), p. 243.

63. Ben J. Davis, Jr. to Carol King, Sept. 6, 1935, accompanied by mimeographed copies of proposed legislation, "Lynching" folder, Schom. An Atlanta lawyer, Davis' father had been a Republican National Committeeman from Georgia. In 1933, the younger Davis headed the Angelo Herndon defense. See Charles H. Martin, *The Angelo Herndon Case and Southern Justice* (Baton Rouge, 1976), chap. 3. Also personal interview with Ted Poston, New York City, Dec. 13, 1962. For further indication of the ILD's campaign against lynching, see press releases and statistical data compiled for distribution by the ILD, vertical file, "Lynching—Statistics" folder, Schom.

64. Clipping from the *Daily Worker* of April 8, 1936, vertical file, "Lynching" folder, Schom. On the change in CP attitudes, see Wilson Record, *The Negro and the Communist Party* (Chapel Hill, 1951), pp. 60–61, 134–36. Actually the Comintern inaugurated the United Front strategy in late 1933, but not all national Communist parties implemented the program immediately. See Wilson Record. *Race and Radicalism: The NAACP and the Communist Party in Conflict* (Ithaca, 1964), pp. 84–88.

65. "Memorandum to the Board of Directors on the *National Negro Congress*, From Mr. Wilkins," March 9, 1936; and "Supplementary Memorandum to the Report on the National Negro Congress, from Mr. Wilkins," March 10, 1936, box A-26, NAACP-LC.

66. White to Houston, Sept. 21, 1934, March 26, 1935, and May 22, 1935 (copies), box C-78, NAACP-LC; Houston to White, April 10, 1935, box C-64, NAACP-LC; White to Eleanor Roosevelt, Feb. 28, 1936, file 100, box 1141, ER; and White to Joel Spingarn, Oct. 9, 1936 (copy), box C-79, NAACP-LC.

67. Record, *Race and Radicalism*, pp. 93–97.

68. For example, in late April 1936, Wilkins advised the NAACP Committee on Administration that since the *Daily Worker* had recently reopened public interest in the men of the Twenty-fourth Infantry still held at Leavenworth prison, the Association should renew its own efforts on their behalf (Minutes of the Committee on Administration, April 27, 1936, box A-26, NAACP-LC).

Chapter 7

1. Sec. Rep., June 8, 1936, and Dec. 9, 1936, NAACP-NY.
2. Walter White, "Memorandum to the Committee on Administration," Aug. 20, 1936, box A-26, NAACP-LC.
3. Charles H. Houston, "Memorandum to Mr. White and the Committee on Administration," Aug. 31, 1936, box A-26, ibid. For an insight into Roy Wilkins' agreement with White on the need to attract support from prominent white sources, see Wilkins to Houston, May 23, 1935, box C-80, ibid.
4. Minutes of the Meeting of the Committee on Administration, Sept. 21, 1936, and "Outline of Proposed Legal Defense–Anti-Lynching Fund Campaign

(as of Dec. 9, 1936)," box A-26, ibid.; Bd. Min. Jan. 4, 1937; and Sec. Rep., Feb. 4, 1937, and April 14, 1937, NAACP-NY. I am also indebted to the comments of Daisy Lampkin in a personal interview, Morris Beach, N.J., Aug. 30, 1962.

5. Treasurer's Reports for Feb. and Nov. 1936, with the Bd. Min. for 1936, NAACP-NY. A year later financial problems persisted, and Daisy Lampkin rejected as unfeasible any reliance on a new button-selling drive. See Roy Wilkins' "Memorandum to the Committee on Administration," Nov. 22, 1937, box A-26, NAACP-LC.

6. Roy Wilkins interview of March 22, 1960, Columbia University Oral History Project, pp. 69–70.

7. White to Wagner, Dec. 10, 1936, RFW. White enclosed the New York *World-Telegram* clipping. Shortly after the first of the year Thurgood Marshall suggested to White that, since the Republican caucus had supported the antilynching bill, and since the Farmer-Laborite bloc in the new Congress wished recognition as a separate entity, the NAACP should attempt to get Farmer-Laborite endorsement of the bill as well (Marshall to White, Jan. 6, 1937, box C-79, NAACP-LC).

8. Sec. Rep., Feb. 4, 1937, and March 8, 1937, NAACP-NY.

9. Sec. Rep., March 8, 1937, NAACP-NY. In this same monthly report, White told his Board that he had "spent the entire week of February 28 in Washington on the matter of the anti-lynching bill."

10. Interview with Joseph Gavagan, Columbia University Oral History Project, 1950, pp. 24–26, 29–31, and 42; personal interview with Joseph Gavagan, New York City, Jan. 17, 1963. See also Houston to White, Feb. 23, 1935, box C-64, NAACP-LC; and White to Houston, Feb. 26, 1935 (copy), box C-78, NAACP-LC. On Gavagan's career, see U.S., Congress, *Biographical Directory of the American Congress*, Senate Document no. 92-8, 92d Cong., 1st sess. (Washington, D.C., 1971), p. 991.

11. U.S., Congress, *Cong. Rec.*, 75th Cong., 1st sess., p. 139 (January 8, 1937). See also Walter White, *A Man Called White* (New York, 1948), p. 172.

12. *Cong. Rec.*, 75th Cong., 1st sess., p. 3252 (April 7, 1937); and ibid., p. 3423 (April 13, 1937).

13. *Crisis*, 44 (April 1937); 113; *New York Times*, April 5, 1937, 4:3.

14. *Cong. Rec.*, 75th Cong., 1st sess., appendix, pp. 721–22; ibid., pp. 2856–57 (March 29, 1937).

15. On Mitchell's background and career, see Maurine Christopher, *Black Americans in Congress* (New York, 1976), pp. 176–84. White to Bill Howard (in Senator Costigan's office), July 29, 1935; Sworn Statement of William E. Howard, July 31, 1935; Lee Johnson to White, Aug. 2, 1935 (copy); and White to Lee Johnson, Aug. 5, 1935, EPC.

16. Sec. Rep., Aug. 2, 1935, NAACP-NY. See also *Crisis* 42 (Oct. 1935): 305.

17. White to Mitchell, a letter of March 1936, cited in *Cong. Rec.*, 74th Cong., 2d sess., pp. 7557–58 (May 19, 1936). Wilkins to White, Aug. 5, 1936, box C-80, NAACP-LC. White to Wilkins, March 18, 1937, ibid., box C-79.

18. Ames to Hatton Sumners, telegram, May 24, 1937; and Mrs. Attwood Martin to Sumners, June 18, 1937; also, Mrs. L. W. Alford to Sumners, May 6, 1937, and Ames to Sumners, July 9, 1937, RG 233, 76th Congress, Judiciary Committee, Anti-Lynching, HR75A-F22.1, NARS. For Martin's given name, see Jacquelyn Dowd Hall, "Revolt against Chivalry: Jessie Daniel Ames and the Women's Campaign Against Lynching" (Ph.D. diss., Columbia University, 1974), p. 359. The same group of committee records contains a letter from Nicholas

Murray Butler to Sumners, April 20, 1937, in which the president of Columbia University deplores lynching but applauds Sumners' opposition to an antilynching bill that threatens constitutional balance.

19. *Cong. Rec.*, 75th Cong., 1st sess., p. 3439 (April 13, 1937); and ibid., pp. 3252–53 (April 7, 1937); and ibid., p. 3205 (April 6, 1937). See also U.S., Congress, House, *Antilynching Bill, Report No. 563*, 75th Cong., 1st sess. (April 6, 1937). Incidentally, Congressman Sumners voted on April 7 to consider the Mitchell bill. Opposition to the Mitchell bill and support for the Gavagan measure are indicated in the columns of the *Amsterdam News*, April 3, 1937, 14:3–5; and April 10, 1937, 1:4 and 14:6.

20. *Cong. Rec.*, 75th Cong., 1st sess., pp. 3423, 3433, 3411 (April 13, 1937); ibid., pp. 3551–52, 3541, 3536, and 3563–64. (April 15, 1937). See also Sec. Rep., April 14, 1937, NAACP-NY.

21. Bd. Min., April 19, 1937, and May 10, 1937; and Sec. Rep., June 9, 1937, NAACP-NY. For indication of the working relationship between Howard Kester and the NAACP, see White to Kester, Dec. 1, 1938 and enclosed copies of letters, M. S. Pickens to White, Nov. 25, 1938, and White to H. H. King, Nov. 30, 1938, reel 4, HAK. Also, White to Bennett Champ Clark, Nov. 15, 1938 (copy), reel 4, ibid.

22. Sec. Rep., May 6, 1937, and June 9, 1937, NAACP-NY. See also White to Lampkin, Sept. 8, 1937 (copy), box C-79, NAACP-LC; and White to Eleanor Roosevelt, June 10, 1937, file 100, ER.

23. James Patterson has very ably analyzed these forces and their consequences for the White House in *Congressional Conservatism in the New Deal: The Growth of the Conservative Coalition in Congress, 1933–1939* (Lexington, 1967), especially chaps. 3–8.

24. MCD to Walter White, telegram, May 18, 1937, and White to Joel Spingarn, May 17, 1937 (copy), box C-79, NAACP-LC.

25. White to Joel Spingarn, May 21, 1937 (copy); White to Frances Williams, May 27, 1937 (copy), box C-79, NAACP-LC; and White to Eleanor Roosevelt, May 21, and June 24, 1937, file 100, ER.

26. U.S., Congress, Senate, *Anti-Lynching Bill, Report No. 793*, 75th Cong., 1st sess. (June 15, 1937); *Cong. Rec.*, 75th Cong., 1st Sess., p. 6613 (June 22, 1937). See also White to Wagner, telegram, June 10, 1937; Wagner to White, June 11, 1937 (copy); and White to Wagner, telegram, June 24, 1937, RFW.

27. Wilkins to White, Aug. 3, 1937, box C-80, NAACP-LC. As J. Joseph Huthmacher has explained, Wagner had to fight a running battle on both ends of Pennsylvania Avenue before seeing the Wagner-Steagall housing act passed in August 1937. J. Joseph Huthmacher, *Senator Robert F. Wagner and the Rise of Urban Liberalism* (New York, 1968), pp. 224–28.

28. White to Wagner, July 16, 1937, and White to Wagner, telegram, Aug. 5, 1937, RFW; Sec. Rep., Aug. 25, 1937, NAACP-NY. For an example of how one railway union leader could help frustrate black workers' hopes for union reforms, see Raymond Wolters, *Negroes and the Great Depression: The Problem of Economic Recovery* (Westport, Conn.), pp. 180–81.

29. White to Wagner, July 26, 1937; copy of White's "Night Letter Sent 25 July 1937 to 59 Senators Listed as Favorable to Anti-Lynching Bill"; and White to Wagner, Aug. 4, 1937, RFW.

30. Wilkins to White, telegram, Aug. 4, 1937, ibid.

31. *Cong. Rec.*, 75th Cong., 1st sess., pp. 8694–97 (Aug. 11, 1937). The Senate was further deprived of a placid closing when Roosevelt nominated Hugo Black to the Supreme Court (Patterson, *Congressional Conservatism*, pp. 157–58).

32. Sec. Rep., Aug. 25, 1937, NAACP-NY. *Cong. Rec.*, 75th Cong., 1st sess., pp. 8758-59 (Aug. 12, 1937). Crop control legislation held assignment as the first order of business. See also White to Wagner, Aug. 13, 1937, RFW.

33. Sec. Rep., Aug. 25, 1937, NAACP-NY. As one former NAACP staff member explained to me in a confidential interview, Minton's effectiveness in countering Borah's pronouncements, resulted, in no small way, from the effect of constitutional and legal points that NAACP representatives kept passing to him during debate. See also White's "Night Letter Sent 25 July 1937 to 59 Senators Listed as Favorable to Anti-Lynching Bill" (copy), RFW.

34. Wagner to White, telegram, Aug. 13, 1937, ibid.

35. Sec. Rep., Oct. 6, 1937, NAACP-NY.

36. The congressional atmosphere was further intensified by the emergence of a conservative coalition (Patterson, *Congressional Conservatism*, chap. 6).

37. Sec. Rep., Nov. 4, 1937, and Dec. 11, 1937, NAACP-NY; and *Cong. Rec.*, 75th Cong., 2d sess, pp. 38-39 (Nov. 16, 1937). See also White to Wagner, Nov. 9, 1937, RFW.

38. *Cong. Rec.*, 75th Cong., 2d sess., pp. 42-52, 39-40 (Nov. 9, 1937).

39. Ibid., p. 68 (Nov. 17, 1937).

40. Ibid., pp. 155-56 (Nov. 19, 1937). See also Franklin L. Burdette, *Filibustering in the Senate* (Princeton, 1940), pp. 193-94.

41. *Cong. Rec.*, 75th Cong., 2d sess., p. 228; (Nov. 22, 1937); ibid., p. 266, (Nov. 23, 1937).

42. White to Wagner, Dec. 11, 1937; Robert W. Horton, "Roosevelt Fails in his Program with Congress," clipping from the New York *World-Telegram* of Dec. 12, 1937; and White's "Memorandum to the Branches of the N.A.A.C.P. and to Organizations Cooperating for Passage of the Gavagan-Wagner-Van Nuys Anti-Lynching Bill," Dec. 21, 1937, RFW; and *Cong. Rec.*, 75th Cong., 2d sess., pp. 1931-34 (Dec. 20, 1937).

43. As quoted in Sec. Rep., Feb. 4, 1937, NAACP-NY. See also *Cong. Rec.*, 75th Cong., 1st sess., p. 3523 (April 15, 1937); and George H. Gallup, ed., *The Gallup Poll: Public Opinion, 1935-1971*, 3 vols. (New York, 1972), 1:48, 75.

44. Sec. Rep., Dec. 11, 1937, NAACP-NY. At the same time, White cited two bitter attacks on the antilynching bill from Mark Sullivan and General Hugh Johnson.

45. Ames to Mrs. W. A. Newell, Christmas season, 1937 (copy), box 3, folder 27, JDA. Also copy of an address for the 1938 meeting of the ASWPL, Piedmont Hotel, Atlanta, Ga. (no indication of author), box 4, folder 34, JDA.

46. White to Charles McNary, Jan. 5, 1938 (copy), file 259-2, NAACP-LC.

47. *Cong. Rec.*, 75th Cong., 3d sess., p. 77 (Jan. 6, 1938); ibid, pp. 138-61, 253-75, 305-18, 362-86, 430-42, 447-52, 493-511, 571-90, 610-32, 682-91, 703-05, 752-71, 813-35, 873-96, 964-1001, 1033-54, 1098-1138, 1168-82, 1197-1213, 1339-47, 1385-1407, 1450-64, 1490-97, 1502-12, 1533-62, 1623-43, 1683-1712, 1924-27, 1945-61, 2022-37, and 2090-2118 (Jan. 7-Feb. 17, 1938). Incidentally, Claude Pepper later recalled that the fight against the antilynching bill was his last active participation against civil rights. He reported learning a good bit about the two sides in the controversy, and thereafter he supported the antilynching, anti-poll tax, and several other civil rights measures (personal interview with Pepper, Washington, D.C., Sept. 19, 1968).

48. *Cong. Rec.*, 75th Cong., 3d sess., p. 310 (Jan. 11, 1938); and p. 892 (Jan. 21, 1938).

49. Wilkins to Houston, Jan. 15, 1938, box C-80, NAACP-LC.

50. Joel Spingarn Memorandum, Jan. 31, 1938 (copy), box C-75, NAACP-LC. For criticisms of the filibuster during the winter of 1938, see "Editorial Opinion

from Southern Daily Papers on the Federal Anti-Lynching Bill," a thirteen-page typescript (n.d.), file 100, ER.

51. Wilkins to Charles Edward Russell, Feb. 1, 1938 (copy), box C-80, NAACP-LC.

52. *Cong. Rec.*, 75th Cong., 3d sess., pp. 1166, 1168 (Jan. 27, 1938). Until 1917, the U.S. Senate had no cloture rule whatever. Furthermore, until cloture was successfully invoked against the satellite communications bill filibuster in the 87th Congress (*New York Times*, Aug. 15, 1962, 1:3; and ibid., Aug. 18, 1962, 1:6), cloture had been secured only four times (see Burdette, *Filibustering*, pp. 222–23). Until the 1964 Civil Rights Act, cloture had never been secured on a piece of civil rights legislation. From 1917 to 1949, cloture required only consent of two-thirds of the members present and voting; because the new rule extended cloture to motions as well as bills, the Senate placated the South by raising the requirement to two-thirds of the entire Senate body (*New York Times*, March 18, 1949, 1:8 and 17:1). See also Marvin E. Stromer, *The Making of a Political Leader: Kenneth S. Wherry and the United States Senate* (Lincoln, 1969), pp. 98–102; and *Congressional Quarterly Guide to the Congress of the United States: Origins, History and Procedure* (Washington, D.C., 1971), pp. 85, 92–93, 117. The author wishes also to thank the late Senate parliamentarian, Charles L. Watkins, for his extensive and informative remarks on these matters during an interview in his Capitol office, Dec. 21, 1962.

53. *Cong. Rec.*, 75th Cong. 3d sess., pp. 1443–49 (Feb. 3, 1938).

54. Wilkins to Joel Spingarn, Feb. 7, 1938 (copy), box C-79, NAACP-LC.

55. Sec. Rep., Feb. 14, 1938, NAACP-NY. See also *New York Times*, Feb. 11, 1938, 1:7.

56. *Cong. Rec.*, 75th Cong. 3d sess., pp. 1887–88 (Feb. 14, 1938); U.S., Congress, *Congressional Directory*, 75th Cong., 3d sess. (Washington, D.C., 1938), pp. 155–57. On Truman's motives, see William C. Berman, *The Politics of Civil Rights in the Truman Administration* (Columbus, 1970), pp. 9–10.

57. *Cong. Rec.*, 75th Cong., 3d sess., pp. 1924–25 (Feb. 15, 1938), and ibid., pp. 2007–08 (Feb. 16, 1938).

58. White to Alben W. Barkley, Feb. 18, 1938 (copy); and White to Franklin D. Roosevelt, Feb. 18, 1938 (copy), RFW.

59. White to William Rosenwald, Feb. 19 and 24, 1938 (copies); and White to Forrester B. Washington in Atlanta, A. C. MacNeal in Chicago, Mrs. Harry Davis in Cleveland, Jennie Young in Detroit, Mrs. Osya Lewis in Kansas City, Mo., Constance Heslip in Toledo, and P. O. Sweeney in Louisville, Feb. 25, 1938 (copies), box C-79, NAACP-LC. Meanwhile, White had made arrangements with Joe Louis and his managers to get antilynching funds from the champion's next fight purse. See White to John Roxborough, February 28, 1938 (telegram, copy), box C-79, NAACP-LC.

60. Sec. Rep., March 10, 1938, NAACP-NY. See also NAACP press release: "Statement of Walter White, Secretary, National Association for the Advancement of Colored People," Feb. 21, 1938, RFW.

61. *Cong. Rec.*, 75th Cong., 3d sess., pp. 2201–10, (Feb. 21, 1938).

62. *Time*, 31 (Jan. 24, 1938); and Bd. Min., April 11, 1938, NAACP-NY.

63. Bd. Min., March 14, 1938, NAACP-NY. *Afro-American*, March 5, 1938, 4:1–2. The question of voting rights, of course, had been opened anew after the Supreme Court's 1935 decision in Grovey v. Townsend, 295 U.S. 45 (1935) which threatened to upend rulings against the white primary in 1927 (*Nixon v. Herndon*, 273 U.S. 536) and 1932 (Nixon v. Condon, 286 U.S. 73).

64. William Hastie to White, March 11, 1938, box C-64, NAACP-LC.

White to Joel Spingarn, March 18, 1938 (copy), and White to Hastie, March 30, 1938 (copy), box C-79, ibid.

65. The dependability of federal agents in the South had long troubled the NAACP. See, for example, White to Homer Cummings, June 26, 1936 (telegram, copy); White to H. L. Mitchell, and White to Howard Kester, both July 15, 1936, reel 2, STFU. The NAACP's Van Nuys resolution in 1936 provided for a Senate, not an agency, investigation.

66. Bd. Min., April 11, 1938, NAACP-NY. At this meeting the Board also urged the inclusion of black troops in active Armed Forces units.

67. "Memorandum on Interview in Senate Reception Room, 3:30 P.M., February 15th, 1938, between Senator Charles L. McNary and Charles H. Houston and Walter White"; White to McNary, Feb. 16, 1938, and Feb. 21, 1938 (copies), file 359, box 2, NAACP-LC. See also Wilkins to Hiram W. Johnson, Feb. 8, 1938 (copy), and Wilkins to John Hamilton, Feb. 9, 1938 (copy), file 359, boxes 2 and 3, respectively, NAACP-LC.

68. Letter to the Editor from John Hamilton, *Afro-American*, Jan. 22, 1938, 1:3–4; and Hamilton to Wilkins, March 14, 1938, file 359, box 3, NAACP-LC. U.S., Bureau of the Census, *Historical Statistics of the United States, Colonial Times to the Present* (Washington, D.C., 1961), p. 691.

69. *Afro-American*, Feb. 12, 1938, 16:1; and April 2, 1938, 5:4 and 17:6–7.

70. White to Hastie, March 30, 1938 (copy), box C-79, NAACP-LC.

71. White to Hastie, April 15, 1938 (copy), box C-79, ibid.

72. *Afro-American*, March 26, 1938, 5:8; Edwin D. Hoffman, "The Genesis of the Modern Movement for Equal Rights in South Carolina, 1930–1939," *Journal of Negro History*, 44 (Oct. 1959): 363–69; and White to Hastie, March 30, 1938 (copy), box C-79, NAACP-LC. See also Robert L. Zangrando, "The NAACP and a Federal Antilynching Bill, 1934–1940," *Journal of Negro History* 50 (April 1965): 106–17.

73. See, for example, John Jasper's front-page column and the editorial on James Weldon Johnson's death (*Afro-American*, July 2, 1938, page 1, 2:4–5, 2:1, and 4:1–2), a report of the eulogy written by Heywood Broun of the Scripps-Howard chain (ibid., July 9, 1938, 6:1–2), and the remarks of Kelly Miller (ibid., July 9, 1938, 1:5 and 2:5).

74. See ibid., June 11, 1938, 1:8 for a report on the events at Coatesville; the editorial and Miller's column appeared in ibid., June 18, 1938, 4:1–2, 4–5.

75. Sec. Rep., April 7, 1938, NAACP-NY; *Afro-American*, April 9, 1938, 17:2–3. See also White to Houston, Marshall, and Wilkins, March 29, 1938 (copy), and White to Hastie, March 30, 1938 (copy), box C-79, NAACP-LC; and Wilkins to Pickens, April 19, 1938, box C-80, NAACP-LC.

76. For insights into Connally's career and attitudes, see Patterson, *Congressional Conservatism*, pp. 111–13. Among the many items on the antilynching bill in the Connally Papers, see Connally letters to Charles O. Andrews and Claude Pepper of Florida, to Walter George and Richard Russell, Jr., of Georgia, to John Overton and Allen Ellender of Louisiana, and to Pat Harrison and Theodore G. Bilbo of Mississippi, Feb. 9, 1939 (copies), Connally to W. E. Neely, ed., *Sheriff's Magazine*, April 3, 1940 (copy); and Connally to Governor Herbert O'Conor of Maryland, Feb. 14, 1940 (wire, copy), box 126, TC; and letter and statistics from the director of the Bureau of the Census to Connally, March 30, 1940; and Senator John H. Bankhead of Alabama to Knox Gilmore of Bessemer, July 7, 1943 (copy), box 127, TC. In 1940, Connally received two letters supporting his opposition to a federal antilynching bill—two letters of special interest because of their authorship: Leonidas C. Dyer of St. Louis to Connally, May 24, 1940, and Congressman Lyndon B. Johnson of Texas to Connally, Jan. 29, 1940, boxes 126 and 127, respectively, TC.

77. Ames to Connally, Jan. 28, 1938; and Connally to Ames, Feb. 7, 1938 (copy), box 127, TC.
78. Ames to Connally, March 7, 1938, box 127, ibid.
79. Ames to Connally, July 14, 1938, box 127, ibid.
80. Thomas A. Krueger, *And Promises to Keep: The Southern Conference for Human Welfare, 1938-1948* (Nashville, 1967), pp. 13-25. "I have just returned from the Southern Conference on [sic] Human Welfare at Birmingham . . . . It was easily the most dynamic interracial meeting I have ever attended" (Jesse Thomas to Eugene Kinckle Jones, Nov. 25, 1938, GOF, box 56, NUL.
81. For a discussion of the attempted "purge," see George B. Tindall, *The Emergence of the New South, 1913-1945* (Baton Rouge, 1967), pp. 625-29.
82. Ames to Bertha Newell, Aug. 25, 1938 (copy), box 3, folder 27, JDA.
83. Ames to Connally, Sept. 25, 1938; and Ames to Connally, Aug. 5, 1940 box 127, TC. With her letter to Connally of early August, she enclosed portions of the July 1940 *The Southern Frontier* (pub. by the Commission on Interracial Cooperation in Atlanta) that urged that every lynching lead to a Justice Department investigation and publication of the findings. For an overall assessment of the ASWPL, see John Shelton Reed, "An Evaluation of an Anti-lynching Organization," *Social Problems* 16 (Fall 1968): 172; and Hall "Revolt against Chivalry," chaps. 6-9.
84. See Table 2, p. 6.
85. Sec. Rep., Sept. 1, 1938, NAACP-NY.
86. *Afro-American*, Sept. 24, 1938, 1:1-3 and 2:6-7, and Sept. 17, 1938, 4:1-2.
87. Bd. Min., Sept. 12, and Nov. 14, 1938, NAACP-NY.
88. For an indication of White's friendships and working relationships with such people, see his autobiography, *A Man Called White* (New York, 1948), pp. 156, 168-69, 175, 179, 181-82, 188, and 192.
89. White to John D. M. Hamilton, Nov. 11, 1938 (copy), file 359, box 3, NAACP-LC. For indications of New Deal losses in the 1938 elections, see Patterson, *Congressional Conservatism*, pp. 286-91, and *Historical Statistics*, p. 691.
90. For a discussion of Murphy's brief, one-year term as attorney general, see Richard D. Lunt, *The High Ministry of Government: The Political Career of Frank Murphy* (Detroit, 1965), chap. 6. See also White to Frank Murphy, Jan. 30, 1939 (copy), box C-79, NAACP-LC.
91. Emphasis added. Sec. Rep., March 9, 1939, and April 7, 1939; and Bd. Min., May 8, 1939, NAACP-NY.
92. W. F. Caldwell to R. B. Eleazer, April 4, 1939, CIC. Three days later, Eleazer wrote the attorney general to argue that the new civil liberties unit should investigate all lynchings (R. B. Eleazer to Frank Murphy, April 7, 1939 [copy], CIC). In response to NAACP and other pressures, the Justice Department did cooperate with state and local officials against the Klan in South Carolina during the Winter of 1940. Sec. Rep., Feb. 13, 1940, NAACP-NY.
93. U.S., Congress, *Congressional Directory*, 87th Congress, 2d sess. (Washington, D.C., 1962), p. 325. For an overview of major international and domestic events, see William E. Leuchtenburg, *Franklin D. Roosevelt and the New Deal: 1932-1940* (New York, 1963), chap. 13.
94. Sec. Rep., March 9, 1939, and April 7, 1939, NAACP-NY.
95. Sec. Rep., May 5, 1939, June 8, 1939, and Sept. 7, 1939; and Bd. Min., June 12, 1939, and June 29, 1939, NAACP-NY.
96. White to Franklin D. Roosevelt, telegram, Sept. 21, 1939, 2538 FDR; and Sec. Rep., Oct. 5, 1939, NAACP-NY.
97. Personal interview with Daisy Lampkin, Morris Beach. N.J., Aug. 30,

1962. For an indication of other issues, see White to Franklin D. Roosevelt, Dec. 23, 1938 (copy), file 100, ER.

98. White to the members of the Board of Directors, Dec. 5, 1939; Bd. Min., Dec. 11, 1939, NAACP-NY. In his memo to the Board, White noted that the Association had applied to the Carnegie Corporation for money to finance informational pamphlets, but the Corporation had postponed a final decision until Gunnar Myrdal and his staff had completed their study, "The Negro in America."

99. The only possible exception to this statement might be the Civil Rights Act of 1968, which contained a passage providing for federal intervention in cases of death or injury to civil rights workers (*New York Times*, April 11, 1968, 34:1).

100. *Afro-American*, Dec. 2, 1939, 1:5 and 2:5; *Cong. Rec.*, 76th Cong., 3rd sess., p. 253 (Jan. 10, 1940); *Daily Worker*, Jan. 11, 1940, clipping vertical file, "Lynching—Legislation" folder, Schom; Sec. Rep., Feb. 13, 1940, NAACP-NY; and U.S., Congress, Senate, Subcommittee of the Committee on the Judiciary, *Hearings, (H.R. 801)*, 76th Cong., 3rd sess. (Feb. 6, 7, and March 5, 12, 13, 1940).

101. Bd. Min., Dec. 14, 1938, NAACP-NY. Following the Molotov-Von Ribbentrop pact of August 1939, the CP-USA yielded to Moscow directives reversing the cooperative policies of the United Front movement. For nearly two years thereafter (until the Nazis invaded the Soviet Union), the CP-USA denounced the war in Europe and renewed its earlier criticisms of moderate black protest groups. In May of 1941, for example, Communist leaders declared that "Walter White and Eugene Kinckle Jones [of the National Urban League], reformers, use the fight against Negro discrimination to win their own people for a war which means continued misery and lynching under the capitalist system" (quoted in Wilson Record, *The Negro and the Communist Party* [Chapel Hill, 1951], pp. 186, 188–89, 325, n. 2).

102. For White's and Spingarn's remarks, see U.S., Congress, Senate, Subcommittee of the Committee on the Judiciary, *Hearings (H.R. 801)*, 76th Cong., 3rd sess., pp. 58–59, 75–79 (Feb. 6, 7, and March 5, 12, 13, 1940). Never overlooking an opportunity to elicit help in the fight for interracial justice, the NAACP first wrote (Sept. 26, 1941), then wired (Nov. 14, 1941) Prime Minister Winston Churchill to complain that prejudice and discrimination in America continued to hamper the general war effort against Germany (Sec. Rep., Dec. 3, 1941, NAACP-NY).

103. White to Edwin M. Watson, Jan. 24, 1940; E. M. W. to Roosevelt, Jan. 26, 1940; and Watson to White, Jan. 27, 1940 (copy), 2538, FDR; Sec. Rep., Feb. 13, 1940; and Bd. Min., Feb. 13, 1940, NAACP-NY. Drew Pearson and Robert S. Allen's "Washington Daily Merry-Go-Round" carried the story of Garner's intentions (clipping from the Washington *Times-Herald*, Jan. 24, 1940, box 127, TC).

104. NAACP Treasurer's Reports, Feb. 1940 and April 1940; Sec. Rep., April 1940 and May 9, 1940, NAACP-NY.

105. White to Lampkin, Nov. 30, 1939 (copy), box C-80, NAACP-LC. Incidentally, Kester's findings and White's fears were independently confirmed by the head of the Association of Southern Women for the Prevention of Lynching, in a pamphlet published two years after the Senate defeat of the Gavagan-Wagner-Capper bill. See Jessie Daniel Ames, *The Changing Character of Lynching* (Atlanta, 1942), pp. 2, 5–7. Typescript copies of Arthur Spingarn, Robert Wagner, and Arthur Capper's radio remarks of April 29, 1940, are available in the Robert F. Wagner Papers at Georgetown University, Washington, D.C.

106. Alben W. Barkley to White, April 22, 1940 (copy), and White to Barkley April 23, 1940 (copy), ER. Portions of the interchange appear in the Sec. Rep., April 1940, and May 9, 1940, NAACP-NY. The Association and Barkley had

had a similar though milder go-round the year before (ibid., May 5, 1939, NAACP-NY).

107. Ibid., Aug. 1, 1940, and Sept. 4, 1940, NAACP-NY. For an indication of earlier NAACP tactics in circulating copies of the Barkley-White correspondence, see Walter White's form letter, "To Organizations Co-operating on the Anti-Lynching Bill," April 24, 1940 (copy), CIC.

108. Arthur Vandenberg to Owen A. Knox, April 29, 1940; see also Knox to Vandenberg, April 24, 1940, ser. 7, box 68, CRC. In his letter to Owen, Vandenberg promised to vote for cloture if continuous sessions failed to break the filibuster.

109. Sec. Rep., April 1940, NAACP-NY.

110. *Cong. Rec.*, 76th Cong., 3rd sess., p. 13353 (Oct. 8, 1940). White's total of seven lynchings explained his continued desire to secure a federal law but also demonstrated the general inability to agree on what constituted a lynching. More recent records cite five. (See Table 2, p. 6). Seeking to resolve discrepancies, Tuskegee Institute held a conference that White attended on December 14, 1940 (NAACP Report of the Department of Branches, Jan. 6, 1941, NAACP-NY). Ralph McGill, publisher of the Atlanta *Constitution*, also attended the Tuskegee meeting (personal interview, Philadelphia, April 4, 1963). See also Bd. Min., Sept. 9, 1940, NAACP-NY; and seven-page typescript "Summary of the Conference on Lynching and Reports on Lynching, Tuskegee Institute, Alabama, December 14, 1940," CIC.

111. *Cong. Rec.*, 76th Cong., 3rd sess., pp. 13353–55 (Oct. 8, 1940); and Sec. Rep., Oct. 14, 1940, NAACP-NY.

112. Bd. Min., May 13, 1940, NAACP-NY.

113. White's own attitudes toward the president and toward the GOP are revealed in Harold L. Ickes, *The Secret Diary of Harold L. Ickes*, vol. 3: *The Lowering Clouds, 1939–1941* (New York, 1954), pp. 516–17. White's complaints after the election displayed a tendency to puff at dying embers (White to Wagner, Nov. 7, 1940, RFW).

114. Jesse W. Reeder, "Federal Efforts to Control Lynching" (Ph.D. diss., Cornell University, 1952), pp. 231–36.

115. Sec. Rep., Feb. 7, 1941, NAACP-NY; *Cong. Rec.*, 77th Cong., 1st sess., index, p. 374 (Jan. 3, 1941, to Jan. 2, 1942); ibid., 77th Cong., 2d sess., index, p. 292 (Jan. 5, 1942, to Dec. 16, 1942).

Chapter 8

1. White to Baldwin, Oct. 1, 1937; Gifts and Loans, 1934–38, Vol. 9, sec. 4, 46, 47, AFPS; and personal interview, confidential source.

2. Sec. Rep., May 5, 1938, and Nov. 1938, NAACP-NY; *New York Times*, Aug. 9, 1940, 13:5.

3. 305 U.S. 337. See also White to Baldwin, Dec. 15, 1938; Applications Favorably Acted Upon, Gifts and Loans, 1934–38, Vol. 9, sec. 4, 125, AFPS; and Loren Miller, *The Petitioners: The Story of the Supreme Court of the United States and the Negro* (Cleveland, 1966), pp. 333–34.

4. White to L. K. Sunderlin (of the Bureau of Internal Revenue), Oct. 21, 1938 (copy); and Guy T. Helvering (commissioner of Internal Revenue), to the NAACP, n.d., but probably late 1938 or early 1939, SJS; White to William Rosenwald, Oct. 10, 1939 (copy), box C-80, NAACP-LC; and Bd. Min., April 8, 1940, NAACP-NY.

5. For a measure of successes in the legal field, see Sipuel v. Board of

Regents, 332 U.S. 631 (1948), Sweatt v. Painter, 339 U.S. 629 (1950), and McLaurin v. Oklahoma State Regents, 339 U.S. 637 (1950), in educational matters; Morgan v. Virginia, 328 U.S. 373 (1946), in transportation; Shelley v. Kraemer, 334 U.S. 1 (1948), in housing; and Smith v. Allwright, 321 U.S. 649 (1944), and Terry v. Adams, 345 U.S. 461 (1953), in voting rights. On defendant's rights see also *Chambers v. Florida*, 309 U.S. 227 (1940). Miller, *The Petitioners*, pp. 334–41, 367–68, 322–23, 294–97, 281.

6. Thomas A. Krueger, *And Promises to Keep: The Southern Conference for Human Welfare, 1938-1948* (Nashville, 1967), pp. 16–17, 38–39, 42–43, and 46–47. See also Richard B. Henderson, *Maury Maverick: A Political Biography* (Austin, 1970), pp. 222–24; Alan Schaffer, *Vito Marcantonio, Radical in Congress* (Syracuse, 1966), pp. 118–20, 133, and 150; and Bd. Min., March 11, 1940, NAACP-NY.

7. See, for example, the NCAPT letterhead stationery of 1942 and 1946, CRC. The basic resumé of the legislative struggle to pass a federal anti–poll tax law appears in Neal R. Peirce, James G. Phillips, and Victoria Velsey, eds., *Revolution in Civil Rights* (Washington, D.C., 1965), pp. 21–23, 33, and 37–38. In 1964 the Twenty-fourth Amendment outlawed the poll tax in federal elections. Two years later the Supreme Court, in Harper v. Virginia Board of Elections, 383 U.S. 663, declared the poll tax unconstitutional in state elections, as well.

8. Bd. Min., June 10, 1940, and Sept. 9, 1940; Sec. Rep., Aug. 1, 1940, and Sept. 4, 1940, and Oct. 14, 1940, NAACP-NY.

9. Minutes of the 32d annual meeting of the NAACP, New York City, Jan. 6, 1941; Bd. Min., Jan. 6, 1941; Sec. Rep., Feb. 7, 1941; and Report of the Department of Branches, Feb. 10, 1941, NAACP-NY.

10. White to Philip Levy (secretary to Senator Robert Wagner), Feb. 13, 1941, RFW. *Cong. Rec.*, 77th Cong., 1st sess., pp. 1150–51 (Feb. 19, 1941); and ibid., p. 1293 (Feb. 24, 1941).

11. For an indication of the Association's dilemma and its responses, see Sec. Rep., March 10, 1941, April 1941, June 5, 1941, and Oct. 8, 1941; and Report of the Department of Branches, April 14, 1941, and Sept. 8, 1941; and Bd. Min., March 10, 1941, NAACP-NY. See also Minutes of the NAACP Staff Conference, Jan. 30, 1941, file 342, box 7, NAACP-LC; White to Senator Harry H. Schwartz (D–Wyo.), March 27, 1941 (copy), and Harry H. Schwartz to Wagner, April 17, 1941, RFW; and Harry H. Schwartz to Senator Robert Taft (R–Ohio), April 17, 1941, box 500, RAT.

12. White to Wagner, April 25, 1941; and White to Franklin D. Roosevelt, June 20, and July 7, 1941 (copies), RFW. Harry S. Truman, *Memoirs*, vol. 1: *Year of Decisions* (Garden City, N.Y., 1955), pp. 166–86. See also White to Truman, July 7, 1941 (copy), and Wilkins to Ira Lewis of the Pittsburgh *Courier*, Sept. 10, 1941 (copy), file 359, box 2, NAACP-LC. William Berman discusses the Truman committee in *The Politics of Civil Rights in the Truman Administration* (Columbus, 1970), pp. 13–15.

13. Herbert Garfinkel, *When Negroes March: The March on Washington Movement in the Organizational Politics for FEPC* (New York, 1969), chaps. 1 and 2, and pp. 186–89. See also Jervis Anderson, *A. Philip Randolph: A Biographical Portrait* (New York, 1972), chaps. 6, 11, and 12, on Randolph's early career, and chap. 16 on the march.

14. Garfinkel, *When Negroes March*, pp. 54–55; Bd. Min., April 14, 1941, NAACP-NY.

15. Bd. Min., May 12, 1941, NAACP-NY; Garfinkel, *When Negroes March*, pp. 53–62; Walter White, *A Man Called White* (New York, 1948), pp.

189–93; Joseph P. Lash, *Eleanor and Franklin* (New York, 1973), pp. 694–96; and Report of the Department of Branches, Sept. 8, 1941, NAACP-NY.

16. National Archives, *Federal Register*, 6 (June 27, 1941), p. 3109.

17. The implications of Executive Order 8802 are discussed in Louis Ruchames, *Race, Jobs, and Politics: The Story of FEPC* (New York, 1953), chaps. 2 and 3; Louis Coleridge Kesselman, *The Social Politics of FEPC: A Study in Reform Pressure Movements* (Chapel Hill, 1948), pp. 16–24; and Richard M. Dalfiume, *Desegregation of the U.S. Armed Forces: Fighting on Two Fronts, 1939–1953* (Columbia, 1969), pp. 117–21.

18. See, for example, the group appeal sent to Franklin Roosevelt by White, Randolph, Roger Baldwin, John P. Davis, Lester Granger, Morris Milgrim (of the Workers Defense League), Willard Townsend (of the CIO), and eight others, March 12, 1943 (copy), file X-36, box 3, NAACP-LC. The status of FEPC and of the MOWM during this period are discussed in Garfinkel, *When Negroes March*, pp. 139–51. On conservative gains, see John Morton Blum, *V Was for Victory: Politics and American Culture During World War II* (New York, 1976), chap. 7.

19. Bd. Min., June 10, 1940; Sec. Rep., June 5, 1941, NAACP-NY.

20. Bd. Min., Sept. 8, 1941, NAACP-NY; and ten-page mimeographed typescript of White's testimony before the Senate Military Affairs Committee on S. 666, the Austin-Wadsworth bill, on April 1, 1943, box 38, OC. For a discussion of the larger issues involved, see Harvard Sitkoff, "Racial Militancy and Interracial Violence in the Second World War," *Journal of American History* 58 (Dec. 1971): 661–81.

21. Sec. Rep., Oct. 5, 1944, NAACP-NY; typescript of NAACP statement regarding the Democratic platform, July 21, 1944, file 367, box 1, NAACP-LC; Minutes of a Special Meeting of the Board of Directors, July 31, 1944; and Bd. Min., Sept. 11, 1944, box A-4, NAACP-LC.

22. Sec. Rep., Feb. 5, 1942, NAACP-NY; White to Wagner, Dec. 5, 1942, with attached resumé of the six lynchings, RFW; and Sec. Rep., Dec. 8, 1942, NAACP-NY.

23. Garfinkel, *When Negroes March*, chap. 3, and pp. 97–102.

24. George Murphy to Adam Clayton Powell, Jr., Oct. 19, 1942, (copy); and Max Yergan to Franklin D. Roosevelt, Oct. 19, 1942 (wire, copy), box 23, NNC.

25. Sec. Rep., July 1943, and July 8, 1944, NAACP-NY; Kirk H. Porter and Donald Bruce Johnson, eds., *National Party Platforms: 1840–1964* (3d ed.; Urbana, Ill., 1966), pp. 406 and 412.

26. Report of the Acting Secretary, Feb. 6, 1945, and April 3, 1945, NAACP-NY. With White in the field, Wilkins often prepared the monthly reports.

27. See, for example, White's letter of protest about the "zoot suit" assaults, White to Franklin D. Roosevelt, Secretary of War Henry L. Stimson, Secretary of the Navy Frank Knox, and Attorney General Francis Biddle, June 11, 1943 (copy), file X-36, box 3, NAACP-LC. White explained the Detroit riot in Sec. Rep., July 1943, and discussed the Detroit and Harlem riots in ibid., Sept. 1943, NAACP-NY. See also White, *A Man Called White*, chaps. 29 and 30; Alfred McClung Lee and Norman Daymond Humphrey, *Race Riot* (New York, 1943), on Detroit; and Dominic J. Capeci, Jr., *The Harlem Riot of 1943* (Philadelphia, 1977).

28. Richard M. Dalfiume has discussed the implications of the war years in "The 'Forgotten Years' of the Negro Revolution," *Journal of American History* 55 (June 1968): 90–106.

29. Muriel S. Outlaw (assistant secretary for membership, NAACP national office) to the author, Aug. 25, 1971.

30. For a discussion of his return to the NAACP, see W. E. B. Du Bois, *The Autobiography of W. E. B. Du Bois* (New York, 1968), chap. 19.

31. Bd. Min., March 12, 1945, and April 9, 1945, box A-4, NAACP-LC; the press release of a telegram sent by White, Du Bois, and Bethune to Edward R. Stettinius, Jr., May 8, 1945, and White's written report to the NAACP Board of Directors from San Francisco, May 8, 1945, NAACP-NY.

32. For information on these and other Association activities at the time, see Sec. Rep., June 5, July 3, Sept. 6, Nov. 8, and Dec. 6, 1945; Du Bois' Report of the Department of Special Research, Oct. 8– Dec. 3, 1945; and Bd. Min., Dec. 10, 1945, NAACP-NY.

33. *Cong. Rec.*, 79 Cong., 1st sess., pp. 5895–96 (June 11, 1945), p. 6003, (June 12, 1945). Peirce, Phillips, and Velsey, *Revolution in Civil Rights*, pp. 21, 33, 37. See also National Federation for Constitutional Liberties "Action Letter," Nov. 22, 1943, and Elayne Goldstein to Jack Raskin (telegram), Nov. 13, 1943, ser. 7, boxes 68 and 69, respectively, CRC.

34. Ruchames, *Race, Jobs, and Politics*, pp. 165–66.

35. Kesselman, *The Social Politics of FEPC*, chap. 2. See also National Council stationery for early 1948, file 386, box 3, NAACP-LC.

36. Sec. Rep., Oct. 5, 1944, NAACP-NY; and Kesselman, *The Social Politics of FEPC*, pp. 206–11; also Bd. Min., Jan. 2, 1945, box A-4, NAACP-LC; Wilkins to Franklin D. Roosevelt Jan. 4, 1945 (copy), file X-36, box 3, NAACP-LC.

37. Mimeographed "Statement of Senator Taft in Connection With the Introduction of a Bill to Establish a Fair Employment Practices Commission" (n.d.—but filed in the 1945 folder); Joseph Newton Pew, Jr. to Taft, March 1, 1945; John Rankin to Taft, June 21, 1945, box 537, RAT. See also, Ruchames, *Race, Jobs, and Politics*, pp. 199–206; and Peirce, Phillips, and Velsey, *Revolution in Civil Rights*, p. 21. The FEPC sponsor was Dennis Chavez (D–N. Mex.).

38. For the maneuvering involved, see National Council for a Permanent FEPC to Truman, June 4, 1945 (telegram, copy); and White to Truman, June 5, 1945 (telegram, copy), file 359, box 2, NAACP-LC. See also Sec. Rep., June 5, 1945, NAACP-NY; and Peirce, Phillips, and Velsey, *Revolution in Civil Rights*, p. 21.

39. Houston to Truman, Dec. 3, 1945 (copy); Truman to Houston, Dec. 7, 1945 (copy); and "Memorandum of Charles H. Houston re President Truman's letter of December 7, 1945" (copy), file 359, box 2, NAACP-LC.

40. *New York Times*, Dec. 16, 1933; and Bd. Min., May 13, 1946, NAACP-NY.

41. Two-page informational memorandum on the "Columbia, Tennessee Race Riot, February 26, 1946," PN. White to Attorney General Tom Clark, Feb. 26, 1946, (telegram, copy); White to Governor Jim McCord of Tennessee, Feb. 26, 27, 1946 (telegrams, copies); and White to Truman, Feb. 28, 1946 (telegram, copy), file 342, box 1, NAACP-LC. In his autobiography, White listed 106 blacks arrested (*A Man Called White*, p. 311).

42. Theron Lamar Caudle (assistant attorney general of the United States) to Thurgood Marshall, March 29, 1946; Marshall to J. Edgar Hoover, May 10, 1946 (copy); White memorandum to Robert Carter, Marian Perry, and Franklin Williams, June 8, 1946 (copy); White to Marshall, June 12, 1946 (copy); White to Truman, June 15, 1946 (telegram, copy); and White to Tom Clark, June 30, 1946 (telegram, copy), file 34, box 1, NAACP-LC. White discussed the harassment of NAACP lawyers in *A Man Called White*, pp. 310–21.

43. The 1946 groups included: the American Federation of Labor,

American Civil Liberties Union, American Council on Race Relations, American Jewish Committee, American Jewish Congress, Catholic Interracial Council, CIO-PAC, Federal Council of Churches, International Ladies' Garment Workers' Union, National Conference of Christians and Jews, National Council of Negro Women, National Education Association, National Urban League, Southern Conference for Human Welfare, Southern Regional Council, Workers Defense League, and the national boards of both the YMCA and YWCA. See Sec. Rep., April 1946, NAACP-NY; letterhead stationery and a list of sponsors for the National Committee for Justice in Columbia, Tenn., file 342, NAACP-LC; and those for the National Emergency Committee Against Mob Violence, file 367, box 2, NAACP-LC.

44. These and parallel examples of racist violence are discussed in the lengthy Sec. Rep., Sept. 1946, NAACP-NY.

45. Ibid. See also *Newsweek* 28 (Aug. 26, 1946): 9; *Saturday Evening Post* 219 (Aug. 24, 1946): 120.

46. White to Truman, November 23, 1945, O.F., folder 1235, HST; White to Truman, May 13, 1946; Philleo Nash to Bill Hassett, June 7, 1946 (copy); and Truman to White, June 11, 1946 (copy), PPF, folder no. 393, HST. See also Alonzo L. Hamby, *Beyond the New Deal: Harry S Truman and American Liberalism* (New York, 1973), chaps. 3 and 5.

47. White to Truman, Sept. 10, 1946 (copy), file 367, box 2, NAACP-LC.

48. Berman, *The Politics of Civil Rights*, pp. 50-52, 55.

49. Leslie S. Perry "Memorandum on the Conference with the President," Sept. 19, 1946, file 367, box 2, NAACP-LC.

50. Memo on a letter from Edward J. Jeffries, Jr., to Truman, Sept. 9, 1946; Paul Robeson to David K. Niles, telegram, Sept. 19, 1946; and Robeson to Truman, telegram, Sept. 13, 1946, official file, lynching folder 93A, HST.

51. Sec. Rep., Oct. 1946, NAACP-NY; and Minutes of the Executive Committee of the National Committee for Justice in Columbia, Tenn., Oct. 9, 1946, file 342, box 2, NAACP-LC.

52. White to Truman, Sept. 20, 1946 (copy); and White to David Niles Sept. 26, 1946 (copy), file 267, box 2, NAACP-LC. U.S., President's Committee on Civil Rights, *To Secure These Rights: The Report of the President's Committee on Civil Rights* (Washington, D.C., 1947), pp. viii, ix, and xii.

53. White to William H. Hastie, Sept. 26, 1946 (copy), file 359, box 3, NAACP-LC.

54. See Hamby, *Beyond the New Deal,* (New York, 1973), chaps. 3 and 5; and Eric F. Goldman, *The Crucial Decade—and After: America, 1945-1960* (New York, 1960), chap. 2, for a discussion of problems facing the White House during 1946.

55. "Statement to be Released by President Truman after 7 P.M., December 5, 1946 (dictated over telephone 12 / 5 / 46)," file 367, box 2, NAACP-LC. The Executive Order itself can be found in National Archives, *Federal Register*, 11 (December 7, 1946), p. 14153.

56. For example, the housing decision in Shelley v. Kraemer (334 U.S. 1) in 1948; the decisions on graduate and professional school training in Sipuel v. Board of Regents (332 U.S. 631) in 1948, and Sweatt v. Painter (339 U.S. 629), and McLaurin v. Oklahoma State Regents (339 U.S. 637) in 1950; and the school desegregation cases headed by Brown v. Board of Education of Topeka (347 U.S. 483) in 1954.

57. James T. Patterson, *Mr. Republican: A Biography of Robert A. Taft* (Boston, 1972), p. 233.

58. Walter White to Wallace White, Nov. 11, 1946 (copy), file 359, box 3, NAACP-LC. A handwritten memo on this copy of the letter indicated that the same message was sent to Massachusetts Congressman Joseph Martin (who headed the new Republican majority in the House and would serve as Speaker) and to Carroll Reece (the Tennessee congressman who would chair the Republican National Committee from 1946 to 1948 [Patterson, *Mr. Republican*, p. 511]).

59. White to "Dear Branch Officer," Jan. 14, 1947 (copy), file 367, box 2, NAACP-LC; and Leslie S. Perry to White, Jan. 15, 1947, file 359, box 3, NAACP-LC.

60. White to Robert K. Carr, Feb. 17, 1947 (copy), file 367, box 2, NAACP-LC.

61. Civil Rights Section of the Department of Justice, twenty-six-page statement submitted to the PCCR, Jan. 15, 1947, box 26, PN. Turner L. Smith to PCCR, Feb. 21, 1947; and Robert Carr memoranda to PCCR, Feb. 21, and Feb. 25, 1947, box 27, PN; and Minutes of the Meeting of the PCCR, March 6, 1947, box 26, PN.

62. Clipping from the *Christian Science Monitor*, March 4, 1947, box 24, PN. See, for example, *Afro-American*, May 3, 1947, 4:1-2; May 10, 1947, 1:2-3; and June 14, 1947, 9:7-8; and Robert Carr memo to PCCR, April 16, 1947, box 27, PN. On the Southern Regional Council, see Wilma Dykeman and James Stokely, *Seeds of Southern Change: The Life of Will Alexander* (Chicago, 1962), pp. 283-85.

63. See the June 1947 files of incoming mail, box 2, PCCR. Monroe Billington seems to have found a parallel phenomenon, in terms of letters from the South generally supportive of Truman's civil rights efforts, *up to the issuance of the PCCR's recommendations in the fall of 1947* ("Civil Rights, President Truman, and the South," *Journal of Negro History*, 58 [April 1973]: 127-33).

64. See, for example, the following memoranda: Robert Carter to Wilkins, Feb. 27, 1947; Wilkins to Madison Jones, March 4, 1947; Jones to Robert Carter, March 10, 1947; Carter to White, March 12, 1947; White to Robert Carter, Oliver Harrington, Madison Jones, Thurgood Marshall, Clarence Mitchell, Leslie Perry, and Roy Wilkins, April 7, 1947; Jones to White April 9, 1947; Leslie Perry to White, April 14, 1947; and Mitchell to White, April 14, 1947, file 367, box 2, NAACP-LC.

65. Jones to Carter, March 10, 1947, file 367, box 2, NAACP-LC.

66. Carter to White, March 12, 1947; and Leslie Perry to White, April 14, 1947, file 367, box 2, NAACP-LC.

67. Hoover's (March 20, 1947) and Clark's (April 3, 1947) testimony before the PCCR is available in transcript, box 26, PN, pp. 85-95, and 114-22, respectively.

68. Transcripts of White and Marshall testimony (April 17, 1947) before the PCCR, box 26, PN, pp. 200-06 and 214-20, respectively. See also Assistant Secretary's Report, May 1947, NAACP-NY. The Court had remanded the conviction of a Georgia sheriff, accused of murdering a black prisoner, on grounds that willfulness was a criterion inadequately explained to the jury. See Screws v. United States, 325 U.S. 9 (1945).

69. Frances Williams to White and Marshall, April 18, 1947, and Frances Williams to Louis T. Wright, March 14, 1947, file 359, box 3, NAACP-LC.

70. Sec. Rep., Feb. 1947, and April 1947; Assistant Secretary's Report, May 1947; and Report of the Washington Bureau, June 1947, NAACP-NY. *Cong. Rec.*, 80th Cong., 1st sess., pp. 9551-52 (July 21, 1947).

71. For these explanations of Michener's conduct, the author is indebted to a former member of the 80th Congress, who asked to remain anonymous (personal interview). For additional insights into Taft's philosophy of government, see Patterson, *Mr. Republican*, pp. 304-05, 320-26, and 429.

72. Earl Michener to Wilkins, May 24, 1947 (copy); Wilkins to Michener, June 2, 1947; and Michener to Wilkins, June 3, 1947 (copy), RG 233, 80th Cong., 1st sess., HR 3488, NARS.

73. Emphasis added. Emanuel Celler to Michener, May 27, 1947; Michener to Celler May 30, 1947 (copy); and Michener to John Blatnik, June 21, 1947 (copy); and see also Michener to Adam Clayton Powell, Jr., Dec. 13, 1947 (copy); RG 233, 80th Cong., 1st sess., HR 3488, NARS.

74. Report of the Washington Bureau, June 1947; Sec. Rep., Sept. 1947, NAACP-NY. For an indication of public antilynching support, see incoming mail of House Committee on the Judiciary, RG 233, 80th Cong., 1st sess., HR 3488, NARS.

75. Although he demonstrated that the theme of a Republican–southern Democratic congressional coalition has been badly overstated, V. O. Key, Jr., did suggest that certain issues of common concern (such as labor bills—and there FEPC qualified) would bring the two groups together in relative harmony. See *Southern Politics in State and Nation* (New York, 1949), pp. 355–59. John A. Salmond has discussed the handiwork of conservative forces in "Postscript to the New Deal: The Defeat of the Nomination of Aubrey W. Williams as Rural Electrification Administrator in 1945," *Journal of American History* 61 (Sept. 1974): 417–36.

76. Michener to Adam Clayton Powell, Jr., Dec. 13, 1947 (copy), RG 233, 80th Cong., 1st sess. HR 3488, NARS. For additional discussions of conservatives, see Susan M. Hartmann, *Truman and the 80th Congress* (Columbia, 1971), pp. 7, 211, and chaps. 4 and 6.

77. Wilkins to Truman (telegram), May 22, 1947, official file, 93A, HST; and *Afro-American*, May 31, 1947, 1:1–2, and 4:1–2. The PCCR reported 31 acquittals in the Earle case (President's Committee on Civil Rights, *To Secure These Rights*, p. 23).

78. *Afro-American*, May 31, 1947, 6:1–2, 5–7. See incoming mail against mob violence and for a federal antilynching law, official file, 93A, HST; and Assistant Secretary's Report, June 1947, NAACP-NY.

79. White to Arthur Spingarn, May 22, 1947, Box 12, ABS. See typescript of speech prepared by Robert K. Carr and Milton Stewart of the PCCR, for Truman to deliver on June 29, 1947, to the NAACP, box 10, PCCR; mimeographed copy of Truman's June 29 speech, CCl; and *New York Times*, June 30, 1947, 1:5 and 3:1–4.

80. See Interim Reports of each of these subcommittees to the full PCCR, each April 17, 1947, boxes 26, 27, PN.

81. "Interim Report of Subcommittee No. 1 on Legislation to the President's Committee on Civil Rights," April 17, 1947, box 26, PN.

82. Carr memorandum to the Members of the PCCR, June 10, 1947, and John L. Vandegrift, Jr., memorandum to Carr, June 27, 1947, PCCR.

83. PCCR Minutes, June 30, 1947, pp. 506–07, 522–23, box 26, PN.

84. For a resumé of the various antilynching bills then pending, see the following PCCR memoranda: Carr to Members of the PCCR, June 10, 1947, and Vandegrift, Jr. to Carr, June 27, 1947, PCCR; and an undated, five-page comparison of three major antilynching bills: the Wagner-Morse Bill in the 80th Congress; the Gavagan-Wagner-Van Nuys measure in the 75th Congress; and the Gavagan bill in the 76th Congress, SJS.

85. See PCCR Minutes, June 30, 1947, pp. 514–26, box 26, PN; and President's Committee on Civil Rights, *To Secure These Rights*, pp. 156–58.

86. Ibid., pp. 139–73. Also personal interview with Morris Ernst, New York City, Nov. 20, 1962.

274 Notes

Chapter 9

1. See records of letters to prominent officials, distributed in Nov., 1947; director of branches Gloster B. Current wrote to "Dear Branch Officer" on Dec. 1, 1947, file 359, box 3, NAACP-LC.

2. Roger Baldwin to the Steering Committee on the Civil Rights Program, March 17 and May 3, 1948 (copies); Louis Wirth to Baldwin, May 14, 1948 (copy), file 408, box 5, NAACP-LC. Wirth sent copies of his letter to Walter White, James Carey of the CIO, and PCCR member Boris Shishkin at the AFL. See also White to David Niles, Nov. 5, Dec. 3, 1947 (copies), file 367, box 2, NAACP-LC.

3. V. O. Key, Jr. *Southern Politics in State and Nation* (New York, 1949), pp. 329-35. Truman's speech can be found in U.S., Congress, House, *Civil Rights Program Message from the President of the United States*, House Doc. 516, 80th Cong., 2d sess. (Feb. 2, 1948).

4. *New York Times*, Jan. 19, 1948, 1:6 and 4:2-5. Cabell L. Phillips, *The Truman Presidency: The History of a Triumphant Succession* (New York, 1966), pp. 148-54; Irwin Ross, *The Loneliest Campaign: The Truman Victory of 1948* (New York, 1969), pp. 23-24; and William C. Berman, *The Politics of Civil Rights in the Truman Administration* (Columbus, 1970), pp. 76, 83.

5. Ross, *The Loneliest Campaign*, pp. 74-77, 109-13; and Phillips, *The Truman Presidency*, pp. 210-11.

6. Bd. Min., Nov. 10, 1947, and Feb. 9, 1948, NAACP-NY.

7. Taft to George H. Bender, Jan. 21, 1948 (copy), box 799, RAT; Neal R. Peirce, James G. Phillips, and Victoria Velsey, eds., *Revolution in Civil Rights*, (Washington, D.C., 1965), pp. 21-23; Bender to Taft, July 28, 1948, box 498, RAT; *Cong., Rec.*, 80th Cong., 2d sess., p. 9353 (July 26, 1948); p. 10251 (Aug. 7, 1948); pp. 9602-04 (Aug. 2, 1948); Berman, *The Politics of Civil Rights*, pp. 120-22); *Congressional Quarterly Guide to the Congress of the United States: Origins, History and Procedure* (Washington, D.C., 1971), pp. 92-93.

8. Personal Interview, Alfred Baker Lewis, Akron, Ohio, Sept. 27, 1973. See National Council for a Permanent Fair Employment Practice Committee stationery of January 1948, file 386, box 3, NAACP-LC. See also *New York Times*, Oct. 12, 1947, 52:3; Oct. 19, 1947, 48:6; and Oct. 24, 1947, 9:5.

9. Sec. Rep., March 1948, NAACP-NY; Robert R. Church to Taft, Feb. 23, 1948; Arnold Aronson, Paul Sifton, and R. R. Church to Taft, n.d., box 537, RAT.

10. See, for example, Madison Jones's memo to White and Wilkins on FEPC, Feb. 7, 1947, file 386, box 3, NAACP-LC.

11. Mary Alice Baldinger (of the National Council for a Permanent FEPC) to Wilkins, May 8, 1948; National Council for a Permanent FEPC press release, May 11, 1948; and White to Wilkins, May 13, 1948, file 386, box 3, NAACP-LC; and Wilkins as chairman of the executive committee of the National Council for a Permanent FEPC to Irving M. Ives, May 20, 1948 (telegram, copy), file 444, box 6, NAACP-LC. See also Elmer Henderson to White, June 10, 1948, file 386, box 3, NAACP-LC.

12. Harry S. Truman, *Memoirs*, vol. 2: *Years of Trial and Hope* (Garden City, N.Y., 1956), p. 280; Dennis v. United States, 341 U.S. 494 (1951); Thomas A. Krueger, *And Promises to Keep: The Southern Conference for Human Welfare, 1938-1948* (Nashville, 1967), pp. 165-81; John Cogley, *Report on Blacklisting*, vol. 1: *Movies* (n.pl., 1956), chap. 1; on Hiss and Chambers, see, for example, *New York Times*, Aug. 26, 1948, 1:8.

13. See, for example, White to Arthur Spingarn, Nov. 13, 1947, Box 12, ABS; Ruth (Ruby) Hurley to White, Dec. 18, 1947, file 386, box 3, NAACP-LC; and Bd. Min. and Sec. Rep. throughout 1947, NAACP-NY. See also Allan Knight

Chalmers and A. Philip Randolph to Members of the Board and all Local Councils of the National Council for a Permanent FEPC, March 13, 1948 (copy), file 386, box 3, NAACP-LC.

14. Bd. Min., May 10, 1948, NAACP-NY; Karl Mundt to White, June 10, and 12, 1948, file 386, box 2, NAACP-LC; Marshall to Houston, Aug. 4, 1949 (copy); and Madison S. Jones, Jr., to Florence Lesueur (president of the Boston NAACP), Nov. 4, 1949 (copy), file 386, box 3, NAACP-LC.

15. Berman, *The Politics of Civil Rights*, pp. 74, 79–85; Ross, *The Loneliest Campaign*, pp. 29–34; undated memorandum, identified in pen as having been "Prepared by GME/parallels memo of Wm. L. Batt," box 20, CCl. ("GME," of course, was George Elsey). Batt directed the Research Division of the Democratic National Committee; internal evidence suggests the memo was written in late summer or early fall of the 1948 campaign. For an indication of the work that went into the president's Feb. 2, 1948 message, see box 31, CCl.

16. See the explanatory memo bearing Stephen Spingarn's initials, dated Jan. 21, 1948, and amended March 15, 1948, box 37, SJS. Stephen J. Spingarn staff memorandum, Jan. 22, 1948, box 31, CCl, suggested White House hopes of a maximum impact from its civil rights proposals.

17. Stephen J. Spingarn memorandum on "Conference in Charles Murphy's Office on Omnibus Civil Rights Bill Draft of 1 / 26 / 48, January 28, 1948"; Wald memorandum to Stephen Spingarn, Jan. 27, 1948, box 37, SJS; and George M. Elsey to Clark Clifford, Jan. 29, 1948, box 31, CCl.

18. Stephen J. Spingarn memo to Charles S. Murphy, Feb. 10, 1948 (copy), box 37, SJS.

19. National Opinion Research Center, *Opinion News* (Feb. 15, 1948), 10, Box 31, CCl; clipping from the *New York Times*, Feb. 27, 1948 OF, Box 1509, HST. See also six-page mimeographed report, "Summary of Southwide Meeting on Human and Civil Rights," Atlanta, Ga., Feb. 27, 1948, GOF, box 98, NUL.

20. Eight-page typescript, "Statement of Charles H. Houston Before the Senate Judiciary Subcommittee, in Support of S. 1352, the Federal Anti-Lynching Bill, January 19, 1948," RG 46, 80th Cong., S. 2860 folder, NARS. See also NAACP Washington Bureau, draft of "Memorandum for a press release," Jan. 21, 1948, file 444, box 6, NAACP-LC.

21. Leslie Perry memorandum to White, Jan. 24, 1948, file 444, box 6, NAACP-LC.

22. See, for example, the twelve-page typescript of a statement in support of the Clifford Case bill (the House counterpart to the Morse-Wagner bill) by Joseph B. Robison of the American Jewish Congress before the House Judiciary subcommittee, Feb. 4, 1948, and the six-page typescript of a statement before the same committee by Mike Masaoka of the Japanese-American Citizens League, Feb. 4, 1948, file 444, box 6, NAACP-LC. See also letters of support for an antilynching bill, RG 233, 80th Cong., 1st sess., HR 3488 folder, NARS.

23. For an assessment of the charges misrepresenting the SCHW as a Communist organization, see Krueger, *And Promises to Keep*, pp. 165–81. See also Clark Foreman to C. Murray Bernhardt (clerk of the House Committee on the Judiciary), Feb. 5, 1948; Joseph Cadden of the Civil Rights Congress to Congressman Earl Michener, Jan. 20, 1948; Arnold Johnson of the CP-USA to Congressman Clifford Case, telegram, Jan. 29, 1948; C. Murray Bernhardt to Joseph Cadden, Jan. 31, 1948 (copy); and Joseph Cadden to Clifford Case, Feb. 4, 1948, RG 233, 80th Cong., 1st sess., HR 3488 folder, NARS.

24. U.S., Congress, House, House Committee on the Judiciary, *Report No. 1597*, 80th Cong., 2d sess., pp. 1–7 (March 23, 1948), copy available, RG 233, 80th Cong., 2d sess., HR 5673, NARS.

25. Ibid., pp. 9–19.

26. Sec. Rep., March 1948, NAACP-NY. See also Leslie S. Perry to Senators Wiley, Langer, Ferguson, Revercomb, Moore, Donnell, Cooper, McCarran, Kilgore, Magnuson, Fulbright, and McGrath, April 28, 1948 (night letter, copy), file 444, box 6, NAACP-LC.

27. Sec. Rep., May and June 1948, NAACP-NY; and draft of White statement to the press on the antilynching bill, June 15, 1948, file 444, box 6, NAACP-LC.

28. Sec. Rep., April 1948, and Bd. Min., June 14, 1948, NAACP-NY; White to J. Howard McGrath, May 20, 1948 (copy), file 367, box 6, NAACP-LC.

29. White to James Roosevelt, Hubert Humphrey, William O'Dwyer, Chester Bowles, and Jacob M. Arvey, July 5, 1948 (telegram, copy); and White to Chester Bowles, July 12, 1948 (copy), file 367, box 6, NAACP-LC.

30. White to William Ritchie, July 12, 1948 (copy); and White to Ritchie, July 12, 1948 (telegram, copy), file 367, box 6, NAACP-LC.

31. In doing so, White used a four-page statement prepared with the help of Henry Lee Moon, NAACP director of public relations, who was just then finishing his own book-length study of black voting power, *Balance of Power: The Negro Vote* (Garden City, N.Y., 1949). See also NAACP press release, July 1, 1948, file 367, box 1, NAACP-LC.

32. "Statement by Continuations Committee of Twenty-One Negro Organizations in Presentation of 'Declaration of Negro Voters' to the Democratic National Platform Committee—Bellevue Stratford Hotel—July 8, 1948," file 367, box 3, NAACP-LC.

33. "Confidential Memorandum to Files from Walter White, July 12, 1948," file 367, box 6, NAACP-LC. See also "Statement Given to Mr. White over Telephone by David Niles July 12, 1948," file 367, box 1, NAACP-LC.

34. For a discussion of these events, see Donald R. McCoy and Richard T. Ruetten, *Quest and Response: Minority Rights and the Truman Administration* (Lawrence, 1973), pp. 124–26.

35. White to J. Howard McGrath, Francis J. Myers, and Oscar Ewing, July 11, 1948 (telegram, copy); White to Paul Fitzpatrick, July 13, 1948 (telegram, copy); and White memorandum on "Telephone Conversation with Emanuel Cellers [sic] from Philadelphia on July 14, 1948—AM," file 367, box 6, NAACP-LC.

36. For a discussion of events at the Democratic convention, see Ross, *The Loneliest Campaign*, pp. 108–25; and Berman, *The Politics of Civil Rights*, pp. 107–14.

37. White to Esther Murray, July 14, 1948 (telegram, copy); and White to Truman, July 14, 1948 (telegram, copy), file 367, box 6, NAACP-LC.

38. McCoy and Ruetten, *Quest and Response*, pp. 138–41.

39. Berman, *The Politics of Civil Rights*, pp. 103–04.

40. "Statement to Republican Platform Committee by Continuations Committee of 21 National Negro Organizations, June 18, 1948," file 367, box 3, NAACP-LC; Kirk H. Porter and Donald Bruce Johnson, eds., *National Party Platforms, 1840–1964* (3d ed.; Urbana, Ill., 1966), pp. 452–53.

41. White to Rexford G. Tugwell, June 16, July 12, 1948 (copies); "Statement by Continuations Committee of Twenty-Two Negro Organizations in Presentation of 'Declaration of Negro Voters' to the Third Party Platform Committee—Convention Hall—July 22, 1948." See also Wilkins to Carl Murphy, Aug. 3, 1948 (copy), file 367, box 3, NAACP-LC. For general information on the Wallace candidacy and the Progressive party, see Ross, *The Loneliest Campaign*, chap. 7; and Phillips, *The Truman Presidency*, pp. 201–05. On Du Bois, see Bd.

Min., Sept. 13, 1948, NAACP-NY; W. E. B. Du Bois, *The Autobiography of W. E. B. Du Bois* (New York, 1968), chap. 19.

42. *New York Times*, July 16, 1948, 1:6–8; Ross, *The Loneliest Campaign*, p. 125; McCoy and Ruetten, *Quest and Response*, p. 127.

43. Leslie Perry to White, July 16, 1948, file 367, box 1, NAACP-LC.

44. "Act *Now* on Civil Rights Legislation: Declaration of 19 national civil rights, labor, church, Negro, Jewish, professional and trade organizations meeting in Washington, D.C., July 22, 1948, on call of the National Association for the Advancement of Colored People," file 367, box 1, NAACP-LC. White had also hoped to attract southern liberals to the meeting (White to Wilkins, July 19, 1948, ibid.).

45. Gloster Current to White, July 23, 1948; White general letter to "Dear Sir," July 26, 1948; and White "Memorandum to the Branches," July 26, 1948, file 367, box 1, NAACP-LC.

46. *New York Times*, July 27, 1948, 1:8. Lee Nichols, *Breakthrough on the Color Front* (New York, 1954), pp. 86–88; Richard M. Dalfiume, *Desegregation of the U.S. Armed Forces: Fighting on Two Fronts, 1939–1953* (Columbia, 1969), pp. 163–72; Donald S. Dawson to Clark Clifford, March 8, 1948, OF, box 1509, HST; Roger Baldwin to the Steering Committee on the Civil Rights Program, May 3, 1948 (copy), file 408, box 5, NAACP-LC, and C. B. Powell of the New York *Amsterdam News* to Arthur Spingarn, July 23, 1948, box 12, ABS.

47. "Statement of 19 Cooperating Organizations Seeking Enactment of Civil Rights Legislation During The Special Session of Congress [:] Released in Washington Friday, July 30, 1948," file 367, box 1, NAACP-LC; and NAACP press release, Aug. 5, 1948, file 367, box 3, NAACP-LC.

48. Lester Granger discussed these matters in a personal interview with the author, at Tuxedo Park, N.Y., July 16, 1964. See also Nichols, *Breakthrough on the Color Front*, pp. 60–64; Dalfiume, *Desegregation of the U.S. Armed Forces*, pp. 102, 175–77; Berman, *The Politics of Civil Rights*, pp. 123–28.

49. *New York Times*, Oct. 30, 1948, 6:1–3; mimeographed copy of Truman's Oct. 29, 1948 Harlem speech, box 36, CCl.

50. On Truman's performance toward Israel, see Truman, *Memoirs*, Vol. 2, pp. 162–65. For the broader picture, see Robert A. Divine, "The Cold War and the Election of 1948," *Journal of American History*, 59 (June 1972), 90–110; *Historical Statistics of the United States*, p. 691.

51. Harvard Sitkoff, "Harry Truman and the Election of 1948: The Coming of Age of Civil Rights in American Politics," *Journal of Southern History*, 37 (Nov. 1971), 597–616.

52. See letters and telegrams between Walter White and the White House, Nov. 5–17, 1948, HST, OF, 413 folder; Bd. Min. Nov. 8, 1948; Meeting of the Board Committee on Legislation, Dec. 14, 1948; and Bd. Min. Jan. 3, 1949, NAACP-NY. See also Minutes of the NAACP Annual Meeting, Jan. 3, 1949, ibid.

53. Table No. 2, p. 6.

54. Copy of *Kiplinger Magazine: The Changing Times*, Vol. 3 (Jan. 1949), pp. 7–12, box 4, CCl.

55. Leslie Perry's special memorandum to the NAACP National Office, Dec. 8, 1948 ABS.

56. Howard Odum to John Steelman, Jan. 19, 1949 (HST), OF, box 1509.

57. *Afro-American*, January 1, 1949, 4:1–2, and 5:3–4; Pittsburgh *Courier*, January 22, 1949, 1–8.

58. Sec. Rep., February 1949, NAACP-NY; Berman, *The Politics of Civil Rights*, pp. 137–45; *Cong. Rec.*, 81st Cong., 1st sess., pp. 10–11 (January 3, 1949).

59. Charles Watkins, personal interview, Washington, D.C., Dec. 21, 1962.

60. See, for example, Leslie Perry to White, Feb. 2, 1949; and White memorandum to the files, Feb. 2, 1949, file 386, box 1, NAACP-LC. See also Perry to White, Jan. 18, 1949, file 386, box 3, NAACP-LC.

61. Pittsburgh *Courier*, Feb. 12, 1949, 14:1–3; and Feb. 26, 1949, 14:1–3; and *New York Times*, March 1, 1949, 1:8.

62. *New York Times*, March 4, 1949, 1:5, 8; March 6, 1949, 40:4–5; and March 12, 1949, 1:8; Bd. Min., March 14, 1949, NAACP-NY; and Berman, *The Politics of Civil Rights*, pp. 146–50.

63. *New York Times*, March 16, 1949, 1:6–8, and 3:2.

64. *Cong. Rec.*, 81st Cong., 1st sess., pp. 2662–2724 (March 17, 1949); *New York Times*, March 17, 1949, 1:8; March 18, 1949, 1:8; Sec. Rep., April 1949, NAACP-NY; and *Congressional Quarterly Guide*, pp. 92–93.

65. *New York Times*, March 17, 1949, 15:5, and March 18, 1949, 17:1–4, carried the Wallace and Vandenberg statements, respectively. Douglas's remarks are found in *Cong. Rec.*, 81st Cong., 1st sess., p. 2665, (March 17, 1949).

66. Chicago *Defender*, March 19, 1949, 6:6–7. The cloture struggle is reviewed in McCoy and Ruetten, *Quest and Response*, pp. 171–77.

67. Chicago *Defender*, March 26, 1949, 1:3–6, 6:6–8. White and McGrath moved quickly to resolve their differences. See White to McGrath, March 15, 1949; McGrath to White, March 15, 1949 (copy); and White to the editor of the Washington, D.C., *Evening Star*, March 18, 1949 (copy), JHM.

68. Remarks of Washington columnist John O'Donnell, reprinted in the Pittsburgh *Courier*, March 26, 1949, 5:3–8.

69. Leslie Perry memorandum to the NAACP branches, youth councils and college chapters, March 31, 1949, file 386, box 3, NAACP-LC.

70. *Cong. Rec.*, 81st Cong., 1st sess., pp. 3152–53 (March 25, 1949); Sec. Rep., April 1949, NAACP-NY.

71. Bd. Min., April 11, 1949, NAACP-NY; and Wilkins to Wilfred C. Leland, Jr., April 6, 1949 (copy), file 386, box 3, NAACP-LC.

72. Chicago *Defender*, March 12, 1949, 1:4, and 7:3–4.

73. Ibid., Feb. 12, 1949, 1:6; Brooks Hays, *A Southern Moderate Speaks* (Chapel Hill, 1959), pp. 25–52; personal interviews with Clifford Case, Washington, D.C., July 11, 1969, and with Brooks Hays, New Brunswick, N.J., June 24, 1964. See also clipping from the *Washington Post*, July 13, 1949, box 24, SJS.

74. Separate drafts and analytical resumés of these bills, dated in early March 1949, SJS. See also Stephen J. Spingarn memorandum to Roger W. Jones March 8, 1949 (copy); and Stephen J. Spingarn memorandum to Clark Clifford March 21, 1949 (copy), SJS.

75. Stephen J. Spingarn to Clark Clifford, April 29, 1949, box 3, CCl; Report by Leslie Perry on Administration Civil Rights Bills, May 6, 1949, and Bd. Min., May 9, 1949, NAACP-NY; NAACP Washington Bureau Report on NAACP Legislative Program, July 8, 1949, file 386, box 3, NAACP-LC; Berman, *The Politics of Civil Rights*, p. 157; and *Cong. Rec.*, 81st Cong., 1st sess., p. 5211 (April 28, 1949), p. 6301 (May 16, 1949), p. 1842 (March 3, 1949), and p. 5382 (April 29, 1949).

76. Leslie Perry memorandum to White, April 27, 1949, file 386, box 3, NAACP-LC; *New York Times*, May 3, 1949, 18:2; and Report by Leslie Perry on Administration Civil Rights Bills, May 6, 1949, NAACP-NY.

77. *New York Times*, May 8, 1949, IV, 9:1–2; and Leslie Perry memorandum to White, April 27, 1949, file 386, box 3, NAACP-LC.

78. Sec. Rep., June 1949, NAACP-NY; Wilkins to Henry Lee Moon, June 9, 1949, file 444, box 6, NAACP-LC; Wilkins to David Niles of the White House

staff, June 20, 1949, PPF, folder 207, HST; and Leslie Perry memorandum to Wilkins, July 8, 1949, file 386, box 3, NAACP-LC. See also *Cong. Rec.*, 81st Cong., 1st sess., p. 7217 (June 6, 1949).

79. *New York Times*, June 22, 1949, 22:4.

80. Peirce, et al., *Revolution in Civil Rights*, p. 24. See, for example, *Cong. Rec.*, 81st Cong., 1st sess., p. 10189 (July 26, 1949), p. 13300 (Sept. 27, 1949), and index, passim; ibid., 81st Cong., 2d sess., index, p. 365.

81. *The Crisis* 56 (July 1949): 213; Poppy Cannon, *A Gentle Knight* (New York, 1956), pp. 15–22; personal interviews with Carl Van Vechten, New York City, Oct. 29, 1962, and with Henry Lee Moon, New York City, April 14, 1978. For an illustration of the controversy that followed White's divorce and remarriage, see clippings from the *Afro-American*, Jan. 21, 1950, 4:2, and Feb. 4, 1950, 4:2, and accompanying correspondence, folder 3, WW.

82. Bd. Min., June 1949, NAACP-NY.

83. Sec. Rep., June 1949; and Bd. Min., July 14, 1949, NAACP-NY.

84. Sec. Rep., Sept. 1949; Bd. Min., Sept. 12, 1949, NAACP-NY; Peirce, et al., *Revolution in Civil Rights*, pp. 23–24; and Berman, *The Politics of Civil Rights*, pp. 170–79. See also Wilkins to A. Philip Randolph, Aug. 23, 1949 (copy), file 386, box 3, NAACP-LC. *Cong. Rec.*, 81st Cong., 1st sess., p. 10647 (Aug. 2, 1949), pp. 14891–92 (Oct. 18, 1949); ibid., 81st Cong., 2d sess., p. 2300–01 (Feb. 23, 1950), pp. 7299–7300 (May 19, 1950), p. 9981–82 (July 12, 1950).

85. Sec. Rep., Sept. 1949, June 1949, NAACP-NY; and Peirce, et al., *Revolution in Civil Rights*, p. 23. The twenty-one-day rule allowed the chairman of the committee that had reported a bill to force it out of the Rules Committee after 21 calendar days (ibid., p. 22); *Cong. Rec.*, 81st Cong., 1st sess., p. 10248 (July 26, 1949); ibid, 81st Cong., 2d sess., index, passim.

Chapter 10

1. Guinn and Beal v. United States, 238 U.S. 347 (1915). On *Guinn*, see Miller, *The Petitioners: The Story of the Supreme Court of the United States and the Negro* (Cleveland, 1966), pp. 219–20. On Du Bois, see *The Crisis* 9 (April 1915): 310–12.

2. On the war, see Joel Spingarn to Edmund Platt, April 7, 1917; Roy Nash to Joel Spingarn, telegram, April 11, 1917; Nash to C. H. Studin, April 12, 1917; and Martin Madden to Joel Spingarn, April 21, 1917, JES; Bd. Min., May 14, 1917, box A-1, NAACP-LC; and Ross, *J. E. Spingarn*, chap. 3.

3. On the general program, see Moorfield Storey to James Weldon Johnson, Dec. 18, 1919, box C-75, NAACP-LC; and Bd. Min., May 10, 1920, NAACP-NY.

4. Morton Sosna, *In Search of the Silent South: Southern Liberals and the Race Issue* (New York, 1977) chaps. 2, 8, and 10; and Jacquelyn Dowd Hall, "Revolt against Chivalry: Jesse Daniel Ames and the Women's Campaign Against Lynching" (Ph.D. diss., Columbia University, 1974), chaps. 7–9.

5. Hall has reviewed some basic explanations for lynching and its decline, ibid., pp. 198–213.

6. *Newsweek* 9 (April 24, 1937): 12; *New York Times*, Feb. 18, 1947, 9:3, and May 22, 1947, 1:5, Sept. 2, 1955, 37:3, and Sept. 24, 1955, 1:2; *Newsweek* 53 (May 4, 1959): 31–32, and *New York Times*, May 5, 1959, 23:1.

7. *Time* 82 (Sept. 27, 1963): 17; *New York Times*, July 9, 1978, 1:1–2.

8. To make the point that violence against black people remained an

unresolved issue, the NAACP continued throughout the 1950s to sponsor an antilynching bill in Congress; this, however, was more a gesture than an expectation of passage (personal interview with Clarence Mitchell, Washington, D.C., Dec. 20, 1962).

9. The Twenty-third Amendment (1961) permitted residents of the District of Columbia to vote in presidential elections; the Twenty-fourth (1964) outlawed the poll tax in elections to federal offices.

10. *Cong. Rec.*, 76 Cong., 3d sess., p. 254 (January 10, 1940); Lyndon B. Johnson to Tom Connally, Jan. 29, 1940, box 127, TC. Four months later, a former NAACP ally expressed the same opposition to the pending antilynching bill: Leonidas C. Dyer to Connally, May 24, 1940, box 126, TC.

11. On the Civil Rights Act, see *New York Times*, April 5, 1964, 1:2; June 7, 1964, 1:5; and June 20, 1964, 1:4. See also Steven F. Lawson, *Black Ballots: Voting Rights in the South, 1944–1969* (New York, 1976), chap. 10. On the missing civil rights workers, see *New York Times*, June 26, 1964, 1:8; Aug. 6, 1964, 1:1.

Bibliography

Manuscripts
Afro-American. Files on Lynching. Baltimore, Md.
Alexander, Dr. Will. Statement. Columbia University Oral History Project, New York City.
American Fund for Public Service Collection. New York City Public Library.
Ames, Jessie Daniel. Papers. University of North Carolina Library, Chapel Hill.
Borah, William E. Papers. Library of Congress, Washington, D.C.
Brotherhood of Sleeping Car Porters. Papers. Library of Congress, Washington, D.C.
Chapman, Oscar. Papers. Harry S. Truman Library, Independence, Mo.
Civil Rights Congress of Michigan. Papers. Archives of Labor History and Urban Affairs, Wayne State University, Detroit, Mich.
Clifford, Clark. Papers. Harry S. Truman Library, Independence, Mo.
Commission on Interracial Cooperation. Papers. Atlanta University Library, Atlanta, Ga.
Connally, Tom. Papers. Library of Congress, Washington, D.C.
Coolidge, Calvin. Papers. Library of Congress, Washington, D.C.
Costigan, Edward P. Papers. Microfilm (reels in the possession of the author). University of Colorado Library, Boulder, Colo.
Daniels, Josephus. Papers. Library of Congress, Washington, D.C.
Du Bois, W. E. B. Papers. Herbert Aptheker Files, New York City.
Du Bois, W. E. B. Papers. Fisk University Library, Nashville, Tenn.
Gavagan, Joseph. Statement, Columbia University Oral History Project, New York City.
Hastie, William. Personal Files. Philadelphia, Pa.
Johnson, James Weldon. Collection. Yale University, New Haven, Conn.
Kester, Howard A. Papers. Microfilm. University of Akron Library, Akron, Ohio (originals at the Southern Historical Collection, University of North Carolina, Chapel Hill).
Lodge, Henry Cabot. Papers. Massachusetts Historical Society, Boston.
McAdoo, William. Papers. Library of Congress, Washington, D.C.
McGrath, J. Howard. Papers. Harry S. Truman Library, Independence, Mo.
Moorland Collection. Howard University Library, Washington, D.C.
Morgan State University Library. Vertical Files. Baltimore, Md.
Nash, Philleo. Files. Harry S. Truman Library, Independence, Mo.
National Association for the Advancement of Colored People. Papers. Library of Congress, Washington, D.C.
National Association for the Advancement of Colored People. Files. National Office, New York City.

National Negro Congress. Papers. Microfilm. Schomburg Collection, New York City Public Library.
National Urban League. Papers. Library of Congress, Washington, D.C.
Overton, Carrie Burton. Papers. Archives of Labor History and Urban Affairs, Wayne State University, Detroit, Mich.
Ovington, Mary White. Papers. Archives of Labor History and Urban Affairs, Wayne State University, Detroit, Mich.
President's Committee on Civil Rights. Files. Harry S. Truman Library, Independence, Mo.
Roosevelt, Eleanor. Papers. Franklin D. Roosevelt Library, Hyde Park, N.Y.
Roosevelt, Franklin D. Papers. Franklin D. Roosevelt Library, Hyde Park, N.Y.
Russell, Charles Edward. Papers. Library of Congress, Washington, D.C.
Schomberg Collection. Lynching Files. New York City Public Library.
Southern Tenant Farmers Union Collection. Microfilm. University of Akron Library (originals at the Southern Historical Collection, University of North Carolina Library, Chapel Hill).
Spingarn, Arthur B. Papers. Library of Congress, Washington, D.C.
Spingarn, Joel E. Papers. Moorland Collection, Howard University, Washington, D.C.
Spingarn, Stephen J. Papers. Harry S. Truman Library, Independence, Mo.
Storey, Moorfield. Papers. Library of Congress, Washington, D.C.
Taft, Robert A. Papers. Library of Congress, Washington, D.C.
Terrell, Mary Church. Papers. Library of Congress, Washington, D.C.
Truman, Harry S. Papers. Harry S. Truman Library, Independence, Mo.
U.S., Congress. Legislative References Files, RG 46. National Archives and Records Service, Washington, D.C.
———. Legislative Reference Files, RG 233. National Archives and Records Service, Washington, D.C.
U.S. Justice Department. Files, RG 60. National Archives and Records Service, Washington, D.C.
Villard, Oswald Garrison. Papers. Houghton Library, Harvard University, Cambridge, Mass.
Wagner, Robert F. Papers. Georgetown University, Washington, D.C.
Washington, Booker T. Papers. Library of Congress, Washington, D.C.
White, Walter. Papers. James Weldon Johnson Collection, Yale University Library, New Haven, Conn.
Wilkins, Roy. Statement. Columbia University Oral History Project, New York City.
Wilson, William, Secretary of Labor. Private File. General Records of the Department of Labor, RG 174, National Archives and Record Service, Washington, D.C.
Wilson, Woodrow. Papers. Library of Congress, Washington, D.C.

U.S. Government Documents

Bureau of the Census. *Fourteenth Census, Abstract.* Washington, D.C.: GPO, 1920.
Bureau of the Census. *Fourteenth Census of the United States: 1920.* Vol. 3, Population Composition and Characteristics of the Population by States. Washington, D.C.: G.P.O., 1961.
———. *Historical Statistics of the United States, Colonial Times to 1957.* Washington, D.C.: G.P.O., 1961.

Commission on Civil Rights. *Freedom to the Free: A Report to the President.* Washington, D.C.: G.P.O., 1963.
Congress. *Congressional Directory.* 66th Cong., 3d sess., Dec. 1920. Washington, D.C.: G.P.O., 1920.
———. *Congressional Directory.* 67th Cong., 2d sess., Jan. 1922. Washington, D.C.: G.P.O., 1922.
———. *Congressional Directory.* 67th Cong., 2d sess., July 1922. Washington, D.C.: G.P.O., 1922.
———. *Congressional Directory.* 68th Cong., 1st sess., Dec. 1923. Washington, D.C.: G.P.O., 1923.
———. *Congressional Directory.* 71st Cong., 3d sess., Jan. 1931. Washington, D.C.: G.P.O., 1931.
———. *Congressional Directory.* 75th Cong., 3d sess., May 1938. Washington, D.C.: G.P.O., 1938.
———. *Congressional Directory.* 87th Cong., 2d sess., Jan. 1962. Washington, D.C.: G.P.O., 1962.
———. *Congressional Record.* 1881–1951.
Congress, House. *Antilynching Bill, Report No. 563.* 75th Cong., 1st sess., April 6, 1937.
———. *Biographical Directory of the American Congress, 1774–1961.* House Document no. 442, 85th Cong., 2d sess. Washington, D.C.: G.P.O., 1961.
———. *Civil Rights Program Message from the President of the United States.* House Doc. 516, 80th Cong., 2d sess., Feb. 2, 1948.
Congress, House. Committee on the Judiciary. *Hearings on the Anti-Lynching Bill.* (H.R. 11279.) 65th Cong., 2d sess., June 6, 1918.
———. Committee on the Judiciary. *Hearings.* (H.R. 11279; ser. 61–pt. 2.) 65th Cong., 2d sess., July 12, 1918.
———. Committee on the Judiciary. Report No. 1597. 80th Cong., 2d sess., Mar. 23, 1948.
———. Committe on Rules. *Ku Klux Klan: Hearings before the Committee on Rules.* 67th Cong., 1st sess., Oct. 11, 1921.
———. Judiciary Committee. *Anti-Lynching Bill, Report No. 452.* 67th Cong., 1st sess., Oct. 31, 1921.
Congress, Senate. *Anti-Lynching Bill, Report No. 793.* 75th Cong., 1st sess., June 15, 1937.
———. *Biographical Directory of the American Congress, 1774–1971.* Senate Document no. 92-8, 92d Cong., 1st sess. Washington, D.C.: G.P.O., 1971.
———. *Miscellaneous, Report No. 1380.* 76th Cong., 3rd sess., April 8, 1940.
———. *Report No. 710 (S. 1978).* 73rd Cong., 2d sess., March 28, 1934.
———. *Senate Report No. 340.* 74th Cong., 1st sess., March 13, 1935.
———. *Senate Report No. 1561.* 74th Cong., 2d sess., 1936.
———. Subcommittee of the Committee on the Judiciary. *Hearings on the Anti-Lynching Bill (S. 121).* 69th Cong., 1st sess., Feb. 16, 1926.
———. *Hearings (S. 1978).* 73rd Cong., 2d sess., Feb. 20, 21, 1934.
———. *Hearings (S. 24).* 74th Cong., 1st sess., Feb. 14, 1935.
———. *Hearings (H.R. 801).* 76th Cong., 3d sess., Feb. 6, 7, and March 5, 12, 13, 1940.
President's Committee on Civil Rights. *To Secure These Rights: The Report of the President's Committee on Civil Rights.* Washington, D.C.: G.P.O., 1947.
National Archives. *Federal Register.*
———. *Statutes at Large.*

Bibliography

Interviews and Correspondence

Adkins, Mark, (special assistant to the president of Paine College, Augusta, Ga.). Letter, March 14, 1979.
Alexander, Raymond Pace, (jurist). Interview, Philadelphia, Aug. 29, 1962.
Ames, Jessie Daniel, (former director of the Association of Southern Women for the Prevention of Lynching). Letter, Tryon, N.C., April 16, 1963.
Baldwin, Roger (former chairman of the board of the American Fund for Public Service). Telephone interview, New York City, Jan. 3, 1963.
Benton, Thomas Hart (artist). Letter, March 1963.
Black, Lucille (national membership secretary of the NAACP). Letter, New York City, July 23, 1962.
Blayton, Reida Dykes (manuscript librarian of Fisk University Library, Nashville, Tenn.). Letter, Dec. 4, 1962.
Bontemps, Arna (librarian, Fisk University). Letter, Sept. 18, 1962.
Case, Clifford (senator from New Jersey). Interview, Washington, D.C., July 11, 1969.
Chalmers, Allan Knight (former president, NAACP Legal Defense and Educational Fund). Interview, New York City, Nov. 19, 1962.
Current, Gloster (deputy to the executive director, NAACP). Interview, New York City, March 14, 1978.
Ernst, Morris (former member President's Committee on Civil Rights). Interview, New York City, Nov. 20, 1962.
Gavagan, Joseph (former congressman from New York). Interview, New York City, Jan. 17, 1963.
Gay, Eustace (member of the editorial staff, Philadelphia *Tribune*). Interview, Philadelphia, Aug. 29, 1962.
Granger, Lester (former executive secretary of the National Urban League). Interview, Sterling Forest near Tuxedo Park, New York, July 16, 1964.
Hastie, William (former member of the NAACP Legal Committee). Interview, Philadelphia, July 25, 1962, and Aug. 15, 1963.
Hays, Brooks (former congressman from Arkansas). New Brunswick, N.J., Interview, June 24, 1964.
Hurley, Ruby (director, NAACP Southeast Regional Offices). Interview, Atlanta, Ga., April 8, 1977, and Feb. 28, 1978.
Jimenez, Lillian B. (assistant to the archivist of Tuskegee Institute). Letters, Feb. 27 and March 29, 1979.
Johnson, Grace Nail (widow of James Weldon Johnson). Interview, New York City, Oct. 16, 1962.
Lampkin, Daisy (former NAACP board and staff member). Interview, Morris Beach, N.J., Aug. 30, 1962.
Lewis, Alfred Baker (former national treasurer of the NAACP). Interview, Akron, Ohio, Sept. 27, 1973.
Marshall, Thurgood (former chief counsel, NAACP). Interview, New York City, April 3, 1963.
McGill, Ralph (publisher, Atlanta *Constitution*). Interview, Philadelphia, April 4, 1963.
Mitchell, Clarence (director, NAACP Washington Bureau). Interview, Washington, D.C., Dec. 20, 1962.
Mitchell, H. L. (a co-founder of the Southern Tenant Farmers Union). Telephone interview, Akron, Ohio, Oct. 27, 1972.
Mitchell, H. L. (co-founder of the Southern Tenant Farmers Union). Interview, Akron, Ohio, Nov. 27–28, 1978.

Moon, Henry Lee (former director of public relations, NAACP). Interview, New York City, April 2, 1963, and April 14, 1978.
Morrow, E. Frederic (former NAACP staff member). Interview, New York City, Feb. 7, 1963.
Morse, Wayne (former senator from Oregon). Interview, Washington, D.C., Dec. 27, 1969.
Murphy, Carl (publisher, *Afro-American*). Interview, Baltimore, Md., Oct. 19, 1962.
Outlaw, Muriel S. (assistant secretary for membership, NAACP). Letter, New York City, Aug. 25, 1971.
Pepper, Claude (congressman from Florida). Interview, Washington, D.C., Sept. 19, 1968.
Poston, Ted (journalist). Interview, New York City, Dec. 13, 1962.
Powell-White, Gladys (first wife of Walter White). Interview, Mainz, Germany, April 22 and 23, 1978.
Randolph, A. Philip (president, Brotherhood of Sleeping Car Porters and Maids). Interview, New York City, Sept. 9, 1964.
Randolph, Richetta (former NAACP staff member). Interview, New York City, Oct. 16, 1962.
Savage, Philip (NAACP field secretary for Delaware, Pennsylvania, and New Jersey). Interview, Philadelphia, Aug. 7, 1962.
Schuyler, George (journalist). Interview, New York City, Jan. 3, 1963.
Sparkman, John (senator from Alabama). Interview, Washington, D.C., Aug. 7, 1969.
Spaulding, Theodore (NAACP board member). Interview, Philadelphia, Oct. 17, 1962.
Spingarn, Arthur B., Interview, New York City, Dec. 9, 1960, and April 2, 1963.
Thomas, Norman (former head of the American Socialist Party). Interview, New York City, July 2, 1964.
Van Vechten, Carl (author). Interview, New York City, Oct. 29, 1962.
Watkins, Charles L. (parliamentarian of the United States Senate). Interview, Washington, D.C., Dec. 21, 1962.
White, Poppy Cannon (widow of Walter F. White). Interview, New York City, Oct. 1, 1962.
Wilkins, Roy (executive director, NAACP). Interview, New York City, June 19, 1970.

Newspapers and Magazines

Afro-American
Amsterdam News
Atlantic Monthly
Birmingham *Age-Herald*
Chicago *Defender*
The Crisis
Daily Worker
Harper's Weekly
The Independent
The Nation
The New Republic
Newsweek
New York *Evening Post*
New York Times
New York *World-Telegram*
Norfolk *Journal and Guide*
North American Review
Pittsburgh *Courier*
St. Louis *Argus*
Saturday Evening Post
South Atlantic Quarterly
Southern Exposure
The Southern Frontier
Survey
Time

Books

Alexander, Charles. *The Ku Klux Klan and the Southwest*. Lexington: University of Kentucky Press, 1966.
Allen, Frederick Lewis. *Only Yesterday*. New York: Bantam Books, 1959.
Alperovitz, Gar. *Atomic Diplomacy: Hiroshima and Potsdam: The Use of the Atomic Bomb and the American Confrontation with Soviet Power*. New York: Vintage Books, 1965.
Anderson, Jervis. *A. Philip Randolph: A Biographical Portrait*. New York: Harcourt Brace Jovanovich, 1972.
Association of Southern Women for the Prevention of Lynching. *Southern Women Look at Lynching*. Atlanta, Ga.: Association of Southern Women for the Prevention of Lynching, 1937.
Baker, Ray Stannard. *Following the Color Line*. New York: Doubleday, Page, 1908.
_____, ed. *Woodrow Wilson, Life and Letters*. 8 vols. Garden City, N.Y.: Doubleday, Page, 1927–1939.
Bardolph, Richard. *The Negro Vanguard*. New York: Vintage Books, 1961.
Beard, Charles. *An Economic Interpretation of the Constitution of the United States*. New York: Macmillan, 1913.
Berman, William C. *The Politics of Civil Rights in the Truman Administration*. Columbus: Ohio State University Press, 1970.
Bernstein, Barton J., and Allen J. Matusow, eds. *The Truman Administration: A Documentary History*. New York: Harper Colophon Books, 1968.
Berry, Mary Frances. *Black Resistance / White Law: A History of Constitutional Racism in America*. New York: Appleton-Century-Crofts, 1971.
Blaisdell, Donald C., ed. *Unofficial Government: Pressure Groups and Lobbies*. Vol. 319 of The Annals of the American Academy of Political and Social Science, ed. Thorsten Sellin. Philadelphia: American Academy of Political and Social Science, September 1958.
Blalock, Hubert M., Jr. *Toward a Theory of Minority-Group Relations*. New York: John Wiley and Sons, 1967.
Blaustein, Albert P., and Robert L. Zangrando, eds. *Civil Rights and the Black American: A Documentary History*. New York: Simon and Schuster, 1970.
Blum, John M. *Joe Tumulty and the Wilson Era*. Boston: Houghton Mifflin, 1951.
_____. *V Was for Victory: Politics and American Culture during World War II*. New York: Harcourt Brace Jovanovich, 1976.
_____. *Woodrow Wilson and the Politics of Morality*. Boston: Little, Brown, 1956.
Boskin, Joseph, ed. *Urban Racial Violence in the Twentieth Century*. 2d ed. Beverly Hills, Calif.: Glencoe Press, 1976.
Bracey, John H., August Meier, and Elliott Rudwick, eds. *Black Nationalism in America*. Indianapolis: Bobbs-Merrill, 1970.
Breitman, George, ed. *By Any Means Necessary: Speeches, Interviews and a Letter by Malcom X*. New York: Pathfinder Press, 1970.
Broderick, Francis L. *W. E. B. Du Bois: Negro Leader in a Time of Crisis*. Stanford, Calif.: Stanford University Press, 1966.
Brown, Richard Maxwell. *Strain of Violence: Historical Studies of American Violence and Vigilantism*. New York: Oxford University Press, 1977.
Brown, Roger. *Social Psychology*. New York: Free Press, 1965.
Brownmiller, Susan. *Against Our Will: Men, Women and Rape*. New York: Simon and Schuster, 1975.
Burdette, Franklin L. *Filibustering in the Senate*. Princeton: Princeton University

Press, 1940.
Butcher, Margaret Just. *The Negro in American Culture.* New York: Mentor Books, 1957.
Cannon, Poppy. *A Gentle Knight.* New York: Rinehart, 1956.
Cantor, Louis. *A Prologue to the Protest Movement: The Missouri Sharecropper Roadside Demonstration of 1939.* Durham, N.C.: Duke University Press, 1969.
Cantril, Hadley. *The Psychology of Social Movements.* New York: John Wiley and Sons, 1941.
Capeci, Dominic J., Jr. *The Harlem Riot of 1943.* Philadelphia: Temple University Press, 1977.
Carter, Dan T. *Scottsboro: A Tragedy of the American South.* Baton Rouge: Louisiana State University Press, 1969.
Cash, W. J. *The Mind of the South.* New York: Vintage Books, 1941.
Chadbourn, James Harmon. *Lynching and the Law.* Chapel Hill: University of North Carolina Press, 1933.
Chalmers, David M. *Hooded Americanism: The History of the Ku Klux Klan.* Chicago: Quadrangle Books, 1968.
Christopher, Maurine. *Black Americans in Congress.* 2d ed. New York: Thomas Y. Crowell, 1976.
Cochran, Thomas, and William Miller. *The Age of Enterprise.* New York: Macmillan, 1942.
Cogley, John. *Report on Blacklisting. Vol. 1: Movies.* N.pl.: Fund for the Republic, 1956.
Cooper, Wayne F., ed. *The Passion of Claude McKay: Selected Poetry and Prose, 1912-1948.* New York: Schocken Books, 1973.
Creel, George. Foreword to *Public Ownership of Government: The Collected Papers of Edward P. Costigan.* New York: Vanguard Press, 1940.
Cripps, Thomas. *Slow Fade to Black: The Negro in American Film, 1900-1942.* New York: Oxford University Press, 1977.
Croly, Herbert. *The Promise of American Life.* New York: Macmillan, 1909.
Cronon, Edmund David. *Black Moses: The Story of Marcus Garvey and the Universal Negro Improvement Association.* Madison: University of Wisconsin Press, 1955.
Cruse, Harold. *The Crisis of the Negro Intellectual.* New York: William Morrow, 1967.
Curtis, James C., and Lewis L. Gould, eds. *The Black Experience in America: Selected Essays.* Austin: University of Texas Press, 1970.
Cutler, James Elbert. *Lynch-Law: An Investigation into the History of Lynching in the United States.* Montclair, N.J.: Patterson Smith, 1969.
Dabney, Virginius. *Below the Potomac.* New York: D. Appleton-Century, 1942.
Dalfiume, Richard M. *Desegregation of the U.S. Armed Forces: Fighting on Two Fronts, 1939-1953.* Columbia: University of Missouri Press, 1969.
Daniel, Pete. *Deep'n as It Come: The 1927 Mississippi River Flood.* New York: Oxford University Press, 1977.
———. *The Shadow of Slavery: Peonage in the South, 1901-1969.* Urbana: University of Illinois Press, 1972.
Davie, Maurice R. *Negroes in American Society.* New York: McGraw-Hill, 1949.
Davis, Allen F. *Spearhead for Reform: The Social Settlements and the Progressive Movement, 1890-1914.* New York: Oxford University Press, 1967.
Davis, Allison, Burleigh B. Gardner, and Mary R. Gardner. *Deep South: A Social Anthropological Study of Caste and Class.* Chicago: University of Chicago Press, 1941.

Davis, George A., and O. Fred Donaldson. *Blacks in the United States: A Geographic Perspective*. Boston: Houghton Mifflin, 1975.
Diner, Hasia R. *In the Almost Promised Land: American Jews and Blacks, 1915-1935*. Westport, Conn.: Greenwood Press, 1977.
Dinnerstein, Leonard. *The Leo Frank Case*. New York: Columbia University Press, 1968.
Dittmer, John. *Black Georgia in the Progressive Era, 1900-1920*. Urbana: University of Illinois Press, 1977.
Divine, Robert A. *Second Chance: The Triumph of Internationalism in America during World War II*. New York: Atheneum, 1971.
Dixon, Thomas. *The Clansman*. New York: Grosset and Dunlap, 1905.
Dollard, John. *Caste and Class in a Southern Town*. 3d ed. Garden City, N.Y.: Doubleday Anchor Books, 1949.
Douglass Frederick. *Why is the Negro Lynched?* Bridgwater, England: John Whitby and Sons, 1895.
Drake, St. Clair, and Horace R. Cayton. *Black Metropolis*. New York: Harcourt, Brace, 1945.
Draper, Theodore. *The Roots of American Communism*. New York: Viking Press, 1963.
Du Bois, W. E. B. *The Autobiography of W. E. B. Du Bois*. New York: International Publishers, 1968.
―――. *Darkwater*. New York: Harcourt, Brace and Howe, 1920.
―――. *Dusk of Dawn: An Essay toward an Autobiography of a Race Concept*. New York: Schocken Books, 1968.
―――. *The Souls of Black Folk*. Greenwich, Conn.: Fawcett Publications, 1961.
―――, ed. *An Appeal to the World. A Statement on the Denial of Human Rights to Minorities in the Case of Citizens of Negro Descent in the United States of America and an Appeal to the United Nations for Redress*. New York: NAACP, 1947.
Duster, Alfreda M., ed. *Crusade for Justice: The Autobiography of Ida B. Wells*. Chicago: University of Chicago Press, 1970.
Dykeman, Wilma and James Stokely. *Seeds of Southern Change: The Life of Will Alexander*. Chicago: University of Chicago Press, 1962.
Embree, Edwin R. *13 Against the Odds* (New York: Viking Press, 1945.
Factor, Robert L. *The Black Response to America: Men, Ideals, and Organization from Frederick Douglass to the NAACP*. Reading, Mass.: Addison-Wesley, 1970.
Feis, Herbert. *From Trust to Terror: The Onset of the Cold War, 1945-1950*. New York: W. W. Norton, 1970.
Filler, Louis. *Crusaders for American Liberalism*. New York: Collier Books, 1961.
Flexner, Eleanor. *Century of Struggle: The Woman's Rights Movement in the United States*. New York: Atheneum, 1970.
Forcey, Charles. *The Crossroads of Liberalism: Croly, Weyl, Lippmann, and the Progressive Era, 1900-1925*. New York: Oxford University Press, 1961.
Fox, Stephen R. *The Guardian of Boston: William Monroe Trotter*. New York: Atheneum, 1970.
Franklin, John Hope. *From Slavery to Freedom: A History of Negro Americans*. 3d ed. New York: Alfred A. Knopf, 1967.
Frazier, E. Franklin. *Black Bourgeoisie: The Rise of a New Middle Class in the United States*. New York: Collier Books, 1962.
―――. *The Negro in the United States*. New York: Macmillan, 1957.
Fredrickson, George M. *The Black Image in the White Mind: The Debate on Afro-*

American Character and Destiny, 1817–1914. New York: Harper and Row, 1971.
Freidel, Frank. *F. D. R. and the South.* Baton Rouge: Louisiana State University Press, 1965.
Fullinwider, S. P. *The Mind and Mood of Black America: 20th Century Thought.* Homewood, Ill.: Dorsey Press, 1969.
Gallagher, Buell G. *American Caste and the Negro College.* New York: Columbia University Press, 1938.
Gambino, Richard. *Vendetta: A True Story of the Worst Lynching in America, the Mass Murder of Italian-Americans in New Orleans in 1891, the Vicious Motivations behind It, and the Tragic Repercussions That Linger to This Day.* Garden City, N.Y.: Doubleday, 1977.
Garfinkel, Herbert. *When Negroes March: The March on Washington Movement in the Organizational Politics for FEPC.* Glencoe, Ill.: Free Press, 1951.
Garraty, John A. *Henry Cabot Lodge, A Biography.* New York: Alfred A. Knopf, 1953.
Ginzburg, Ralph. *100 Years of Lynchings.* New York: Lancer Books, 1962.
Glazer, Nathan. *The Social Basis of American Communism.* New York: Harcourt, Brace and World, 1961.
Goldman, Eric F. *The Crucial Decade—and After: America, 1945–1960.* New York: Vintage Books, 1960.
———. *Rendezvous with Destiny.* New York: Alfred A. Knopf, 1958.
Gosnell, Harold F. *Negro Politicians.* Chicago: University of Chicago Press, 1935.
Gossett, Thomas F. *Race: The History of an Idea in America.* Dallas: Southern Methodist University Press, 1963.
Grant, Donald L. *The Anti-lynching Movement, 1883–1932.* San Francisco: R and E Research Associates, 1975.
Greenbaum, Fred. *Fighting Progressive: A Biography of Edward P. Costigan.* Washington, D.C.: Public Affairs Press, 1971.
Grimké, Francis J. *The Lynching of Negroes in the South: Its Consequences and Remedy.* Washington, D.C.: n. pub., 1899.
Grimshaw, Allen D., ed. *Racial Violence in the United States.* Chicago: Aldine, 1969.
Hair, William Ivy. *Carnival of Fury: Robert Charles and the New Orleans Race Riot of 1900.* Baton Rouge: Louisiana State University Press, 1976.
Hamby, Alonzo L. *Beyond the New Deal: Harry S Truman and American Liberalism.* New York: Columbia University Press, 1973.
Handlin, Oscar. *The American People in the Twentieth Century.* Cambridge: Harvard University Press, 1954.
———. *Race and Nationality in American Life.* Garden City, N.Y.: Doubleday, 1957.
Hareven, Tamara. *Eleanor Roosevelt: An American Conscience.* Chicago: Quadrangle Books, 1968.
Harlan, Louis. *Booker T. Washington: The Making of a Black Leader, 1856–1901.* New York: Oxford University Press, 1972.
Harris, William H. *Keeping the Faith: A. Philip Randolph, Milton P. Webster, and the Brotherhood of Sleeping Car Porters, 1925–1937.* Urbana: University of Illinois Press, 1977.
Hartmann, Susan M. *Truman and the 80th Congress.* Columbia: University of Missouri Press, 1971.
Hauptman, Laurence M. *The Lake Mohonk Conference on the Negro Question: Guide to the Annual Reports.* New York: Clearwater, 1975.

Hayes, Laurence J. W. *The Negro Federal Government Worker—A Study of His Classification Status in the District of Columbia, 1883-1938.* Washington, D. C.: Howard University, 1941.
Haynes, Robert V. *A Night of Violence: The Houston Riot of 1917.* Baton Rouge: Louisiana State University Press, 1976.
Hays, Brooks. *A Southern Moderate Speaks.* Chapel Hill: University of North Carolina Press, 1959.
Heaton, J. L. *Cobb of "The World."* New York: E. P. Dutton, 1924.
Henderson, Richard B. *Maury Maverick: A Political Biography.* Austin: University of Texas Press, 1970.
Henri, Florette. *Black Migration: Movement North, 1900-1920.* Garden City, N.Y.: Anchor Books, 1976.
Herndon, Angelo. *You Cannot Kill the Working Class.* New York: International Labor Defense and the League of Struggle for Negro Rights, n.d. (c. 1934).
Higham, John. *Strangers in the Land: Patterns of American Nativism, 1860-1925.* New York: Atheneum, 1963.
Hixson, William B., Jr. *Moorfield Storey and the Abolitionist Tradition.* New York: Oxford University Press, 1972.
Hofstadter, Richard. *The Age of Reform.* New York: Vintage Books, 1960.
―――. *The American Political Tradition and the Men Who Made It* (New York: Vintage Books, 1959).
―――. *Social Darwinism in American Thought.* Boston: Beacon Press, 1955.
―――, and Michael Wallace. *American Violence: A Documentary History.* New York: Vintage, 1971.
Huggins, Nathan Irvin. *Harlem Renaissance.* New York: Oxford University Press, 1973.
Holmes, John Haynes. *I Speak for Myself.* New York: Harper and Brothers, 1959.
Howe, M. A. DeWolfe. *Portrait of an Independent: Moorfield Storey.* Boston: Houghton Mifflin, 1932.
Hughes, Langston. *Fight for Freedom: The Story of the NAACP.* New York: Berkley, 1962.
Huthmacher, J. Joseph. *Senator Robert F. Wagner and the Rise of Urban Liberalism.* New York: Atheneum, 1968.
Ickes, Harold L. *The Secret Diary of Harold L. Ickes.* Vol. 3: *The Lowering Clouds, 1939-1941.* New York: Simon and Schuster, 1954.
Jack, Robert L. *The History of the National Association for the Advancement of Colored People.* Boston: Meador Publishing Co., 1943.
Jacques-Garvey, Amy. *Garvey and Garveyism.* London: Collier Books, 1970.
―――, ed. *Philosophy and Opinions of Marcus Garvey.* Vols. 1 and 2. New York: Universal Publishing House, 1925.
Johnson, Charles S., Edwin R. Embree, and Will W. Alexander. *The Collapse of Cotton Tenancy.* Chapel Hill: University of North Carolina Press, 1935.
Johnson, James Weldon. *Along This Way.* New York: Viking Press, 1933.
―――. *The Autobiography of an Ex-coloured Man* (New York: Alfred A. Knopf, 1976).
―――. *Black Manhattan* (New York: Atheneum, 1968).
―――. *Negro Americans, What Now?* New York: Viking Press, 1935.
Kellogg, Charles Flint. *NAACP: A History of the National Association for the Advancement of Colored People.* Vol. I: *1909-1920.* Baltimore: The Johns Hopkins Press, 1967.
Kesselman, Louis Coleridge. *The Social Politics of FEPC: A Study in Reform Pressure Movements.* Chapel Hill: University of North Carolina Press, 1948.

Kester, Howard. *Revolt among the Sharecroppers*. New York: Covici Friede, 1936.
Key, V. O., Jr. *Southern Politics in State and Nation*. New York: Vintage Books, 1949.
Kipnis, Ira. *The American Socialist Movement, 1897–1912*. New York: Columbia University Press, 1952.
Kirby, Jack Temple. *Darkness at the Dawning: Race and Reform in the Progressive South*. Philadelphia: J. B. Lippincott, 1972.
Kolko, Gabriel. *The Politics of War: The World and United States Foreign Policy, 1943–1945*. New York: Vintage Books, 1968.
Kraditor, Aileen S. *The Ideas of the Woman Suffrage Movement, 1890–1920*. Garden City, N.Y.: Anchor Books, 1971.
Krueger, Thomas A. *And Promises to Keep: The Southern Conference for Human Welfare, 1938–1948*. Nashville: Vanderbilt University Press, 1967.
Lacy, Dan. *The White Use of Blacks in America*. New York: Atheneum, 1972.
Lash, Joseph P. *Eleanor and Franklin*. New York: New American Library, 1973.
Lawson, Steven F. *Black Ballots: Voting Rights in the South, 1944–1969*. New York: Columbia University Press, 1976.
Lee, Alfred McClung, and Norman Daymond Humphrey. *Race Riot*. New York: Dryden Press, 1943.
Lee, Harper. *To Kill a Mockingbird*. (Philadelphia: J. B. Lippincott, 1960.
Lester, Julius, ed. *The Seventh Son: The Thoughts and Writings of W. E. B. Du Bois*. New York: Random House, 1971.
Leuchtenburg, William E. *Franklin D. Roosevelt and the New Deal: 1932–1940*. New York: Harper Torchbooks, 1963.
_____. *The Perils of Prosperity, 1914–32*. Chicago: University of Chicago Press, 1958.
Levy, Eugene. *James Weldon Johnson: Black Leader, Black Voice*. Chicago: University of Chicago Press, 1973.
Lincoln, Eric C. *The Black Muslims in America*. Boston: Beacon Press, 1961.
Link, Arthur S. *Wilson: The New Freedom*. Princeton: Princeton University Press, 1956.
_____. *Wilson: The Road to the White House*. Princeton: Princeton University Press, 1947.
Lipset, Seymour. *Political Man*. Garden City, N.Y.: Doubleday, 1960.
Locke, Alain, ed. *The New Negro: An Interpretation*. New York: Albert and Charles Boni, 1925.
Logan, Rayford W. *The Betrayal of the Negro: From Rutherford B. Hayes to Woodrow Wilson*. New York: Collier Books, 1967.
_____. *What the Negro Wants*. Chapel Hill: University of North Carolina Press, 1944.
Lord, Walter. *The Good Years*. New York: Bantam Books, 1962.
Lowitt, Richard. *George W. Norris: The Persistence of a Progressive, 1913–1933*. Urbana: University of Illinois Press, 1971.
Lunt, Richard D. *The High Ministry of Government: The Political Career of Frank Murphy*. Detroit: Wayne State University Press, 1965.
Mangum, Charles S., Jr. *The Legal Status of the Negro*. Chapel Hill: University of North Carolina Press, 1940.
Martin, Charles H. *The Angelo Herndon Case and Southern Justice*. Baton Rouge: Louisiana State University Press, 1976.
Martin, Tony. *Race First: The Ideological and Organizational Struggles of Marcus Garvey and the Universal Negro Improvement Association*. Westport, Conn.: Greenwood Press, 1976.

McCoy, Donald R., and Richard T. Reutten. *Quest and Response: Minority Rights and the Truman Administration.* Lawrence: University Press of Kansas, 1973.

McCullers, Carson, "The Member of the Wedding," *Famous American Plays of the 1940's,* ed. Henry Hewes. New York: Dell, 1960.

McKay, Claude. *Harlem Shadows.* New York: Harcourt, Brace, 1922.

McKenna, Marian C. *Borah.* Ann Arbor: University of Michigan Press, 1961.

McPherson, James M. *The Abolitionist Legacy: From Reconstruction to the NAACP.* Princeton: Princeton University Press, 1975.

Meier, August. *From Plantation to Ghetto.* New York: Hill and Wang, 1966.

─────, and Elliott Rudwick. *Negro Thought in America, 1880–1915: Racial Ideologies in the Age of Booker T. Washington.* Ann Arbor: University of Michigan Press, 1966.

─────. *CORE: A Study in the Civil Rights Movement, 1942–1968.* New York: Oxford University Press, 1973.

Miller, Loren. *The Petitioners: The Story of the Supreme Court of the United States and the Negro.* Cleveland: World, 1966.

Milton, George Fort. *Lynchings and What They Mean: General Findings of the Southern Commission on the Study of Lynching.* Atlanta, Ga.: The Commission, 1931.

─────. *The Plight of Tuscaloosa: A Case Study of Conditions in Tuscaloosa County, Alabama, 1933.* Atlanta, Ga.: Southern Commission on the Study of Lynching, 1933.

Minor, Robert. *Lynching and Frame-up in Tennessee.* New York: New Century, 1946.

Mitchell, H. L. *Mean Things Happening in This Land: The Life and Times of H. L. Mitchell, Co-Founder of the Southern Tenant Farmers Union.* Montclair, N.J.: Allanheld, Osmun, 1979.

Mitchell, Margaret. *Gone with the Wind.* New York: Macmillan, 1936.

Moon, Henry L. *Balance of Power: The Negro Vote.* Garden City, N.Y.: Doubleday, 1949.

Morison, Elting E., John M. Blum, and Alfred D. Chandler, Jr., eds. *The Letters of Theodore Roosevelt.* Vol. 8: *The Days of Armageddon, 1914–1919.* Cambridge, Mass.: Harvard University Press, 1954.

Murphy, Edgar Gardner. *Problems of the Present South: A Discussion of Certain of the Educational, Industrial and Political Issues in the Southern States.* New York: Longmans, Green, 1916.

Murray, Robert. *The Harding Era: Warren G. Harding and His Administration.* Minneapolis: University of Minnesota Press, 1969.

─────. *Red Scare: A Study of National Hysteria, 1919–1920.* New York: McGraw-Hill, 1964.

Myrdal, Gunnar. *An American Dilemma.* 2 vols. New York: McGraw-Hill, 1964.

Newby, I.A. *Jim Crow's Defense: Anti-Negro Thought in America, 1900–30.* Baton Rouge: Louisiana State University Press, 1965.

Nichols, Lee. *Breakthrough on the Color Front.* New York: Random House, 1954.

Nolen, Claude H. *The Negro's Image in the South: The Anatomy of White Supremacy.* Lexington: University of Kentucky Press, 1967.

Odum, Howard W. *Southern Regions of the United States.* Chapel Hill: University of North Carolina Press, 1936.

Olsen, Otto H. *Carpetbagger's Crusade: The Life of Albion Winegar Tourgée.* Baltimore: The Johns Hopkins Press, 1965.

─────. *The Thin Disguise: Turning Point in Negro History. Plessy v. Ferguson, a Documentary Presentation (1864–1896).* New York: Humanities Press, 1967.

Osofsky, Gilbert. *Harlem: The Making of a Ghetto. Negro New York, 1890–1930.* New York: Harper Torchbooks, 1968.
Ottley, Roi. *"New World A-Coming."* Boston: Houghton Mifflin, 1943.
_____ and William J. Weatherby, eds. *The Negro in New York: An Informal Social History, 1626–1940.* New York: Praeger, 1969.
Ovington, Mary White. *The Walls Came Tumbling Down.* New York: Schocken, Books, 1970.
Owen, Chandler. *The Remedy.* Pub. in 1 vol. with Randolph, *The Truth about Lynching.* New York: Cosmo-Advocate, [1917].
Patterson, Haywood, and Earl Conrad. *Scottsboro Boy.* New York: Bantam Books, 1951.
Patterson, James T. *Congressional Conservatism and the New Deal: The Growth of the Conservative Coalition in Congress, 1933–1939.* Lexington: University of Kentucky Press, 1967.
_____. *Mr. Republican: A Biography of Robert A. Taft.* Boston: Houghton Mifflin, 1972.
Patterson, William L., ed. *We Charge Genocide: The Historic Petition to the United Nations for Relief from a Crime of the United States Government against the Negro People.* New York: Civil Rights Congress, 1951.
Peirce, Neal R., James G. Phillips, and Victoria Velsey, eds. *Revolution in Civil Rights.* Washington, D.C.: Congressional Quarterly Service, 1965.
Pickens, William. *The New Negro: His Political, Civil and Mental Status and Related Essays.* New York: Negro Universities Press, 1969.
Phillips, Cabell L. *The Truman Presidency: The History of a Triumphant Succession.* New York: Macmillan, 1966.
Polenberg, Richard. *War and Society: The United States, 1941–1945.* Philadelphia: J. B. Lippincott, 1972.
Powdermaker, Hortense. *After Freedom. A Cultural Study in the Deep South.* New York: Viking Press, 1939.
Proceedings of the National Negro Conference, 1909. New York: Arno Press and the *New York Times*, 1969.
Randolph, Asa Philip. *The Truth about Lynching: Its Causes and Effects.* Pub. in 1 vol. with Owen, *The Remedy.* New York: Cosmo-Advocate, [1917].
Raper, Arthur F. *The Tragedy of Lynching.* Chapel Hill: University of North Carolina Press, 1933.
Raucher, Alan R. *Public Relations and Business, 1900–1929.* Baltimore: The Johns Hopkins Press, 1968.
Record, Wilson. *The Negro and the Communist Party.* Chapel Hill: University of North Carolina Press, 1951.
_____. *Race and Radicalism: The NAACP and the Communist Party in Conflict.* Ithaca, N.Y.: Cornell University Press, 1964.
Robinson, James Harvey. *The New History.* New York: Macmillan, 1912.
Rose, Arnold. *The Negro in America.* Boston: Beacon Press, 1962.
_____. *The Negro's Morale.* Minneapolis: University of Minnesota Press, 1949.
Ross, B. Joyce. *J. E. Spingarn and the Rise of the NAACP, 1911–1939.* New York: Atheneum, 1972.
Ross, Irwin. *The Loneliest Campaign: The Truman Victory of 1948.* New York: Signet Books, 1969.
Rosenman, Samuel I., ed. *The Public Papers and Addresses of Franklin Delano Roosevelt.* 13 vols. New York: Macmillan, 1938–*1950*.
Ruchames, Louis. *Race, Jobs, and Politics: The Story of FEPC.* New York: Columbia University Press, 1953.

Rudwick, Elliott M. *W. E. B. Du Bois: Propagandist of the Negro Protest.* New York: Atheneum, 1968.

———. *Race Riot at East St. Louis July 2, 1917* (New York: Atheneum, 1972).

St. James, Warren D. *The National Association for the Advancement of Colored People: A Case Study in Pressure Groups.* New York: Exposition Press, 1958.

Schaffer, Alan. *Vito Marcantonio, Radical in Congress.* Syracuse: Syracuse University Press, 1966.

Scott, Emmett J. *Negro Migration during the War.* New York: Arno Press and the New York Times, 1969.

Seale, Bobby. *Seize the Time: The Story of the Black Panther Party and Huey P. Newton.* New York: Vintage Books, 1970.

Seligmann, Herbert J. *The Negro Faces America.* New York: Harper and Brothers, 1920.

Shay, Frank. *Judge Lynch: His First Hundred Years.* Montclair, N.J.: Patterson Smith, 1969.

Sherman, Richard B. *The Republican Party and Black America: From McKinley to Hoover, 1896-1933.* Charlottesville: University Press of Virginia, 1973.

Sinclair, Andrew. *The Available Man: The Life behind the Masks of Warren Gamaliel Harding.* Chicago: Quadrangle Books, 1969.

Sinkler, George. *The Racial Attitudes of American Presidents: From Abraham Lincoln to Theodore Roosevelt.* Garden City, N.Y.: Doubleday, 1972.

Sitkoff, Harvard. *A New Deal for Blacks: The Emergence of Civil Rights as a National Issue.* Vol. 1: *The Depression Decade.* New York: Oxford University Press, 1978.

Smelser, Neil J. *Theory of Collective Behavior.* New York: Free Press, 1963.

Sosna, Morton. *In Search of the Silent South: Southern Liberals and the Race Issue.* New York: Columbia University Press, 1977.

Spear, Allan H. *Black Chicago: The Making of a Negro Ghetto, 1890-1920.* Chicago: University of Chicago Press, 1967.

Spero, Sterling D., and Abram Harris. *The Black Worker: The Negro and the Labor Movement.* New York: Columbia University Press, 1931.

Stearns, Harold. *Liberalism in America.* New York: Boni and Liveright, 1919.

Sterner, Richard. *The Negro's Share.* New York: Harper and Brothers, 1943.

Sternsher, Bernard, ed. *The Negro in Depression and War: Prelude to Revolution, 1930-1945.* Chicago: Quadrangle Books, 1969.

Strickland, Arvarh E. *History of the Chicago Urban League.* Urbana: University of Illinois Press, 1966.

Stromer, Marvin E. *The Making of a Political Leader: Kenneth S. Wherry and the United States Senate.* Lincoln: University of Nebraska Press, 1969.

Swanberg, W. A. *Citizen Hearst.* New York: Bantam Books, 1963.

Swisher, Carl Brent, ed. *Historic Decisions of the Supreme Court.* Princeton: D. Van Nostrand, 1958.

———. *Selected Papers of Homer Cummings.* New York: Charles Scribner's Sons, 1939.

Tatum, Elbert Lee. *The Changed Political Thought of the Negro, 1915-1940.* New York: Exposition Press, 1951.

Thelen, David P. *Robert M. La Follette and the Insurgent Spirit.* Boston: Little, Brown, 1976.

Thomas, Lewis F. *The Localization of Business Activities in Metropolitan St. Louis.* Washington University Studies, n.s. no. 1. St. Louis: Washington University, 1927.

Thornbrough, Emma Lou. *T. Thomas Fortune: Militant Journalist.* Chicago: University of Chicago Press, 1972.

Tindall, George B. *The Emergence of the New South, 1913–1945.* Baton Rouge: Louisiana State University Press, 1967.
Toomer, Jean. *Cane.* New York: Liveright, 1975.
Truman, Harry S. *Memoirs. Vol. 1: Year of Decisions.* Garden City, N.Y.: Doubleday, 1955.
──────. *Memoirs. Vol. 2: Years of Trial and Hope.* Garden City, N.Y.: Doubleday, 1956.
Tuttle, William M., Jr. *Race Riot: Chicago in the Red Summer of 1919.* New York: Atheneum, 1970.
Veblen, Thorstein, *The Theory of Business Enterprise.* New York: Charles Scribner's Sons, 1904.
──────. *The Theory of the Leisure Class.* New York: Macmillan, 1899.
Villard, Oswald Garrison. *Fighting Years.* New York: Harcourt, Brace, 1939.
Vincent, Theodore G. *Black Power and the Garvey Movement.* Berkeley, Calif.: Ramparts Press, 1971.
Vose, Clement E. *Caucasians Only: The Supreme Court, the NAACP, and the Restrictive Covenant Cases.* Berkeley: University of California Press, 1967.
Waldron, Edward E. *Walter White and the Harlem Renaissance.* Port Washington, N.Y.: Kennikat Press, 1978.
Walling, William English. *Progressivism—and After.* New York: Pickwell, 1914.
Walters, Alexander. *My Life and Work.* New York: Fleming H. Revell, 1917.
Walton, Hanes, Jr. *Black Politics: A Theoretical and Structural Analysis.* Philadelphia: J. B. Lippincott, 1972.
Waskow, Arthur I. *From Race Riot to Sit-In, 1919 and the 1960s: A Study in the Connections between Conflict and Violence.* Garden City, N.Y.: Doubleday, 1966.
Weatherford, W. D. *The Negro from Africa to America.* New York: Negro Universities Press, 1969.
Weinstein, James. *The Decline of Socialism in America, 1912–1925.* New York: Vintage Books, 1969.
Weiss, Nancy J. *The National Urban League, 1910–1940.* New York: Oxford University Press, 1974.
Wells-Barnett, Ida B. *On Lynchings: Southern Horrors, a Red Record, Mob Rule in New Orleans.* New York: Arno Press, 1969.
White, Walter. *How Far the Promised Land?* New York: Viking Press, 1955.
──────. *A Man Called White.* New York: Viking Press, 1948.
──────. *Rope and Faggot: A Biography of Judge Lynch.* New York: Alfred A. Knopf, 1929.
Wiebe, Robert H. *The Search for Order, 1877–1920.* New York: Hill and Wang, 1967.
Williams, Robin M., Jr. *The Reduction of Intergroup Tensions: A Study of Research on Problems of Ethnic, Racial, and Religious Group Relations.* New York: Social Science Research Council, 1947.
Wolseley, Roland E. *The Black Press, U.S.A.* Ames: Iowa State University Press, 1971.
Wolters, Raymond. *Negroes and the Great Depression: The Problem of Economic Recovery.* Westport, Conn.: Greenwood, 1970.
──────. *The New Negro on Campus: Black College Rebellions of the 1920s.* Princeton: Princeton University Press, 1975.
Woodward, C. Vann. *Origins of the New South, 1877–1913.* Baton Rouge: Louisiana State University Press, 1966.
──────. *The Strange Career of Jim Crow.* New York: Oxford University Press, 1960.

Wreszin, Michael. *Oswald Garrison Villard: Pacifist at War*. Bloomington: Indiana University Press, 1965.
Wynn, Daniel Webster. *The NAACP versus Negro Revolutionary Protest*. New York: Exposition Press, 1955.
Zinn, Howard. *La Guardia in Congress*. New York: W. W. Norton, 1959.

Articles

Alexander, Raymond Pace. "The Upgrading of the Negro's Status by Supreme Court Decisions." *Journal of Negro History* 30 (April 1945): 117–49.
Allswang, John M. "The Chicago Negro Voter and the Democratic Consensus: A Case Study, 1918–1936." In Bernard Sternsher, ed., *The Negro in Depression and War: Prelude to Revolution, 1930–1945*, pp. 234–57. Chicago: Quadrangle Books, 1969.
Athey, Louis L. "Florence Kelley and the Quest for Negro Equality." *Journal of Negro History* 56 (Oct. 1971): 249–61.
Bailey, J. W. "Some Thoughts on Lynching." *South Atlantic Quarterly* 5 (Oct. 1906): 353–54.
Barber, Henry E. "The Association of Southern Women for the Prevention of Lynching, 1930–1942." *Phylon* 34 (Dec. 1973): 378–89.
Billington, Monroe. "Civil Rights, President Truman, and the South." *Journal of Negro History* 58 (April 1973): 127–33.
Blumenthal, Henry. "Woodrow Wilson and the Race Question." *Journal of Negro History* 48 (Jan. 1963): 10–15.
Bond, Horace M. "What Lies behind Lynching." *The Nation* 128 (March 27, 1929): 370–71.
Calista, Donald J. "Booker T. Washington: Another Look." *Journal of Negro History* 49 (Oct. 1964): 240–55.
Carter, Charles Frederick. "The Lynching Infamy." *Current History* 15 (March 1922): 897–902.
Chatfield, Charles. "World War I and the Liberal Pacifist in the United States." *American Historical Review* 75 (Dec. 1970): 1920–37.
Cooney, Charles F. "Walter White and the Harlem Renaissance." *Journal of Negro History* 57 (July 1972): 231–40.
Contee, Clarence G. "Du Bois, the NAACP, and the Pan-African Congress of 1919." *Journal of Negro History* 57 (Jan. 1972): 13–28.
Cothran, Ben. "Ousting Judge Lynch." *The Forum* 98 (Oct. 1937): 158–63.
Cripps, Thomas R. "*The Birth of a Race* Company: An Early Stride toward a Black Cinema." *Journal of Negro History* 59 (Jan. 1974): 28–37.
———. "The Myth of the Southern Box Office: A Factor in Racial Stereotyping in American Movies, 1920–1940." In Curtis, James C., and Lewis L. Gould, eds., pp. 116–44. *The Black Experience in America: Selected Essays* Austin: University of Texas Press, 1970.
———. "The Reaction of the Negro to the Motion Picture *Birth of a Nation*." *The Historian* 25 (May 1963): 344–62.
Crofts, Daniel W. "The Black Response to the Blair Education Bill." *Journal of Southern History* 37 (Feb. 1971): 41–65.
Crowe, Charles. "Racial Massacre in Atlanta, September 22, 1906." *Journal of Negro History* 54 (April 1969): 150–73.
Dabney, Virginius. "Dixie Rejects Lynching." *The Nation* 145 (Nov. 27, 1937): 579–80.
Dalfiume, Richard M. "The 'Forgotten Years' of the Negro Revolution." *Journal of American History* 55 (June 1968): 90–106.

Daniel, Pete. "The Metamorphosis of Slavery, 1865–1900." *Journal of American History* 66 (June 1979): 88–99.

Davis, Horace B. "A Substitute for Lynching." *The Nation* 130 (Jan. 1, 1930): 12–14.

Divine, Robert A. "The Cold War and the Election of 1948." *Journal of American History* 59 (June 1972): 90–110.

Douglass, Frederick. "Lynch Law in the South." *North American Review* 155 (July 1892): 117–24.

Du Bois, W. E. B. "Criteria of Negro Art." *Crisis* 32 (Oct. 1926): 296–97.

———. "The Immediate Program of the American Negro." *Crisis* 9 (April 1915): 310–12.

———. "Of the Culture of White Folk." *Journal of Race Development* 7 (April 1917): 434–37.

———. "Opinion." *Crisis* 18 (May 1919): 13–14.

"W. E. B. Du Bois' Confrontation with White Liberalism during the Progressive Era: A *Phylon* Document," with an Introduction by William M. Tuttle, Jr. *Phylon* 35 (Sept. 1974): 241–58.

Durbin, Winfield T. "The Mob and the Law." *The Independent* 55 (July 30, 1903): 1790–93.

Filene, Peter G. "An Obituary for 'The Progressive Movement.'" *American Quarterly* 22 (Spring 1970): 20–34.

Fishel, Leslie H., Jr. "The Negro in the New Deal Era." *Wisconsin Magazine of History* 48 (Winter 1964–1965): 111–23.

Galloway, Charles B. "Some Thoughts on Lynching." *South Atlantic Quarterly* 5 (Oct. 1906): 351–53.

Garner, James Wilford. "Lynching and the Criminal Law." *South Atlantic Quarterly* 5 (Oct. 1906): 333–41.

Gerber, David A. "Lynching and Law and Order: Origin and Passage of the Ohio Anti-lynching Law of 1896." *Ohio History* 83 (Winter 1974): 33–50.

Gibbons, His Eminence, Cardinal. "Lynch Law: Its Causes and Remedy." *North American Review* 181 (Oct. 1905): 502–09.

Gillard, John T. "Lynching and Lunching." *Commonweal*, 20 (May 25, 1934): 95–97.

Glasson, William H. "The Statistics of Lynchings." *South Atlantic Quarterly* 5 (Oct. 1906): 342–48.

Grantham, Dewey W., Jr. "The Progressive Movement and the Negro." *South Atlantic Quarterly* 54 (Oct. 1955): 461–77.

Greenbaum, Fred. "The Anti-Lynching Bill of 1935: The Irony of 'Equal Justice— Under Law.'" *Journal of Human Relations* 15 (Third Quarter 1967): 72–85.

Grimshaw, Allen D. "Factors Contributing to Colour Violence in the United States and Britain." *Race* 3 (1962): 3–19.

———. "Lawlessness and Violence in America and Their Special Manifestations in Changing Negro-White Relationships." *Journal of Negro History* 44 (Jan. 1959): 52–72.

———. "Three Major Cases of Colour Violence in the United States." *Race* 5 (1963): 76–86.

"A Growing Social Effort in the South." *Survey* 36 (May 20, 1916): 196.

Gruening, Martha. "Democratic Massacres in East St. Louis." *Pearson's Magazine* 38 (Sept. 1917): 106–08.

———. "The Truth about the Crawford Case." *New Masses* 14 (Jan. 8, 1935): 9–14.

Hall, Jacquelyn. "Women & Lynching." *Southern Exposure* 4 (Winter 1977): 52–54.

Harlan, Louis R. "Booker T. Washington in Biographical Perspective." *American Historical Review* 75 (Oct. 1970): 1581–99.

Hixson, William B., Jr. "Moorfield Storey and the Defense of the Dyer Anti-Lynching Bill." *New England Quarterly* 42 (March 1969): 65–81.
_____. "Moorfield Storey and the Struggle for Equality." *Journal of American History* 55 (Dec. 1968): 533–54.
Hoffman, Edwin D. "The Genesis of the Modern Movement for Equal Rights in South Carolina, 1930–1939." *Journal of Negro History* 44 (Oct. 1959): 363–69.
Hope, Cecil S. "The Flames of Lynch-Law Spread." *Labor Defender*. No. v. (Dec. 1931): 237. In "Lynching—Statistics" folder, Schomburg Collection, New York City Public Library.
_____. "Halt Lynch Terror!" *Labor Defender* (Feb. 1932): 26. In "Lynching—Statistics" folder, Schomburg Collection, New York City Public Library.
Inverarity, James M. "Populism and Lynching in Louisiana, 1889–1896: A Test of Erikson's Theory of the Relationship between Boundary Crises and Repressive Justice." *American Sociological Review* 41 (April 1976): 262–80.
Johnson, James Weldon. "Lynching—America's National Disgrace." *Current History* 19 (Jan. 1924): 596–601.
_____. "The Practice of Lynching," *Century* 115 (Nov. 1927), 65–70.
_____. "Report of the Department of Justice on Sedition among Negroes." Editorial in the New York *Age*, Dec. 20, 1919. In "Pamphlets," James Weldon Johnson Collection, Yale University, New Haven, Conn.
Kaiser, Ernest. "The Federal Government and the Negro, 1865–1955." *Science and Society* 20 (Winter 1956): 27–58.
Key, V. O., Jr. "Secular Realignment and the Party System." *Journal of Politics* 21 (May 1959): 198–210.
Kirby, John B. "The Roosevelt Administration and Blacks: An Ambivalent Legacy." In Barton J. Bernstein and Allen J. Matusow, eds., *Twentieth-Century America: Recent Interpretations*. 2d ed., pp. 265–88. New York: Harcourt Brace Jovanovich, 1972.
Labor Defender, June 1930, p. 126. In "Lynching—Case Stories" folder, Schomburg Collection, New York City Public Library.
Lerner, Gerda. "Early Community Work of Black Club Women." *Journal of Negro History* 59 (April 1974): 158–67.
Levy, Eugene. " 'Is the Jew a White Man?': Press Reaction to the Leo Frank Case, 1913–1915." *Phylon* 35 (June 1974): 212–22.
Link, Arthur, and Jerold S. Auerbach. Letters to the editor. *Journal of American History* 55 (June 1968): 231–38.
Link, Arthur S. "The Negro as a Factor in the Campaign of 1912." *Journal of Negro History* 32 (Jan. 1947): 81–99.
McCoy, Donald R., and Richard T. Reutten. "Towards equality: blacks in the United States during the Second World War." In A. C. Hepburn, ed., pp. 135–53. *Minorities in History* London: Edward Arnold, 1978.
Meier, August, and Elliott Rudwick. "Attorneys Black and White: A Case Study of Race Relations within the NAACP." *Journal of American History* 62 (March 1976); 913–46.
_____. "The Rise of the Black Secretariat in the NAACP, 1909–1935." *The Crisis* 84 (Feb. 1977): 58–61, 64–68.
Miller, Robert M. "The Attitudes of American Protestantism toward the Negro, 1919–1939." *Journal of Negro History* 41 (July 1956): 215–40.
_____. "The Protestant Churches and Lynching,1919–1939." *Journal of Negro History* 42 (April 1957): 118–31.
Minor, Robert. "The Negro and His Judases." *The Communist* 10 (July 1931): 632–39.

Mintz, Alexander. "A Re-examination of Correlations between Lynchings and Economic Indices." *Journal of Abnormal and Social Psychology* 41 (April 1946): 154–60.
Murray, Hugh T., Jr. "The NAACP versus the Communist Party: The Scottsboro Rape Cases, 1931–32." *Phylon* 28 (3d qtr. 1967): 276–87.
Nash, Roy. "The Lynching of Anthony Crawford." *The Independent* 88 (Dec. 11, 1916): 456, 458, 460–62.
Page, Thomas Nelson. "The Lynching of Negroes—Its Cause and Its Prevention." *North American Review* 178 (Jan. 1904): 33–48.
Page, Thomas Walker. "Lynching and Race Relations in the South." *North American Review* 206 (Aug. 1917): 241–50.
Pillsbury, Albert E. "A Brief Inquiry into a Federal Remedy for Lynching." *Harvard Law Review* 15 (May 1902): 707–13.
Poe, Clarence H. "Lynching: A Southern View." *Atlantic Monthly* 93 (Feb. 1904): 155–65.
Pope, Whitney, and Charles Ragin. "Mechanical Solidarity, Repressive Justice, and Lynchings in Louisiana." *American Sociological Review*, 42 (April 1977): 363–68.
"A Practical Way to Cut Down Lynchings." *Survey* 37 (Jan. 20, 1917): 461.
Randolph, A. Philip. "Why Should We March?" *Survey Graphic* 31 (Nov. 1942): 488–89.
"Recent Comments on Lynching and the New Negro Crime." *Harper's Weekly* 47 (Aug. 29, 1903): 1395–96.
Record, Wilson. "Negro Intellectual Leadership in the National Association for the Advancement of Colored People: 1910–1940." *Phylon* 17 (4th qtr., 1956): 375–89.
Reed, John Shelton. "A Note on the Control of Lynching." *Public Opinion Quarterly* 33 (Summer 1969): 268–71.
―――. "An Evaluation of an Anti-lynching Organization." *Social Problems* 16 (Fall 1968): 172–82.
―――. "Percent Black and Lynching: A Test of Blalock's Theory." *Social Forces* 50 (March 1972): 356–60.
Rudwick, Elliott. "W. E. B. Du Bois in the Role of *Crisis* Editor." *Journal of Negro History* 43 (July 1958): 214–40.
Salmond, John A. "Postscript to the New Deal: The Defeat of the Nomination of Aubrey W. Williams as Rural Electrification Administrator in 1945." *Journal of American History* 61 (Sept. 1974): 417–36.
Sherman, Richard B. "The Harding Administration and the Negro: An Opportunity Lost." *Journal of Negro History* 49 (July 1964): 151–68.
Sitkoff, Harvard. "Harry Truman and the Election of 1948: The Coming of Age of Civil Rights in American Politics." *Journal of Southern History* 37 (Nov. 1971): 597–616.
―――. "Racial Militancy and Interracial Violence in the Second World War." *Journal of American History* 58 (Dec. 1971): 661–81.
Sledd, Andrew. "The Negro: Another View." *Atlantic Monthly* 90 (July 1902): 65–73.
Smith, T. Lynn. "The Redistribution of the Negro Population of the United States, 1910–1960." *Journal of Negro History* 51 (July 1966): 153–73.
"The So-Called Race Riot at Springfield, Illinois." In Allen D. Grimshaw, ed., *Racial Violence in the United States*, pp. 51–56. Chicago: Aldine, 1969.
Strange, Robert. "Some Thoughts on Lynching." *South Atlantic Quarterly* 5 (Oct. 1906): 349–51.

Thornbrough, Emma Lou. "Booker T. Washington as Seen by his White Contemporaries." *Journal of Negro History* 53 (April 1968): 161–82.
——. "The Brownsville Episode and the Negro Vote." *Mississippi Valley Historical Review* 44 (Dec. 1957): 469–93.
Tucker, David M. "Miss Ida B. Wells and Memphis Lynching." *Phylon* 32 (Summer 1971): 112–22.
Tuttle, William M., Jr. "Labor Conflict and Racial Violence: The Black Worker in Chicago, 1894–1919." *Labor History* 10 (Summer 1969): 408–32.
Villard, Oswald Garrison. "The President and the Segregation at Washington." *North American Review* 198 (Dec. 1913): 800–07.
Walling, William English. "The Race War in the North." *The Independent* 65 (Sept. 3, 1908): 529–34.
Wasserman, Ira M. "Southern Violence and the Political Process." *American Sociological Review* 42 (April 1977): 359–62.
Weiner, Jonathan M. "Class Structure and Economic Development in the American South, 1865–1955." *American Historical Review* 84 (October 1979): 970–92.
Weiss, Nancy J. "From Black Separatism to Interracial Cooperation: The Origins of Organized Efforts for Racial Advancement, 1890–1920." In Barton J. Bernstein and Allen J. Matusow, eds., *Twentieth-Century America: Recent Interpretations*. 2d ed. pp. 52–87. New York: Harcourt Brace Jovanovich, 1972.
Wells-Barnett, Ida B. "Lynching and the Excuse for It." *The Independent* 53 (May 16, 1901): 1133–36.
——. "The Negro's Case in Equity." *The Independent* 52 (April 26, 1900): 1010–11.
White, Walter. "I Investigate Lynchings." *American Mercury* 16 (Jan. 1929): 77–84.
——. "The Negro and the Communists." *Harper's Magazine* 164 (Dec. 1931): 62–72.
——. "U.S. Department of (White) Justice." *Crisis* 42 (Oct. 1935): 309–10.
Wolgemuth, Kathleen L. "Woodrow Wilson's Appointment Policy and the Negro." *Journal of Southern History* 24 (Nov. 1958): 457–71.
——. "Woodrow Wilson and Federal Segregation." *Journal of Negro History* 44 (April 1959): 158–73.
Young, Erle Fiske. "The Relation of Lynching to the Size of Political Areas." *Sociology and Social Research* 12 (March-April 1928): 348–53.
Zangrando, Robert L. "Black Protest: From the Politics of Entree to the Politics of Liberation." *Afro-American Studies* 1 (May 1970): 29–40.
——. "The NAACP and a Federal Antilynching Bill, 1934–1940." *Journal of Negro History* 50 (April 1965): 106–17.
——. "The 'Organized Negro'; The National Association for the Advancement of Colored People and Civil Rights." In James C. Curtis and Lewis L. Gould, eds., pp. 145–71. *The Black Experience in America*. Austin: University of Texas Press, 1970.
Zeichner, Oscar. "The Legal Status of the Agricultural Laborer in the South." *Political Science Quarterly* 55 (Sept. 1940): 412–28.

Pamphlets and Reports

Ames, Jessie Daniel. *The Changing Character of Lynching*. Atlanta: Commission on Interracial Cooperation, 1942.

Bibliography

Amis, B. D. *Lynch Justice at Work*, American Negro Labor Congress, n.d. In "Lynching" folder, Schomburg Collection, New York City Public Library.
Anti-lynching Crusaders. *The Ninth Crusade*. New York: NAACP, 1922.
Association of Southern Women for the Prevention of Lynching. *A New Public Opinion on Lynching*. Atlanta, Ga.: April 1933. Johnson Collection, Yale University Library, New Haven, Conn.
Burroughs, Nannie. *Lynchers*. District One for the Suppression of Lynching and Mob Violence, n.d. In "Lynching" folder, Schomburg Collection, New York City Public Library.
Commission on Interracial Cooperation. *Mob Murder in America*. Atlanta, Ga.: The Commission, n.d. In "Lynching" folder, Schomburg Collection, New York City Public Library.
———. *The Mob Still Rides*. Atlanta, Ga.: The Commission, 1936. In "Lynching" folder, Schomburg Collection, New York City Public Library.
Commission on Race Relations of the Federal Council of Churches. *Horrible and Shameful*. New York: The Commission, 1931. In "Lynching" folder, Schomburg Collection, New York City Public Library.
Du Bois, W. E. B., John Garfield, Oscar Hammerstein, II, et al. *American Crusade to End Lynching*. Throw-away pamphlet, 1946. In "Lynching" folder, Schomburg Collection, New York City Public Library.
Edmonds, Dr. Henry M. *The Cost of the Mob*. Rpt. from the Birmingham *Age-Herald*, Oct. 8, 1933. Atlanta, Ga.: Commission on Interracial Cooperation, 1933. In "Lynching" folder, Schomburg Collection, New York City Public Library.
Gregg, James E. *Lynching: A National Menace*. Hampton Institute, c. 1919. In "Lynching" folder, Schomburg Collection, New York City Public Library.
Haywood, H., and M. Howard. *Lynching*. New York.: International Pamphlets, 1932. In "Lynching" folder, Schomburg Collection, New York City Public Library.
Johnson, James Weldon. *The Changing Status of Negro Labor*. From an address to the National Conference of Social Work at Kansas City, Mo., May 20, 1918. In "Pamphlets," blue box, Johnson Collection, Yale University Library, New Haven, Conn.
———. *Self-determining Haiti*. New York: *The Nation*, for the NAACP, 1920. In Mary White Ovington Papers, Archives of Labor History and Urban Affairs, Wayne State University, Detroit, Mich.
Lynching Goes Underground. Sponsored by Senators Robert Wagner, Arthur Capper, and Congressmen Joseph Gavagan and Hamilton Fish, Jan. 1940. In "Lynching—Causes" folder, Schomburg Collection, New York City Public Library.
Methodist Federation for Social Service. *The Social Service Bulletin*. n.p.: The Federation, 1, 1930. In "Lynching—Case Stories" folder, Schomburg Collection, New York City Public Library.
Nash, Roy. *The Lynching of Anthony Crawford*. New York: NAACP, 1916.
The National Board of the National Sharecroppers Fund. *End the Shame of Lynching*. New York: The Board, n.d. In "Lynching" folder, Schomburg Collection, New York City Public Library.
NAACP. *Annual Reports*. New York: NAACP, 1911–1950.
———. *An Appeal to the Conscience of the Civilized World*. New York: NAACP, 1920.
———. *Can the States Stop Lynching?* New York: NAACP, 1937.
———. *Fighting a Vicious Film*. Boston: NAACP, 1915.

302   Bibliography

_____. *Fortieth Spingarn Medal.* New York: NAACP, June 24, 1955.
_____. *NAACP, An American Organization.* New York: NAACP, 1956.
_____. *The Lynching of Claude Neal.* New York: NAACP, 1934.
_____. *The N.A.A.C.P.: Its History, Achievements, Purposes.* New York: NAACP, n.d.
_____. *Notes on Lynching in the United States.* New York: NAACP, 1912.
_____. *Racial Inequalities in Education.* New York: NAACP, 1938.
_____. *The Recent Record of the Ku Klux Klan—As Set Forth by 2 Alabama Editors.* New York: NAACP, n.d.
_____. *A Ten-Year Fight against Lynching.* New York: NAACP, 1920?.
_____. *Thirty Years of Lynching in the United States, 1889-1918.* New York: NAACP, 1919, and Yearly Supplements, 1920-1946.
Nordyke, Lewis T. *Ladies and Lynchings.* From *Survey Graphic*, Nov. 1939. Rpt. for the Association of Southern Women for the Prevention of Lynching. Loaned to the author by Jessie Daniel Ames, former director of the group.
Ovington, Mary White. *How the National Association for the Advancement of Colored People Began.* New York: NAACP, 1914.
Pickens, William. *Lynching and Debt-Slavery.* New York: American Civil Liberties Union pamphlet, 1921. In "Lynching" folder, Schomburg Collection, New York Public Library.
Waldron, J. Milton, and J. D. Harkless. *The Political Situation in a Nut-Shell: Some Un-colored Truths for Colored Voters.* Washington, D.C.: n.p., 1912.
Weatherford, W.D. *Lynching*—Removing Its Causes. N.p., Y.M.C.A., 1916. In "Lynching" folder, Schomburg Collection, New York City Public Library.
The Writers' League Against Lynching. *Support the Federal Anti-lynching Bill!* New York: NAACP, April 1934.

Supreme Court Cases

Brown v. Board of Education of Topeka, 347 U.S. 483 (1954).
Brown et al v. Mississippi, 297 U.S. 278 (1936).
Buchanan v. Warley, 245 U.S. 60 (1917).
Chambers v. Florida, 309 U.S. 227 (1940).
Corrigan v. Buckley, 271 U.S. 323 (1926).
Dennis v. United States, 341 U.S. 494 (1951).
Frank v. Mangum, 237 U.S. 309 (1915).
Grovey v. Townsend, 295 U.S. 45 (1935).
Guinn and Beal v. United States, 238 U.S. 347 (1915).
Harper v. Virginia Board of Elections, 383 U.S. 663 (1966).
Herndon v. Lowry, 301 U.S. 242 (1937).
Hodges v. United States, 203 U.S. 1 (1906).
McLaurin v. Oklahoma State Regents, 339 U.S. 637 (1950).
Missouri ex rel. Gaines v. Canada, 305 U.S. 337 (1938).
Moore v. Dempsey, 261 U.S. 86 (1923).
Morgan v. Virginia, 328 U.S. 373 (1946).
Nixon v. Condon, 286 U.S. 73 (1932).
Nixon v. Herndon, 273 U.S. 536 (1927).
Norris v. Alabama, 294 U.S. 587 (1935).
Plessy v. Ferguson, 163 U.S. 537 (1896).
Powell v. Alabama, 287 U.S. 45 (1932).
Screws v. United States, 325 U.S. 9 (1945).
Shelley v. Kraemer, 334 U.S. 1 (1948).
Sipuel v. Board of Regents, 332 U.S. 631 (1948).

Slaughter-House Cases, 16 Wall., 36 (1873).
Smith v. Allwright, 321 U.S. 649 (1944).
Sweatt v. Painter, 339 U.S. 629 (1950).
Terry v. Adams, 345 U.S. 461 (1953).
United States v. Cruikshank, 92 U.S. 542 (1876).
Watson v. Memphis, 373 U.S. 526 (1963).

Reference Works

Complete Presidential Press Conferences of Franklin D. Roosevelt. New York: DeCapo Press, 1972. Vols. 3–5, 9–11, 15.
Congressional Quarterly Guide to the Congress of the United States: Origins, History and Procedure. Washington, D.C.: Congressional Quarterly Service, 1971.
Corwin, Edward S., Norman J. Small and Lester S. Jayson, eds. *The Constitution of the United States of America: Analysis and Interpretation.* Washington, D.C.: G. P. O., 1964.
Fleming, G. James, and Christian E. Burckel, eds. *Who's Who in Colored America.* 7th ed. Yonkers-on-Hudson, N.Y.: Christian E. Burckel Associates, 1950.
Gallup, George H., ed. *The Gallup Poll: Public Opinion, 1935–1971*, 3 Vols. Vol. 1. New York: Random House, 1972.
Garraty, John A., and Jerome L. Sternstein, eds. *Encyclopedia of American Biography.* New York: Harper and Row, 1974.
Marquis, Albert Nelson, ed. *Who's Who in America.* Vol. 11: *1920–1921.* Chicago: A. N. Marquis, 1920.
National Cyclopaedia of American Biography. New York: James T. White, 1922.
Ploski, Harry A., ed. *Reference Library of Black America*, Bk. 3. New York: Bellwether, 1971.
Porter, Kirk H., and Donald Bruce Johnson, eds. *National Party Platforms: 1840–1964.* 3d ed.; Urbana: University of Illinois Press, 1966.
Rywell, Martin, ed. *Afro-American Encyclopedia.* 10 Vols. Vol. 5. North Miami, Fla.: Educational Book Publishers, 1974.
Zangrando, Robert L., "Walter Francis White," in John A. Garraty and Jerome L. Sternstein, eds. *Encyclopedia of American Biography* (New York: Harper and Row, 1974), pp. 1188–89.

Unpublished Materials

Bunche, Ralph J. "The Programs, Ideologies, Tactics and Achievements of Negro Betterment and Interracial Organizations." Typescript (copy) prepared for the Carnegie Corporation-Gunnar Myrdal study of The Negro in America, 1940. In Schomburg Collection, New York Public Library.
Du Bois, W. E. B. "My Relations with the N.A.A.C.P." (Mimeograph 15 pp.). In "vertical file," 1948, Moorland Collection, Howard University, Washington, D.C.
Eisenberg, Bernard. "James Weldon Johnson and the National Association for the Advancement of Colored People, 1916–1934." Ph.D. diss., Columbia University, 1968.
Grant, Donald L. "The Development of the Anti-lynching Reform Movement in the United States, 1883–1932." Ph.D. diss., University of Missouri-Columbia, 1972.

Grimshaw, Allen D. "A Study in Social Violence." Ph.D. diss., University of Pennsylvania, 1959.
Hall, Jacquelyn Dowd. "Revolt against Chivalry: Jessie Daniel Ames and the Women's Campaign against Lynching." Ph.D., diss. Columbia University, 1974.
Kifer, Allen F. "The Negro Under the New Deal, 1933–1941." Ph.D. diss., University of Wisconsin, 1961.
Lawrence, Charles R. "Negro Organizations in Crisis: Depression, New Deal, W. W. II." Ph.D. diss., Columbia University, 1953.
NAACP. "Chronology of a Crusade." mimeographed list of NAACP activities, 1909–1959. In NAACP files, National Office, New York City.
Reeder, Jesse Woodland. "Federal Efforts to Control Lynching." Ph.D. diss., Cornell University, 1952.
Stubbs, Carolyn Amonitti. "Angelina Weld Grimké: Washington Poet and Playwright." Ph.D. diss., George Washington University, 1978.
Tillman, Nathaniel P. "Walter Francis White: A Study in Interest Group Leadership." Ph.D. diss., University of Wisconsin, 1961.
Wright, Richard. "Repeating a Modest Proposal (with Apologies to Old Jonathan)." Unpub. article submitted to *Race*, in mid-1930s. Now held by Henry L. Moon, former NAACP director of public relations, New York.
Zangrando, Robert L. "The Efforts of the National Association for the Advancement of Colored People to Secure Passage of a Federal Anti-lynching Law, 1920–1940." Ph.D. diss., University of Pennsylvania, 1963.

Index

Abbott, Robert S., 101
Addams, Jane, 24
"An Address to the Nation on Lynching" (1919), 50
Afro-American, 64, 73, 74, 75, 78, 124, 153, 155, 158, 177, 184, 201
Alexander, Will W., 58, 102-3, 104, 116-17, 126-27, 132, 157
Amenia conferences, 31, 32, 107, 109
American Civil Liberties Union (ACLU), 111, 187
American Council on Race Relations, 187, 190
American Fund for Public Service (AFPS; Garland Fund), 68, 81-82, 87-88, 96-97, 101, 106, 131, 166
American Negro Labor Congress, 94
Ames, Jessie Daniel, 4, 102-3, 126, 143, 149, 156-58
Amsterdam News, 124
Antilynching Conference of 1919, 46, 48-50
Anti-Lynching Crusaders, 78, 81, 98
Anti-Poll Tax Drive, 167, 181, 183, 189, 208
Armwood, George, 103-4
Art Commentary on Lynching, 125-26
Ashurst, William (D-Ariz.), 133, 142, 146
Association of Southern Women for the Prevention of Lynching (ASWPL), 4, 100, 102-3, 105, 116, 126, 135, 143, 149, 156-57, 213

Bagnall, Robert, 72-73, 81, 106
Bailey, Josiah W. (D-N.C.), 144
Baldwin, Roger, 82, 173, 187, 189
Barbour, (William) Warren (R-N.J.), 164, 168
Barkley, Alben W. (D-Ky.), 145, 152-53, 163-65, 182, 202-3, 204
Bender, George H. (R-Ohio), 189, 190, 198

Bethune, Mary McLeod, 169, 171
Bilbo, Theodore (D-Miss.), 150, 152, 179
Binga, Jesse, 73
The Birth of a Nation, 33-34
Black, Hugo (D-Ala.), 144
Blair, Henry W. (R-N.H.), 15
Borah, William (R-Ida.), 65, 66, 129, 135-36, 149, 164
Borchard, Selma, 125
Bromley, Dorothy Dunbar, 149
Brown, Charlotte Hawkins, 155
Brown v. *Board of Education of Topeka*, 82, 178
Byrnes, James (D-S.C.), 133, 150

Capper, Arthur (R-Kan.), 145, 163, 168, 189
Carey, James B., 173, 176
Carr, Robert K., 179, 180, 185
Case, Clifford (R-N.J.), 185, 193
Case antilynching bill, 193, 197, 198
Celler, Emanuel (D-N.Y.), 183, 185, 195, 206
Chadbourn, James Harmon, 102, 117
Chicago *Defender*, 74, 79, 91, 101, 176, 177, 199, 204, 205
Chisum, Melvin J., 77
Christian, George B., Jr., 66, 70
Church, Robert R., Jr., 190
Civil Rights Congress, 193
Clark, Bennett Champ (D-Mo.), 145-46, 147
Clark, Tom, 180-81, 184
Clarke, Edward Young, 92
Clifford, Clark, 191, 208
Cloture, 71, 151, 163, 189, 200, 202-4
Coatesville, Pa., lynching, 26-27, 155, 212
Cobb, James, 65, 76
Cold War attitudes, 191
Columbia, Tenn., riot, 172-74, 176

306   Index

Commission on Interracial Cooperation (CIC), 11, 19, 58, 100, 102–3, 105, 116, 132, 135, 213
Communist Party—USA (CP-USA), 19, 94–95, 99–100, 115, 136–38, 177, 191, 193
Connally, Tom (D–Tex.), 147, 152, 156–58
Constitutionality, question of, 44, 55, 59, 65, 117, 185–86
Coolidge, Calvin, 64
Copeland, Royal S. (D–N.Y.), 145
Costigan, Edward P. (D–Col.), 111–12, 119–20, 126, 128, 131, 142
Costigan-Wagner antilynching bill, 114–15, 117–18, 121, 158
"Court packing" of 1937, 144, 145
Crumpacker, Edgar D. (R–Ind.), 16
Cummings, Homer, 122–24, 127, 133, 158
Curtis, Charles (R–Kan.), 54–56, 67, 69, 71

Dabney, Virginius, 149
Daily Worker, 136, 137, 177
Daugherty, Harry, 56, 60
Davis, Benjamin J., Jr., 136–37, 177
Davis, Harry E., 56
Davis, John P., 106, 109, 110, 137–38, 155–56
Delany, Hubert, 141
Democratic National Convention (1948), 194–96
Department of Justice, 59, 60, 122–24, 133, 154, 160, 173, 174, 179–81, 191, 192
De Priest, Oscar (R–Ill.), 16, 73, 115, 142
Detroit, 86–88, 171
"Dixiecrats," 187, 204, 215
Dorsey, Hugh M., 42, 57–58, 93
Douglas, Helen Gahagan (D–Calif.), 173, 185
Douglass, Frederick, 13, 17
Du Bois, W. E. B., 13, 24, 28, 32, 33, 37, 53–54, 56, 73, 105, 106–8, 131, 171, 197
Duck Hill, Miss., lynching, 143, 213
Dungee, Roscoe G., 77
Durbin, Winfield T., 14
Dyer, Leonidas, (R–Mo.), 25, 42–45, 54–57, 59–63, 77, 78, 83–85, 121
Dyer antilynching bill, 43–45, 54–55, 57, 64, 66–69, 78–79, 83, 84–85

Early, Stephen, 121
Eastman, Elizabeth, 119, 125, 126
East St. Louis, Ill., riot, 36–38, 43
Eightieth Congress (1947–48), 178, 182–84
Elaine (Phillips County), Ark., 85–86, 173
Eleazer, Robert, 102, 160

Embree, Edwin, 104, 113
Employment discrimination, 167, 198
Ernst, Morris, 96, 177, 179

Fair Employment Practice Committee (FEPC), 168–69, 170, 171–72, 181, 183, 188–91, 198, 205, 208
Federal Bureau of Investigation (FBI), 154, 180–81
Filibuster, 69–71, 128, 149–53, 154, 189, 202
Fish, Hamilton, Jr. (R–N.Y.), 99, 161, 162
Flynn, Mike, 125, 130, 140
Ford, James W., 100, 136, 137
Ford, Thomas (D–Calif.), 115, 134
Fortune, T. Thomas, 12, 13
Frank, Leo, 28, 58, 60, 85–86
Freeman, Douglas, 105
Freeman, Elizabeth, 29–30
Frelinghuysen, Joseph (R–N.J.), 74, 132
Fury, 135

Gallinger, Jacob H. (R–N.H.), 16, 23
Gannett, Lewis, 96
Garland, Charles, 81
Garland Fund. *See* American Fund for Public Service
Garrett, Finis J. (D–Tenn.), 63
Garvey, Marcus, 19, 53, 79–80, 90–92
Gavagan, Joseph (D–N.Y.), 134, 141, 144, 161–62, 165
Gavagan antilynching bill, 141, 143, 161, 170
Gelders, Joseph, 157, 167
George, Walter (D–Ga.), 157–58
Geyer, Lee E. (D–Calif.), 165, 167
Goff, Guy, 60
Graves, Dixie Bibb (D–Ala.), 149
Greenville, S. C., lynching, 179, 180, 184
Grimké, Angelina Weld, 89
Grimké, Archibald, 26, 55, 64
Grimké, Francis, 13
Gruening, Martha, 27, 37, 83

Haiti, 57
Hamilton, John, 129, 154, 159
Hammond, Lily H., 31
Harding, Warren G., 56–57, 73–74, 77
Harlem Renaissance, 89–90
Harris, Abram L., 109–10
Harrison, Byron (Pat) (D–Miss.), 67, 113, 146
Harvier, Ernest, 73
Hastie, William, 137, 139, 153, 166
Hayden, Carl (D–Ariz.), 201, 203, 204

Haynes, George E., 155
Hays, Brooks (D–Ark.), 205–6
Hodges v. *United States*, 15
Holmes, John Haynes, 17
Hoover, Herbert, 93, 98, 104, 105–6
Hoover, J. Edgar, 180–81
Hornblower, George S., 44–45, 169
Houston, Charles, 106, 110, 119, 124, 125, 126, 127, 130, 131, 139, 166, 172, 192
Houston, Tex., riot, 39–40
Howard, Perry, 62, 75, 89, 142
Humphrey, Hubert H. (D–Minn.), 188, 190, 195, 204–5, 208

The Independent, 15, 30
International Labor Defense (ILD), 94, 99–101, 103

Johnson, Georgia Douglas, 89
Johnson, Grace Nail, 82
Johnson, Henry Lincoln, 62, 89
Johnson, James Weldon, 31–33, 35–39, 48, 53, 64, 76, 80–81, 82, 89, 93, 96, 98, 100, 101, 102, 109, 111, 132, 155, 204, 211, 212; as lobbyist, 55–57, 59, 61–63, 68–70, 83–85
Johnson, Lee, 115, 142
Joint Committee on National Recovery (JCNR), 109, 110, 138
Jones, Scipio Africanus, 85–86, 100

Kelley, Florence, 24, 28
Kester, Howard, 143, 163
Keyserling, Leon, 115, 117
King, William (D–Utah), 145, 149
Ku Klux Klan, 33, 57, 62, 76, 81, 83, 87–88, 91–94

La Follette, Robert M., Jr. (Progressive–Wisc.), 152
La Follette, Robert M., Sr. (R–Wisc.), 71
Lampkin, Daisy, x, 140, 163
League of Struggle for Negro Rights (LSNR), 94, 99, 100, 104
Lewis, J. Hamilton (D–Ill.), 142, 146
Lewis, William H., 65, 76–77
Lindbergh Act, 123, 127
Lodge, Henry Cabot (R–Mass.), 15, 64, 65–67, 68–71, 79, 196, 204
Logan, John A. (R–Ill.), 15
Lucas, Scott (D–Ill.), 202–3, 205
Lynching: cases of, 13, 26–27, 28, 29, 30, 35, 39, 41–42, 92–93, 103–4, 117, 122–23, 127–28, 158, 170, 174–75, 176, 180, 181,
192, 213; causes of, 8–10; decline of, 10–12, 98–99, 200; early Congressional reactions to, 15–16; early protests against, 12–17; statistics, 4–8, 18, 26, 28, 29, 35, 97, 98–99, 117–18, 163, 192, 200; theories about, 4, 8, 9–12

Maclean, Mary, 27
Madden, Martin (R–Ill.), 61, 63, 74, 83
March on Washington Movement (MOWM), 168, 170
Margold, Nathan, 97, 110
Marshall, Louis, 60, 83, 86, 212
Marshall, Thurgood, 139, 166, 173, 181
Martin, Joseph W., Jr. (R–Mass.), 179, 182
Maverick, Maury (D–Tex.), 143
McGrath, J. Howard (D–R.I.), 195, 204, 206
McIntyre, Marvin, 127–28, 155
McKay, Claude, 89–90
McKellar, Kenneth (D–Tenn.), 120, 156
McKinley, William, 13, 15
McLeod, Thomas, 92
McNary, Charles (R–Ore.), 129, 153, 154, 163–65, 196, 204
Mencken, H. L., 117
Michener, Earl C. (R–Mich.), 182–84
Milholland, John E., 14
Military desegregation, 167, 198
Milton, George Fort, 102
Minton, Sherman (D–Ind.), 146, 152
Mississippi Valley flood, 104–5
Missouri ex rel. Gaines v. *Canada*, 166
Mitchell, Arthur (D–Ill.), 141–43
Moores, Merrill (R–Ind.), 43, 44, 45, 60
Moore v. *Dempsey*, 84, 85–86
Morse, Wayne L. (R/D–Ore.), 173, 179, 185, 197, 201, 204–5
Moton, Robert Russa, 48, 76
Murphy, Carl, 155
Murphy, Frank, 88, 159–60

Nash, Royal Freeman, 29–30, 32
National Association for the Advancement of Colored People (NAACP): alternative programs, 107–10, 130–31, 132–33, 161–62, 166–68, 180–81, 188, 199–200, 205, 212; finances, 30, 46, 68, 81–82, 84, 87, 96–97, 98, 106–7, 126, 130, 131, 139–40, 163, 177; Legal Defense and Educational Fund, Inc., 166–67; organizational developments, ix, 17, 22–24, 171; and reformist elements, 82–83, 87–88, 111, 113–14, 125, 135, 155, 159, 163, 173–74, 176, 188, 189–

Index

90, 194, 205, 208, 211; tactics, 17–21, 23, 26, 34, 36–38, 44–45, 48–49, 73–75, 83–84, 94–95, 110–11, 115, 121, 125–26, 169, 180, 184–85, 207, 208, 210–11
National Emergency Committee Against Mob Violence, 175, 184
National Equal Rights League (NERL), 49, 68, 79
National Negro Congress (NNC), 137–38, 155–56, 170, 177
National Urban League (NUL), 109, 199
Neal, Claude, 122–23, 127, 133
Neely, Matthew (D–W.Va.), 151, 163
The Negro in Georgia, 42, 57–58
Negro Silent Protest Parade, 37–38
Nerney, May Childs, 27
Niles, David, 175, 177
Nixon v. *Condon*, 88
Nixon v. *Herndon*, 88
Norris, George (R–Neb.), 150
Norton, Mary T. (D–N.J.), 172, 206, 208

O'Day, Caroline (D–N.Y.), 125, 126
Omaha riot, 54
Ovington, Mary White, 22, 26, 37, 62, 80, 96, 107–8, 109, 212

Pan-Africanism, 53, 171
Parker, John J., 99, 105
Peabody, George Foster, 48, 113, 157
Peabody, Philip G., 28–29
Pepper, Claude (D–Fla.), 157, 201
Perry, Leslie, 179, 180, 197–98, 201, 204, 206–7
Pickens, William, 106
Pillsbury, Albert E., 16, 23, 27, 55, 60, 212
Pittsburgh *Courier*, 75, 79, 177, 201
Plessy v. *Ferguson*, 15
Powell, Adam Clayton, Jr. (D–N.Y.), 184, 185, 206, 208
Powell v. *Alabama*, 86
President's Committee on Civil Rights (PCCR), 175–78, 194, 199, 207, 214; hearings, 179–82; recommendations, 185–86
Princess Anne, Md., lynching, 103–4, 117
Progressivism, 24–25, 58, 115
"Purge" of the Democratic Party, 157–58

Race riots, 8, 14, 22, 34, 45, 54, 170–71
Randolph, A. Philip, 155, 168, 170, 198
Raper, Arthur F., 102, 117, 132
Ritchie, Albert C., 104

Robinson, Joseph T. (D–Ark.), 119–20, 124, 127, 145
Rolph, James, 104
Roosevelt, Eleanor, 113, 118, 119–20, 123–24, 133, 134, 135, 138, 144
Roosevelt, Franklin D., 101, 102, 104, 112–13, 118, 119, 127, 131, 133, 134, 135, 140, 154, 155, 162–63, 168–69, 170
Roosevelt, Theodore, 14, 39
Russell, Charles Edward, 24, 151
Ryan, Thomas Fortune, 131

Scott, Emmett J., 40, 48
Scottsboro cases, 99–100, 135
Seligmann, Herbert J., 48, 93, 106
Shelley v. *Kraemer*, 191
Shillady, John R., 32, 41, 46, 48–50, 51–53, 212
Shortridge, Samuel (R–Calif.), 67–69
Slemp, C. Bascom, 76–77
Smith, Harry C., 13
Southern Commission on the Study of Lynching, 100, 102, 115
Southern Conference for Human Welfare (SCHW), 157, 167, 193, 213
Southern Regional Council (SRC), 11, 19, 180, 192, 213
Spingarn, Arthur, 55, 81–82, 107, 108, 118, 152, 162, 163
Spingarn, Joel, 27, 28, 30, 44–45, 55, 107, 109, 121, 140, 150–51, 169, 212
Spingarn, Stephen J., 191
Springfield, Ill., riot, 22–23
State actions against lynching, 20, 42, 46–47, 57, 79, 119, 205
Stockton, Herbert, 65, 81, 118
Storey, Moorfield, 24–25, 29, 30, 44–45, 46, 48–50, 52, 54–55, 56, 58–59, 211
Studin, Charles, 60
Sumners, Hatton (D–Tex.), 61, 64, 125, 134, 141–42, 143, 156
Sweet, Henry, 87–88
Sweet, Ossian, 86–88

Taft, Robert A. (R–Ohio), 172, 179, 182–83, 189, 190
Talbert, Mary B., 78, 81
Taylor, Edward (D–Col.), 134
Terrell, Mary Church, 78-79
Thirty Years of Lynching in the United States, 41, 48, 93
Till, Emmett, ix, 213

Title 18 of the U.S. Code, 19, 181, 185–86, 206
Tobias, Channing H., 169, 176, 177, 179
Toomer, Jean, 90
To Secure These Rights, 175, 186
Tourgée, Albion, 14
Trotter, William Monroe, 13, 49, 53, 56, 66, 68, 79, 171
Truman, Harry S., 59, 152, 168, 171, 175–78, 187–88, 197–98, 199, 201, 202, 209
Turner, Henry M., 12
Tuscaloosa, Ala., lynching, 103, 104
Twenty-fourth Infantry, 39–40, 57, 86
Tyler, Elizabeth, 92

Underwood, Oscar (D–Ala.), 69
Unemployed Councils, 103–4
United Nations, 171
Universal Negro Improvement Association (UNIA), 19, 53, 79–80, 91, 94

Vandenberg, Arthur (R–Mich.), 189, 202–3, 204
Van Nuys, Frederick (D–Ind.), 127, 132–33, 141, 144, 145, 152, 153, 161
Villard, Oswald Garrison, 14, 22–23, 24, 26, 27, 29, 40–41, 109

Wagner, Robert F. (D–N.Y.), 106, 111, 117, 119, 131, 145–46, 148, 161, 163, 168, 174, 185, 197, 204–5
Wagner–Van Nuys–Gavagan antilynching bill, 147, 149–53, 154, 161
Wald, Lillian, 24
Walker, Madame C. J., 49
Walker, Zachariah, 26, 155
Wallace, Henry A., 178, 187, 197, 204
Walling, William English, 22, 28, 30, 43, 46, 48
Walters, Alexander, 13, 24
Washington, Booker T., 13–14, 16, 211
Watson, James (R–Ind.), 56, 67, 69–71, 83
Weatherford, Willis D., 14, 29
Weaver, Robert C., 109, 110
Wells-Barnett, Ida B., 4, 13, 23, 53
Wherry, Kenneth (R–Neb.), 202–3, 204
White, George (R–N.C.), 16
White, Wallace (R–Me.), 178, 182
White, Walter F., 4, 31, 33, 44–45, 53, 55, 58–59, 62, 72, 100, 101, 107, 129, 140, 153, 156, 167–69, 171, 175–76, 184, 190, 207–8, 211, 212; as lobbyist, 105, 107, 111, 112, 117, 120–21, 124, 125–26, 130–31, 133, 142, 144–45, 148, 152, 155, 159, 182, 204, 207; on lynching, 10, 11, 41–42, 90, 92–93, 176; and 1948 election, 194–97, 199; and PCCR, 175–78, 180–81, 187
Wickersham, George W., 60, 93, 212
Wilkins, Roy, 107, 108, 109, 124, 130, 131, 137, 140, 142, 150, 153, 183, 184, 189, 190, 205, 208, 213
Williams, Frances, 133, 136, 155, 181–82
Wilson, Butler R., 64, 65
Wilson, Woodrow, 38, 40–41, 45
Wise, Stephen S., 24, 81
Woodward, Isaac, 174–75, 176, 181
Writers' League Against Lynching (WLAL), 112, 114

Yergan, Max, 137, 170, 176, 177

"Zoot Suit Riots," 170–71